'The global pandemic
migration is essential to
role of migration in revita
agriculture afloat cannot
book that investigates the social and economic implications of international labour migration to Europe's rural regions from both empirical and analytical perspectives.'

Anna Triandafyllidou, *Ryerson University, Canada*

'This is book is a must-read for anyone interested in understanding the phenomenon of internal rural migration in Europe, its diversity of local practices and similarity in outcomes for social groups, rural industries and rural societies across and within countries in Europe. It is the combination of empirically rich, in-depth case studies that portray the human element of migration with discussions of their significance against the background of labour market and migration theories and the specificity of the rural context that makes the book so particularly insightful.'

Bettina Bock, *Wageningen University and Research, Netherlands*

'In fourteen expertly-crafted chapters, this collection offers a historically-informed snapshot of the living and working conditions of people who migrate to rural areas of Europe and the US for agricultural work. Never flinching from sharp critical analysis of the racial capitalism that often seeks to divide workforces in order to weaken them, *International Labour Migration to Europe's Rural Regions* also engages with rural workers' responses to the multiple structures of oppression they face. This book could not be more timely. Emerging as it does during a pandemic that has seen agricultural workers finally gain recognition as "key workers" it challenges the lie of "unskilled work" and the stigma that often accompanies agricultural wage work.'

Ben Rogaly, *University of Sussex, UK*

International Labour Migration to Europe's Rural Regions

Emerging in the throes of a global pandemic that threatens Europe's economies and food security, *International Labour Migration to Europe's Rural Regions* combines a diverse range of empirically rich, in-depth case studies, analysis of their rural context specificities, and insights from labour market and migration theories to critically examine the conditions and implications of rural labour migration.

Despite its growing political, economic, and social importance, our understanding of international labour migration to Europe's rural regions remains limited. This edited volume provides intricate descriptions of lived experience, critical theoretical analyses, analytical synthesis, and policy recommendations for this novel and developing phenomenon which has the potential to transform the lives of international migrants and local communities. The book's 25 authors represent a wide range of social science disciplines, with coverage of a vast range of Europe's rural regions, and diverse types of rural labour in areas such as horticulture, shepherding, wild berry picking and fish processing.

The volume will be of interest to policy-makers at local, regional, national and European levels, and scholars and students in a broad range of areas, including migration, labour markets, and rural studies.

Johan Fredrik Rye is Professor in Sociology at the Department of Sociology and Political Science at the Norwegian University of Science and Technology. He has studied various forms of mobility in late modern societies, including international labour migration, domestic migration of youths, and leisure mobilities, combining a range of qualitative and quantitative materials and research methods. Rye is currently leading the international comparative research project Global Labour in Rural Societies (Glarus).

Karen O'Reilly is Emeritus Professor of Sociology at Loughborough University and an Independent Research Academic. She has been researching migration since the early 1990s and is author of numerous books and articles including *The British on the Costa del Sol*, *Ethnographic methods*, and *International Migration and Social Theory*. She is currently co-investigator on the ESRC-funded project Brexit Brits Abroad and is on the International Advisory Board of Glarus.

Routledge Advances in Sociology

289 Thinking Through Dilemmas: Schemas, Frames, and Difficult Decisions
Lawrence H. Williams

290 Classifying Fashion, Fashioning Class: Making Sense of Women's Practices, Perceptions and Tastes
Katherine Appleford

291 Women and Work in Ireland: A Half Century of Attitude and Policy Change
Margret Fine-Davis

292 Housing and Domestic Abuse: Policy into Practice
Yoric Irving-Clarke and Kelly Henderson

293 Mobilising Place Management
Claus Lassen and Lea Holst Laursen

294 International Labour Migration to Europe's Rural Regions
Edited by *Johan Fredrik Rye and Karen O'Reilly*

295 The Subjectivities and Politics of Occupational Risk: Mines, Farms and Auto Factories
Alan Hall

296 Civil Society: Between Concepts and Empirical Grounds
Edited by *Liv Egholm and Lars Bo Kaspersen*

297 The Economy of Collaboration: The New Digital Platforms of Production and Consumption
Francesco Ramella and Cecilia Manzo

For more information about this series, please visit: www.routledge.com/Routledge-Advances-in-Sociology/book-series/SE0511

International Labour Migration to Europe's Rural Regions

Edited by
Johan Fredrik Rye and
Karen O'Reilly

Routledge
Taylor & Francis Group
LONDON AND NEW YORK

First published 2021
by Routledge
2 Park Square, Milton Park, Abingdon, Oxon OX14 4RN

and by Routledge
52 Vanderbilt Avenue, New York, NY 10017

Routledge is an imprint of the Taylor & Francis Group, an informa business

British Library Cataloguing-in-Publication Data
A catalogue record for this book is available from the British Library

Library of Congress Cataloging-in-Publication Data
Names: Rye, Johan Fredrik, editor. | O'Reilly, Karen, editor.
Title: International labour migration to Europe's rural regions /
edited by Johan Fredrik Rye and Karen O'Reilly.
Description: First Edition. | New York: Routledge, 2020. |
Series: Routledge advances in sociology |
Includes bibliographical references and index.
Identifiers: LCCN 2020026262 (print) | LCCN 2020026263 (ebook) |
ISBN 9780367900717 (hardback) | ISBN 9781003022367 (ebook)
Subjects: LCSH: Migrant labor–Europe–Case studies. |
Occupational mobility–Europe–Case studies.
Classification: LCC HD5856.E78 I68 2020 (print) |
LCC HD5856.E78 (ebook) | DDC 331.6/2094091734–dc23
LC record available at https://lccn.loc.gov/2020026262
LC ebook record available at https://lccn.loc.gov/2020026263

ISBN: 978-0-367-90071-7 (hbk)
ISBN: 978-1-003-02236-7 (ebk)

Typeset in Times New Roman
by Newgen Publishing UK

Contents

List of tables ix
List of figures x
List of contributors xi
Acknowledgements xvi

SECTION I
Transforming Europe's rural industries 1

1 New perspectives on international labour migration to Europe's rural regions 3
JOHAN FREDRIK RYE AND KAREN O'REILLY

2 Are the guest-worker programmes still effective? Insights from Romanian migration to Spanish agriculture 22
MONICA ŞERBAN, YOAN MOLINERO-GERBEAU AND ALEXANDRA DELIU

3 The social and spatial mobility strategies of migrants: Romanian migrants in rural Greece 37
LOUKIA-MARIA FRATSEA AND APOSTOLOS G. PAPADOPOULOS

4 Ghettos, camps and dormitories: migrant workers' living conditions in enclaves of industrial agriculture in Italy 52
CRISTINA BROVIA AND VALERIA PIRO

5 Lessons from the mountains: mobility and migrations in Euro-Mediterranean agro-pastoralism 70
DOMENICA FARINELLA AND MICHELE NORI

6 Temporary farmworkers and migration transition: on a changing role of the agricultural sector in international labour migration to Poland 86
AGATA GÓRNY AND PAWEŁ KACZMARCZYK

7 'Living on the edge'? A comparative study of processes of marginalisation among Polish migrants in rural Germany and Norway 104
JAKUB STACHOWSKI AND KAMILA FIAŁKOWSKA

8 Changing labour standards and 'subordinated inclusion': Thai migrant workers in the Swedish forest berry industry 121
AINA TOLLEFSEN, CHARLOTTA HEDBERG, MADELEINE ERIKSSON AND LINN AXELSSON

SECTION II
Transforming Europe's rural societies **139**

9 Agricultural employers' representation and rationalisation of their work offer: the 'benevolent moderator' 141
JOHAN FREDRIK RYE AND SAM SCOTT

10 Emotions and community development after return migration in the rural Arctic 159
MARIT AURE AND LARISSA RIABOVA

11 Does international labour migration affect internal mobility in rural Norway? 175
MARIE HOLM SLETTEBAK

12 'If we do not have the pickers, we do not have the industry': rural UK under a Brexit shadow 193
KEITH HALFACREE

SECTION III
Concluding remarks **209**

13 Farm labour in California and some implications for Europe 211
PHILIP MARTIN

14 The (re)production of the exploitative nature of rural migrant labour in Europe 228
KAREN O'REILLY AND JOHAN FREDRIK RYE

Index 246

Tables

6.1 Selected job characteristics of Ukrainian migrants by sector of employment, 2017 94
6.2 Selected characteristics of Ukrainian migrants by sector of employment, 2017. Mazonvian region 96
6.3 Selected characteristics of Ukrainian migrants by sector of employment, 2017. Other regions than the Mazovian region 97
8.1 Costs and earnings of Thai berry pickers (per season) 129
8.2 Distribution of berry pickers by system of payment 131
11.1 Descriptive statistics (variables used in Tables 11.2 and 11.3) 184
11.2 Fixed effects linear regression, out-migration and in-migration of Norwegian-born 185
11.3 Fixed effects linear regression, out- and in-migration of low- and high-educated Norwegian-born 186
11.4 Sensitivity analysis. Fixed effects linear regression with different model specifications 187
13.1 US agricultural employment (including forestry, fishing, and hunting), 2006–2026. 1,000s 220
13.2 Full time and actual average pay of California farm workers, 2016 222

Figures

4.1	The Transformed Littoral Strip (TLS) landscape, 2013	56
4.2	Greenhouses in the Transformed Littoral Strip (TLS), 2013	59
4.3	The agricultural plane around Saluzzo, 2014	62
4.4	Entrance of the camp managed by the association Caritas, summer 2016	64
6.1	Foreigners aged 18 years and more residing in Poland, by regions, 2016	89
6.2	Selected modes of recruitment of Ukrainian workers in various sectors of the Polish economy. Percentages. 2017	100
7.1	Accommodation of seasonal migrant workers in Germany, 2010	113
7.2	An example of migrants' housing in the Norwegian case	115
8.1	The distribution of reported earnings (USD) after deductions (n=152)	130

Contributors

Marit Aure is Professor in Sociology at UiT, The Arctic University of Norway. She holds a Ph.D. in Planning and Community Studies. Her research interests encompass international and national migration and integration, gender, masculinity, employment-related mobility, (coastal) rural and urban development. Aure engages in participatory action research and co-production of knowledge. She is currently leading the international research project Sustainable diverse cities: innovation in integration (Cit-egration).

Linn Axelsson is a Research Fellow in Human Geography at Stockholm University. Her research interests include critical border studies, migration governance, international labour migration, and precarious work. She is currently leading a research project on the growing involvement of non-state actors in the regulation of international labour migration.

Cristina Brovia is a political scientist. She obtained her Ph.D. in Political Science at the University of Turin and University of Paris 1 – Pantheon Sorbonne, with a thesis addressing the question of seasonal migrant workers' camps in intensive agricultural areas in northern Italy. Her main research interests concern political sociology, migration in rural areas, ghettos and camps, migrants' mobilisations, local policy-making linked to migration issues, and integration issues

Alexandra Deliu finished her Ph.D. in Sociology at the University of Bucharest and, since 2014, has been is a researcher at the Research Institute for Quality of Life, within the Romanian Academy. Her research interests are focused on topics such as migration and identity, mainly explored with a qualitative methodology including discursive, and narrative analysis.

Madeleine Eriksson is Senior Lecturer in Human Geography at Umeå University, Sweden. She has studied representations of the rural and the urban with focus on the northern periphery and urban regeneration and the disciplining of labour migrants. One important element in her research is the study of representations of 'the other' in relation to discourses of globalisation, new forms of mobility and different social categories such as gender, race, and class.

Domenica Farinella is Lecturer in Economic and Environmental Sociology at Messina University, Italy. Her recent topics include rural and local studies with a specific concern for change in pastoralism, multifunctionality in agriculture, new peasantries, informal economy, and the southern Italy question. In the last years she has been conducting ethnographic research in sheep dairy value-chains and changes in Sardinian pastoralism.

Kamila Fiałkowska is Researcher at the Centre of Migration Research, University of Warsaw. Her research focuses on emigration from Poland, specifically seasonal migration from Poland to Germany and post-accession emigration of Poles to the UK. Her research interests revolve around gender relations in migratory settings, masculinity studies and family relations, construction of national and gender identities, and qualitative research methods in migration studies.

Loukia-Maria Fratsea is Researcher at the Department of Geography, Harokopio University and holds an Integrated Masters in Agricultural Economics and a M.Sc. in Rural Development and Management of Rural Space, both from the Agricultural University of Athens. She is finishing her Ph.D. in Geography (jointly supervised at Harokopio University and Università della Calabria). Her research interests include rural transformation, migration and social change, and social stratification and mobility.

Agata Górny is Head of Demography and Population Economics, Chair at the Faculty of Economic Sciences, University of Warsaw, and Deputy Director of the Centre of Migration Research, University of Warsaw; Vice-President of the Committee for Migration Studies at the Polish Academy of Sciences. Her research interests include temporal patterns of migration, illegal migration, citizenship and migration, immigration to Poland, socio-economic integration of immigrants and the research methods in migration studies.

Keith Halfacree is Reader at the Department of Geography at Swansea University and an internationally acknowledged specialist in the field of rural studies. He has published widely on key topics in rural migration research, covering both domestic and international migration, and has been in the forefront to develop novel theoretical approaches for the understanding of rurality, rural migration, and rural change.

Charlotta Hedberg is Associate Professor in Human Geography at Umeå University, Sweden. Her research deals with migration studies in relation to low-wage labour, rural and regional development, labour market integration, and lifestyle migration. Her research on labour migration relates to the example of Thai wild berry pickers in Sweden, which has been analysed through ethnographic research from a transnational and translocal perspective.

Paweł Kaczmarczyk is Director of the Centre of Migration Research at the University of Warsaw and an Assistant Professor at the Faculty of Economic Sciences, University of Warsaw; IZA fellow, and SOPEMI correspondent for Poland at OECD. His main research areas include causes and consequences of labour migration, highly skilled mobility, methodology of migration research, migration policy, labour economics, population economics and demography, and international economics.

Philip Martin is Professor Emeritus of Agricultural and Resource Economics at the University of California-Davis, US, Editor of *Rural Migration News*, and the author of numerous research publications on migration and farm labour. His most recent book is *The Prosperity Paradox: Fewer and More Vulnerable Farm Workers* (2020).

Michele Nori is based at the Global Governance Programme of the European University Institute (EUI), Firenze. A tropical agronomist as educational background, with a Ph.D. in rural sociology, he has worked extensively in pastoral areas in Africa, Asia, and recently in the Mediterranean region. He has recently completed a Marie Curie Fellowship on migration and pastoralism. Nori is currently engaged with the ERC-funded PASTRES project which studies the interfaces among pastoralism, resilience and uncertainty.

Yoan Molinero-Gerbeau is Ph.D. in Political Science and International Relation and Researcher at the Institute of Economy, Geography and Demography (CSIC) at the Spanish National Research Council (CSIC). He has been working for several years on the link between migrations, agriculture and global chains from an International Relations perspective, principally developing the world-ecology perspective.

Karen O'Reilly is Emeritus Professor of Sociology at Loughborough University and an Independent Research Academic. She has been researching migration since the early 1990s and is author of numerous books and articles including *The British on the Costa del Sol*, *Ethnographic Methods*, and *International Migration and Social Theory*. She is currently co-investigator on the ESRC-funded project Brexit Brits Abroad, and is on the International Advisory Board of Glarus.

Apostolos G. Papadopoulos is Director of the Institute of Social Research (IKE) at the National Centre of Social Research (EKKE) and Professor of Rural Sociology and Geography at Harokopio University. He is Chair of the CIHEAM Advisory Board and Vice-President of the European Sociological Association. His research has focused on family farming, rural development and policy, socio-spatial transformations in rural areas, social class and stratification, international migration, migrant labour and integration.

Valeria Piro is a Post-Doc Fellow at the Department of Sociology at the University of Padova, working on a project concerning migrant labour conditions in meat processing plants. She is currently teaching Sociology of Migration at the University of Bologna. She holds a Ph.D. in Sociology and Methodology of Social Research. Her main research interests concern migration and labour studies, spatial sociology, and ethnographic methodologies.

Larissa Riabova is Acting Research Director and Head of Department of Social Policy in the North at the Institute for Economic Studies of the Kola Science Centre of the Russian Academy of Sciences. She holds a Ph.D. in Economics. Her research interests are social sustainability, social policy and community studies in the Arctic. She studies mining, forestry and fishery-based communities, and is a Co-Editor of the peer-reviewed academic journal *Barents Studies: Peoples, Economies and Politics*.

Johan Fredrik Rye is Professor in Sociology at the Department of Sociology and Political Science at the Norwegian University of Science and Technology. He has studied various forms of mobility in late modern societies, including international labour migration, domestic migration of youths, and leisure mobilities, combining a range of qualitative and quantitative materials and research methods. Rye is currently leading the international comparative research project Global Labour in Rural Societies (Glarus).

Sam Scott is Senior Lecturer in Geography at the University of Gloucestershire, UK. His research focuses on international labour migration and workplace exploitation. Recently he has been involved in the Global Labour in Rural Societies (Glarus) project funded by the Norwegian Research Council (2017–2021) and in work for the UK Government's Director of Labour Market Enforcement (DLME) looking at non-compliance and precarious work in the UK labour market (2018–2020).

Monica Șerban is a Senior Researcher at the Research Institute for Quality of Life, Romanian Academy. She holds a Ph.D. in Sociology. Her current research interests are clustering around migration policies from the perspective of origin area, return migration and re-migration.

Marie Holm Slettebak is a Ph.D. candidate in Sociology at the Department of Sociology and Political Science at the Norwegian University of Science and Technology. Her current research focuses on the interplay of migration, labour markets and social inequality. Her research interests include migration, mobility, social inequality, rural and urban areas, and quantitative research methods.

Jakub Stachowski is Ph.D. candidate at the Department of Sociology and Political Science, NTNU. Jakub explores the process of integration of Eastern and Central European migrants in rural areas in Norway. By using ethnographic methods and employing the perspective of migrants, he studies spatial, labour-market related, social and transnational aspects of migrants' integration in the rural community. Research areas and interests include labour migration, transnationalism, urban and rural areas, criminality, social theory, and ethnographic research methods.

Aina Tollefsen is Associate Professor in Human Geography at Umeå University, Sweden and has researched processes of migration, return, and circulation in different geographical contexts. She has conducted biographical interviews with labour migrants and refugees and expert interviews in Sweden, the US, and Mexico. Her experience includes research on globalising working conditions in a transnational corporation, drawing on interviews with workers in factories in South Africa, Mexico, and Sweden.

Acknowledgements

The book has been initiated and edited as part of the 2017–2022 *Global Labour in Rural Societies* research project financed by the Norwegian Research Council (grant no. 261854/F10). All chapters have been peer reviewed and the editors wish to thank the many external reviewers for their constructive comments to the chapters. Funding from the Norwegian University of Science and Technology (NTNU), UiT The Arctic University of Norway, Harokopio University (Greece), Umeå University (Sweden) and Centro de Ciencias Humanas y Sociales del CSIC (Spain) has made possible Open Access publishing of the volume.

Section I

Transforming Europe's rural industries

Chapter 1

New perspectives on international labour migration to Europe's rural regions

Johan Fredrik Rye and Karen O'Reilly

Migrants at work transforming rural Europe

International labour migrants no longer settle mainly in urban gateways but are more evenly spread across Europe's urban and rural spaces (McAreavey 2018, Bock *et al.* 2016, Corrado *et al.* 2016). Estimates suggest that more than 5 million international migrants currently live in the EU's rural regions, though actual numbers are likely to be even higher (Natale *et al.* 2019). In some rural industries, such as horticulture and food processing, migrant workers make up the majority in manual, low-skilled positions, and many rural communities today host large populations of migrant workers from across the globe (Rye and Scott 2018). As a result, even the very idea of everyday rural life is changing as traditional notions associating the rural with a quaint backwardness and sedentarism are challenged by changing social dynamics, cosmopolitanism, and mobility (Burdsey 2013, Woods 2018, 2007, Rye 2018, Bell and Osti 2010). In this book we provide rich detailed descriptions and theoretical analyses of this novel phenomenon which has the potential to transform the lives of both the international labour migrants arriving in Europe's rural regions and the rural communities in which they arrive.

At the time of concluding the volume – spring 2020, in the midst of the Covid-19 pandemic – the complexities of the migrant labour phenomenon in Europe's rural regions were more evident than ever. State borders – as well as key aspects of everyday life inside the borders – were practically shut down. Many migrant workers in the food industries could not travel to workplaces abroad to make a living for themselves and their households. Others, in place, were severely affected by government measures to limit the spread of the virus, which, for some, led to reduced work hours or even lay-offs. The shutdown also created havoc for other actors in the food production industries, including fears for fields neither planted nor harvested, short- and long-term market failures and large numbers of bankruptcies. In response, a variety of regulative measures were enacted to counter effects of the pandemic that demonstrates the crucial role of migrant labour in Europe's food industries. For instance, the European Commission (2020) issued, in late March, an emergency notice stating that seasonal farmworkers were to be treated in the same manner as 'critical occupations' in terms of cross-border travelling. The individual chapters in the volume were finalised just before the outbreak of the Covid-19 pandemic (papers were accepted after peer review in January/February 2020). However, they all provide invaluable knowledge about the international labour migration phenomenon and its transformative powers in the rural industries and rural society at large, and as such provide a sound foundation for future endeavours to develop sustainable food production and labour practices in rural Europe. These are insights that will be more important than ever as Europe strives to get back to the 'new normal' after the Covid-19 pandemic.

International labour migration in rural Europe as a multiscalar phenomenon

International labour migration to Europe's rural regions is located within *global* systems, especially those related to labour markets, and *European* societal, cultural and economic structures, and political shifts. Migration regimes are also constantly being shaped at every level and in all aspects by *nation*-states, although there is great variation within states, notably between urban and rural regions but also between rural localities. We argue that every understanding of a specific migration flow needs to examine this wider picture and how larger societal structures shape the current context of labour migration, through a range of possibilities and impossibilities, assumptions and dreams, actions and inactions.

Most importantly, while international rural labour migrants and their host localities each have their unique experiences and practices in relation to the labour migration phenomenon at large, they nevertheless operate within the same globalised international society, as do urban regions. If anything, the 2020 Covid-19 pandemic demonstrates starkly how all localities – whether urban neighbourhoods, small towns, or rural villages – are interconnected and interdependent. Over the last decades these interlinkages have become increasingly evident in the enhanced levels of international migration across the globe, which has led to the coinage of the now widely used term 'Age of Migration' (Castles *et al.* 2014). According to the *International Organisation of Migration* (IMO 2019), there are today some 272 million people residing in a country other than that of their birth. Two thirds of these are considered 'labour migrants,' of which increasing numbers find employment in rural industries in Europe and in other regions of the western world (Dufty-Jones 2014).

These flows of labour migration are closely related to the emergence of global food systems, in which international conglomerates exert control over food production through ownership structures and technological regimes, which impact processing, distribution, and retailing. As shown in several chapters of this volume, labour migration is largely demand-driven and responds to the dynamics of the current global modes of industrialised and intensive food production, which in turn rely on access to what seems like inexhaustible pools of inexpensive, flexible and docile migrant labour. The international industry of labour recruiters (Martin 2017) and other mediators (Krifors 2020) further work to facilitate these flows in – at least for the employers – 'frictionless' manners. Further, the emergence of new communication technologies – both virtual (internet, telephony, and so forth) and physical (such as transport routes and low-fare flights) – has been pivotal in facilitating the recruitment of migrants workers from just about anywhere to jobs just about anywhere. As such, the phenomenon of rural labour migration is deeply related to general globalisation processes which work to reduce physical barriers for personal mobility, and thus labour. This applies both to the food industries – which are in focus in the present volume, reflecting their central role in the rural migration nexus – but also to other parts of rural labour markets (such as tourism and hospitality, health, and service provision) which increasingly recruit workers internationally. These global developments serve to shape or frame every migrant flow we discuss in this book, not simply as macro-level structures but also as everyday practices, ideas, attitudes, and outcomes (O'Reilly 2012).

Europe's leading position in the world economy and relative affluence makes it an attractive destination for workers seeking better paid jobs and improved working conditions. There are no sound estimates for the total number of labour migrants in rural Europe. However, analysing available survey materials, Natale *et al.* (2019) suggest that about 5.1 million international migrants *reside* in the EU countries' rural regions, less than half of whom were born in an EU country. The share of international migrants in rural areas varies greatly between states, from near zero in Romania and Bulgaria to 40 per cent in Luxemburg. In total, Natale *et al.* (2019: 5) estimate that five-and-a-half per cent of the EU's rural population is made up of international migrants. This is about half the number of those living in towns (10.2 per cent) and one third compared with cities (14.5 per cent). In other words, while Europe's rural regions house larger numbers of migrants, their populations nevertheless appear more homogeneous when compared with urbanised regions. These numbers include diverse categories of migrant, including workers, refugees, students, and retirees. In terms of labour migration specifically, Natale *et al.* (2019) estimate there were approximately 575,000 migrants working in the EU's agricultural industries, which reflects an increase of 33 per cent between 2011 and 2017. However, real numbers are likely to be far higher (Natale *et al.* 2019, 12), and even more so if circular, non-residential migrants are included. For instance, more than 300,000 migrants, mostly Ukrainians, were given admittance for seasonal work in the Polish agricultural sector in 2017 (see Górny and Kaczmarczyk, Chapter 6). In conclusion (and accepting that records are likely to underestimate actual numbers), this circularity underlines the pivotal role of agriculture in the context of EU migration, both for its rural regions and more broadly, which features prominently in this volume's composition.

Over the last three decades various geopolitical changes have propelled cross-border labour migration across the European continent, among which the collapse of the Communist regimes (1989–1990) and EU enlargements (2004 and 2007) stand out as particularly significant. Migration has largely flown westwards across the European continent, reflecting strong regional economic disparities within Europe, most pronounced between 'old' and 'new' EU members. In addition, many European countries recruit workers from the African countries, the Middle East and beyond. In several chapters of this volume, these recruitment practices form an important backdrop in understanding the potential of wealthier countries to capitalise upon poorer ones, as well as how such notions become taken for granted and therefore unquestioned by policy-makers and other powerful players, and sometimes the migrants themselves.

Furthermore, three 'European crises' provide an important backdrop for understanding international migration to Europe's rural regions. The first is the 2008 financial crisis, which among other things led to mass unemployment and downscaling of welfare services across the continent. These are not static events that provide a simple backdrop to lives but are triggers promoting action and inaction, as is starkly illustrated in Fratsea and Papadopoulos' chapter in this volume (Chapter 3) about the struggles of Romanian migrants in Greece to ameliorate the profound effects of the Greek crisis.

Second, the 2015 refugee crisis refers to the large numbers of refugees fleeing the Syrian war and other destinations in the Middle East and beyond, who eventually made their way to EU member states. Many of these 2015 migrants arrived in rural destinations and would try to find work in rural industries (see for instance Brovia and Piro, Chapter 4). These events demonstrated Europe's role in the global migration nexus and raised questions about key facets of EU migration policies.

Third, political reconfigurations of the European Union, in part following and interlinked with effects of the financial and refugee crises, changed the willingness and ability to host migrant populations among both policy-makers and the public. Mamonova and Franquesa (2019) contend that right-wing populism has found its 'greatest support among rural communities.' These developments are more likely to be relevant for some flows than others. For instance, Iocco, Lo Cascio and Perrotta (2020) show how Italian right-wing populism established powerful anti-immigration discourses with reference to 'Italian' agricultural and food traditions ('nativism'). Another example is UK's withdrawal from the EU ('Brexit'), which for many voters was motivated by a wish to restrict labour migration from Central and Eastern Europe, and implies that the UK is expected to set up and enforce more restrictive labour migration policies. This, Halfacree argues in Chapter 12 of this volume, has the potential to restructure the very social fabric and cultural imaginary of the UK's countryside. These are processes that challenge the idea of an 'all-White countryside' (Neal and Agyeman 2006) and actualise the (still) underdeveloped question of 'rural racism' (Chakraborti and Garland 2011) in the rural studies tradition.

There are other political events with profound and ongoing implications for specific labour migration patterns across Europe. For instance, the Ukraine/Russia conflict in 2014 saw large numbers of Ukrainians migrating westwards to Poland, making that country a main receiver of labour migrants in Europe (Górny and Kaczmarczyk, Chapter 6).

The 2020 Covid-19 pandemic represents yet another 'crisis,' with a global character that unfolds in unique ways across – and within – the European continent. Its long-term effects for migrant labour are still unknown: it may result in reduced mobility across spaces, or it may create a reconfiguration of the food production industries and the ways in which they mobilise migrant labour.

Despite strong structural forces at the global and European scales, the chapters in this volume demonstrate substantial heterogeneity in labour migration practices across Europe's rural regions. National and local contexts each impact rural labour migration, as global change and far-reaching structural shifts are understood and performed in different contexts in diverse ways. Thus, labour migration across European rural spaces represents highly diverse personal characteristics and migration regimes, labour conditions, and overall life situation. Each rural community represents a unique social context for migrants' everyday lives, due to demographic, economic, and sociopolitical characteristics of local communities, and former experiences with international migration. As such, and as argued more extensively by O'Reilly and Rye in the final chapter of this volume, labour migration in Europe's rural regions needs to be researched as a multiscalar spatial phenomenon, where the ongoing outcomes of labour migration emerge from the interaction of the everyday practices of actors, and the dynamics of local, regional, national, European, and global societal structures.

The rural migration context

It is necessary to address some further contextual dimensions of international labour migration, specifically the phenomena conceptualised as 'labour migration' and as 'rural space.' We begin with the latter. Our objective in this volume is to describe and theorise labour migration to Europe's *rural* regions and to understand how it diverges from its urban counterpart. While we acknowledge the many similarities across the rural/urban dimension, this endeavour rests on a belief that the social fabric of rural localities is distinct from that of urban regions, and that these differences inform the social practices that constitute labour migration and are essential for understanding the wider international labour migration phenomenon. The following chapters provide ample evidence that this is the case, and that the rural context generates different migration practices. Thus, while the very concept of 'rural' has been a contested term in the social sciences, with some even suggesting it should be abandoned (Hoggart 1990), it nevertheless enables us to conceptualise the specific and unique contextual conditions that pertain 1) to rural labour markets (for example, the reliance on specific primary industries such as agriculture, forestry and fisheries, and the food processing industries), 2) to demographic characteristics of rural areas (such as scattered settlement structures), and 3) to the degree of peripherality (such as distance to administrative centres). However, most importantly for the present volume's focus on international migrant workers has been the rural labour markets' dependency on agriculture and the other industries that recruit large numbers of manual and low-skilled workers.

Despite the arguments above, we are not employing the term 'rural' to identify, demarcate, or define places on a map, not least because, in practice, it can be impossible to draw clear-cut lines between rural and urban spaces. As Martin's chapter (Chapter 13) demonstrates, most of California's rural labour migrants work and reside in 'metropolitan' areas, as do many in the EU when population density is used to distinguish rural from urban (Davidova *et al.* 2019). Nevertheless, places can be geographically urban yet culturally rural. We therefore need to be flexible in our application and understanding of the term as a multidimensional context, defining it in terms of how it shapes the lives of labour migrants in each case.

This volume thus addresses 'rural' as a multidimensional territorial and social construct, primarily conceptualised by reference to labour market characteristics – especially the predominance of agriculture and other food industries – which are further interrelated with demographic characteristics and characteristics of peripherality, including those associated with the imagination and emotions. This definition of 'the rural' is intentionally imprecise. We are using it as an analytical tool (Benson and O'Reilly 2015), a concept that is valuable for its power to identify contextual structural and agentic properties of the emerging labour migration phenomenon across the European continent.

While 'labour migration' is another contested expression in the field of migration studies, in the present volume it has been crucial to emphasise the labour market *context* of migration. The majority of international migrants arriving in Europe's rural regions, as elsewhere (Dufty-Jones 2014), have been motivated mainly by work prospects, and their experiences are defined by the characteristics of their relationship to the labour market, often a generally precarious position as manual workers in low-skilled positions. Other migrants, for instance refugees from the Middle East or, at the other end of the spectrum, western 'lifestyle' migrants, arrive in rural regions primarily for other reasons and will gain different experiences in rural communities, even where they, at times, undertake work (Benson and O'Reilly 2015, Huete *et al.* 2013).

A further important analytical distinction is between citizens, or residents, of a given nation-state, and those who are considered 'other.' In the literature, the former are interchangeably denoted as 'nationals,' 'natives,' 'locals,' or even, at times, the 'domestic' labour force. In the chapters of this volume, we use the term 'local' to distinguish labour migrants from those who work or live locally, while acknowledging that this can be complicated, and providing further explanations as necessary. A further conceptual confusion is between 'temporary,' 'circular,' and 'permanent' migrants, which may be more clearly defined by state authorities, for instance, in visa regulations and guest-worker schemes, than in migrants' actual practices. What begins as 'temporary' migration may turn out to be repetitive and circular, then permanent.

Finally, the chapters in this volume generally refer to 'international migrants,' or simply to 'migrants' rather than 'immigrants' or 'emigrants' – except where such a distinction is required for clarity. As O'Reilly (2000) argued 20 years ago, migration terms are often used in value-laden ways linked to status, and assuming stasis. For similar reasons, we are careful with our use of the term mobility (Sheller and Urry 2006). Our aim is not to perpetuate normative assumptions about migration as either perpetually mobile or inevitably leading to settlement, but instead to leave such desires, imaginations, practices, and outcomes as questions for each case to examine as relevant.

Emerging literatures – diversity of approaches and common themes

The present volume seeks to contribute intricate analyses of labour migration processes in Europe's rural regions by providing richly detailed, in-depth accounts of a variety of cases. Each of these cases illustrates how migration practices are specific in time, place, and societal context, but there are also some shared characteristics which suggest that individual cases are informed by similar social dynamics. Building on Rye and Scott (2018), in this section we review the rapidly emerging literature on international labour migration to rural societies to identify such key themes. We have identified five strands of literature that stand out as particularly relevant for the understanding of international labour migration to Europe's rural regions, and which provide an important backdrop for the present volume's chapters.

First, there is a large and continually evolving body of research on labour migration to rural localities in the US which is valuable in helping us understand the European experience, despite important differences. As Martin (Chapter 13) demonstrates in his chapter, US agriculture, particularly in the western states, has longstanding historical experiences with employment of salaried migrant labour. However, since the early 1990s, several authors have noticed the even more widespread distribution of international migration across the US (Massey 2008, Hernández-León and Zúñiga 2005), with most rural industries (including meatpacking, tourism and private service providers) today employing large-scale international migrant labour. While many-faceted, a key theme is that labour migrants are found in the secondary labour market in poorly paid jobs that are difficult, dirty and sometimes dangerous (Leach and Bean 2008). It appears that US labour arrangements are even more exploitative than noted in the European literature, possibly due to the more 'mature' capitalist mode of US food production. The US literature also tends to emphasise the role of migration regulations, possibly because so many migrant workers originate from Mexico and other Latin-American countries and their admittance to the US labour market is subject to strict border regulations (Martin 2019). The result is large-scale clandestine migrant flows; today, approximately half of farmworkers in the US are 'undocumented.' European clandestine flows appear much smaller but, as US studies demonstrate, should not be ignored given these migrants' legally vulnerable position. The US society details the many hardships experienced (Holmes 2013) by these groups, with many 'living in limbo' as a perpetual condition (Keller 2019). The US literature is further instructive in its emphasis on race and racialisation as key dimensions, which appears less emphasised in the European literature but nonetheless surfaces as important in understanding migrants' position in rural labour markets and rural society, as noted in many of this volume's contributions. Finally, the US experience is informative for its relative lack of welfare state arrangements, even for 'documented' workers, which further adds to migrants' 'structural vulnerability' (Quesada *et al.* 2011) and marginalised position. The failure to collectively organise labour interests in the US, and even more so in the rural industries, has also led to disempowerment of migrant workers. As such, Martin's chapter in this volume (Chapter 13) – as well as the general US literature on rural labour migration – may be read as an informative comparative case for the European situation, and as a warning about possible future developments in European agriculture and rural society if Europe should follow the same developmental trajectory. This strand of literature is evidence of why our analyses (as argued above, and in Chapter 14) must include an overview of broader structural shifts such as understanding regulatory procedures, welfare state arrangements, mode of production, and the historical sedimentation of practices and assumptions (O'Reilly 2012).

Second, in the European context, literature has emerged from an initial focus on the large-scale influx of labour migrants that first appeared in the Mediterranean horticultural industries (Rye and Scott 2018). A milestone publication is Hoggart and Mendoza's (1999) analysis of the extensive recruitment of migrant workers in Spain's horticulture industries, which they argue constitutes a 'secondary labour market' which in ways resembles the US experiences. Later works have focused on how the industrialisation of Mediterranean horticulture has made it increasingly reliant on imported labour – first from countries outside the EU, later supplemented by migrants from the new EU states – and the consequences thereof for the workers. While Almeria's 'Sea of Plastic,' a 450 square kilometre area covered by greenhouse plastic in southern Spain, illustrates the transformation of the agricultural landscape both literally and metaphorically, the 'ghettos' of southern Sicilia illustrate the severe implications for the migrant agricultural workers in such rural enclaves. If the US literature is instructive in its illustration of what the rural labour migration phenomenon may imply for Europe at large, the Mediterranean literature provides an important message about what is already taking place within the European context.

The Mediterranean literature has developed into a strong research network exploring the migration/agricultural nexus, which has become institutionalised in the extensive research network on migrations, agriculture and food sustainability. This body of literature demonstrates the strong linguistic barriers that exist in the research field in Europe, as most contributions are published in languages other than English, and are thus often inaccessible or largely ignored by the English research community. Important exceptions are the two edited volumes by Gertel and Sippel (2014) and Corrado *et al.* (2016), which have been instrumental in presenting Mediterranean experiences to the wider European audience. A key objective of the present volume is to create a further bridge between the Mediterranean and English-speaking literatures.

Third, reflecting the more recent flows of migrant labour, a parallel literature has developed in the English-language research community. This has focused also on the industrial and labour market context of labour migration and the often exploitative character of migrant work, for instance in the British horticulture industry (Rogaly 2008, Ivancheva 2007), the wild berry industries in Finland and Sweden (Ahlo and Helander 2016, Eriksson and Tollefsen 2018), and the fish-processing industry in coastal Norway (Aure 2008, Rye 2018). These studies are important both in their documentation of exploitative labour arrangements beyond the Mediterranean region, but they also clearly demonstrate efforts to – and potential of – state interventions through welfare state and labour market arrangements in Europe's more regulated economies, even though this potential is often not realised. For instance, while marginalisation and invisibility appear to be constant, the everyday lives of Polish farm workers in Germany differ from that of salmon assembly-line workers in Norway's fish-processing industry, and these differ even further compared with Sub-Saharan workers in Mediterranean horticulture. As such, this strand of literature is instructive to understand the large regional diversity within the European context, as well as providing insights into the effects of migration, labour market and welfare policies. Several of the present volume's contributions draw on and expand these insights.

A fourth strand of literature focuses on questions of place, identity, and belonging, and migrants' position in host rural communities. This literature analyses the labour market as just one among many social domains, and labour migrants as one type of migrant among many. A central topic in this literature is the question of migrants' integration into host communities and how they negotiate their everyday lives as migrants. For instance, Flynn and Kay (2017) demonstrate how Polish migrants seek 'security' and 'normal life' in the rural UK, where employment is just one among many aspects of their striving for better lives. Other major contributions are McAreavey (2018) and Kordel *et al.* (2019), who demonstrate the many analytical interlinkages between labour and migration with sociological perspectives on society. This is important to understand the complexities of the *labour* migration phenomenon and demonstrates that *labour* migration cannot been conceptualised by labour market theories alone. As Şerban *et al.* emphasise in Chapter 2 of this volume, employers – and states – often attempt to recruit abstract 'labour' but overlook that 'labour' arrives as human beings, and, as demonstrated by Aure and Riabova in this volume (Chapter 10), analyses of rural labour migration need to incorporate emotions and aspirations for the future, at both individual and community levels.

A fifth strand of literature further extends the perspective from labour market dynamics to how international migration both challenges and changes traditional conceptions of rural society. As above, the *labour* migrant often appears as just one among many kinds of international migrant, reflecting the often-blurred distinctions between migrant categories. Early examples include Hedberg and do Carmo's (2012) edited volume on rural translocalism, which demonstrates how contemporary rural societies have, through international migration, become inherently multilocal, and Burdsey's (2013) argument that 'issues related to integration, conflict, conviviality and prejudice between different ethnic groups are no longer purely the preserve of towns and cities.' Woods' (2017, 2018) work on 'rural cosmopolitanism' similarly emphasises the 'global' character of rural life and migration. Moore (2019) identifies processes of both exclusion and inclusion of Central and East European migrants in a UK rural village, and, in the Mediterranean context, Alegret-Móren and Wladyka's (2020) work on the relationship between rural migration and rural society analyses communities' demographic sustainability. A final theme, which links back to the more developed US literature's focus on race and ethnicity, is the question of how migrants are treated as 'others,' and, as such, less deserving of labour market and welfare state entitlements, and as a challenge to the traditional image of the rural countryside as essentially 'white' (Hedberg and Haandrikman 2014). Several of this volume's chapters provide examples of such discriminatory social practices that invoke sociological questions of race, racialisation, and ethnicity. However, these dimensions are often referred to – both in lay discourses and in academic works, including many of the chapters in this volume – by use of 'nationality' as a proxy.

Taken together, these strands portray a multifaceted picture of international labour migration to Europe's rural regions, and, as such, mirror the very diverse character of the phenomenon as it unfolds across rural space. This is anything but a field of research with one or a few dominant perspectives, and we have not been able to be comprehensive in our review (but see Rye and Scott 2018). Substantively, we suggest a few overarching traits which we find instructive for the further advancement of the research field and to which we hope the present volume contributes. First, we hold that the international rural labour migration phenomenon needs to be analysed in the analytical intersection between migration theories, labour market theories and rural studies. Second, we find comparative analysis – across Continents, nation-states and sub-state regions – instructive to understand both commonalities across rural spaces as well as their differences. Third, and despite the emerging literature, which largely relies on qualitative and case-oriented methodologies, we notice a lack of a more overarching theoretical lens that provides a coherent account of the contemporary labour migration phenomenon in Europe's rural regions. This has been the rationale for the book at large but also this volume's final chapter, where we employ practice theory to provide a theoretical framework.

Putting the pieces together in the puzzle of rural labour migration in Europe

The labour migration phenomenon transforms not just the everyday lives of European rural labour migrants but also Europe's rural spaces. Each chapter contributes important pieces to this intricate puzzle, and together they paint a fuller picture of the role of labour migration in contemporary rural Europe. The book is structured in three sections. The first section, 'Transforming Europe's rural industries,' analyses rural industries' increasing reliance on migrants to perform low-skilled, manual labour. Its seven chapters analyse different labour migration flows across the European continent. The first four of these concentrate on the Mediterranean region, which, as noted above, figures as the longest established case of rural labour migration in the European context. Şerban, Molinero-Gerbeau and Deliu (Chapter 2) analyse Romanian migration to Spanish horticulture to question the popular 'triple win' approach to labour migration, which proclaims benefits for migrants, and sending and receiving countries alike. They find that migration is scarcely beneficial for the individual migrants, regardless of changing regulative arrangements. Fratsea and Papadopoulos (Chapter 3) provide a contrasting case of Romanian migration to Greece, accentuating the scope of migrants' agency and strategies for social mobility in the context of the 2008 financial crisis. Taken together, these two chapters demonstrate the relevance of unique features of the social structure in receiving societies for labour migrants' experiences.

Brovia and Piro (Chapter 4) discuss contrasting experiences *within* nation-states in their comparison of migrant housing conditions in two Italian regions which host large numbers of migrant workers: the Transformed Littoral Strip in Sicily and Saluzzo in Piedmont. Their analysis demonstrates how both a policy focus and a labour market focus are required to understand the farm workers' generally poor work and life conditions, in the context of differing forms of settlement and housing structure.

Analysis of Mediterranean agriculture and its use of migratory labour has largely focused on the intensive horticulture industries. Farinella and Nori's (Chapter 5) illustrate how agro-pastoralism – a multifunctional rural system based on extensive livestock rearing complemented by other agricultural activities – in mountainous regions of Greece, Spain, and Italy is similarly reliant on access to migrant labour, notably shepherding. Despite recognising some individual agency, and more horizontal interactions with their hosts than in other cases, they demonstrate how the farmers' rhetoric of the 'good worker' serves to maintain subordination of the migrant shepherds.

The next three chapters expand the perspective to rural regions and industries that more recently, yet now extensively, recruit migrant labour. Górny and Kazcmarczyk (Chapter 6) address the extensive migration of recent years from Ukraine to Poland, which has served to counterbalance the similarly impressive migration from Poland to western European countries. The demand for foreign farm workers was the initial impetus for Ukraine to provide labour migration to Poland, but these authors find the role of agriculture in the employment of foreign labour has been diminishing in more recent years as Ukrainian migrants use work in agriculture as a gateway to other sectors with better conditions. Stachowski and Fiałkowska (Chapter 7) contrast two different cases of Polish migration: seasonal, circular work in the German agricultural industry, and more permanent employment in Norway's fish-processing industries. Their analysis details the marginalisation of Polish migrants in both rural contexts. However, they find the specific social processes leading to marginalisation – and the shape it takes – are variable. Analysis of the outcomes also rely on understanding the specific working arrangements, the specific challenges labour migrants face, and the role of migrants' strategies in counterbalancing their less privileged positions. In the last chapter of this section, Tollefsen, Hedberg, Eriksson and Axelsson (Chapter 8) analyse an even more marginalised group of labour migrants in rural Europe, Thai berry pickers in the Swedish forests. As larger society acknowledged the poor wage and working conditions of these migrants, legal regulations were introduced to improve conditions. However, the Thai migrant berry pickers continue to be exploited, and fulfilment of their formal rights is still lacking, as a result of processes the authors theorise as 'subordinated inclusion.'

Taken together, the chapters of this volume demonstrate the variety of the labour migration phenomenon in rural Europe, but also point to the many shared characteristics of the rural industrial and societal context. For instance, the dominance of precarious work and living conditions and processes of marginalisation and subordination in host rural communities appears universal, regardless of policy or legislative attempts to ameliorate them. Their invisible, or even actively ignored, position in the rural localities similarly appears as another general characteristic of the phenomenon of international labour migration to Europe's rural regions. A final common theme is the relatively restricted scope for migrant agency and long-term improvement of their conditions.

The second section is titled 'Transforming Europe's rural societies' and extends the perspective from that of the migrants to the many other agents involved in the rural labour migration phenomenon, such as employers, local populations, and societies at large. The chapters thus demonstrate how international migration at the same time is embedded within but also changes the social structures of the host rural communities, regions, and nation-states. Rye and Scott (Chapter 9) take the perspective of the rural employers, the farmers, who recruit migrant labour to perform manual work tasks in the fields and asks how they make sense of wage and work conditions that are so often characterised as exploitative, at times even 'gruelling' (Guthman 2017, 24). In the course of their in-depth interviews, the Norwegian, UK and US strawberry farmers alike all emphasised what they find to be rather attractive features of migrants' work, not least because, they suggest, the migrant workers have no better job option 'at home.' The chapter clearly demonstrates the presence of different narratives on rural migrant labour, which is important in order to understand the potential of – and barriers to – labour market and migration reforms. Aure and Riabova (Chapter 10) analyse the role of emotions in understanding the long-term experiences of Russian female migrants who participated in a programme to recruit Russian workers to the fish-processing industry in rural Norway around the turn of the century. There was an assumption that the migration would improve the migrants' economic situation and spur development in the home community, but these goals barely materialised. The analysis shows how rural labour migration – before, during, and after migration – is imbued with hopes, aspirations, and dreams, not only by the migrants themselves but also by their local communities. Another example of the interlinkages between labour migration flows and everyday life in rural communities is given by Slettebak (Chapter 11), who utilises registration data from Norway to analyse how international migration streams are reflected in Norwegians' migratory patterns. Effects are minor and labour migrants appear, if anything, to be an addition to expanding populations and labour markets, rather than displacing Norwegian-born workers. As such they can function as a much needed 'demographic refill' for rural regions facing depopulation. Halfacree (Chapter 12) concludes this section by discussing how the UK's withdrawal from the Europe Union in different ways could change rural communities, as well as the everyday lives of their populations. He suggests that sentiments of the 'revanchist rural' has grown in the country, which challenges the status of, and ambition for, the UK countryside to be a diverse, welcoming, and modern space, not least for labour migrants.

The book's final section – 'Concluding remarks' – contains two chapters which, from quite different angles, provide directions for the further study of international labour migration to rural Europe. Martin (Chapter 13) gives first an overview of how US agriculture developed its current dependence on the recruitment of an internationally recruited labour force from Mexico and other Latin-American countries. The US, in particular Californian horticulture, provides an instructive scenario for how Europe's agricultural industries may evolve in years to come if current global agri-food dynamics are continued. The enduring pursuit of more 'efficient' production – often involving the replacement of smaller family farms with large industrial units reliant on migrant labour, and increased intensification of food production processes – has resulted in rural poverty, migrant marginalisation, and exploitative labour relations. As shown in other chapters in the volume, some parts of rural Europe already resemble the Californian model, and others are apparently following suit. In the final chapter, O'Reilly and Rye outline an overall theoretical framework, a practice theory of rural labour migration, and utilise this framework to identify some key challenges for the study of the phenomenon.

Futures of labour migration to Europe's rural regions

Together, the chapters in this edited volume demonstrate how recent labour migration processes in Europe have changed the social fabric of rural localities across the continent. These processes unfold in diverse ways, with very different consequences for migrants and local populations, and with major differences across rural spaces. International labour migration to Europe's rural regions truly is – to twist Vertovec's (2007) expression – a 'super-diverse' phenomenon. Detailing the many different manifestations of the phenomenon has been a key objective of the current volume. However, taken together, the book's contributions also provide a fuller account of the international labour migration phenomenon currently unfolding in Europe's rural regions. We shall here suggest three kinds of key insights that emerge from the chapters of the book.

New knowledge about the rural labour migration phenomenon

The wage and working conditions of labour migrants may vary across Europe's rural regions, nevertheless, they are generally poor in both absolute and relative terms, and in many instances working conditions are overtly exploitative. Also, many migrants' overall living conditions are clearly sub-standard judged by commonly held standards. These conditions result from the very character of migrants' work in the rural industries, which are characterised by low productivity and wage capacities, and the fact that most migrants perform the least profitable work tasks – that is, manual and low-skilled jobs. There is also an implicit assumption, shared by many players, that these migrants cannot (and should not) expect better. They are often viewed as 'labour' rather than as 'human beings,' as Şerban *et al.* (Chapter 2) demonstrate in their chapter. Another key factor appears to be the relative invisibility of migrant workers in rural regions, as they often work and reside in sparsely settled communities, their living conditions circumscribed by the suppositions above. The invisibility is often related to ethnicity and racialisation processes, as the labour migrants are conceived of as 'others' and less deserving of inclusion in hosting communities and societies. Finally, many of the chapters illuminate the scope of migrant agency and demonstrate the wide range of strategies employed by the migrants to cope with their marginalised positions in the rural labour markets and rural societies. However, as elaborated in O'Reilly and Rye's concluding chapter in this volume, the analyses more often highlight how, and why, their room for manoeuvre is so often restricted.

New theoretical perspectives on rural migration

The volume also adds to scientific perspectives making sense of labour migration in Europe's rural regions and beyond. In their totality, the volume's chapters clearly demonstrate the benefits of integrating the many dimensions of migration in a coherent analysis that considers how scales play out in practice. While the labour market necessarily provides a focal point in analysis of work-related migration, migrant workers' experiences need to be analysed within their larger social reality, otherwise we are complicit in viewing them as labour rather than as people. Social practices take place in everyday local contexts, and thus need to be studied in their localised contexts; any analysis should also strive to conceptualise the actors' practices within a framework that accounts for the interplay of larger societal structures in contiguity. Theories of migration, labour markets, and rural society would all benefit from cross-fertilisation of their perspectives. O'Reilly and Rye (Chapter 14) outline in the final chapter a practice theory approach that seeks to establish such a conceptual framework that avoids single factored theoretical discussions and conclusions. Other approaches are to be welcomed.

New migration and labour market policies

Finally, while our primary aim was not to provide detailed policy recommendations, the analysis suggests some important insights of relevance for policy-makers. First, the book's contribution confirms that rural labour migrants constitute a large rural population with precarious living conditions. Specific living conditions may vary, but the overall image is one of marginalisation, invisibilisation, and exploitation. Addressing these conditions is a major challenge for policy objectives of social equality and cohesion in European societies. Second, rural localities invite different policy measures than urban regions. The rural industries, such as those we have focused on here (agriculture and fish processing), largely recruit migrants to manual and low-skilled positions which are among the least attractive in western European labour markets. However, there are also important differences within the rural industries, which means policy measures need to be sensitive not only to the rural societal context but also industrial characteristics, and how they vary over time and place. The chapters may even suggest that rural industries are particularly evasive, though not totally immune (Rye 2017), to nation-state's attempts to regulate labour market conditions. An especially instructive case is Tollefsen *et al.*'s (Chapter 8) analysis of the Swedish attempt to enforce regulations for the benefit of Thai berry pickers, which they demonstrate largely failed. There is a risk that rural labour migrants, due to their general invisibility in rural society, fall under the radar of the general public and policy-makers. Third, the book provides important lessons on the shape that future developments may take and raises the importance of realising the implications of certain choices, such as intensification and consolidation. Here, Martin's (Chapter 13) sketch for what may happen if Europe follows the Californian route is instructive. In some regards, this has already come to pass in Mediterranean horticulture, and it is also noticeable in other parts of rural Europe's industries.

Conclusion

Taken together, the chapters in this volume demonstrate the diversity of labour migration in rural Europe. The phenomenon encompasses highly diverse social practices in terms of personal characteristics and migration regimes, labour conditions, and overall life situation. Each rural community represents a unique social context for migrants' everyday lives, due to demographic, economic, and sociopolitical characteristics of local communities, and former experiences with international migration.

This volume also points to the many shared characteristics of the rural industrial and societal context nested within European labour migration's diverse manifestations. For instance, the dominance of precarious work and living conditions, and processes of marginalisation and subordination in host rural communities appears universal, regardless of policy or legislative attempts to ameliorate them. Another common theme is the relatively restricted scope for migrant agency and long-term improvement of their conditions. They provide, as such, a sound foundation for future endeavours to develop sustainable food production and labour practices in rural Europe. These are insights that will be more important than ever as Europe strives to get back to the 'new normal' after the Covid-19 pandemic.

We have argued here that labour migration in Europe's rural regions thus needs to be researched as a multiscalar spatial phenomenon, where the ongoing outcomes of labour migration are understood to emerge out of the interaction between everyday practices of actors and the dynamics of local, regional, national, European, and global societal structures. Further, we argue that the international rural labour migration phenomenon needs to be analysed in the analytical intersection between migration theories, labour market theories, and rural studies.

Acknowledgements

The chapter, as well as the overall book project, is the result of the 2017–2022 Global Labour in Rural Societies research project financed by the Norwegian Research Council (grant no. 261854/F10). The authors wish to thank the external reviewers for their constructive comments on the manuscript.

References

Alegret-Móren, R. and D. Wladyka. 2020. *International Immigration, Integration and Sustainability in Small Towns and Villages. Socio-Territorial Challenges in Rural and Semi-Rural Europe*. London: Palgrave MacMillan

Alho, R.J. and M.J. Helander. 2016. 'Foreign Seasonal Farm Workers' Strategies at the Margins of the Finnish Welfare State: Informal Networks and Weak Ties.' *Nordic Journal of Migration Research* 6(3): 148–157.

Aure, M. 2008. 'Arbeidsmigrasjon fra Teriberka til Båtsfjord 1999–2002.' Ph.D. diss, University of Tromsø.

Bell, M.M. and G. Osti. 2010. 'Mobilities and Ruralities. An Introduction.' *Sociologia Ruralis* 50(3): 199–204. DOI: 10.1111/j.1467-9523.2010.00518.x.

Benson, M. and K. O'Reilly 2015. 'From Lifestyle Migration to Lifestyle in Migration: Categories, Concepts and Ways of Thinking.' *Migration Studies* 4(1): 20–37.

Bock, B., G. Osti and F. Ventura. 2016. 'Rural Migration and New Patterns of Exclusion and Integration in Europe.' In *The Routledge International Handbook of Rural Studies* edited by M. Shucksmith and D. Brown, 71–84. New York, Routledge.

Burdsey, D. 2013. '"The Foreignness is Still Quite Visible in This Town": Multiculture, Marginality and Prejudice at the English Seaside.' *Patterns of Prejudice* 47(2): 95–116.

Castles, S., H.D. Haas and M.J. Miller. 2014. *The Age of Migration. International Population Movements in the Modern World*. Basingstoke: Palgrave Macmillan.

Chakraborti, N. and J. Garland, eds. 2011. *Rural Racism*. London: Routledge.

Corrado, A., C. de Castro and D. Perrotta, eds. 2016. *Migration and Agriculture Mobility and Change in the Mediterranean Area*. London: Routledge.

Davidova, S.M., K.J. Thomson and A.K Mishra, eds. 2019. *Rural Policies and Employment: TransAtlantic Experiences*. Singapore: World Scientific Books, number q0210, March.

Dufty-Jones, R. 2014. 'Rural Economies in the "Age of Migration": Perspectives from OECD Countries.' *Geography Compass* 8(6): 368–380.

Eriksson, M. and A. Tollefsen. 2018. 'The Production of the Rural Landscape and its Labour: The Development of Supply Chain Capitalism in the Swedish Berry Industry.' *Bulletin of Geography. Socio-economic Series* 40: 69–82.

European Commission. 2020. 'Guidelines Concerning the Exercise of the Free Movement of Workers during Covid-19 Outbreak.' Communication from the Commission. 30 March 2020 (eur-lex.europa.eu/ legal-content/EN/TXT/?uri= CELEX:52020XC0330(03).

Flynn, M. and R. Kay. 2017. 'Migrants' Experiences of Material and Emotional Security in Rural Scotland: Implications for Longer-term Settlement.' *Journal of Rural Studies* 52: 56–65.

Gertel, J. and S.R. Sippel, eds. 2014. *Seasonal Workers in Mediterranean Agriculture*. Abingdon: Routledge.

Guthman, J. 2017. 'Paradoxes of the Border: Labour Shortages and Farmworker Minor Agency in Reworking California's Strawberry Fields.' *Economic Geography* 93(1): 24–43.

Hedberg, C. and R. Miguel do Carmo. 2012. *Translocal Ruralism. Mobility and Connectivity in European Rural Spaces*. London: Springer.Hedberg, C. and K. Haandrikman. 2014. 'Repopulation of the Swedish Countryside: Globalisation by International Migration.' *Journal of Rural Studies* 34: 128–138.

Hernández-León, R. and V. Zúñiga, eds. 2005. *New Destinations: Mexican Immigration in the United States*. New York: Russell Sage Foundation.

Hoggart, K. 1990. 'Let's Do Away with Rural.' *Journal of Rural Studies* 6(3): 245–257.

Hoggart, K. and C. Mendoza. 1999. 'African Immigrant Workers in Spanish Agriculture.' *Sociologia Ruralis* 39(4): 538–562.

Holmes, S.M. 2013. *Fresh Fruit, Broken Bodies: Migrant Farmworkers in the United States*, Berkeley: University of California Press.

Huete, R., A. Mantecon and Estevez, J. 2013. 'Challenges in Lifestyle Migration: Reflections and Findings about the Spanish Crisis.' *Mobilities* 8(3): 331–348.

International Organisation for Migration (IMO). 2019. World Migration Report 2020. Geneva: International Organization for Migration.

Iocco, G., M. Lo Cascio and D. Perrotta. 2020. '"Close the Ports to African Migrants and Asian Rice!": The Politics of Agriculture and Migration and the Rise of a "New" Right-wing Populism in Italy.' *Sociologia Ruralis*: Unpaginated. DOI: 10.1111/soru.12304.

Ivancheva, M. 2007. 'Strawberry Fields Forever? Bulgarian and Romanian Student Workers in the UK.' Journal of Global and Historical Anthropology 49: 110–117.

Keller, J.C. 2019. *Milking in the Shadows: Migrants and Mobility in America's Dairyland*. New Brunswick: Rutgers University Press.

Kordel, S., T. Weidinger and I. Jelen, eds. 2019. *Processes of Immigration in Rural Europe*. Cambridge: Cambridge Scholars Publishing.

Krifors, K. 2020. 'Logistics of Migrant Labour: Rethinking how Workers "Fit" Transnational Economies.' *Journal of Ethnic and Migration Studies*, DOI: 10.1080/1369183X.2020.1754179.

Leach, M.A. and F.D. Bean. 2010. 'The Structure and Dynamics of Mexican Migration to New Destinations in the United States.' In *New Faces in New Places* edited by D.S. Massey, 51–74. New York: Russell Sage Foundation.

Mamonova, N. and J. Franquesa. 2019. 'Populism, Neoliberalism and Agrarian Movements in Europe. Understanding Rural Support for Right-wing Politics and

Looking for Progressive Solutions.' *Sociologia Ruralis*: Unpaginated. DOI: 10.1111/soru.12291.

Martin, P. 2019. 'Trump, Migration, and Agriculture.' *Crossing Borders* 9: 9–27.Martin, P. 2017. *Merchants of Labor: Recruiters and International Labor Migration*. Oxford: Oxford University Press.

Massey, D.S., ed. 2008. *New Faces in New Places: The Changing Geography of American Immigration*. New York: Russell Sage Foundation.

McAreavey, R. 2018. *New Immigration Destinations: Migrating to Rural and Peripheral Areas*. London: Routledge.

Moore, H. 2019. 'Perceptions of Eastern European Migrants in an English Village: The Role of the Rural Place Image.' *Journal of Ethnic and Migration Studies*. https://www.tandfonline.com/doi/full/10.1080/1369183X.2019.1623016

Natale, F., S. Kalantaryan, M. Scipioni, A. Alessandrini and A. Pasa. 2019. *Migration in EU Rural Areas*. Luxemburg: Publications Office of the European Union.

Neal, S. and J. Agyeman. 2006. *The New Countryside? Ethnicity, Nation, and Exclusion in Contemporary Rural Britain*. Bristol: Policy Press.

O'Reilly, K. 2000. *The British on the Costa del Sol*. London: Routledge.

O'Reilly, K. 2012. *International Migration and Social Theory*. Basingstoke: Palgrave.

Quesada, J., L.K. Hart and P. Bourgois. 2011. 'Bourgois Structural Vulnerability and Health: Latino Migrant Laborers in the United States.' *Medical Anthropology* 30(4): 339–362.

Rogaly, B. 2008. 'Intensification of Workplace Regimes in British Horticulture: The Role of Migrant Workers.' *Population, Space and Place* 14(6): 497–510.

Rye, J.F. 2017. 'Negotiating Neoliberalism: Informalisation and Reformalisation of Industrial Relations in Norway's Agricultural Industry in the 21st Century.' *Population, Space and Place* 23: Unpaginated.

Rye, J.F. 2018. 'Labour Migrants and Rural Change: The "Mobility Transformation" of Hitra/Frøya, Norway, 2005–2015.' *Journal of Rural Studies* 64: 189–199.

Rye, J.F. and S. Scott. 2018. 'International Labour Migration to/in Rural Europe: A Review of the Evidence.' *Sociologia Ruralis* 8(4): 928–954.

Sheller, M. and J. Urry. 2006. 'The New Mobilities Paradigm.' *Environment and Planning A* 38: 207–226.

Vertovec, S. 2007. 'Super-diversity and its Implications.' *Ethnic and Racial Studies* 30(6): 1024–1054.

Woods, M. 2007. 'Engaging the Global Countryside: Globalization, Hybridity and the Reconstitution of Rural Place.' *Progress of Human Geography* 31(4): 485–507.Woods, M. 2017. 'Rural Cosmopolitanism at the Frontier? Chinese Farmers and Community Relations in Northern Queensland, c.1890–1920.' Australian Geographer 49: 107–131.

Woods, M. 2018. 'Precarious Rural Cosmopolitanism: Negotiating Globalization, Migration and Diversity in Irish Small Towns.' *Journal of Rural Studies* 64: 164–176. DOI.org/10.1016/j.jrurstud.2018.03.014.

Chapter 2

Are the guest-worker programmes still effective?

Insights from Romanian migration to Spanish agriculture

Monica Şerban, Yoan Molinero-Gerbeau and Alexandra Deliu

Migration, development and guest-worker programmes

In 1986, Castles published an article titled 'The guest-worker in western Europe – an Obituary' in the *International Migration Review*. Twenty years later, the same renowned scholar authored 'Guestworkers in Europe: A Resurrection?' in the same prestigious journal. The two titles reflect the major changes defining the way scholars, and even more so policymakers, have positioned themselves in relation to migration and development during the last decades.

When the first article was written, pessimism dominated the migration–development debate, fed by the perceived failure of the post-Second World War European guest-worker programmes. At the beginning of the millennium, when the second article was published, new evidence and theoretical frameworks to interpret it stimulated a rather optimistic view (De Haas 2010). Within this context, a new wave of guest-worker programmes has developed in Europe (Rye and Scott 2018). According to their promoters, these programmes would be more than a way to open safe channels for migration, as they would also promote co-development experiences (Macías Llaga *et al.* 2016). This perspective, stressing the benefits of migration for individuals, their countries of origin, and their destinations, has been actively promoted under the label *triple-win*.

By investigating Romanians' migration to work in the intensive agriculture sector of Huelva, Spain, this chapter questions the idea that the triple-win approach offers overall benefits, primarily at the migrant level. To assess the tenets of the triple-win approach, the cases of the Huelvan guest-workers programme and Romanian migrants are particularly relevant. The Huelvan programme, one of the new wave of European guest-workers programmes, has attracted the attention of both scholars (e.g. Plewa 2009) and policy-makers (e.g. Wickramasekara 2011) and is often labelled as 'good practice' in the field (López-Sala 2016). On the other hand, Romanians have been one of the most numerous migrant groups working in Huelva agriculture in the past 20 years (Molinero-Gerbeau 2018). Since Spain and Romania both belong to the European Union (EU), which promotes free circulation of labour, Romanian migration to Huelva has evolved through a complex history from managed migration to free circulation; this makes the case even more interesting. To emphasise this change, we distinguished two phases in the history of this migration: The first lasted from 2002 to 2008, when migration developed on the basis of a bilateral agreement, and the recruitment was managed at the source by public authorities: it is therefore called the *public* phase of migration. The second began in 2009 and is still underway. During this phase, Romanians, as EU citizens, have had the right to sign a work contract directly in Spain without the need for a visa. Spanish employers have taken the lead in recruiting the migrants: it is therefore called, as expressed by Molinero-Gerbeau (2018), the *private* phase of migration.

Our analysis is based on two approaches: first, using legal and official documents, we investigate the context within which this migration was initiated and how it was implemented. Our primary aim in this direction is to understand whether the managed migration intentionally addressed positive effects and development goals. Our analysis points to the predominance of the Spanish employers' needs, without any attention directed towards other consequences of migration.

The second approach is based on qualitative research with Romanian workers in Huelvan agriculture, both at the origin and the destination. Our analysis investigates the differences in migration practices associated with the two identified phases as well as the benefits of migrating abroad at the individual level. We argue that the passage from managed migration to free migration did not fundamentally impact the way migration was experienced by the participants. We argue that, even if the migration is profitable for participants, its impact ultimately remains limited; this argument holds even for individuals involved in circular patterns of mobility for a long time.

Who benefits from circular/temporary guest-worker programmes? The triple-win approach

The *win-win-win* approach, also known as the *triple-win* approach, is intimately linked to the promotion of circular mobility as a beneficial form of migration. The advocates of this type of temporary migration claim that migrating under circular schemes stimulates co-development (Macías Llaga *et al.* 2016), bringing benefits to the three involved entities: the countries of origin, the destination, and the migrants themselves. Developed by think-tanks (Agunias 2006) and endorsed by international bodies such as the Global Forum on Migration and Development (GFMD 2007), the International Organization for Migration (IOM 2010) or the European Migration Network (EMN 2011), the triple-win approach has become the most widespread argument for legitimising the initiation of new temporary circular initiatives. This type of safe migration would have advantages for destination countries, as they would receive the required workforce, avoiding both irregular migration, and the social costs of long-term integration. For origin countries, it would bring economic and social remittances, limiting the effects of brain drain and, given the contexts at the origin, fostering development. Migrants themselves would also benefit by gaining economic and human capital – professional and language skills – and resources to improve their lives at home, while working abroad under legal conditions. They would also be able to return to their origin country, thus avoiding family breakups (Agunias 2006, López-Sala and Godenau 2015, Agunias and Newland 2007, Newland 2007).

Advised by EMN, the European Commission (2007) adopted this approach and decided to test it by financing, among other programmes, two pilots in Spain's seasonal agriculture, one in the province of Lleida and the other in Huelva. The objective was to evaluate the impact of circular migration programmes to promote their implementation throughout the EU. Even if the Spanish programmes were considered successful by their promoters (Molinero-Gerbeau and Avallone 2018), some academics remained sceptical, highlighting that triple-win served only as an argument to legitimise the circular/temporary programmes whose winning effects had not been proven empirically (López-Sala and Godenau 2015).

The discussion about Spanish programmes thus resumed a long debate in migration studies that debunked the optimistic view of guest-worker programmes, especially in their seasonal/circulatory version, as the 'best' way to manage migration in relation to development (e.g. Rush 2002, Rush and Martin 2008, Martin 2003, Wickramasekara 2011, Castles and Ozkul 2014). We here contribute to this debate by reviewing how Romanian migration was channelled to the agriculture of Huelva and the effects of this experience, especially on migrants.

Investigating Romanian migration to Huelva

Our analysis is based on qualitative research on Romanians' seasonal migration to work in the Huelvan agriculture. We base our text on 16 interviews (four men and 12 women) with former or current Romanian workers in Huelva. Their ages varied from 30 to 39 (men) and 20 to 55 (women). The majority of respondents were married (10), five were single, and one was divorced.

In Romania, the fieldwork was carried out from November to December 2016 and August 2017 in one village in the south of the country. In Spain, it was conducted in May to June 2015 in five towns in the province of Huelva. The interviewees were selected according to two criteria: the year of first departure from Romania (before versus after 2007) and the pattern of migration (single versus repeated migration). This way, the sample became heterogeneous in terms of phases (the *public* phase of migration versus the *private* one) and circularity. The interview protocol was the same for the two countries. Interviewees were openly asked to evaluate their migration experience and prompted to discuss its positive and negative facets. In addition to interviews, we also inspected official documents, legislation, and administrative data. These all formed the basis of how migration to Huelva was initiated, from a top-down perspective.

Agri-food industry in Huelva and its need for seasonal workers

Huelva is an Andalusian province, famous as producer of strawberries. Yearly, about 80 per cent of Huelvan strawberry production is exported, generating a total turnover of around 250 to 300 million euro (López-Sala 2016). Since the 1970s, 'a post-Fordist, ultra-modern [and] technologically advanced agriculture, well embedded in the global value chain' (Caruso 2016, 265) has developed in the region. The production is highly dependent not only on constant capital but also on variable capital – mainly on labour. For every hectare of strawberry crop, five to six workers are required, totalling 40,000–60,000 every campaign (Plewa 2009).

In the 1990s, the 'huge workforce problem' (Reigada 2012, 109) of Huelvan agriculture found its first solution in employing Moroccans and Sub-Saharan Africans already living in Spain, most with irregular status. After massive regularisations in 2000 and 2001, when their status was legalised, these migrants moved to other economic sectors with better working conditions and higher salaries. Pressed to find a solution, employers tried to bring the workers needed directly from abroad (Gualda Caballero 2012). The micro-guest programmes were therefore designed by Huelvan authorities, employers, and trade unions. Based on bilateral agreements, these programmes recruited directly in the origin countries; they have been implemented since 2001. With Romania, a bilateral agreement was signed in 2002, initiating the migration of interest for us here.

Romanians working in Huelva agriculture – a top-down perspective

The agreement with Romania was similar to the agreements Spain concluded with other countries during the same period (Ferrero-Turrión and López-Sala 2009). Its lack of specificity pointed to a focus on the Spanish side's needs, without considering those of the origin countries. *On paper*, the agreement with Romania was rather large in scope, addressing not only seasonal workers but also permanent workers and trainees. *De facto*, it functioned mainly with regard to agricultural seasonal workers, as the official data prove. The agreement revolved around the idea that one migrant equals one worker. The aim was to select the workers best fitting the employer's needs, transfer them safely abroad, guarantee they offered their labour under regulated conditions and, then, once they were no longer needed at the destination, transfer them back to their place of origin. In this vein, the legal document devoted large sections to the selection process, the work contract and its associated rights and to the workers' return. The migrant worker, rather than the migrant human being, to refer to Max Frisch' famous words, was the key perspective, and the effort went towards transferring the labour back and forth safely and lawfully.

There was only a vague connection between the agreement and any development goal. The legal text addressed the benefits Romania would gain through the return of migrants (as they would bring valuable skills) and mentioned 'measures to promote the reintegration of migrant workers in the origin state' to be implemented, without providing any specific details on this (Law 2002, 464).

In implementation, the agreement favoured setting up the Romanian institutional apparatus for sending a labour force abroad: the Office for Labour Migration Abroad (OLMA), a public institution that was established shortly before the agreement was signed, was in charge of implementing it. This state 'monopoly' simplified the process for the Spanish side but excluded other actors (e.g. private recruitment companies) who could compete with public authorities in recruiting.

Recruitment was a multistep process involving trips to Bucharest, where the OLMA offices were located. Long queues and people sleeping overnight in the front of OLMA offices were the typical images spread by the Romanian media during the selection campaigns.

Together with the contract (limited to a maximum of nine months per year), the workers were bound to sign a commitment to return to Romania at the end of the contract, and to visit the Spanish Consulate in Bucharest within a month after return. It is interesting to note here that migrants were not only pressed to return, they also paid the cost of proving that they were back in the origin country. Those not obeying were banned from participating in the programme for three years; there were additional sanctions if they tried to obtain a residence or work permit in Spain.

Without explicitly mentioning circularity, the agreement allowed for it. The employers encouraged the 'good' workers to come back for the next season, offering them a nominal contract that was sent directly to the Spanish Consulate in Bucharest. In this way, the migrants avoided the costs of repeating the recruitment. Apparently to the advantage of the migrant, the procedure excluded the Romanian authorities (and their control) from the process and pressed the workers to better conform to the employers' requirements. The number of 'repeaters' was probably substantial: a short comparison of the figures published by Romanian and Spanish sources points to a difference in the number of contracts of about 21,000 up to 2008. This suggests that circularity was relatively high among the Romanians working in Huelva and that the Spanish employers' practice of contacting the Romanian workers directly was widespread.

These procedures, set up in 2002, remained basically unchanged until 2007, when Romania became an EU member. That event impacted the way Romanian authorities approached managed migration. In 2007, OLMA was disbanded and all its tasks related to migrant recruitment were transferred to the National Agency for Employment. Placing all the national/international issues of employment under the same umbrella was a clear sign that Romanian authorities were ready to fully embrace the EU concept of mobility. However, as a new EU member, Romania was subject to transitional arrangements. On assessment, every (long-standing) member of the EU had the right to impose restrictions on Romanians' access to its labour market. As in 2007, the Spanish authorities decided to not open the labour market for Romanians, and the bilateral agreement continued to be applied. This lasted until 2009, when Spain dropped the transitional arrangements and Romanian workers could freely sign a contract with the Spanish employers.

For Romanian migration to Huelva, 2008 marks the end of publicly managed recruitment, the *public* phase; however, the event did not put a stop to migration. Spanish employers took the initiative themselves to recruit in Romania as the national government froze the programme with Morocco, and eastern European citizens became the only reliable source for the workforce. For that purpose, they used different strategies: contacting the former migrants directly, asking them to bring new workers, using former migrants as recruiting intermediaries, working with private recruiting companies or using the services of the publicly managed EURES network. Previous studies (e.g. Lopez-Sala 2016) suggested that the practices of contacting the former 'good' workers directly, offering them a new contract, and using their social network to attract new workers became widespread. This is, at least in the Romanian case, just the extension of the nominal contract form of recruiting used previously.

In 2011, as an effect of the economic crisis, the Spanish government reintroduced the labour market restrictions for Romanians. This lasted until 2013, when all the transitional arrangements related to the incorporation of Romania in the EU ended. However, the restrictions only marginally affected the migration practices in this case, as Romanians already had the right to free movement (granted in 2007), and for their work contracts, the employers only needed special approval (not related to any quotas). As such, this new *private* phase of migration did not seem to bring substantive changes in the way migration was experienced by Romanians recruited to work in Huelvan agriculture.

Romanians working in Huelva agriculture – a bottom-up perspective

The involvement of the Romanian public authorities in recruitment introduced differences between the two identified phases, mainly with regard to the selection process in origin and return obligations. Apparently, according to our informants, the rest of the process/conditions (work at destination, housing, and social integration at destination, including earnings) remained mostly undisturbed by the changes during the two periods.

When organised by state agencies in Romania, the selection process prioritised the Spanish employers' preferences. Middle-aged women with work experience in agriculture and healthy physical appearances were, in the words of migrants, the perfect candidates. Word-of-mouth dissemination of information about recruitment campaigns involved the programme's participants in the selection process itself. They added their own evaluation of who was the most 'fit' according to the promoted criteria. One of the women, for example, was convinced she had been rejected at her first attempt to gain a contract in Spain, when the agreement was operational, because she was 'too' tall.

> *They were looking for shorter persons. This is what I gathered the first time. Because with strawberries, it's truly very hard for the tall ones. Because I used to work on my knees.*
>
> (Woman, age 48, repeated migration)

Following this, migrants themselves caused the selection to evolve into a more complex process that reinforced, and even strengthened, the Spanish employers' criteria by reducing the costs of selection (for instance, only those who previous migrants appreciated as 'fit' were advised to apply for this migration), and increasing migration selectivity on the basis of their network. The interposition of former participants in the programme as recruiting agents added a new layer to selection. Driven by the willingness to bring 'proper' workers to the employer and/or to reduce the risk of an inappropriate migration experience for the candidates, the participants in migration became themselves instances of selection. During the private phase, this process seemed to be accentuated. Talking about a departure in 2009, one of the circular migrants told us the story of a selection through an intermediary, a Romanian woman, who came directly to her village.

I: *And she took everyone who wanted to go, or was there some sort of preselection on her part?*

R: *There was some sort of preselection, you had to… it was, it was also the age at that moment, because they would only take [women] up to a certain age, up to 50 years old, and she had to see them, to make sure they are not… Oh! And we also had… But no, she did not take her. Yes, another girl came and*

> *she was deaf. She could hear, but it was very difficult for her, and she [the woman in charge with finding women to work in Spain] did not take her.*
>
> (Woman, age 48, repeated migration)

From the very beginning of the migration to Huelva, between the moment of selection and the departure, there was an unspecified waiting period. The departure time used to be announced from day to day, via a phone call. This seemed to be the main instrument to manage the departures, and it appeared repeatedly in the interviews. Whether the caller was the public agency, the Spanish employer himself, the intermediary, or the private company, the call provided brief news about departure. The cost that migrant labour had incurred for employers in the non-activity period was thus transferred to the origin, transforming the potential migrants into migrants for the shortest term possible, when their labour force was fully needed at the destination. One of the women recalled that, in December 2008, she participated in a selection organised by the state agency, but she only left in February 2009, as briefly announced via a phone call.

> *(...) I think, around 6th- 7th- 8th of December. This was on a Saturday when the preselection took place. We went there, to C., they made us fill out some forms, some papers to fill out and they say: [provide] the phone numbers where you can be reached at and... The truth is that they called us in February, around the 15th of the month...*
>
> (Woman, age 52, single migration)

Once departure was announced, the potential migrant had to arrive (even from one day to the next) at the place communicated by her recruiter as the journey's starting point. The buses still prevailed in employers' preferences. The low cost and quick decisions about the dates of the trip probably favoured this choice. The freedom to decide on the time of the migrants' departure was also a means to reduce the costs associated with labour, as the migrants could be sent back gradually when the campaign reached its final stage.

Most employers paid half the cost of the trip. The journey from Romania to Spain was usually handled by the migrants (employers might advance the money and then deduct it from the workers' salaries), while the employer paid for the return. Our data suggested that the practice was common to the two phases. It is interesting that the cost of the trip back was transformed over time, at least by some employers, into a means to control the departure time. The practice of not paying for the migrants' return until the moment the employer chose put pressure on the workers to comply with the employer's will. All the women seemed to share this knowledge about the trip back.

> *So, they used to pay, we paid one trip, and they paid the other, right? And, for example, lately, we would pay the ticket towards Spain and they would*

pay for the trip back to Romania, and if you wouldn't stay for the campaign to be over, they wouldn't pay.

(Woman, age 48, repeated migration)

Once in Spain, the migrants were quickly integrated into the work. The daily work activities were described as difficult and physically exhausting. Migrants worked six days a week, six-and-a-half hours per day. The supervision was tight and the migrants shared a perception of 'being watched.' Generally, the accommodation was isolated, near the field, and was characteristic of temporary/short-term housing. Normal conditions included sharing common spaces (kitchen and bathroom) and sleeping three to seven in a room. Contact with the host society was minimal, as the living quarters were isolated, and the workplace was temporary. Moreover, and more importantly, the employer mediated these contacts. He arranged trips to the grocery store and visits to the doctor, if needed.

I spent the Easter there. Yes, the Easter. But they have nothing to do with it. (...) I mean, we didn't go to church to see how Catholics celebrate Easter, because the farm was in the middle of the field, and for us to go to town we would take the bus. So, when we received the salary, they would ask: Do you want to go to town? Yes. And they [the employers] would order a bus. Yes. So, it was all organized, one couldn't go as she pleased...

(Woman, age 52, single migration)

As the employer facilitated, approved, or mediated every contact or need outside the field, the degree of perceived dependence was high, and migrants tended to act in a way that was pleasing to the employer. One migrant spoke of this type of migration as being a period of 'staying in order.' The explanation for this high conformism probably lies in translating different interests into behaviours that were beneficial for both sides – migrants and employers – framed by the pressure of the limited seasonal time. The migrants' motivations clearly pointed to the need to accumulate as much money as possible. The limited duration of migration meant that time was perceived primarily as a time of work, favouring migrants' availability for overtime. Isolation from the host community, which limited alternative ways to spend (free) time, favoured the openness to work extra hours.

I: *And was it mandatory to work the extra hours if the employers needed it, or...?*
R: *Yes. Well, no, it wasn't. It wasn't, but, as we were far away, what could we do? You didn't have the bus ready... to leave [go to town].*

(Woman, age 43, repeated migration)

The power of the employer over the migrants seemed to be linked mainly to the conviction that he was the one who controlled the time–money association.

The tendency to please the employer became understandable from this perspective. The fact that migrants in their first work experience were perceived as the most obedient (see also Plewa 2009) further supports this. The fear of being sent home – meaning the interruption of the time–money series – played a central role in the entire process. However, during the overall migration experience, respecting the initial deal was the essential measure against which the relation with the employer was evaluated. As the expectations were generally met, the migrants positively evaluated the employers and repeatedly qualified them as 'sympathetic.'

I: *And what did you think about the employer?*
R: *He was very nice. (…) As long as he didn't pressure us or stress us or anything… I don't know if I ever saw his face. So, haven't seen him, ever. So, no… We would see the boss in the morning, sometimes. If only!*
(Woman, age 52, single migration)

Earnings were evaluated by comparing them with those acquired in a similar timeframe at the origin. As the comparison was always to the advantage of the destination, even if some rights were not fully respected (e.g. paying overtime hours at a higher rate), the payment was acceptable because it was considerably higher than what migrants could access at the origin. As one woman told us:

> *…and better payment. Because there, so what I earned in two months there, a hundred million, a hundred and something, well, go figure… You do the math: how many months would it have taken me to earn as much here, with a salary of seven million per month?*
> (Woman, age 52, single migration)

Defined as a period in which to earn money, the time spent in migration was structured around the idea of accumulating as much as possible. That was why consumption was reduced to a minimum and social life was curtailed to costless activities. The different interests of the employer (to have hard workers uninterested in connected activities) were satisfied by the behaviour of the carefully selected migrants.

I: *And you worked the extra hours if you wanted to, or was it mandatory?*
R: *Well, in a way you wanted to work overtime, because this was why you were there, to earn money, not to stay in your room. What were you supposed to do in your room from 2PM until the evening… until the next day?*
(Woman, age 45, repeated migration)

Although the difference between the origin and the destination in terms of earnings was high, this did not mean that migrants remitted or returned home with large amounts of money. The time spent in migration was too short to allow for significant accumulations. About 1,000 euros per worked month did not allow large investments, even if pooled. That is why remittances were mainly a way to preserve or consolidate a predeparture position rather than to foster upward moves in the social structure at the origin. One of the women, after 11 years of repeated seasonal migration to Spain, explained what she used the money for:

> *Rather daily expenses. Paying for the children's accommodation in Bucharest, for schools. Less for investments.*
>
> (Woman, age 48, repeated migration)

Given the duration of the contract, the migrants strove to integrate the experience of working abroad in their household's ordinary life at the origin. If the effort was not successful, migration was abandoned. If they succeeded, then the migrants made the step towards circularity. However, circularity was not simply implemented by the employer. Rather, it was built based on both the employers' needs and the ability of the first-time migrants to integrate their migration experience in their ordinary life in Romania. Three to six months per year working in agriculture in Spain also meant six to nine months of not working in Romania, and the migrant had to solve this problem. The initial tendency was to exit the labour market while living at home between two successive migrations. Flexible arrangements on the labour market at the origin become part of the story (e.g. working as a seller for the small shop of a family member at the origin). However, in many cases, the strategy was not to find a work arrangement at the origin, but to increase the time in migration. This could be translated into an attempt to gain a longer contract or to combine temporary contracts in different EU countries; this strategy was easily accessible to Romanians beginning in 2014, when they enjoyed the full right of mobility within the EU. The case of one woman in particular is illustrative. Now aged 46, she entered migration in 2015, with a contract in German agriculture. In 2016, she had her first contract in Spain to supplement the departures to Germany, limited to one per year. Her motivations for working abroad were related to meeting the needs of the household and providing for her children. At the time of the interview, she had her bags ready, waiting for the phone call from her Spanish employers to start a new three-month contract there.

The skills migrants achieved during their experience in Spain were rather limited. The migrants were aware that the knowledge they accumulated abroad was highly specific to a type of crop that was not grown in Romania. The difficulty of the work lay not in its complexity but in the conditions. Good health was a prerequisite for success because perseverance was key to fulfilling the contract. The migrants did not value the experience for the skills they acquired but in rather general terms as nonspecific knowledge about a different type of work, in a different culture, in interaction with different individuals. In itself, the experience was characterised as a mind-opening one.

> *And you got to see something different. Something different, and not just that, but also, another kind of life style, lots of things, I learned a lot. (…) I don't know, I think I changed, you change and you find a new perspective, you see things differently… and now, a person who was away, even for a little bit, I think that she sees things differently compared to those who didn't get out of here at all.*
>
> (Woman, age 45, repeated migration)

Guest-worker programmes – the best way to manage migration?

In examining the case of Romanian migration to Huelva, this chapter aimed to contribute to the renewed debate around migration and development issues, discussing the so-called triple-win approach. Largely promoted by some international organisations and think-tanks, triple-win has lately served to justify setting up a new wave of guest-worker programmes in Europe. We focused our attention at the individual level, trying to assess the benefits that seasonal migration to the intensive agriculture sector of Huelva brings to Romanian workers. The expectation was for our findings to reflect the triple-win approach's central tenet of benefits for the origin, the migrants, and the destination. This expectation was based on previous evaluations of the Huelvan programme as an exemplary one and the dynamics of Romanian migration, including its transformation from managed to free migration. However, our findings suggested that the wins for migrants were rather limited and fragile, whereas co-development, the major win for the origin, was not claimed or formulated explicitly in legal documents. In fact, while implemented on the basis of a bilateral agreement from 2002 to 2009, Romanian migration in the Huelvan agriculture sector mainly served the need of Spanish employers to build their labour force in a legal and orderly way.

The agreement signed with the Romanian authorities was only one of the protocols concluded by Spain with different countries in the same period. The similarity of these documents (Ferrero-Turrión and López-Sala 2009) suggests that the specifics of the origins were not actually taken into account and hints that the promoted model of migration was defined in the destination area and simply exported to the origin. The aim of the agreement was to select the workers best fitted to the Spanish requirements (without questioning them), to transfer them safely abroad, and to transfer them back to Romania once their job was complete. Workers entered the programme without a history, future, or present life at the origin. They were just workers whose labour was needed somewhere else.

The bilateral accord made only vague references to the return and measures to help returnees reintegrate at the origin, but no empirical or administrative information has suggested that this was more than a paper approach. The lack of any action to enhance the positive effects was striking, and the expectation that migration would produce such effects points to a simplistic understanding of the entire process.

The passage from the *public* phase to the *private* phase did not seem to change the practices associated with migration in any fundamental way, according to our data. The strategies of recruitment were different, based more on direct contact between employers and future employees, and involving social networks more extensively. However, the right of free work in Spain did not significantly modify the way Romanians travelled, lived, and worked in the agricultural sector in Huelva. Additional research is needed to better grasp why this happened. To our understanding, a certain inertia in migration practices was partially responsible. Moreover, the careful selection of the migrants as individuals with few occupational alternatives in their origin countries, prone to constituting a docile and disciplined labour force, and the power of social networks made up of migrants who learned to embody and enact employers' demands in selection probably played a role in the explanation.

Our informants pointed to limited individual benefits associated with this form of migration. Seasonal migration was accessed for its monetary value and evaluated comparing the job opportunities and wages at the origin (usually the poorest rural areas of Romania) and the destination. The short duration of the contract shaped the entire experience of working abroad and living under the pressure of the time–money association. While the amounts of money earned abroad were considerably higher than what migrants would achieve working at the origin, they were not large enough to allow for major investments. This migration was a strategy for surviving and making minor household improvements, rather than achieving prosperity. As the work was unskilled and performed in isolation from Spanish society, the migrants' benefits in terms of human capital were rather limited as well, and migration was valued by participants rather as a new experience associated with gaining diffuse knowledge of the world.

The repeated involvement of some workers in this type of migration was a sign that seasonal work in agriculture was a valuable option for them. However, the lack of any support to incorporate the season in Spain into normal life at the origin was a substantial difficulty that migrants had to manage alone. From this perspective, extending the duration of the contract was only one of the available solutions to increase the benefits of migration. Supporting flexible work arrangements at the origin, which would allow individuals to go to work abroad temporarily, could also be an option for consideration.

While far from suggesting that the Huelva programme was a failed experience, our analysis of Romanian migration invites a less optimistic view of its effects than triple-win implies. The triple-win discourse serves to legitimise this type of initiative. However, to foster true experiences of co-development, more ambitious objectives are required, including explicitly mentioning co-development as a goal and more effective instruments that acknowledge the needs of migrants and origins.

Acknowledgements

The research leading to these results received funding from the EU's Seventh Framework Programme for research project TEMPER (Temporary versus Permanent Migration, under grant agreement no. 613468) and the University of Bucharest project 86INT/2014. We wish to thank the anonymous reviewers for their comments on the manuscript. Funding from the Centro de Ciencias Humanas y Sociales del CSIC (Spain) has made possible open access publishing of the chapter.

References

Agunias, D.R. 2006. 'From a Zero-Sum to a Win-Win Scenario? Literature Review on Circular Migration.' Washington DC. www.migrationpolicy.org/pubs/CircularMigrationLitReview_9.06_DAgunias.pdf

Agunias, D.R. and K. Newland. 2007. 'Circular Migration and Development: Trends, Policy Routes and Ways Forward.' Policy Brief Migration Policy Institute. Washington DC.

Caruso, F. 2016. 'Fragole Amare: Lo Sfruttamento Del Bracciantato Migrante Nella Provincia Di Huelva.' In *Agromafie e Caporalato – Terzo Rapporto*, edited by FLAI-CGIL, 265–280. Roma: Ediesse.Castles, S. 1986. 'The Guest-worker in Western Europe – An obituary.' *International Migration Review*, 20(4): 761–778.

Castles, S. 2006. 'Guestworkers in Europe: A Resurrection?' *International Migration Review*, 40(4): 741–766.

Castles, S. and D. Ozkul. 2014. 'Circular Migration: Triple Win, or a New Label for Temporary Migration?' In *Global and Asian Perspectives on International Migration*, edited by G. Battistella, 266. Cham: Springer.

De Haas, H. 2010. 'Migration and Development: A Theoretical Perspective.' *International Migration Review* 44(1): 227–264.

EMN. 2011. 'Temporary and Circular Migration: Empirical Evidence, Current Policy Practice and Future Options in EU Member States.' Brussels.

EU Commission. 2007. 'Communication on Circular Migration and Mobility Partnerships between the European Union and Third Countries.' Brussels.

Ferrero-Turrión, R. and A. López-Sala. 2009. 'Nuevas Dinámicas de Gestión de Las Migraciones En España El Caso de Los Acuerdos Bilaterales de Trabajadores Con Países de Origen,' *Revista Del Ministerio de Trabajo e Inmigración* 80: 119–132.

GFMD. 2007. 'Human Capital Development and Labor Mobility: Maximizing Opportunities and Minimizing Risks.' Brussels.

Gualda Caballero, E. 2012. 'Migración Circular En Tiempos de Crisis. Mujeres de Europa Del Este y Africanas En La Agricultura de Huelva.' Papers. Revista de Sociologia 97(3): 613–640.

IOM. 2010. 'World Migration Report 2010.' Geneva.López-Sala, A. 2016. 'Producing Temporariness, (Re)Producing Precariousness: Regulation, Rights and Non-Citizenship Status of Temporary Immigrant Workers.' *Arbor* 192(777): 1–4.

López-Sala, A. and D. Godenau. 2015. 'En Torno a La Circularidad Migratoria: Aproximaciones Conceptuales, Dimensiones Teóricas y Práctica Política.' *Migraciones* 38: 9–34.

Macías Llaga, I., J.A. Márquez Domínguez and J.M. Jurado Almonte. 2016. 'La Contratación En Origen de Temporeros Marroquíes Para Los Campos Españoles Como Experiencia de Codesarrollo.' *Cuadernos Geográficos* 55(2): 173–194.

Martin, P. 2003. 'Managing Labor Migration: Temporary Worker Programs for the 21st Century.' International Labour Organisation, Geneva: 117–131.

Molinero-Gerbeau, Y. 2018. 'La Privatización de Los Programas de Migración Temporal En España Como Efecto Poscrisis.' In *Anuario Cidob de La Inmigración*, edited by J. Arango, R. Mahía, D. Moya and E. Sánchez-Montijano, 284–206. Barcelona: Cidob.

Molinero-Gerbeau, Y. and G. Avallone. 2018. 'Migration and Labour Force Needs in Contemporary Agriculture: What Drives States to Implement Temporary Programs? A Comparison among the Cases of Huelva, Lleida (Spain) and Piana Del Sele (Italy).' *Calitatea Vietii* 29(1): 3–22.

Newland, K. 2007. 'Can Migrants, Countries of Origin and Countries of Destination All Win from Circular Migration?' Global Forum on Migration and Development, Civil Society Day. Belgium.

Plewa, P. 2009. 'Administration of Seasonal Foreign Worker Admissions to Huelva' s Strawberry Agriculture.' 1–52. http://migration.ucdavis.edu/cf.

Reigada, A. 2012. 'Más Allá Del Discurso Sobre La "Inmigración Ordenada": Contratación En Origen y Feminización Del Trabajo En El Cultivo de La Fresa En Andalucía.' *Política y Sociedad* 49(1): 103–122.

Rye, J.F. and S. Scott. 2018. 'International Labour Migration and Food Production in Rural Europe: A Review of the Evidence.' *Sociologia Ruralis* 58(4): 928–952.

Wickramasekara, P. 2011. Circular Migration: A Triple Win or a Dead End. International Labour Office, Bureau for Workers' Activities (ACTRAV). Geneva: ILO, 2011 114p. (GURN discussion paper, no.15)

Chapter 3

The social and spatial mobility strategies of migrants

Romanian migrants in rural Greece

Loukia-Maria Fratsea and Apostolos G. Papadopoulos

Introduction

Most of the literature on migration in Greece highlights the country's transformation from an emigration country in the post-war period to an immigrant receiver from the 1970s onwards. Indeed, as was the case with other southern European countries such as Italy, Spain and Portugal, Greece had become an immigration country by the early 1990s (King, Lazaridis and Tsardanidis 2000). In the scholarly literature, migration was perceived as a primarily 'urban' phenomenon in Greek research (Papadopoulos and Fratsea 2019) and in European literature alike (Jentsch and Simard 2009). However, labour market incorporation and the employment structure of migrants in Greek rural areas also became an important subject in the literature around the turn of the century and onwards (Vaiou and Hadjimichalis 1997, Kasimis and Papadopoulos 2005, Labrianidis and Sykas 2009, Kasimis, Papadopoulos and Pappas 2010, Papadopoulos and Fratsea 2017). In this literature, the employment characteristics of migrants in rural areas, their livelihoods, and the implications of migrant labour for the Greek countryside have been at the core of conversations. The larger presence of migrants in rural Greece has furthermore been connected to a combination of demographic, social, economic, and structural factors linked to labour shortages in local host societies (Kasimis and Papadopoulos 2005, Kasimis, Papadopoulos and Pappas 2010). Migrants were conceived as a 'multifunctional' labour force that responded to various labour needs in rural areas, for example in farming, construction, tourism, and personal services. However, the undertaking of different jobs/tasks also led to significant differentiation among migrants. In fact, migrants' deeper integration into the local labour markets resulted in a range of social mobility patterns in both rural and peripheral labour markets. At the same time, migrants' geographical mobility became more complex (Papadopoulos 2009).

The economic crisis after 2008 has disrupted and challenged migrants' integration pathways in Greece. Indeed, the worsening economic situation has greatly affected the social mobility strategies which migrants had built up so carefully on both an individual and a family level. In this adverse economic situation, migrants have elaborated a number of practices in order to cope, or even to improve, their economic situation.

This chapter analyses the role migrants' agency plays in shaping their social and spatial mobility trajectories, taking the migratory patterns of Romanians in Greece as an example. We use a transnational approach to examining social and spatial pathways, emphasising that social status and wellbeing are perceived and expressed in relational terms. Hence, Romanians' active engagement with practices and strategies for social mobility is connected with their perception of existing inequalities, which mobilises them to develop aspirations for moving forward and/or moving up.

The chapter is structured as follows: first, a theoretical discussion is developed, based on a review of key works addressing the concepts of migrant agency and mobility. This is followed by a brief account of Romanian migration to Greece and of migrants' spatial mobility patterns between the two countries and within Greece. The empirical part of the chapter analyses the social and spatial mobility strategies of Romanian migrants in Western Greece and their attempts to improve their wellbeing and social standing, not only in Greece but also in their country of origin. The concluding part summarises the main empirical findings and articulates some interesting insights into the relationship between migrant agency and mobility.

Revisiting migrant agency and mobility

Contemporary theoretical and empirical debates on migrant integration in the labour market focus on migrants' precarious status and their limited ability to alter their working or living conditions. There is also an ongoing discussion about 'agency,' however, which recognises migrants as active agents able to impact on their working life (Bakewell 2010, Papadopoulos, Fratsea and Mavrommatis 2018). More particularly, migrant agency is an emerging subject in both migration studies and wider social science literature. Since agency is a complex concept in itself (Emirbayer and Mische 1998), the definition of migrant agency faces several challenges and frequently causes confusion and/or misunderstandings among scholars (Bakewell 2010, Castles 2010, Portes 2010). The debate on agency and structure lies at the heart of the social sciences, while the relationship and interdependencies between agency and structure is still one of the 'core enigmata in social science and theory' (Fuchs 2001, 24). According to one of the main theorists of the interplay between agency and structure, 'being an agent means to be capable of exerting some degree of control over the social relations in which one is enmeshed, which in turn implies the ability to transform those social relations to some degree' (Sewell 1992, 20). Although there are valid concerns about the degree of control and strength that migrants enjoy in shaping their external conditions, it is often stressed that the study of migrant agency provides a key axis for studying both the migration process and market integration (Coe and Lier 2010, Anderson and Ruhs 2010, O'Reilly 2012).

In the relevant literature, the concept of agency is closely associated with the concepts of strategy and practice. Although a plethora of definitions have been offered, scholars do agree that strategies are adopted by individuals, families, or collectives to change or manage existing conditions (Crow 1989, Morgan 1989). The study of strategies is recognised as an important conceptual and analytical tool in social research (Wallace 2002). Notions of, and strategies, for 'coping,' 'getting by,' or 'moving ahead' are important for understanding the actions of individuals or families. In this context, people's agency creates a solid basis for devising and (re)formulating strategies. It is by building or adopting creative strategies that people can stay afloat and even reformulate the conditions and possibilities of their everyday lives (Katz 2004, Coe and Lier 2010). Using the analysis of Katz (2004) and focusing the discussion on the labour market, three broad categories of strategies are worth highlighting: 'resilience' strategies, 'reworking' strategies, and 'resistance' strategies. Resilience strategies refer to the actions that individuals and/or families use to cope with everyday life (Katz 2004, 243–244). Reworking strategies include practices and actions that introduce conditions that make people's lives more functional and allow them to maintain better survival opportunities (Katz 2004, 247). Finally, resistance strategies build and shape a critical consciousness through which historical and geographical conditions of oppression and exploitation can be dealt with at various spatial levels (Katz 2004, 252).

Unquestionably, the concept of mobility has come to dominate migration studies. The concept transcends the movement/fixity divide and 'encompasses both the large-scale movements of people, objects, capital and information across the world, as well as the more local processes of daily transportation, movement through public space and the travel of material things within everyday life' (Hannam, Sheller and Urry 2006, 1). The 'new mobilities paradigm' (Sheller and Urry 2006) calls for examination of the various facets of mobility/immobility and their interconnections. A mobilities approach gets past both the micro versus macro scale and the agency/structure divide, 'exploring connections across scales and envisions a distributed agency that is both human and non-human' (Sheller 2014, 49). Hence, we refer to mobilities as a complex assemblage of movement, social imaginaries, and experience (Glick Schiller and Salazar 2013).

Thus, a key aspect of examining migrant integration processes in the labour market is recognising migrants as active agents and identifying to what extent they are able to influence their working life by adopting individual and/or family strategies (Papadopoulos and Fratsea 2013, Pereira 2014, Papadopoulos, Fratsea and Mavrommatis 2018). Particularly in the current economic context, there is a growing interest in the type of strategies developed by migrants to mitigate the adverse effects of the recession.

Certainly, these specific ethnic strategies (Aldrich and Waldinger 1990) are not limited to the labour market (Bauder 2005, Herrera 2012, Maroukis 2013, Domínguez-Mujica, Guerra-Talavera and Parreño-Castellano 2014), but also include wider geographical mobility strategies (Pereira 2012, Cadena and Kovak 2016, Marcu 2018). In fact, the rigid differentiation between labour market strategies and mobility strategies is challenging, as there is a constant interplay between them. In other words, instead of distinguishing between different types of strategy, we may refer to a 'repertoire of strategies and practices' that migrants adopt or create to improve their wellbeing. Thus, in a micro-perspective, the life strategies of migrants are 'fundamental choices, under competition-like pressure, that are dealt with in a sequence/algorithm-like manner by resource mobilization and by capital conversion' (Sandu 2005, 37). Additionally, there is a micro-macro interaction and interconnection when examining migrants' strategies. In this sense, migrants as agents interact with the existing opportunity structure in host societies and actively pursue specific occupational, social integration, and mobility goals in response to the changing opportunities or challenges both in the host and origin society. Nevertheless, those practices and strategies are relational. Put differently, migrants develop strategies not by making a comparison between 'here' and 'there,' but by simultaneously being here and there. This is a transnational approach to how migrant agency is expressed that warrants further research in migration studies.

Romanian migration in Greece before and during the economic crisis

Since 1990, Romania has experienced the highest increase in emigration of all EU countries, and emigration has affected highly skilled and medium/low-skilled migration alike. Between 1990 and 2017, Romania registered the highest increase in its migration stock, at 287 per cent, while the UN estimates 3.58 million Romanians live abroad (Dospinescu and Russo 2018). Different stages of migration and different types of movement have affected post-socialist Romania. Internal migration from rural to urban areas and vice versa has coexisted with international migration, on a temporary or permanent basis, creating a complex web of transnational relations between Romania and the rest of Europe (Sandu 2005, Horváth and Gabriel Anghel 2009, Potot 2010).

Southern European countries – particularly Italy and Spain – ranked among the basic destinations for Romanians during the mid-2000s. In the years that followed, Germany became their main destination country, while the second top destination country is the UK with more than 50,000 long-term Romanian migrants in 2016 (OECD 2018, 46). Currently, 1.94 million Romanians live in southern European countries, of which 49,276 live in Greece (Eurostat 2020). It is important to note that empirical evidence suggests that many Romanians have moved from Greece to Western European countries during the country's economic recession.

Until recently, migration from Albania was at the heart of the migration debate in Greece, in both public and academic discourse. As a consequence, Romanian migrants are a rather neglected migrant group in the Greek migration research, despite their being (at 5.1 per cent) among the top three national migrant groups after Albanians (52.7 per cent) and Bulgarians (8.3 per cent). Romanian migration to Greece dates back to the early 1990s, following the collapse of the socialist regime. At that time, Romanian migrants amounted to just 1,941 people. By 2001, this figure had risen to 23,206 people, while in 2011 their number had doubled to 46,524. Notably, the number of Romanians who have taken Greek citizenship has increased significantly (Population Census 2011). In terms of geographical distribution, the majority of Romanians live in urban areas, with over 40 per cent of all Romanian migrants living in Athens. In the Peloponnese and Crete, which are characterised as more rural/coastal areas, this figure amounts to 23.8 per cent and 9.6 per cent respectively. Generally, the gender distribution appears to be relatively balanced, although women seem to be slightly more numerous, at 54 per cent.

Initially, in both rural and urban areas, the majority of Romanian migrants supplied the so-called 'secondary labour market' (Reich, Gordon and Edwards 1973, Piore 1979), which consists of seasonal, menial, low-wage, unstable jobs. However, the Greek regularisation laws (1997–1998, 2001 and 2005) paved the way for migrants to seek better, more skilled, more secure, better-paid and, in some cases, higher-status employment, both in rural areas or in the construction/service sector in island/urban areas. Additionally, the right of free circulation for Romanians within the Schengen region from 2002 on, and Romania's accession to the EU in 2007, brought about new opportunities for spatial mobility both between Romania and Greece, and within Greece, along with new pathways of occupational and social mobility. In 2011, the majority of Romanian migrants were employed in services (48 per cent), with one third in the secondary and 17 per cent in the agricultural sector (Population Census 2011).

However, the economic recession in Greece has impacted on the occupational mobility of migrants in many ways and posed grave challenges for their occupational and social mobility. Empirical evidence suggests that, in numerous cases, the crisis had a devastating impact on the lives of Romanian migrants: unemployment sky-rocketed and many Romanians decided either to move to another country or to return to their country of origin. Indeed, the social cost of the economic recession and the implementation of fiscal austerity measures and economic adjustment programmes was particularly high. The risk of poverty and income inequality increased (Ketsetzopoulou 2017, Mitrakos 2018), while Greece's GDP shrunk by 26 per cent since the economic recession in 2008, with unemployment rising to 27.5 per cent in 2013, affecting a quarter of the labour force, with youth unemployment exceeding 50 per cent (OECD 2016, 20).

It should be noted that the impact of the economic downturn has varied between regions and urban/rural areas, as well as between different social groups (Hadjimichalis 2011, Dijkstra, Garcilazo and McCann 2015, Ketsetzopoulou 2017, Artelaris 2017, Papadopoulos 2019). Recent research has shown that, in general, rural areas appear to have a higher degree of resilience to the implications of the crisis compared with large urban centres (Balourdos 2017, Papadopoulos *et al.* 2019).

In an attempt to alleviate the implications of the economic recession, some Romanians expanded and/or invented new strategies and practices by establishing new pathways to improving their wellbeing. In the following section, we will analyse certain aspects of the social and spatial mobility practices and strategies of Romanian migrants who live in a predominantly rural region in Western Greece.

Facets of Romanian migrant agency in Greece

The study area in Western Greece

The study area consists of two regional units in the Peloponnese peninsula, Ilia and Achaia, which administratively are part of the Western Greece Region. The area has an extensive coastline and borders the Ionian Sea and the Gulf of Patras. The plains of the regional unit of Ilia are the largest in the Peloponnese, however, the region is also known for the coastal wetlands of Kotichi and Kaïafa, which are areas of rare natural beauty and ecological value. Historically, agriculture and stock breeding have been the main economic activities of the local population, alongside tourism. Olive, grains, wine, pepper, fruit, vegetables, dairy and fish products are important for the local economy, supplying the food-processing industries that operate in the area. Even though employment in the region's primary sector has fallen over the last 20 years, from 35 per cent in 1991 to 18 per cent in 2011, the primary sector is still considered a fundamental pillar of the region's growth and development. There has been an expansion in horticulture and greenhouses in the valley of Ilia, where 3 per cent of Greece's total agricultural production is cultivated, while strawberry cultivation in the area has been expanding since the 1970s; currently, over 90 per cent of Greece's strawberries are grown in Western Greece (Papadopoulos and Fratsea 2017).

In the early 1990s, a 'mobility transformation' (Rye 2018) emerged in the wider region: this included the movement of international migrants who had been living and working in different urban or rural regions of Greece and saw new employment prospects in the intensive agricultural sector, but also internal migrants originating from large urban centres who settled in the area, combining employment opportunities with quality of life. More recently, a number of Syrian refugees have been living in the Myrsini Open Reception Centre, while they wait for their asylum claim to be accepted and/or to be recognised under the refugee regime.

Romanian migration to the area dates back to early 1990s and the collapse of the socialist regime, when a small number of Romanian migrants arrived in the area. Currently, there are 1,758 Romanians in our study area, although many more arrive in the area from urban centres in Greece and/or directly from Romania at the harvesting season. The majority of Romanian migrants are employed in the local agricultural (42.3 per cent) and tertiary (37.5 per cent) sectors, while one fifth are employed in the local construction or local food processing sectors (Population Census 2011).

Methodologically, the following analysis is based on two studies carried out consecutively in the wider area of Western Greece: one investigated the various patterns of migrants' social and spatial mobilities, while the other study focuses on the relationship between migrant mobilities and spatial inequalities. The first study utilised the life history approach as a basic method that looks into the stories of migrants living in the area who originated from Albania, Romania and Bangladesh. The 'built-in historical perspective' (Rogaly 2015) of life histories allows for the study of migrants' individual and family trajectories. In fact, both the life history approach and the biographical method are important methodologies when examining various social and spatial mobilities (Halfacree and Boyle 1993, Thompson 2004, Frändberg 2008, Bertaux and Thompson 2009, Adey 2010, Rogaly 2015). The second study, conducted in the context of the IMAJINE project, focuses on the relationship between migrant mobilities and spatial inequalities and utilises the semi-structured interview as its core tool for connecting individual and family histories to various local, regional and statistical data. The second study, which is in process, has also included a number of interviews with local stakeholders.

In total, 13 interviews with Romanian migrants have been conducted in the wider area of Western Greece, while 11 additional interviews were conducted with local stakeholders (e.g. the local mayors, the Migrant Integration Centre, farmers), key informants and local residents. We conducted thematic analysis on the data, looking at migrant agency along with their responses to government policies, and we followed Charmaz's (2006) 'flexible' grounded theory approach in data coding and analysis.

Particular emphasis is given to the analysis of individual and family attitudes, aspirations, perceptions and experiences with a view to understanding and interpreting the movements and integration patterns of the various migrant groups being researched. The interviews were carried out in Greek and/or Romanian and were recorded with the participants' permission. To protect the co-workers and interviewees, their names and the place of the fieldwork have been anonymised.

Deciphering Romanian migrants' mobility strategies

Prior to the economic recession, the rural labour market in the area was characterised by an 'ethnic' and gender hierarchy: skilled and permanent jobs were mainly filled by Albanian men, who had a longer presence in the area, while seasonal and back-breaking agricultural tasks were performed by migrant women and newly arrived migrants. Although the recent economic recession has disrupted and challenged the social and economic incorporation of migrants in the local area, it seems that a number of migrants have made a virtue out of a necessity and expanded or invented new strategies and practices to alleviate the implications of the economic recession – what Katz (2004) calls resilience and reworking strategies – or even to establish new pathways for their social upgrading. In what follows, we identify the strategies that Romanian migrants have employed for social and geographical mobility – strategies that respond to the existing spatial inequalities. In contrast to traditional narratives of migrants as 'passive victims' of external events, these strategies underscore the migrants' role as active agents in the migration process, who seek to improve their social position in the host country and/or to establish their position in their origin country.

Transnational entrepreneurship

Although Romanian migrant entrepreneurship in Greece remains at relatively low levels compared with Albanian migrants, in recent years a number of Romanian business have been established in the area. We may discern three types of ethnic business: first, local barbecue restaurants/tavernas, which were initially opened by Albanian migrants, and this strategy was then followed by Romanian migrants. This strategy signalled an improved socio-economic status following many years of hard work in the fields or of working as waiters in the service sector. These restaurants offer Greek cuisine to Greeks, migrants living in the areas and other Romanians. For Romanian migrants, these restaurants are generally also places where they can spend their free time with their compatriots. Second, in recent years, transport companies have emerged which work between Greece and Romania. As Ana (50 years old) and her husband described after many years working in rural areas moving through agriculture to food manufacturing, services and construction, their upward trajectory was interrupted by the collapse of the construction sector in Greece. Given their knowledge and the networks they had formed over the years, they purchased a truck and currently specialise in the transportation of vegetables. Initially, they transported goods domestically; today, however, they have expanded their activities and established an office in Romania.

A third type of entrepreneurial activity is that pursued by Ioan, a 38-year-old who has lived in the study area for more than a decade. He related that after many years living in the area and moving from agricultural job to agricultural job and then to caring for the elderly, he inherited a house in the area. Given the increased housing needs of the migrants who work in the agricultural sector, particularly during high season, he transformed his residence into a kind of rural 'Airbnb' for Romanian migrants and other migrant workers. In this way, he increased his income and can support his extended family, who live permanently in Romania.

All these entrepreneurial strategies point to the fact that there are certain specific labour market niches in rural areas that have been capitalised on by migrants during the downturn. These entrepreneurial practices involve both formal and informal economic activities, which may have significant implications for the process of the migrants' social and economic integration (Kloosterman and Rath 2002). Nevertheless, Romanian migrants themselves consider social networks to play a crucial role in the success of any entrepreneurial activity. As Matei eloquently describes, after many years living in Greece during which he moved from agriculture to construction, his upward trajectory was interrupted by the collapse of the construction sector. However, he managed during the crisis to establish a local wood-processing facility. For him, the networks he had established with the locals acted as a buffer during the economic crisis. He attributes his upward social mobility, despite the economic crisis, to his investment in building a 'good' reputation – a good 'name' in local society. 'Wherever I went, I sat down and said, "hello and good morning."' He actually compares himself with the other Romanian migrants who did not invest time in interacting with the locals.

> *After I finished work, I sat down with my boss for a beer or a souvlaki... and as a result I returned home late at night. The other Romanians saw this as a form of 'overtime'; they didn't want to do it. But how can you get ahead if you don't look right and left to see what's happening? How will you ever learn Greek if you don't talk to the Greeks? The others [Romanians] used to 'hide' after work. Why are you hiding? Get out and say good morning! Those of them who didn't invest in this [practice] didn't succeed. They went back to Romania.*
>
> Matei (53 years old)

In other words, in the current economic situation, the embeddedness of migrant entrepreneurs in social networks is considered an important factor in the success of migrant businesses (Kloosterman and Rath 2001).

Devising spatial mobility strategies

During fieldwork, it became apparent that various types of spatial mobilities strategies are aiming to improve Romanian migrants' wellbeing, as identified in our study area. First, there is a circulatory mobility, in the form of continual movements that connect urban and rural places in Romania with our research area. More to the point, based on our interviews, Romanian migrants migrate directly from Romania to Western Greece in the peak strawberry-picking season. As one interviewee says, 'they [Romanian migrants] come for strawberry picking. They know when to come to the right place,' (Ioan, 38 years old). Their arrival in the region thus clearly relates to the information that family members and friends have provided regarding employment opportunities. The integration of Romania and Bulgaria into the EU (2007), which favoured the free movement of its citizens, facilitated this spatial mobility strategy. In this case, Romanian migrants' movement is for a limited period of time for employment, and increases their income in their origin country, supporting their households. This type of Romanian mobility, as a household 'support strategy' (Marcu 2018) or survival strategy (Potot 2010), is also documented in other countries in southern Europe, and in particular in Italy and Spain, while it has also been evident recently in the agro-food sector in the UK (Scott 2015).

Nevertheless, depending on their life stage and family status, temporary movements of this sort may result for some Romanian migrants in a more permanent stay in the area, although the 'dream of return' remains vivid in their future plans: As Anton recalls:

> *I came here [to Western Greece] for a month to see my father who have been working in the fields (…) and now 15 years have gone by (…) Recently, I said to my wife that we should buy a house here [in Western Greece]. Think about it I said to her – […] a house for our child to grow up in. No, she said (…), but inside I know she wants to stay here. Maybe not for ever, but…I am thinking about staying here. Because the first 15 years have gone by… friends have come and gone… Someday, of course, I will return my country.*
>
> (Anton 37 years old)

Conclusions

A number of social and spatial mobility strategies and practices have emerged among Romanian migrants in rural Greece during the period of austerity in Greece; the two types of strategy cannot be easily disentangled because it is acknowledged that upward social mobility is linked to an individual's geographical mobility (Savage 1988). Many of these resilience and reworking strategies may have started as 'coping' mechanisms designed to help migrants 'get by' or survive under the pressure of the economic recession, but they have been upgraded in the meantime into more elaborate plans for bettering their way of life and, eventually, for improving their status both in Greece and in their country of origin. We have therefore expanded Katz's (2004) scheme to include aspects of social upgrading and future wellbeing as a reminder of the fact that migrants themselves tend to develop some sort of 'substantive rationality' (a term coined by Weber) to guide their lives. This chapter argues that, apart from illustrating the socio-economic trajectories of individual Romanian migrants and families, the strategies and practices they employ should also be seen as making inroads into Greek society in general and the rural communities in particular. By examining Romanian migrants' practices during the economic crisis, their agency becomes apparent in contradistinction to the traditional narratives of migrants as 'passive victims' of external conditions. In other words, there are various conventional and non-conventional strategies that migrants have devised as tools for accomplishing and maintaining their social status in the host society. This implies that migrants strengthen their function(s) as social actors and, more importantly, that they are conscious of the existing system of social stratification but are actively seeking ways to improve their class position and wellbeing. Migrants' active engagement with practices and strategies aiming at their social upgrading also illustrates that there is a constant comparison, at least in their minds, between the place where they are currently living and an imaginary place that they can move to in the future. In this context, the 'imaginaries of mobility' (Glick Schiller and Salazar 2013) play a predominant role in shaping their migration plans, aspirations and expectations. Their perception of the prevalent inequalities mobilises them to develop aspirations embedded in their own capabilities and networks, with the expressed aim of moving ahead. Moving ahead means that they may opt to move back-and-forth to Romania, or to move forward into a different economic sector, occupation or region. Migrant agency offers a means of considering migrants' trajectories within the host society, while at the same time implying that they are part and parcel of the social structure in rural areas.

Acknowledgements

The Integrative Mechanisms for Addressing Spatial Justice and Territorial Inequalities in Europe (IMAJINE) project has received funding from the European Union's Horizon 2020 Research and Innovation Programme, under Grant Agreement no. 726950. This chapter reflects only the authors' views. The EU Commission is not responsible for any use that may be made of the information it contains. The authors wish to thank the external reviewers for their comments on the manuscript.

References

Adey, P. 2010. *Mobility*. New York: Routledge.

Aldrich, H.E. and R. Waldinger. 1990. 'Ethnicity and Entrepreneurship.' *Annual Review of Sociology* 16(1): 111–135.

Anderson, B. and M. Ruhs. 2010. 'Researching Illegality and Labour Migration.' *Population, Space and Place* 16(3): 175–179.

Artelaris, P. 2017. 'Geographies of Crisis in Greece: A Social Well-being Approach.' *Geoforum* 84: 59–69.

Bakewell, O. 2010. 'Some Reflections on Structure and Agency in Migration Theory.' *Journal of Ethnic and Migration Studies* 36(10): 1689–1708.

Balourdos, D. 2017. 'Αστική φτώχια και 'καλή διακυβέρνηση' στην Ελλάδα: Μία πρώτη προσέγγιση.' Στο *Το κοινωνικό πορτραίτο της Ελλάδας 2016–2017, επιμέλεια* Ν. Δεμερτζής, Δ. Μπαλούρδος, Η. Κικίλιας, Ν. Σπυροπούλου και Μ. Χρυσάκης. Αθήνα: ΙΩΝ, 375–400.

Bauder, H. 2005. 'Habitus, Rules of the Labour Market and Employment Strategies of Immigrants in Vancouver, Canada.' *Social and Cultural Geography* 6(1): 81–97.

Bertaux, D. and P.R. Thompson. 2009. *Pathways to Social Class: A Qualitative Approach to Social Mobility*. New Brunswick: Transaction Publishers.

Cadena, B.C. and B.K. Kovak. 2016. 'Immigrants Equilibrate Local Labor Markets: Evidence from the Great Recession.' *American Economic Journal: Applied Economics* 8(1): 257–290.

Castles, S. 2010. 'Understanding Global Migration: A Social Transformation Perspective.' *Journal of Ethnic and Migration Studies* 36(10): 1565–1586.

Charmaz, K. 2006. *Constructing Grounded Theory: A Practical Guide Through Qualitative Analysis*. London: Sage.

Coe, N.M. and D.C. Jordhus-Lier. 2010. 'Constrained Agency? Re-evaluating the Geographies of Labour.' *Progress in Human Geography* 35(2): 211–233.

Crow, G. 1989. 'The Use of the Concept of "Strategy" in Recent Sociological Literature.' *Sociology* 23(1): 1–24.

Dijkstra, L., E. Garcilazo and P. McCann. 2015. 'The Effects of the Global Financial Crisis on European Regions and Cities.' *Journal of Economic Geography* 15(5): 935–949.

Domínguez-Mujica, J., R. Guerra-Talaver and J.M. Parreño-Castellano. 2014. 'Migration at a Time of Global Economic Crisis: The Situation in Spain.' *International Migration* 52(6): 113–127.

Dospinescu, A. and G. Russo. 2018. *Romania. Systematic Country Diagnostic: Background Note – Migration. From Uneven Growth to Inclusive Development: Romania's Path to Shared Prosperity – Systematic Country Diagnostic.* Washington DC: World Bank.

Emirbayer, M. and A. Mische. 1998. 'What is Agency.' *American Journal of Sociology* 103(4): 962–1023.

Eurostat 2020. Population on 1 January by Age Group, Sex and Citizenship. Statistical Database. Accessed 9 February 2020. https://appsso.eurostat.ec.europa.eu/nui/show.do?dataset=migr_pop1ctz&lang=en.

Frändberg, L. 2008. 'Paths in Transnational Time-Space: Representing Mobility Biographies of Young Swedes.' *Geografiska Annaler: Series B, Human Geography* 90(1): 17–28.

Fuchs, S. 2001. 'Beyond Agency.' *Sociological Theory* 19(1): 24–40.

Glick Schiller, N. and N.B. Salazar. 2013. 'Regimes of Mobility Across the Globe.' *Journal of Ethnic and Migration Studies* 39(2): 183–200.

Hadjimichalis, C. 2011. 'Uneven Geographical Development and Socio-spatial Justice and Solidarity: European Regions After the 2009 Financial Crisis.' *European Urban and Regional Studies* 18(3): 254–274.

Halfacree, K.H. and P.J. Boyle. 1993. 'The Challenge Facing Migration Research: The Case for a Biographical Approach.' *Progress in Human Geography* 17(3): 333–348.

Hannam, K., M. Sheller and J. Urry. 2006. 'Editorial: Mobilities, Immobilities and Moorings.' *Mobilities* 1(1): 1–22.

Herrera, G. 2012. 'Starting Over Again? Crisis, Gender, and Social Reproduction among Ecuadorian Migrants in Spain.' *Feminist Economics* 18(2): 125–148.

Horváth, I. and R. Gabriel Anghel. 2009. 'Migration and its Consequences for Romania.' *Südosteuropa* 57(4): 386–403.

Jentsch, B. and M. Simard, eds. 2009. *International Migration and Rural Areas*. Farnham: Ashgate.

Kasimis, C. and A.G. Papadopoulos. 2005. 'The Multifunctional Role of Migrants in the Greek Countryside: Implications for the Rural Economy and Society.' *Journal of Ethnic and Migration Studies* 31(1): 99–127.

Kasimis, C., A.G. Papadopoulos and C. Pappas. 2010. 'Gaining from Rural Migrants: Migrant Employment Strategies and Socioeconomic Implications for Rural Labour Markets.' *Sociologia Ruralis* 50(3): 258–276.

Katz, C. 2004. *Growing Up Global: Economic Restructuring and Children's Everyday Lives*. Minneapolis: University of Minnesota Press.

Ketsetzopoulou, M. 2017. 'Κατανομή εισοδήματος και επίπεδο διαβίωσης στην Ελλάδα της κρίσης.' Στο Το κοινωνικό πορτραίτο της Ελλάδας 2016–2017, επιμέλεια Ν. Δεμερτζής, Δ. Μπαλούρδος, Η. Κικίλιας, Ν. Σπυροπούλου και Μ. Χρυσάκης, 359–373.

King, R., G. Lazaridis and C. Tsardanidis, eds. (2000). *Eldorado or Fortress? Migration in Southern Europe*. London: Macmillan.

Kloosterman, R. and J. Rath. 2001. 'Immigrant Entrepreneurs in Advanced Economies: Mixed Embeddedness Further Explored.' *Journal of Ethnic and Migration Studies* 27(2): 189–201.

Kloosterman, R. and J. Rath. 2002. 'Working on the Fringes: Immigrant Businesses, Economic Integration and Informal Practices.' *Marginalisering eller Integration*. NUTEK, Stockholm, 177–188.

Labrianidis, L. and T. Sykas. 2009. 'Migrants, Economic Mobility and Socio-Economic Change in Rural Areas: The Case of Greece.' *European Urban and Regional Studies* 16(3): 237–256.

Marcu, S. 2018. 'Mobility as a Support Strategy: Linked Lives Through the Life Course among Eastern Europeans in Spain.' *Geoforum* 97: 335–342.

Maroukis, T. 2013. 'Economic Crisis and Migrants' Employment: A View from Greece in Comparative Perspective.' *Policy Studies* 34(2): 221–237.

Mitrakos, T. 2018. 'Economic Inequalities, Poverty and Social Exclusion: International Experience and the Case of Greece in the Recent Crisis.' *Social Policy* 9: 7–24.

Morgan, D.H.J. 1989. 'Strategies and Sociologists: A Comment on Crow.' *Sociology* 23(1): 25–29.

OECD 2016. *OECD Economic Surveys: Greece 2016*. Paris: OECD Publishing.

OECD 2018. *International Migration Outlook 2018*. Paris: OECD Publishing.

O'Reilly, K. 2012. *International Migration and Social Theory*. Basingstoke: Palgrave Macmillan.

Papadopoulos, A.G. 2009. 'Begin from the Bottom and Move up: Social Mobility of Immigrant Labour in Rural Greece.' *Méditerranée*. 113: 25–39.

Papadopoulos, A.G. 2019. 'Rural Planning and the Financial Crisis.' In *Routledge Companion to Rural Planning* edited by M. Scott, N. Gallent and M. Gkartzios, 183–191. Oxon: Routledge.

Papadopoulos, A.G. and L-M. Fratsea. 2013. 'Η κοινωνική και γεωγραφική κινητικότητα των μεταναστών ως μορφή ένταξής τους στην αγορά εργασίας' *Γεωγραφίες* 22: 73–90.

Papadopoulos A.G. and L-M. Fratsea. 2017. 'Migrant Labour and Intensive Agricultural Production in Greece: The Case of Manolada Strawberry Industry.' In *Migration and Agriculture: Mobility and Change in the Mediterranean Area,* edited by A. Corrado, D. Perotta and C. de Castro, 128–144. Oxon: Routledge.

Papadopoulos, A.G. and L-M. Fratsea. 2019. 'Migrant Labour and Spatial Justice in Rural Greece: Taking Stock of Recent Research.' Paper presented at the Rural History Conference – EURHO, EHESS, in Paris, 10–13 September 2019.

Papadopoulos, A.G., L-M. Fratsea and G. Mavrommatis. 2018. 'Governing Migrant Labour in an Intensive Agricultural Area in Greece: Precarity, Political Mobilization and Migrant Agency in the Fields of Manolada.' *Journal of Rural Studies*, 64: 200–209.

Papadopoulos, A.G., L-M. Fratsea, P. Karanikolas and S. Zografakis. 2019. 'Reassembling the Rural: Socio-Economic Dynamics, Inequalities and Resilience in Crisis-Stricken Rural Greece.' *Sociologia Ruralis* 59(3): 474–493.

Pereira, S. 2012. 'Immigrant Workers' (Im)mobilities and their Re-migration Strategies.' *Employee Relations* 34(6): 642–657.

Pereira, S. 2014. 'Migrant Workers and Labour Agency Social Actors or Submissive Players?' IMI Working Papers Series, Paper 99, International Migration Institute, University of Oxford.

Piore, M.J. 1979. *Birds of Passage.* Cambridge: Cambridge University Press.

Potot, S. 2010. 'Transitioning Strategies of Economic Survival: Romanian Migration during the Transition Process.' In *A Continent Moving West? EU Enlargement and Labour Migration from Central and Eastern Europe,* edited by B. Richard, G. Engbersen and M. Okólski, 249–270. Amsterdam: Amsterdam University Press.

Population Census. 2011. Population by nationality. Accessed 14 May 2020. www.statistics.gr/el/statistics/-/publication/SAM03/-.

Portes, A. 2010. 'Migration and Social Change: Some Conceptual Reflections.' *Journal of Ethnic and Migration Studies* 36(10): 1537–1563.

Reich, M., D.M. Gordon, and Edwards, R.C. 1973. 'Dual Labor Markets: A Theory of Labor Market Segmentation.' *American Economic Review* 63(2): 359–365.

Rogaly, B. 2015. 'Disrupting Migration Stories: Reading Life Histories Through the Lens of Mobility and Fixity.' *Environment and Planning D: Society and Space* 33(3): 528–544.

Rye, J.F. 2018. 'Labour Migrants and Rural Change: The "Mobility Transformation" of Hitra/Frøya, Norway, 2005–2015.' *Journal of Rural Studies*, 64: 189–199.

Sandu, D. 2005. 'Dynamics of Romanian Emigration After 1989: From a Macro- to a Micro-Level Approach.' *International Journal of Sociology* 35(3): 36–56.

Savage, M. 1988. 'The Missing Link? The Relationship between Spatial Mobility and Social Mobility.' *The British Journal of Sociology* 39(4): 554–577.

Scott, S. 2015. 'Making the Case for Temporary Migrant Worker Programmes: Evidence from the UK's Rural Guestworker ('SAWS') scheme.' *Journal of Rural Studies* 40: 1–11.

Sewell, W.H.Jr. 1992. 'A Theory of Structure: Duality, Agency, and Transformation.' *American Journal of Sociology* 98(1): 1–29.
Sheller, M. and Urry, J. 2006. 'The New Mobilities Paradigm.' *Environment and Planning A*, 38(2): 207–226.
Sheller, M. 2014. 'Sociology after the Mobilities Turn.' In *The Routledge Handbook of Mobilities,* edited by A. Peter, D. Bissell, K. Hannam, P. Merriman and M. Sheller, 45–54. Oxon: Routledge.
Thompson, P. 2004. 'Researching Family and Social Mobility with Two Eyes: Some Experiences of the Interaction Between Qualitative and Quantitative Data.' *International Journal of Social Research Methodology* 7(3): 237–257.
Vaiou, D. and C. Hadjimichalis. 1997. *Με τη ραπτομηχανή στη κουζίνα και τους Πολωνούς στους αγρούς: πόλεις, περιφέρειες και άτυπη εργασία*, Αθήνα: Εξάντας.
Wallace, C. 2002. 'Household Strategies: Their Conceptual Relevance and Analytical Scope in Social Research.' *Sociology* 36(2): 275–292.

Chapter 4

Ghettos, camps and dormitories

Migrant workers' living conditions in enclaves of industrial agriculture in Italy

Cristina Brovia and Valeria Piro

Migrant farm workers' settlements in enclaves of intensive agriculture

In recent decades, in many countries, and not just in the global north, migrants have represented a relevant share of the workforce employed in low-paid and 'dirty' jobs in the agricultural sector, especially in areas characterised by intensive production and low levels of mechanisation (see, among others, Corrado, de Castro and Perrotta 2016, Gertel and Sippel 2014). The Italian situation is similar to other contexts where local producers require the presence of a cheap and flexible labour force able to meet the needs of a just-in-time system of fresh food production. The temporality of the employment coupled with low and uneven salaries, and the shortage of renting opportunities has forced many migrant farm workers to look for cheap and informal living arrangements near to the areas of agricultural production. This fosters the mushrooming of numerous informal settlements in the countryside made of self-constructed shacks or tents, with poor access to water and other services. These settlements, usually known as 'ghettos,' '*tendopoli*,' or 'camps,' are spread out in the north and in the south of the country, lodging from a few dozen to several thousand migrants. The *Grand ghetto di Rignano* in Apulia, for example, provided precarious shelter for up to 2,000 workers per season before it was evicted in 2017 (Filhol 2016).

By focusing on two different areas of intensive agriculture, this chapter explores farm workers' living conditions in Italy in order to understand how these living arrangements have emerged and developed through time due to the interplay between several structural factors and farm workers' mobility strategies. Moreover, we aim to show the effects of these living arrangements on workers' everyday lives as well as on the local contexts. In particular, we discuss the case of the Transformed Littoral Strip (TLS), in the province of Ragusa (Sicily, in the south of Italy), the biggest Italian greenhouse district, which produces fresh crops all year long. Here, many migrant farm workers, especially Romanians, find accommodation 'on-site' as companies accommodate them within their land. Secondly, we focus on the region of Saluzzo (Piedmont, in the north of Italy), one of the main areas of fruit production, where seasonal labour is essential during the picking season. Here, a larger informal settlement, hosting mostly Sub-Saharan workers, emerged in 2012 and has been progressively institutionalised and transformed into a camp. Although these cases represent two different forms of living arrangement for migrant farm workers in Italy, they both underline migrants' experiences of spatial and social isolation in the local context.

The analysis of the case studies relies on our primary ethnographic data gained through long-term fieldwork in both areas. In the TLS, the empirical research has been carried out since 2013 by use of several qualitative methodologies: participant observation as a farm worker inside greenhouses and packinghouses for two months; observation inside trade union offices and medical clinics for eight months; 53 semi-structured interviews with farm workers, employers, trade unionists, and other relevant actors collected in 2013, 2015 and 2019. In the area of Saluzzo, the empirical research was carried out between 2014 and 2017 which combined various qualitative methodologies: participant observation during the harvesting season within migrant camps and political organisations, 62 semi-structured interviews with relevant actors (in particular migrant workers, employers, members of political organisations, and the local administration), and the analysis of local press concerning migrant camps and agricultural labour in the region. All names of interviewees are pseudonyms to protect their anonymity.

Throughout the chapter, we argue that different types of settlements emerge and develop according to the interplay of four main factors: 1) the organisation of production (a seasonal versus a de-seasonalised form of agriculture); 2) the set of migration policies that channel migrants into specific areas while, at the same time, defining their differentiated legal status; 3) the regulations of labour market and recruitment procedures; 4) migrants' self-tailored mobility strategies. The interplay between these factors produces a certain type of living arrangement for the workforce that in turn shapes labour markets (by affecting the level of salaries or the forms of recruitment), showing how the productive sphere and the sphere of domesticity, which constitutes a relevant aspect of workforce reproduction, are highly intertwined.

Before the analysis of the two case studies, in the next section we discuss the literature dealing with migrant farm workers' living conditions by highlighting two perspectives – policy focused and labour-market focused – that emerge from recent scholarship looking at migrant labour in enclaves of intensive agriculture, and we underline the importance of merging these two approaches. Finally, the last section discusses similarities and differences between the two cases and includes some conclusive remarks.

Migrant living arrangements in rural areas

The majority of the scholarship dealing with migrant living arrangements in the country of migration focuses on urban contexts. Less attention has been devoted to studying migrants' presence in rural areas, although there are some exceptions (Kordel, Weidinger and Jelen 2018, Membretti, Kofler and Viazzo 2017). Nevertheless, the literature dealing with migrant workers in agriculture is contributing to filling this gap by coupling the interests in farm workers' labour conditions with an attention toward their living arrangements (Torres Pérez 2011, Gadea, Ramírez and Sánchez 2014, Gertel and Sippel 2014, Corrado, de Castro and Perrotta 2016). All this research converges in describing migrants' living situations near the agricultural enclaves as problematic: shanty towns with no access to water and electricity emerge right behind the greenhouses in the Plain of Sousse, in Morocco, as well as in Andalusia, Spain (El Haiba 2018, Hellio 2014); in the Canadian countryside, farm workers live inside the farms that hire them with no possibility of leaving without losing their legal status (Castracani 2019, Perry 2018); in northern Mexico, worker encampments, located on the companies' private land, are policed by *camperos* paid by the employers to avoid workers escaping (Sánchez Saldaña and Flores 2019). In several countries, male and female workers experience difficulties due to their isolation and separation from the local population, with restriction in accessing hospitals, schools, trade unions, and similar services (Perry 2018, Torres Pérez 2011, Gadea, Ramírez and Sánchez 2014).

These sets of studies also disentangle some causal factors leading to migrants' problematic living conditions in rural areas. Although intrinsically connected, we single out two different perspectives which the literature offers to better understand why ghettos and other forms of farm worker segregation continue to emerge and develop in several countries: policy focused and labour-market focused analytical perspectives.

On the one hand, scholars look at the role played by local and national policies in tackling, ignoring, or fostering these forms of isolation experienced by migrants in rural areas (Brovia 2018, Caruso 2018, Lo Cascio and Piro 2018, Semprebon, Marzorati and Garrapa 2017). According to these scholars, local and national policymakers often fail to improve the workforce's living conditions, since they do not consider the farm workers' presence as structural. As a consequence, they usually adopt an 'emergency approach,' that means considering the migrant presence as an 'extraordinary' and unpredictable phenomenon, which needs to be dealt with through 'extraordinary' means and budgets (Semprebon, Marzorati and Garrapa 2017). In the enclaves of intensive agriculture, the emergence of reception centres, which are usually dismantled at the end of each picking season, unfolds from this logic and underlies the temporary presence of migrants in the local context and their undesirability when the working season comes to an end (Brovia 2018, Lo

Cascio and Piro 2018). This perspective focuses on policies and understands migrants' living arrangements as a consequence of the lack of state action, and so could envisage possible solutions to improve migrants' living conditions through a mindful and effective policy intervention (Caruso 2018).

On the other hand, scholars look at the organisation of production, at the employers' recruitment strategies, and ultimately at the function that migrant living arrangements have for the local labour markets. According to this second perspective, informal settlements, camps, and other forms of spatial isolation do not represent just a 'side-effect' of labour market distortions, but rather are deeply constitutive of a certain labour regime based on the reproduction of flexible and cheap labour (Garrapa 2016, Castaracani 2019, Sanò 2018). The main features of these settlements, namely their proximity to the areas of production as well as their role in limiting workers' mobility, are functional to the just-in-time agricultural labour market. Perrotta and Sacchetto (2012), for instance, describe rural ghettos as spaces of migrant 'seclusion,' meaning a particular type of labour force placement characterised by the overlap between the production and the reproduction of everyday life. Differently from other types of camp, workers living in ghettos are not deprived formally of freedom of movement, but they are *de facto* captives, since they seldom move from rural areas.

Similar forms of immobilisation and control over migrant labour are found in other countries and sectors (Agier 2014, Bernardot 2008, Bruslé 2014). Manufacturing companies in China and eastern Europe, for instance, implement what Smith (2003) calls a 'dormitory labour regime'; the existence of dormitories near the factories where migrants are hired allows the employers that provide them to extend their control over employees' domestic spaces as well as their working ones, and to contain wages due to a reduction in the workforce's reproductive costs (see also Pun and Smith 2007, Ceccagno and Sacchetto 2020). Thus, according to this second perspective that focuses on labour markets' internal dynamics, there are no policies that can be implemented to radically improve farm workers' living arrangements, since segregation in the rural areas is a direct spatial effect of the labour market's structural need for cheap and nearby labour.

By discussing and comparing our case studies, we show that these two analytical perspectives, focusing alternatively on the policies or on the labour market, are not necessarily mutually exclusive. Indeed, they need to be merged in order to analyse the interplay between numerous causal factors (i.e. the organisation of production, labour market regulation, and migration laws, the effects of local and national policies) in shaping the forms assumed by farm workers' living arrangements. Moreover, to understand how living arrangements emerge and develop, we need to consider migrants' strategies of adapting to their living spaces, but also their strategies to 'escape' from them in order to increase their bargaining power (Mezzadra 2006, Smith 2006).

Greenhouse agriculture and migration in the Transformed Littoral Strip

The Transformed Littoral Strip (TLS) represents the biggest area of greenhouses in Italy, running alongside the coastline for 150km in south-eastern Sicily, mainly encompassed by the province of Ragusa (Figure 4.1). The district is specialised in the cultivation of vegetables such as courgettes, aubergines, peppers, and especially tomatoes, among them, 'high quality' tomatoes exported all over Europe, such as the *ciliegino* or *datterino* types.

According to last Census data (ISTAT 2013), 70 per cent of the greenhouse companies in the TLS municipality is constituted by small and medium-size enterprises (comprising land of less than two hectares). Of these, 94 per cent are registered as an 'individual company,' meaning that they are directly managed by the landowner (or renter), who works in the fields with one to four salaried workers who are employed for six days per week, eight or nine hours per day, for almost the entire year. Aside from picking, farm workers are busy with other tasks, such as transplanting and 'cleaning' the plants to increase their productivity, which means that waged labour inside greenhouses is needed the entire year, except from a brief interruption to 'sterilise' the land in the summertime. Employers are directly responsible for worker recruitment, and they usually rely on word-of-mouth, casual picking in some strategic spots, and very rarely on intermediaries. Employers directly control the teams or, alternatively, hire a foreman for this task.

Figure 4.1 The Transformed Littoral Strip (TLS) landscape, 2013 (Photo credit: Valeria Piro)

According to the National Institute for Social Service (INPS), in the province of Ragusa around 28,000 people were employed in agriculture in 2017, and among them around 8,000 were European and non-European migrants. Nevertheless, this data largely underestimates the number of migrant workers, who are generally hired irregularly – that is, with no contract and no registration for social services – and who, according to our interviewees and previous research, represent around 46–47 per cent of the total workforce (Battistelli et al. 2018).

The number of migrants in the TLS has increased constantly since early 1980s. The first migrants to reach the area were Tunisian men, due to the geographical proximity of the two regions and to the high permeability of the Italian southern border. Since their arrival, Tunisian farm workers and their families have started to reside in the city centres in the municipalities of the TLS, renting empty houses in an area characterised by the emigration of its former inhabitants.

During the 2000s, the TLS labour market underwent another significant transformation, especially in terms of the gender and the nationality of its workforce, with a significant increase in the number of Romanian male and female labourers hired in this sector. The access of Romanian citizens into the European Union in 2007 has accelerated their migration towards Sicily, allowing their free movement within the Schengen area. To these workers, often hired as a couple, employers offered precarious accommodation in the countryside, in shelters built on their private property. In the last few years, due to relevant geopolitical transformations, the increase in the number of people seeking asylum in Europe also fostered the mushrooming of reception centres in Sicilian rural areas (Dines and Rigo 2015). Thus, since 2015, refugees and asylum seekers, coming mainly from Sub-Saharan Africa, have been temporarily integrated into the agricultural labour market, while Romanian farm workers have started to leave the area.

The presence of different national groups has caused harsh conflicts between previously hired farm workers and newcomers (Cortese and Palidda 2018, Kilkey and Urzì 2017, Urzì and Williams 2016). The local labour market competition has been stimulated by paying workers undertaking the same tasks and the same number of hours a different salary according to their nationality. In 2013, for instance, a daily salary for a Tunisian man consisted of 35-30 euros per day for an average of 9 hours of work; by contrast a Romanian male or female worker was paid 25-20 euros per day. A few years later, in 2015, salaries turned out to be on average five euros lower due to the economic crisis affecting several labour market sectors. Recently, in 2019, salaries have slightly increased for Tunisian and Romanian workers who, at 40-35 euros per day, earn more than Sub-Saharan refugees and asylum seekers, who obtain 25-20 euros per day.

These differences in salaries between nationalities can be partially explained by the differences in migrants' arrivals and length of stay, and by the assumption that longer-term migrants have gradually experienced processes of upward social mobility, partly thanks to the presence of more vulnerable newcomers in the locality (Cortese and Palidda 2018). At the same time, as research in other areas and contexts also demonstrates (Hellio 2014, Preibisch and Binford 2007), it is relevant to also consider the employers' role in recruiting newcomers with the purpose of fuelling competition among the workforce segments and, consequently, depressing wage demand under the threat of unemployment. In the section below, we have chosen to focus on (mainly Romanian) farm workers living inside their workplace to highlight the effects that this peculiar form of accommodation produces on rural areas and on workers' everyday life.

Living inside the companies

When visiting TLS for the first time, the newcomer is struck by the huge amount of plastic stretching all over the land with no breaks until the coast (Figure 4.2). At first glance, it is difficult to notice the numerous shacks located near to the greenhouses. These shacks are small, crumbling buildings, often with no plaster or paving, and sometimes no windows. According to the size of the companies, these buildings could host anything from a single worker to dozens of employees. Usually, each couple or single person occupies a room, the space properly experienced by them as 'home,' while toilets are shared with other workers hired by the same company. Employers provide spaces previously used to repair work equipment, now turned into proper 'dormitories.' According to the employers interviewed, to cover the costs for these 'houses' Romanian farm workers are paid less than their Tunisian workmates, who live in the city centre.

Romanian farm workers we met during fieldwork explained their decision to live in the countryside as a solution that allows them to avoid commuting and to save much more money compared with renting a private apartment in the city centre. Nevertheless, they also highlighted numerous shortcomings experienced while living near the greenhouses.

First, the overlapping of spaces of work and life demands a flexibilisation of the working hours that, in turn, increase workers' uncertainty and difficulties in managing their lives. Since farm workers live inside the companies, employers usually do not plan shifts in advance, organising them daily according to the contingent needs of production, assuming workers' total availability. Overworking is thus common in periods of picking, while unpaid days off are also frequent when production slows down during the summertime. Nicola, a Romanian worker employed inside one of the company sites where the author experienced a period of participant observation, was always complaining about 'the impossibility of organising his own time' and having to look for another job during the period of forced work reduction.

Figure 4.2 Greenhouses in the Transformed Littoral Strip (TLS), 2013 (Photo credit: Valeria Piro)

Second, for farm workers living near the greenhouses, companies represent the space where they generally spend the whole day, both work and spare time, due to the difficulties of leaving the countryside without a private car, and without money to pay for an 'informal' taxi driver. The money shortage is also caused by the fact that salaries are frequently postponed until the end of the working season (apart from a small amount provided to cover basic needs). Reaching supermarkets, hospitals, schools, trade union offices, or bars is thus expensive, time-consuming, and often not affordable for many farm workers, who are consequently forced to reduce their needs to a minimum or to rely on charities to make their ends meet. Adrian and Catrina, a couple of Romanian farm workers in their 50s we met during the fieldwork, relied on Antonio, a Sicilian driver in his 60s, who charged them 10 euros to cover the 15km that separates the couples' 'house' in the countryside from the city centre.

Finally, the overlapping of the workplace and the domestic sphere leads to a loss of intimacy, de-structuring it as a place ('home') that is not safe and secure, since it is not private and protected from the employers' presence. Gabriela, a Romanian farm worker in her 40s, expressed this feeling by explaining:

> *Gabriella: I didn't like to work for* Stimolo [fictitious name for a local company]. *When I was employed there, the boss used to enter our place every*

morning to wake up us. We were just drinking our coffee, and he didn't care, came inside shouting 'good morning' and asking us to get ready as soon as possible. (Informal conversation, TLS)

Employers often 'exceed' their role by charging farm workers with extra tasks, such as cleaning the company offices for the same amount of money, as Ana, another Romanian farm worker, recounted during our conversations. This increased workers' vulnerability, especially for women who sometimes report cases of sexual harassment by their employers (Palumbo and Sciurba 2018).

For workers experiencing these living conditions, one of the few feasible forms of resistance is to threaten to or actually quit their job – and therefore their house – and move to another company (*cf.* also Perrotta 2015). Indeed, the turnover inside the companies is quite high, and Romanian workers, enjoying their freedom of movement within the Schengen Area, often interrupt their permanence in the TLS for more or less extended periods, moving within Romania or in other European countries. The following fieldnote reports the story of a couple of Romanian farm workers living between Romania and the TLS.

> *I spent the entire afternoon with Lorina and Patriciu in their house in the city centre in Vittoria* [city in the TLS]. *While Patriciu was watching Romanian TV, Lorina was chatting animatedly with me about her new flat: 'Do you remember when you came to visit me at* Battaglia's [fictitious name of a local company]*? We were living in a small room, it was always smelly and we had to drink coffee sitting on our bed! While now we have a proper bedroom, a kitchen and a place on our own.' Since 2013, when we first met, I have visited four of Lorina's and Patriciu's place out of seven they have been working and living in between 2013 and 2019, aside from periods spent in Romania and in Germany. Since their arrival, their new employer rents them this house in the city centre for 200 euros per month. While I thought it was great to live in a 'proper' house, Lorina explained that, all in all, it was not: now their salaries were a bit higher (40 euros a day, instead of the 25–30 earned before) but when they factored in rent, bills, and 'taxi' to drive to the countryside every morning, they were not able to save so much money. That's why, she explained, many Romanians were deciding to leave the TLS. When I asked her why they weren't living close to the greenhouses anymore, she explained that employers didn't allow it because controls over worker exploitation were now much more numerous.*
>
> (Fieldnote, TLS)

As Lorina's and Patriciu's story epitomises, migrants often exert their 'mobility power' by leaving the company or the country, for short periods or definitively, in order to look for better opportunities (Smith 2006). According to several informants, the law 199/2016, well known as the law anti-*caporalato* (informal brokers), has recently increased attention on migrant working and living conditions in rural areas. Following this law, in 2017 local and national institutions signed an inter-ministerial agreement (*Protocollo sperimentale contro il caporalato e lo sfruttamento in agricoltura. Cura – Legalità – Uscita dal ghetto*) forcing them to guarantee decent living solutions for migrant farm workers. Notwithstanding some relevant improvements, the law to a certain extent has negatively affected Romanian migrants' real salaries, pushing some of them to move out of the TLS. The interplay between employers' interests, legislation requirements, and migrants' mobility strategies is thus shaping farm workers' living arrangements in the countryside of the TLS (see also Tollefsen *et al.*, Chapter 8).

Agricultural production and seasonal labour market in the region of Saluzzo

The agricultural area of Saluzzo (Figure 4.3) extends over a vast plain at the foot of the Alps in the northwest of Italy (in the province of Cuneo, Piedmont), and encompasses 18 municipalities around the town of Saluzzo. This area represents one of the main Italian sites of fruit production by size: about 15,000 hectares and 300,000 tonnes of fruits produced in 2017 (Camera di Commercio di Cuneo 2018). The production is mainly destined for sale without processing through large-scale cooperatives and wholesalers.

As in the case of TLS, the last agricultural census (ISTAT 2013) has shown a significant reduction in the province of the number of farms (-30.7 per cent) but a moderate decrease in the farms' surface area (-8.8 per cent) and of the total agricultural land (-5.3 per cent). These data are consistent with an ongoing process of land concentration, usually leading to the disappearance of smaller farms, typical of monoculture and intensive agricultural areas. The harvest season in Saluzzo lasts about six months, from June to the end of October. During this period, different types of fruit are picked such as, in order of importance for quantity produced, apples, kiwis, nectarines, peaches, plums, and pears. Fruit harvesting is rarely mechanised and demands a lot of seasonal labour. As happens in the TLS, the local population is not attracted by these low-paid and demanding positions, which are now mainly filled by foreign workers.

As in the TLS, the analysis of working conditions in this area has shown the spread of partially irregular work situations, in which the employer issues a regular work contract but declares a very limited number of hours on the payslips, the rest being paid informally. The salary is usually paid on an hourly basis, the average wage being around five euros per hour. Unlike many other agricultural enclaves (but similar to the recruitment situation in the TLS), labour intermediation, both formal and informal, is not widespread in this area, and the recruitment and management of the workers are usually handled directly by employers.

Figure 4.3 The agricultural plane around Saluzzo, 2014 (Photo credit: Cristina Brovia)

The research carried out has underlined a variety of situations concerning migrant seasonal workers in terms of origins, migratory trajectories, and working and living conditions. We chose to focus in particular on Sub-Saharan African migrants who experience particularly difficult living conditions and whose situation is instructive to understand the social dynamics in this area. Data collected by the *Centro per l'impiego* (the Public Employment Service) show that 2,147 people from Sub-Saharan African countries held an agricultural employment contract during the harvest season in the region of Saluzzo in 2017 (*La Stampa*, 6 March 2018).

According to the data processed by the humanitarian organisation Caritas and published on the project website page *Saluzzo migrante*, they are exclusively men, mainly aged between 20 and 30. The most represented countries are Mali, Ivory Coast, Burkina Faso, Senegal, and Gambia. Most of them are asylum seekers or hold a humanitarian residence permit.

Living inside labour camps

The presence of seasonal migrants from Sub-Saharan Africa has been registered in Saluzzo since 2009, the year in which the first informal concentration of about

30 workers was noticed at the railway station, a place used as a meeting place and informal settlement (*Corriere di Saluzzo*, 3 September 2009). In the following years, this number increased to 100 people camped inside some abandoned train carriages, then in a disused warehouse next to the station. In June 2012, the municipal administration forced migrants to move to a peripheral area, the Foro Boario, and provided a big tent as a shelter. An informal settlement was formed around the tent, which by 2013 hosted up to 1,000 workers, living in extremely precarious conditions. Following a spontaneous demonstration organised in this camp in August 2013 to demand access to drinking water, the so-called 'water riot,' the municipality entrusted the management of the settlements to some local associations, in particular to Caritas Diocesana of Saluzzo. Caritas managed the camp at the Foro Boario for three years (from 2014 to 2016), providing tents, a range of services, and legal, administrative, and health assistance (Figure 4.4). In 2017, however, Caritas decided to withdraw from the management of the camp, which returned to being an informal settlement.

In 2018, the Municipality of Saluzzo inaugurated the PAS (*Prima Accoglienza Stagionali* – First Seasonal Reception Centre), a dormitory placed in the premises of an abandoned barracks adjacent to the Foro Boario, including 386 beds and access to services. However, these facilities are insufficient to accommodate all the people flowing into the region during the picking season.

Dozens of people continue to live in informal settlements: during the summer of 2018, they lived inside a closed factory, and in 2019 they lived in another tented encampment near the PAS. Apart from this main camp, both Caritas and the agricultural trade union Coldiretti organise accommodations for seasonal workers in 'container camps,' located in Saluzzo and some other villages in the area.

The attempts to gradually institutionalise the informal settlements have been accompanied by a slight improvement in living conditions: access to drinking water and services (although insufficient), a transition from an open-air camp to a dormitory inside a building, and easier access to health and legal assistance. But this process has also led to a greater controls on people, not only in terms of the workers but also activists, journalists, researchers, and others. For example, the PAS is monitored 24/7 by guardians and social workers operating in partnership with the local administration. The access to the court and the building is granted only to registered workers with a pass and to other people with the direct authorisation of the mayor.

Every year, the local administration has systematically closed the formal camp and dismantled the informal settlements at the end of each agricultural season. In some cases, the evacuation of groups of workers who wish to remain in the region, or have no other place to go, is managed with the intervention of the local police.

The research has underlined that the implementation by the local administration, and in some cases by humanitarian organisations, of these kinds of

Figure 4.4 Entrance of the camp managed by the association Caritas, summer 2016 (Photo credit: Cristina Brovia)

facilities is underpinned by an approach based on an emergency dimension, built on the temporary character of the migrants' presence during the season. In this sense, the main actors involved in this processes, in particular agricultural trade unions and the municipality, have often emphasised the temporality of the migrants' presence, considered above all as a disposable seasonal workforce. In this regard, the institutional camps are configured as 'natural' extensions of the informal ones, without considering any other structural solutions.

These forms of labour camp seem to represent, above all, an acceptable compromise for the main actors involved, namely the local administration worried about the emergence of problematic situations, and employers, who benefit from the presence in the region of a cheap workforce. Indeed, these camps allow an available stock of labour on the territory during the season, concentrated in limited areas, and generally easily identifiable and controllable, by giving the means to simplify the dispersion of this labour force when it is no longer needed.

The implementation of this kind of solution is not without consequences for the workers themselves. Being confined to a restricted place in peripheral areas and spending most of the time between the camps and the place of work, they have few occasions to interact with the local population, except for social workers or the few people accessing the camps. Moreover, the constant overcrowding inside the camps causes a lack of any form of intimacy and very poor hygiene conditions, increasing mental and physical health issues for many workers who are already weakened by hard working hours and often difficult life paths. A statement read by a farm worker during a demonstration in 2014 details the hardships of the migrant workers.

> *We are a group of farm workers and unemployed people who have come to Saluzzo for the fruit harvest season, some for the first year, others for several years. (…) Many of us are political refugees who have been thrown out of the reception centres, we have been disoriented, without a home, without a job, without having the opportunity to learn Italian, so we started to travel all over Italy looking for work (…). Work in the countryside is uncertain, poorly paid, and it is difficult to find a means of dignified housing. Last year we lived in the shacks of Guantanamò* [term used by migrants and activists to name the informal settlement formed in 2013], *at the Foro Boario, this year in the tents of the Campo Solidale Caritas, which, although they offer more comfort, are not an ideal solution. The cold, the humidity, the sharing of very small spaces, the difficulties in washing and preparing food make life difficult and expose us to various health problems. Every year, once the season is over, the camps are evacuated and we are forced to leave. Some of us return to our places of residence, others go to other camps and seasons in other parts of Italy, others simply have no place to go (…).*
>
> (Text read by a farm worker during a demonstration, Saluzzo, 12 October 2014)

The analysis has also shown that these labour camps are often managed with a paternalistic and authoritarian attitude by organisations or institutions, who aim to become the privileged interlocutor concerning the inhabitants' lives outside work, such as the organisation of the collective spaces in the camp, medical and legal assistance, the organisation of sports and recreational activities, and so on (Hmed 2008). Moreover, although camps can also represent a fertile ground for socialisation, collective identification, and collective action (Bernardot 2008), the research has illustrated that the progressive institutionalisation of these spaces, along with an increased control over the hosted people, has concurred to inhibit collective and political dynamics.

Conclusions

Throughout this chapter, we dealt with two forms of territorial segregation experienced by migrant farm workers in areas of intensive agriculture. For each of the two case studies, we described the characteristics of the agricultural production and farm workers' living conditions, with particular attention to the processes leading to these forms of segregation. Then, we analysed how different forms of settlement have emerged and developed according to the interplay of several factors, such as the type of production, the organisation of the labour market, the regulation of migration flows, and migrants' mobility strategies.

In this way, we highlighted that the temporality of agricultural production (seasonal versus de-seasonalised agriculture) strongly shapes the temporality of the migrants' presence and influences the modality of settlements. On the one hand, the case of TLS showed that the de-seasonalisation of agriculture goes along with farm workers' sedentarisation in certain territories and the permanence of a portion of these workers inside the companies. On the other hand, the case of Saluzzo showed how the seasonal organisation of production, characterised by the arrival of hundreds of Sub-Saharan African workers during the picking season, goes along with the emergence of precarious and temporary accommodation, i.e. informal 'ghettos' and institutional camps, dismantled at the end of each working season.

The analysis of these two cases also suggests that the diversification of settlements is also conditioned by workers' legal status as it is defined by migration policies. In the case of TLS, workers come mainly from Tunisia and Romania and they usually have a history of long-term settlement in the region thanks to a more stable legal status. In Saluzzo, African workers living in camps are mainly refugees and asylum seekers, and they experience extremely precarious living conditions, moving between several reception centres, and constantly worrying about the renewal of their documents.

Concerning the regulation of the labour market, and especially the recruitment procedures, the analysis of the two cases showed that there is a predominance of direct hiring and a reduced recourse to intermediaries, dissimilarly from many other agricultural enclaves in Italy. Nevertheless, the recent legislation tackling informal brokerage (the anti-*caporalato* law, n. 199/2016) and the following agreement also concerning farm workers' living conditions had a certain impact on the areas under concerns. In the TLS, the pressures exerted over the employers pushed them to relocate part of the workforce to the city centres. Therefore, although the majority of Romanian farm workers are still living inside the companies, some are now moving into rented houses in the city centres, while others are leaving Sicily due to a reduction in their savings. In the area of Saluzzo, the effect of the legislation was to accelerate the process of institutionalisation of informal settlements into camps, although they are still dismantled at the end of each working season.

Although all these structural constraints strongly shape the working and living conditions of migrant labour, the analysis shows that migrants are sometimes able to cope with these situations through their own strategies and autonomy. For example, the case of TLS shows how, for Romanian workers as European citizens, mobility is a resource they can mobilise to bargain for better labour and living conditions with their employers (Smith 2006). In contrast, Sub-Saharan farm workers in Saluzzo are often not able to exert this 'mobility power' in the European territory and remain trapped into a 'circular mobility' between the north and south of Italy until they find opportunities to abandon seasonal agriculture in search of better opportunities in other labour market sectors.

By discussing and comparing our case studies, we show that in order to analyse the emergence and development of migrants' settlements we need to take into account several factors that literature often deals with separately by privileging either a policy focused or a labour-market focused analytical perspective. As our analysis shows, these two perspectives need to be merged in order to analyse the interplay between numerous factors, namely the organisation of production, the effects of local and national policies, and migrants' mobility strategies, in shaping the forms assumed by farm workers' living arrangements.

Acknowledgements

Although the chapter overall is the result of collaborative research and analysis, sections four and five were written by Cristina Brovia, while sections one, two and three were written by Valeria Piro. The authors wish to thank the external reviewers for their comments on the manuscript.

References

Agier, M., ed. 2014. *Un monde de camps.* Paris: La Découverte.

Battistelli, S., P. Campanella, V. Comito, V. Papa and Ruggeri, A. 2018. 'I presidi di Noto e di Ragusa.' In *Vite sottocosto*, edited by P. Campanella, 159–208. Roma: Aracne.

Bernardot, M. 2008. *Camps d'étrangers*. Bellecombe-en-Bauges: Éditions du croquant.

Brovia, C. 2018. 'Migrants de saison: les camps de travailleurs agricoles étrangers comme problème public: le cas de Saluzzo (Italie),' Ph.D. diss., University of Turin and Paris 1.

Buslé, T. 2014. 'Qatar. Vie quotidienne et intimité dans un camp de travailleurs migrants.' In *Un monde de camps*, edited by M. Agier, 287–299. Paris: La Découverte.

Camera di Commercio di Cuneo. 2018. *Rapporto Cuneo* 2018. *L'economia reale dal punto di osservazione della camera di commercio.*

Caruso, F.S. 2018. 'Dal ghetto agli alberghi diffusi: L'inserimento abitativo dei braccianti stagionali nei contesti rurali dell'Europa meridionale.' *Sociologia Urbana e Rurale*, 116: 78–92.

Castracani, L. 2019. *Ils viennent pour travailler: Enquête ethnographique parmi les ouvriers agricoles migrants au Québec.* Montréal: Presse de l'Université du Québec.

Ceccagno, A. and D. Sacchetto. 2020. 'The Mobility of Workers Living at Work in Europe.' *Current Sociology*: 68(3): 299–315.

Corrado, A., C. de Castro and D. Perrotta, eds. 2016. *Migration and Agriculture: Mobility and Change in the Mediterranean Area.* London-New York: Routledge.

Cortese, A.M. and R. Palidda. 2018. 'Concorrenza imperfetta: Strategie competitive di migranti tunisini e rumeni nell'agricoltura del ragusano.' *Mondi Migranti*: 49–66.

Dines, N. and E. Rigo. 2015. 'Postcolonial Citizenships Between Representation, Borders and the "refugeeization" of the workforce.' In *Postcolonial Transitions in Europe*, edited by S. Ponzanesi and G. Colpani. London: Rowman and Littlefield.

El Haiba, B. 2018. 'Dynamique agricole, migration et production du logement ouvrier dans la région du Souss Massa.' Paper presented at the 6th International Seminar: Migrations, Agriculture, Food and Sustainable Development, Agadir, 21–23 March.

Filhol, R. 2016. 'Vivre au "Grand Ghetto."' In *Mobil Hom(m)es*, edited by E. Canepari E., B. Mésini and S. Mourlane, 135–143. Ed. de l'Aube: La Tour d'Aigues.

Gadea, E., A. Ramírez and J. Sánchez. 2014. 'Estrategia de reproducciòn social y circulaciones migratorias de los trabajadores en los enclaves globales.' In *De cadenas, migrantes y jornaleros: Los territorios rurales en las cadenas globales agroalimentarias*, edited by A. Cánovas Pedreño, 134–149, Madrid: Talasa Ediciones.

Garrapa, A.M. 2016. *Braccianti Just in Time*. Lucca: La Casa Usher.

Gertel, J. and S.R. Sippel, eds. 2014. *Seasonal Workers in Mediterranean Agriculture: The Social Costs of Eating Fresh*. London: Routledge.

Hellio, E. 2014. '"We Don't Have Women in Boxes": Channelling Seasonal Mobility of Female Farmworkers Between Morocco and Andalusia.' In *Seasonal Workers in Mediterranean Agriculture: The Social Costs of Eating Fresh*, edited by J. Gertel and S.R. Sippel, 141–157, London: Routledge,.

Hmed, C. 2008. 'Des mouvements sociaux 'sur une tête d'épingle': le rôle de l'espace physique dans le processus contestataire à partir de l'exemple des mobilisations dans les foyers de travailleurs migrants.' *Politix* 84(4): 145–165.

ISTAT (Istituto Nazionale di Statistica). 2013. *6° censimento generale dell'agricoltura. Atlante dell'agricoltura italiana.*

Kilkey, M. and D. Urzì. 2017. 'Social Reproduction in Sicily's Agricultural Sector: Migration Status and Context of Reception.' *Journal of Ethnic and Migration Studies* 43(15): 2573–2590.

Kordel S., T. Weidinger and I. Jelen. 2018. *Processes of Immigration in Rural Europe*. Newcastle: Cambridge Scholars Publishing.

Membretti, A., I. Kofler and P. Viazzo. 2017. *Per forza o per scelta. L'immigrazione straniera nella Alpi e negli Appennini*. Roma: Aracne.

Lo Cascio, M. and V. Piro. 2018. 'Ghetti e campi. La produzione istituzionale di marginalità abitativa nelle campagne siciliane.' *Sociologia Urbana e Rurale* 117: 77–97.

Mezzadra, S. 2006. *Diritto di fuga*. Verona: Ombre Corte.

Palumbo, L. and A. Sciurba. 2018. *The Vulnerability to Exploitation of Women Migrant Workers in Agriculture in the EU: The Need for a Human Rights and Gender Based Approach*. European Parliament Study. www.europarl.europa.eu/RegData/etudes/STUD/2018/604966/IPOL_STU%282018%29604966_EN.pdf.

Perrotta, D. 2015. 'Agricultural Day Laborers in Southern Italy: Forms of Mobility and Resistance.' *South Atlantic Quarterly* 114(1): 195–203.

Perrotta, D. and D. Sacchetto. 2012. 'Il ghetto e lo sciopero: braccianti stranieri nell'Italia meridionale.' Sociologia del Lavoro 128: 152–166.

Preibisch, K. and L. Binford 2007. 'Interrogating Racialized Global Labour Supply: An Exploration of the Racial/National Replacement of Foreign Agricultural Workers in Canada.' *The Canadian Review of Sociology and Anthropology* 44(1): 5–34.

Perry, J.A. 2018. 'Living at Work and Intra-worker Sociality Among Migrant Farm Workers in Canada.' *Journal of International Migration and Integration* 19(4): 1021–1036.

Pun, N. and C. Smith. 2007. 'Putting Transnational Labour Process in its Place: The Dormitory Labour Regime in Post-socialist China.' *Work, Employment and Society* 21(1): 27–45.

Sánchez Saldaña, K. and S.M.L. Flores. 2019. 'La vulnerabilità 'socialmente costruita' dei lavoratori agricoli in Messico: paternalismo e lavoro non libero.' *Cartografie Sociali* IV: 65–86.

Sanò, G. 2018. *Fabbriche di plastica: Il lavoro nell'agricoltura industriale*. Verona: Ombre Corte.

Semprebon, M., R. Marzorati and A.M. Garrapa. 2017. 'Governing Agricultural Migrant Workers as an "Emergency": Converging Approaches in Northern and Southern Italian Rural towns.' *International Migration* 55(6): 200–215.

Smith, C. 2003. 'Living at Work: Management Control and the Dormitory Labour System in China.' *Asia Pacific Journal of Management* 20(3): 333–358.

Smith, C. 2006. 'The Double Indeterminacy of Labour Power. Labour Effort and Labour Mobility.' *Work, Employment and Society* 20: 389–402.

Torres Pérez, F. 2011. *La inserción de los inmigrantes: luces y sombras de un proceso*. Madrid: Talasa Ediciones.

Urzì, D. and C. Williams. 2016. 'Beyond Post-National Citizenship: An Evaluation of the Experiences of Tunisian and Romanian Migrants Working in the Agricultural Sector in Sicily.' *Citizenship Studies* 21(1): 136–150.

Chapter 5

Lessons from the mountains

Mobility and migrations in Euro-Mediterranean agro-pastoralism

Domenica Farinella and Michele Nori

International migrant workers and extensive agricultural systems

This chapter explores the role of international migrant workers in mountainous, island, and inner territories that cover large parts of Mediterranean Europe (Greece, Spain, and Italy), where intensive and mechanised agriculture is not feasible due to agro-ecological features and the nature of the terrain (steep, remote, rocky). The modernisation process that unfolded in the aftermath of the Second World War has further pushed agriculture towards more market-oriented and capital-based patterns. As a result, these settings have been marginalised and undergone longstanding decline, leading to economic crisis, demographic regression, and land abandonment (Jentsch and Simard 2009, Nori and Farinella 2020). Here agro-pastoral systems – the extensive livestock rearing of mostly sheep and goats (but also cattle, horses, and pigs) based on natural or cultivated grazing and complemented by forms of crop farming – still represent a main source of local livelihood. As shepherding has become a less attractive opportunity for local populations, labour is today increasingly provided by international migrants.

This chapter presents the results of extensive fieldwork based on ethnographic observations, field notes, and semi-structured interviews with some 170 stockbreeders and 50 international migrant shepherds over the last five years in different regions of Mediterranean Europe: Greece (Peloponnese and Thessaly), Spain (Cataluña), and Italy (Piedmont, Trivento, Abruzzo, and Sardinia). Qualitative research was conducted by the authors, with semi-structured interviews collected both directly and through collaborators. Agro-pastoral settings provide an original perspective because most European literature (among others, Ortiz-Miranda *et al.* 2013, Gertel and Sippel 2014, Corrado *et al.* 2016) focuses on migrants' presence in intensive agricultural systems that characterise high-potential areas, while limited research explores other production systems (Rye and Scott 2018).

Since the mid-1990s, the exploitation of international migrant workers has been analysed as a structural component of commercial agriculture

(Martin 2016), driven by agricultural modernisation and the global integration of agri-food chains. The intensification of productive processes has led to the decline of peasant agriculture, a drop in agricultural employment, and its proletariatisation with a shift from family labour to wage work. The neo-liberal restructuring of agri-food controlled by multinationals and the supermarket revolution (Burch and Lawrence 2007) increased small farmers' dependence on the market and reduced their negotiating power. This agricultural squeeze forced independent farmers to cut down on production costs, including labour. Similar trends can be observed in both northern and southern Europe (Reigada 2017, Rye, Slettebak and Bjørkhaug 2018), as well as in other global regions (Martin 2016).

Segmented market theory (Piore 1979) has been commonly used to explain the consequent exploitation of international migrant workers to reduce costs, as they offered a new reserve labour pool willing to accept low-wage and sub-standard work conditions refused by local people (Castles and Kosack 1973). For migrants, agriculture remains a sponge sector and viable gateway to local labour markets, where even precarious opportunities are appealing compared with those in their country of origin (the so-called dual frame of reference) (Waldinger and Lichter 2003). The constant pressure of such a 'reserve army' swelled by new migratory waves consolidates exploitative conditions, as evidenced by the continuous replacement of migrant labour with new arrivals and different ethnic groups (Waldinger and Lichter 2003, Gertel and Sippel 2014). This competition is powered by the 'good worker' rhetoric employers use to essentialise stereotypes and prejudices as 'natural attributes,' justifying 'changes in labour force hiring, to reject one group and legitimate the next one' (Hellio 2017, 212).

Within this framework, agro-pastoralism provides a unique perspective compared with more intensive agricultural sectors, emphasising the variability of farming systems and their environmental embeddedness, the relevance of peasant strategies and family labour, pluri-activism, socio-ecological services, and other 'off-market' factors relevant in contrasting agricultural squeeze and the abandonment of marginal settings (Van der Ploeg 2008, 2013).

In intensive farming, work is seasonal and requires a certain number of workers concentrated in the field or in greenhouses to carry out simple and repetitive tasks. Labour relations are very hierarchical: employers are separated from migrants and interact with them through intermediaries such as '*caporali*' for hiring, pay, accommodation, and other aspects linked to their work (Corrado *et al.* 2018). Migrant workers' segregation and exploitation are thus evident and bolstered by workers' concentration in rural ghettos with sub-standard living conditions.

In agro-pastoral farms, self-employment and unpaid family work is fundamental and migrant work is often complementary. The stockbreeder works alongside the wage worker, merging exploitation with self-exploitation. This has important implications in terms of personal relations, which seem more horizontal and less hierarchical. However, employers develop hidden forms of control, subordination, and exploitation: a prime example is the rhetoric of the 'good worker.' In addition, agro-pastoral labour is multifunctional and less stereotyped than in intensive agriculture, thus generating spaces of autonomy and freedom within which workers exercise their own agency.

The next section presents the main results of our research, analyses how agro-pastoral systems respond to the pressures from global agri-food chains and examines international migrant workers' role in this process. The third section discusses 'good worker' rhetoric as a means of exercising power over migrant shepherds and their response in terms of migrant agency. The final section summarises some conclusions to be drawn from this research.

Migrant shepherds in agro-pastoral systems: a patchy mosaic

Extensive rearing of goat and sheep represents a minor segment of the broader livestock sector in the European Union which hinges on more intensive breeding of cattle, poultry, and pigs. Sheep's and goat's milk totalled about three per cent of total EU milk production for 2015, while small ruminants 'represented less than 2 per cent of total EU meat production [...] and less than 6 per cent of its value' (BEPRS 2017, 3). However, this sector is strategic for Euro-Mediterranean countries, where extensive livestock breeding is a main economic activity in the mountainous territories, inner regions, and islands that are not suited to intensive agriculture. In these settings, agro-pastoralism provides critical contributions in managing landscape and ecological resources, supporting employment and income of local communities, and helping to avert depopulation. In 2015, Greece, Spain, and Italy concentrated 39 and 67 per cent, respectively, of all sheep and goats in the EU, and among the largest producers of sheep milk, with Greece accounting for 31 per cent, Spain 25.2 per cent, and Italy 21.4 per cent in 2018 (ISMEA 2019). Sheep milk is used to produce standardised cheeses that are relevant in local food culture, such as Italy's Pecorino Romano, Greece's Feta, and Spain's Manchego.

Meat production is another important component of the agro-pastoral economy. For example, in Greece 'the value of sheep and goat meat production represents almost half of the total livestock production value' (BEPRS 2017, 3), while Spain ranks second in production of lamb meat after the UK (EC 2020).

Dairy products and meat, however, are also commodities in international markets and within global agro-food chains, and therefore subject to international competition and price volatility (Farinella 2019). For example, from 2000 to 2017, sheep milk price averaged €0.80/litre in Italy and Spain and €0.90/litre in Greece (our calculations, Eurostat 2020), with negative peaks reaching €0.60/litre. When mentioning the agricultural squeeze, many respondents indicated that the price to ensure adequate profitability for sheep farms is at least €1.00/litre.

Recent decades have witnessed a growing global competition on these markets. Many agro-pastoral farms have been forced to either close or restructure their farms by expanding their herd and reorganising land and labour resources in order to adjust cost-benefit ratios (Hadjigeorgiou 2011, Ragkos and Nori 2016, Mattalia *et al.* 2018, Farinella 2019). This has resulted throughout the region in fewer agro-pastoral enterprises with larger flock size. Eurostat (2016) data show the number of sheep farms have roughly halved since 1990, with a 68.1 per cent drop in number in Italy, a 50.6 per cent drop in Spain, and 46.4 per cent drop in Greece. Respective national flocks also decreased, albeit at lower rates, during the same period: 0.4 per cent in Greece, 9.4 per cent in Spain, and 19.4 per cent in Italy, underscoring an expansion in size for the remaining farms.

Despite this common process of intensification, agro-pastoralism in Mediterranean Europe remains territorially diversified and adapted to local ecological conditions. Using the results of our research, a broad classification could combine the magnitude and intensity of livestock mobility, and the scale of agricultural farming:

a) Transhumant systems (from *trans-humare*, moving through lands) based on seasonal mobility of livestock, which are grazing outdoors and get their nutrients from the natural pasture. These farms of medium- to small-sized flocks are typical of mountainous settings and often devoted to meat production.
b) Extensive or semi-extensive systems, often associated with inner and hilly areas, where animals spend most of their time in pastures nearby or at short distance. These farms have small or medium size, with some of their land partly devoted to their own production of feed, forage, and cultivated pastures.
c) Semi-intensive systems, typically for large farms in the plains, whereby livestock are kept mainly inside stables; animal feed is partially produced by the farm and supplemented with the purchase of external inputs, with limited degrees of open grazing.

The pastoral territories of Mediterranean Europe display agro-ecological and socio-cultural diversity, as well as important similarities. In Greece, sheep and goats represent about 75 per cent of overall grazing units, contributing significantly to local income and the GDP. Agro-pastoralism is territorially diversified: in mainland territories (Thrace, Macedonia, Thessaly, and Peloponnese) a patchy mosaic is found, with more intensive farming in lowland plains characterised by high investment and modern infrastructure, especially since the 2000s. Mixed systems of transhumance and semi-extensive breeding prevail in mountainous areas, where agro-pastoralism accounts for 17 per cent of employment and 6.5 per cent of local production (Ragkos and Nori 2016). In most Greek island communities, lower scale extensive grazing of sheep and goats represents an important source of livelihood through the processing and sale of traditional cheeses in tourist networks (Ragkos *et al.* 2018).

In Spain, sheep and goat farming represents about one third of all livestock units. There is great territorial diversity, from the northern mountainous ranges to central mountainous *meseta*, and to drier southern pasturelands. Pastoral systems in Spain have changed dramatically in recent decades, towards enlarged flock size and reduced mobility, often with a view to enhance per capita milk production. Evolving from the traditional system that connected grazing areas in Castilla y León to Extremadura and Andalusia according to the season, transhumance is still quite popular throughout the country, especially for meat production. While the distances covered today are limited, the living and working conditions during some of the year remain difficult due to geographical isolation and climate conditions. Extensive rearing of small ruminants remains important throughout the country; sheep and cattle breeding with mixed orientation predominates in the northern temperate regions, while extensive beef and pig production is more typical in the western and southwestern peninsular lands.

In Italy, agro-pastoral breeding of sheep, goats, and even cattle is widespread in the inner territories; important agro-ecological differences exist across regions and between alpine, apennine, and insular areas. In the northern alpine settings from Piedmont to Veneto, seasonal transhumance from lower to higher altitudes is a most-performed activity, with small ruminant flocks often devoted to meat production, while cattle herds are raised for mixed purposes. In the apennine systems typical of central and southern Italy, as well as in Sardinia, the characteristic transhumance systems have almost disappeared to the benefit of semi-extensive permanent ones. Here, sheep and goat are mostly raised for milk production to supply local dairy value chains. Driven by Pecorino Romano marketing, semi-intensive farms are increasingly spreading throughout Sardinia (Farinella 2019), though more extensive grazing and artisanal dairies are important for local tourism.

Common traits of agro-pastoral systems include technical, policy, as well as socio-economic aspects. Mechanisation is limited and labour continues to be mostly physical and manual. Productivity rates have increased more slowly than production costs, whose rise has often been on the shoulders of the shepherding workforce: wages have not improved through time, while working conditions have intensified. Since 2003 the reorientation of the Common Agricultural Policy (CAP) towards rural development has enabled recognising agro-pastoral practices in managing landscape and ecological resources of marginal territories. Public support has shifted accordingly from remunerating production to a multifunctional vision of agriculture (Kerven and Behnke 2011, Nori and de Marchi 2015). The constant decline in the number of agro-pastoral farms suggests though that CAP schemes are not an adequate guarantee for these systems' permanence and reproduction (Farinella *et al.* 2017). Eurostat figures indicate that conditions are not attractive and/or enabling for new generations: in 2016 46.8 per cent of farm heads in Greece, 49.2 per cent in Spain, and 42.2 per cent in Italy were aged 55 and older.

Through these lenses one can understand the crisis of the agro-pastoral 'vocation' and the relative lack of workforce on pasturelands in the Alps, Epirus, Apennines, and Pyrenees which rank among the areas most exposed to the risk of abandonment (Nori 2017).

This is the context in which international migrant workers have come to provide a skilled labour force at a relatively low cost. Based on our research, the typical profile of a migrant shepherd is: a male, aged between 25 and 40; a native of a Mediterranean country (predominantly Romania, Morocco, Albania, or North Macedonia) and more recently Asia (i.e., Pakistan, India), and sub-Saharan Africa (i.e., Ghana, Senegal); often issued from pastoral settings and thus have some experience and skills related to livestock husbandry. History, language, and migration networks have shaped the different migratory patterns and presence. For instance, Romanians are found mostly in Italy and parts of Spain, while Moroccans are more usually found in Spain and Albanians in Greece (Nori 2017).

In Greece, the influx of international migrant workers began in the 1990s, after the collapse of the Albanian regime and the opening of Albania's borders. Apart from their contributions to the extensive livestock sector, Albanian migrant workers have also played a critical role in revitalising the local social, economic, and demographic fibres in many rural communities (Kasimis *et al.* 2010, Kasimis and Papadopoulos 2013). These early flows slowly opened the way to shepherds originating from eastern Europe (Bulgaria and Romania) and, more recently, to workers from India and Pakistan. Today, migrants represent about half of the agro-pastoral salaried workforce in Epirus and Peloponnese, and about one third in Crete (Ragkos and Nori 2016). On one hand, the migrant workforce has supported the development of large, innovative, and specialised dairy farms, while, on the other, it has contributed to the endurance of more traditional transhumance systems. As a substitute for family labour, the recruitment of migrants has allowed household members to pursue other activities or to look for employment outside the agricultural sector (Papadopoulos and Roumpakis 2009, Ragkos and Nori 2016, Papadopoulos and Fratsea 2017). Contracts are completely informal, and salary ranges between 300–600 euros per month according to the region and system.

Also, in Spain, migration from several countries has contributed to the labour reconfiguration of existing agro-pastoral systems. In areas where wildlife predation is encroaching, the presence of shepherds is increasingly important for tending flocks and because it is difficult to source local workers, most shepherds are of foreign origin. Traditionally migrant shepherds originate from Morocco and Romania, but more recently also from Bulgaria, Ukraine, and from Sub-Saharan Africa and Latin-Americas. In the Catalan Pyrenees, international migrants constitute about half of the waged shepherding workforce (Nori and López-i-Gelats 2017). The ratio of migrant to local shepherding labour drops to one in three in central Spain, Galicia, and Extremadura – where migrant labour is usually from Portugal (Nori 2017). Some of these workers have benefited from some form of training in one of the country's six pastoral regional schools. Monthly salary averages 600–700 euros, with higher rates in the northern regions.

As in the case of Spain, the growing presence of predators has contributed to the reincorporation of shepherds in many areas of Italy. In the northern alpine regions, where transhumant systems are characterised by lengthy and harsh periods of constant mobility, two out of three salaried shepherds are international migrants (Nori and de Marchi 2015). In the northern Italian lowland areas, migrant shepherds are also the main labour source in intensive cattle stockbreeding linked to the production of Parmigiano cheese (Lum 2011). In Abruzzo, a region with important pastoral traditions, official data indicate a long-established presence of shepherds from North Macedonia and Romania (Coldiretti 2010). In Sardinia, which holds over 40 per cent of the national sheep flock, one in three hired shepherds is an international migrant (Farinella and Mannia 2017); Albanians have been replaced over time by Romanians and, more recently, by Moroccans and Indians. Salaries range from 500–900 euros monthly, depending mostly on the size of the flock (Farinella and Mannia 2017).

Migrant shepherds and the 'good workers' rhetoric

The dynamics characterising migrant workers in agro-pastoralism present some continuity but mostly differ from those typical of other agricultural systems. Conditions of illegality, limited rights, low wages, and poor living and working standards are typical and common. International migrant shepherds show high degrees of mobility, often moving from one farm to another seeking better working and living conditions (Farinella 2019). Recruitment is mostly by word of mouth through personal networks and individual arrangements among migrant communities who often engage friends and relatives. The contractual arrangements are often quite informal and precarious, although in many cases there is a formal contract that covers only partially the worker's rights and social insurance.

The main differences concern the type of work and the employment relationships. As noted earlier, harvesting in more intensive agriculture systems is a strenuous physical activity, stereotyped, and monotonous, temporally and spatially concentrated, and often carried out in work groups. The organisation of the work is hierarchical, with a separation of employer from workers through the presence of several intermediaries. Supervision is close and constant, with pay set by the piece. Picking fruits and filling boxes as quickly as possible, for example, represent simple goals connected to standardised tasks that subordinate the worker to the production chain according to Marx's description of the worker as the 'living appendix of the machine.'

Agro-pastoralism is more multifunctional: in addition to livestock shepherding and its overall management, there are collateral tasks such as clearing lands, building fences, collecting timber, and building or mechanical activities on the farm. Sometimes migrant shepherds carry out tasks requiring 'high' skills, such as cheesemaking or land cultivation and the related use of agricultural vehicles. While the workload is widespread throughout the year, some tasks are seasonal, such as lambing, milking, dairy processing, shearing, and farming. However, the main task remains accompanying the grazing flock. This is not particularly strenuous or physically demanding, but rather requires the ability to adapt to harsh environmental conditions, flexibility, and the management of risk and uncertainty that open spaces entail. Time management may be flexible during the day, but milking periods are intense and the livestock requires continuous care, including at night.

Migrant shepherds are scattered across the countryside and generally work alone or at most in pairs, live in isolated sheepfolds, often in areas remote from villages and with limited means to move and socialise or to organise collective forms of mobilisation (as it is the case for other contexts, see Perrotta and Sacchetto 2014, Corrado *et al.* 2018). However, isolation and solitude are typical features of this profession (Meuret 2010). These conditions improve when more migrants work together, when the sheepfolds are near to rural towns, or if the workers own a vehicle (car, bicycle, or scooter). The relationships between the employer and the hired shepherd seem horizontal and direct. Stockbreeders are involved in daily activities, and they share the same work environment and conditions with their workers, with the ambiguity of stockbreeders representing themselves as 'self-exploited' like the migrant. This does not mean that there are no conflicts or exploitation. Working relationships are embedded within a complex family fabric in which bonds are limited, personal, and constant: the forms of subordination and exploitation become more subtle and less explicit. Furthermore, the informality that characterises the contractual arrangements offers ample room for ambiguity and uncertainty. In the case of Romanian shepherds working in Sardinia, the monthly salary for a full-time activity with limited holidays or spare time is quite low; board and lodging is generally provided on the farm, often associated with the sheepfold. According to employers, the provision of food and accommodation in kind implies significant savings for the worker, around 400–500 euros per month. According to the workers, however, sometimes the accommodation is not comfortable, and the food provided may not be appropriate in type or quality. This kind of arrangement enables farmers to underpay workers and maintain forms of control over them. Family practices presented as neutral or even 'helping' express a governmental power on migrant life. Following Foucault (1982, 790):

> *"Government" did not refer only to political structures or to the management of states; rather, it designated the way in which the conduct of individuals or of groups might be directed – the government of children, of souls, of communities, of the sick It did not only cover the legitimately constituted forms of political or economic subjection, but also modes of action, more or less considered and calculated, which were destined to act upon the possibilities of action of other people. To govern, in this sense, is to control the possible field of action of others.*

When the farmer's family establishes what and when to eat, how and when to sleep, how to dress, and when to wash, this structures the migrants' field of action, determining their subjection (Farinella and Mannia 2018).

However, the uncertainty related to shepherding gives to the migrant workers the opportunity to mobilise numerous 'weapons of the weak' (Scott 1985) and survival strategies. They carve out wide spaces of freedom and autonomy through the daily practices that 'build' pastoralism as an open and multifunctional activity in an uncertain context. This becomes visible both in the routine tasks of tending the flock (as, for example, in the personal style with which the flock is led to grazing), as well as in all those complementary activities important to the overall income. As recalled by an interviewed shepherd:

> *First of all I have experience, I know everything, so I don't have problems […] In addition to what I earn [as a shepherd], I am a handyman, I do a little bit of everything […] I am free because I can manage myself, […] the basis is here [the shepherd's salary]. I can fix things, I did that walker, I fixed it, I fix chainsaws and I get paid of course. […] Here I gain €500, but cutting the wood and with other things […] my annual count is more than €1,000 per month […] And I have bed and board […] I don't have to pay my rent so… Of course we have to buy children's stuff, but the primary needs such as eating, meat, bread, and wine and other things are provided by our shepherds! […] I have a vegetable garden, I always had one […] I have it since the day I arrived. Yes. We breed chickens, quails […] We sell them. I mean, my wife is a housewife and she takes care of it to raise some money, with mushrooms, with the hens or its eggs, with quails, and then when we have them with tomatoes, I mean we know how it works! We get by and we are doing well!! […]*
>
> (Romanian shepherd, Sardinia, Italy, aged 33)

This excerpt shows how the migrant shepherd bases his 'agency' on a set of everyday practices of existence (De Certeau 1980) related to agro-pastoral work and is thus able to limit subordination and increase autonomy.

To counter this, the rhetoric of the 'good worker' is used. According to all stockbreeders interviewed, willingness to adapt, flexibility, a spirit of sacrifice, endurance, familiarity with harsh living conditions in the countryside, and acceptance of working conditions and pay generally rejected by the local population are some of the reasons they prefer hiring foreigners rather than 'lazy' young locals (Hoggart and Mendoza 1999, MacKenzie and Forde 2009):

> *People from here do not want to do that job. It is a hard job, with scarce holidays. There are no people from here available. Those that would, they are all too old. Romanians are hard workers and experienced. In their country the situation is more difficult than here.*
>
> (Spanish stockbreeder, Tartareu, aged 60)

> *Reliable, always there. Greeks would only take this job if they were completely desperate.*
>
> (Greek stockbreeder, Vlohos, age not recorded)

> *They adapt to everything and they work under the terms and the conditions we set! Those who resist and continue to work with us are the ones who like the job enough and are comfortable with the stockbreeders. They do what you tell them. They have reduced economic needs compared to Italians.*
>
> (Italian stockbreeder, Friuli Venezia Giulia, aged 33)

The 'good worker' rhetoric expresses the stockbreeders' need to affirm their power and control through ethnic essentialisation mechanisms (Balibar 1991). The migrant shepherds need 'willingness to accept the hard conditions of this business' and to be 'hard working,' 'trustworthy,' 'clever,' 'skilled,' 'quick learners,' and, at the same time, 'cheaper' and 'obedient':

> *He is very obedient and trustworthy. Does not say 'no.'*
>
> (Greek stockbreeder, Anilio/Zarko, age not recorded)

This excerpt shows all the ambivalence of a performative sentence: the migrant is trustworthy because he does not say 'no': that is, he remains subordinate. This mechanism of essentialising subordination is very evident towards a main ethnic group of shepherds, the Romanians. The stockbreeders interviewed emphasised that, on one hand, Romanians are selected precisely because of the cultural correspondence to local populations, for example originating from rural areas, being in contact with animals, their 'white' skin and more 'European' culture and traditions:

> *Ours is a particular lifestyle, no Saturdays or Sundays: Italians would not live this way. We are comfortable with Romanians, they adapt. 90 per cent are children of shepherds, they have sheep in Romania.*
>
> (Italian stockbreeder, Lentiai, Veneto, aged 35)

On the other hand, it is implicitly emphasised that, despite these similarities, migrant shepherds originate from more *backward* areas.

> *They are like us 40 years ago, they can do without medicines; they adapt, they have no specific needs. For our work this means a lot!*
>
> (Italian stockbreeder, Pergine Val Sugana, Trentino, aged 43)

> *They are like we were 50 years ago. Tough and hard workers and ready to overcome hardships.*
>
> (Spanish stockbreeder, Estorm, aged 55)

> *Work in Romania is completely different. […]. They make a grim life for 200 euros a month.*
>
> (Italian stockbreeder, Veneto, aged 49)

This 'imagined backwardness' allows stockbreeders to assert a sort of moral, cultural, and technical superiority over the foreign worker that legitimises the low wage and the demand of obedience. For example, employers claim that previous experience with animals is of limited use since sheep farming in the country of origin is different, simpler, and not advanced; the migrant 'needs a lot of training' and lacks specific skills especially in the case of large flocks (such as in Sardinia or in Spain). Similarly, migrants are presented as having lower economic needs and therefore able to accept a wage rejected by locals.

> *They pretended to be able to do everything, but when it was time to work they didn't know where to begin. Some of them liked to work, and others didn't, that was eventually clear from the early morning. They did it but didn't want to. They are good as welders and bricklayers; not so much with animals. […] And if you are not there, they don't do anything. They need to be monitored otherwise they won't do anything at all. They are fast learners though, but they aren't reliable.*
>
> (Italian stockbreeder, Sardinia, aged 60 about)

In the stories told by the interviewees, the 'good Romanian' turns into 'a savage' when he stops being docile and obedient, even going as far as quitting the job without notice, inexplicably turning into a drunk and untrustworthy (Farinella and Mannia 2018).

> *[The Romanians] are 'unreliable in that they can leave at any time.'*
>
> (Greek stockbreeder, Lefktra, Viotias, aged 50)

This last excerpt shows a paradoxical situation in which informality stops being passively suffered by the worker as a means for the employer to impose bad conditions and low wages, and instead becomes a weapon to claim his own power of action. The act of 'leaving' as a unilateral choice, without notice, reaffirms the migrant's agency.

In addition, the 'good worker' rhetoric conceals stockbreeders' tendency to tackle the continuous need for labour without increasing wages, according to a short-term strategy by which they switch employment from one ethnic group to another, sustaining 'a competitive advantage based on minimizing labour costs to the lowest point of regulatory compliance' (McKenzie and Forde 2009, 147).

This seems to happen in the recent phenomenon of replacing Romanians with Indians and north Africans to whom, once again, 'essentialised' characteristics are attributed: a Sardinian interviewee claimed, for example, that their Muslim faith would make them more reliable because it refrains them from getting drunk.

Conclusions

This chapter shows the complexity of migration patterns within Euro-Mediterranean agro-pastoral systems based on multifunctional family farming. As a primary source of livelihood, agro-pastoralism has proved to be a resilient practice in face of many and growing embedding uncertainties affecting inner and mountainous rural settings, where alternative opportunities for income and employment are limited. These areas are characterised by important phenomena of socio-economic marginalisation, demographic decline, land abandonment, and problems of generational renewal.

Global competition has forced most agro-pastoral farms to restructure their practices, pushing towards an expansion of flock size and the intensification of its management. Socio-economic conditions have hardly improved, while responsibilities and costs have grown. As it becomes increasingly difficult to recruit local workers for shepherding tasks, international migrants have become a strategic asset for these systems. In recent decades, the supply of 'good migrant workers' has sustained agro-pastoral farming, with relevant implications as well for keeping marginal territories vibrant and productive.

As it is more broadly the case for capitalistic agriculture, the migrant workforce serving agro-pastoral farms is subject to high degrees of exploitation and precariousness, expressed by low pay, harsh living and working conditions, and the limited formalisation of contractual relationships. International migrant shepherds are caught in a 'bad job' with limited options for improving their situation and upgrading their conditions. However, the relationships between local employers and migrant workers are more complex than in other contexts. On the one hand, exploitation is more nuanced and less visible because it is embedded in family bonds and articulated in more horizontal interactions. On the other, the unpredictability and multifunctionality of agro-pastoral work leaves vast spaces of autonomy and agency for migrant shepherds.

In a constant tension between the employer's need to exercise control and the worker's will to reaffirm his own agency, the rhetoric of the 'good worker' emerges in the stories of the interviewed stockbreeders. This rhetoric functions to essentialise and subordinate the migrant workers, but also to maintain competition between different groups in a segmented market: the shepherd is a 'good worker' only as long as he is docile, obedient, and willing to accept low wages. The migratory paths remain circular and international migrants move from one farm to another, from one territory to another; they cannot think of shepherding as a 'career' with opportunities for social mobility, but only as a precarious and uncertain employment and temporary source of income.

Such dynamics explain to a good degree the limited effectiveness of the migratory phenomena in tackling the generational renewal problems that affect the European agrarian world and that jeopardise its reproduction. These also help unveiling the inconsistencies of the political and financial engagements that aim to support agriculture and rural development in Europe.

Acknowledgements

The chapter is part of the European Research Council (ERC) project *PASTRES (Pastoralism, Uncertainty and Resilience)*. Data and interviews have been mostly sourced through two projects: the European Commission Marie Curie project *TRAMed – Transhumances in the Mediterranean* (2015–2018), coordinator: Michele Nori, and the ethnographic research *Changes of the Sardinian Pastoralism: Shepherds and Romanian Workers* (2016–2019), coordinator: Domenica Farinella. We wish to thank the anonymous reviewers for their comments on the manuscript.

References

Balibar, E. 1991. 'Preface.' In *Race, Nation, Class: Ambiguous Identities*, edited by B.E.I., Wallerstein, 1–13. London, New York: Verso.

BEPRS. 2017. 'The Sheep and Goat Sector in the EU Main Features, Challenges and Prospects.' Briefing European Parliamentary Research Service www.europarl.europa.eu/RegData/etudes/BRIE/2017/608663/EPRS_BRI(2017)608663_EN.pdf.

Burch, D. and G. Lawrence. 2007. *Supermarkets and Agri-food Supply Chains Transformations in the Production and Consumption of Foods*. Cheltenham: Elgar.

Castles, S. and G. Kosack. 1973. *Immigrant Workers and Class Structure in Western Europe*. London: Institute of Race Relations, Oxford University Press.

Coldiretti. 2010. Complemento al *Dossier immigrazione Istat 2010*. www.coldiretti.it/archivio/istat-nelle-stalle-dove-si-ottiene-il-latte-per-il-parmigiano-reggiano-1-lavoratore-su-3-e-indiano-12-10-2010.

Corrado, A., C. De Castro and M. Perrotta, eds. 2016. *Migration and Agriculture. Mobility and Change in the Mediterranean Area*. London: Routledge.

Corrado, A., L. Palumbo, F.S. Caruso, M. Lo Cascio, M. Nori and A. Triandafyllidou. 2018. *Is Italian Agriculture a 'Pull Factor' for Irregular Migration – and, If So, Why?* Open Society Foundations. https://cadmus.eui.eu/handle/1814/60950.

De Certeau, M. 1980. *L'invention du quotidien. Tome I. Arts de faire*. Paris: UGE.

EC. 2020. *Market Situation for Sheep and Goat Meats.* Committee for the Common Organisation of the Agricultural Market. Bruxelles: European Commission. https://circabc.europa.eu/sd/d/c23fa87f-fecf-45cf-91e8-223c5735cc4d/0%20Sheep%20no%20link%20pdf.pdf.

Eurostat. 2016. *Agriculture, Rural Development Statistics 2016*. Luxemburg: Eurostat.

Farinella, D. 2019. 'The Case of the Pecorino Romano Dairy Production Chain in Sardinia, Italy.' In *Food Track. A Transparent and Traceable Supply Chain for the Benefit of Workers, Businesses and Consumers*, edited by M. Migliorini, 130–163. Rome: CGIL.

Farinella, D. and S. Mannia. 2017. 'Migranti e pastoralismo. Il caso dei servi pastori romeni nelle campagne sarde.' *Meridiana* 88: 175–196.

Farinella, D. and S. Mannia. 2018. '«Mi chiamo Serban e non sono il romeno di nessuno, sono il romeno di me stesso». Pratiche di assoggettamento e soggettivazione tra pastori sardi e servi pastori romeni.' *Etnografia e ricerca qualitativa* 3: 405–426.

Farinella, D., M. Nori and A. Ragkos. 2017. 'Change in Euro-Mediterranean Pastoralism: Which Opportunities for Rural Development and Generational Renewal?' In *Grassland Resources for Extensive Farming Systems in Marginal Lands,* edited by C. Porqueddu, A. Franca, G. Molle, G. Peratoner and A. Hokings, 23–36. Wageningen: Wageningen Academic Publishers. https://doi.org/10.1002/ldr.764.

Foucault, M. 1982. 'The Subject and Power.' *Critical Inquiry* 8(4): 777–795 https://doi.org/10.1086/448181.

Gertel, J. and R.S. Sippel, eds. 2014. *Seasonal Workers in Mediterranean Agriculture: The Social Costs of Eating Fresh.* London: Routledge.

Hadjigeorgiou, I. 2011. 'Past, Present and Future of Pastoralism in Greece.' *Pastoralism: Research, Policy and Practice* 1: 1–24. DOI:10.1186/2041-7136-1-24.

Hellio, E. 2017. '"They Know That You'll Leave, Like a Dog Moving onto the Next Bin": Undocumented Male and Seasonal Contracted Female Workers in the Agricultural Labour Market of Huelva, Spain.' In *Migration and Agriculture. Mobility and change in the Mediterranean area,* edited by A. Corrado, C. De Castro and M. Perrotta, 198–216. London: Routledge. https://doi.org/10.1186/2041-7136-1-24.

Hoggart, K. and C. Mendoza. 1999. 'African Immigrant Workers in Spanish Agriculture.' *Sociologia Ruralis* 39(4): 538–562 https://doi.org/10.1111/1467-9523.00123.

ISMEA, 2019. *Settore ovicaprino, Scheda di settore.* www.ismeamercati.it/lattiero-caseari/latte-derivati-ovicaprini.

Jentsch, B. and M. Simard, eds. 2009. *International Migration* and *Rural Areas. Cross-National Comparative Perspectives*. London: Ashgate.

Kasimis, C. and A.G. Papadopoulos. 2013. 'Rural Transformations and Family Farming in Contemporary Greece.' In *Agriculture in Mediterranean Europe: Between Old and New Paradigms*, edited by D. Ortiz-Miranda Moragues-Faus A. and E. Arnalte-Alegre, 283–293. UK: Emerald.

Kasimis, C., A.G. Papadopoulos and C. Pappas. 2010. 'Gaining from Rural Migrants: Migrant Employment Strategies and Socioeconomic Implications for Rural Labour Markets.' *Sociologia Ruralis* 50(3): 258–276. doi.org/10.1111/j.1467-9523.2010.00515.x.

Kerven, C. and R. Behnke. 2011. 'Policies and Practices of Pastoralism in Europe.' *Pastoralism: Research, Policy and Practice* 1: 1–28. DOI:10.1186/2041-7136-1-28.

Lum, K.D. 2011. *The Quiet Indian Revolution in Italy's Dairy Industry*. Firenze: European University Institute. https://doi.org/10.1186/2041-7136-1-28.

MacKenzie, R. and C. Forde. 2009. 'The Rhetoric of the "Good Worker" versus the Realities of Employers' use and the Experiences of Migrant Workers.' *Work, Employment and Society.* 23(1): 142–159. https://doi.org/10.1177/0950017008099783.

Martin, P.L. 2016. *Migrant Workers in Commercial Agriculture*. Geneva: ILO.

Mattalia, G., G. Volpato, P. Corvo and A. Pieroni. 2018. 'Interstitial but resilient: nomadic shepherds in Piedmont amidst spatial and social marginalization.' *Human Ecology* 46: 747–757. https://doi.org/10.1007/s10745-018-0024-9.

Meuret, M. 2010. *Un savoir-faire de bergers.* Versailles: Editions Qua Beaux livres.

Nori, M. 2017. 'Migrant Shepherds: Opportunities and Challenges for Mediterranean.' *Journal of Alpine Research* 105(4): 0–14. doi.org/10.4000/rga.3544.

Nori, M. and D. Farinella. 2020. *Migrations, Agriculture and Rural Development. Mobility and Migrations in European Agro-Pastoralism.* Switzerland: Springer. www.springer.com/gp/book/9783030428624.

Nori, M. and F. López-i-Gelats. 2017. 'Relevo generacional e inmigrantes en el mundo pastoril: el caso del Pirineo catalán.' Paper presented at 4th International Seminar on Migrations, Agriculture and Food Sustainability of the Spanish National Research Council (CSIC). Madrid, 26–27January.

Nori, M. and V. de Marchi. 2015. 'Pastorizia, biodiversità e la sfida dell'immigrazione: il caso del Triveneto.' *Culture della sostenibilità* 8(15): 78–101.

Ortiz-Miranda, D., A. Moragues-Faus and E. Arnalte-Alegre, eds. 2013. *Agriculture in Mediterranean Europe: Between Old and New Paradigms. Research in Rural Sociology and Development, Volume 19.* UK: Emerald.

Papadopoulos, T. and A. Roumpakis. 2009. *Familistic Welfare Capitalism in Crisis: The Case of Greece.* ERI Working Paper Series, WP-09-14. UK: European Research Institute, University of Bath.

Perrotta, D. and D. Sacchetto. 2014. 'Migrant Farmworkers in Southern Italy: Ghettoes, Caporalato and Collective Action.' *Workers of the World – International Journal on Strikes and Social Conflicts* 1(5): 75–98.

Piore, M. 1979. *Birds of Passage. Migrant Labor and Industrial Societies.* Cambridge: Cambridge University Press.

Ragkos, A. and M. Nori. 2016. 'The Multifunctional Pastoral Systems in the Mediterranean EU and Impact on the Workforce.' *Options Méditerranéennes, Série A Séminaires Méditerranéens* 114(15): 325–328. Saragoza: CIHEAM.

Ragkos, A., S. Koutsou, A. Theodoridis, T. Manousidis and V. Lagka. 2018. 'Labor Management Strategies in Facing the Economic Crisis. Evidence from Greek Livestock Farms.' *New Medit, A Mediterranean Journal of Economics, Agriculture and Environment 2018* 1. DOI: 10.30682/nm1801f.

Reigada, A. 2017. 'Family Farms, Migrant Labourers and Regional Imbalance in Global Agri-food Systems. On the Social (Un)sustainability of Intensive Strawberry Production in Huelva (Spain).' In *Migration and Agriculture. Mobility and change in the Mediterranean area*, edited by A. Corrado, C. De Castro and M. Perrotta, 95–110. London: Routledge.

Rye, J.F. and S. Scott. 2018. 'International Labour Migration and Food Production in Rural Europe: A Review of the Evidence.' *Sociologia Ruralis* 58(4): 928–952. https://doi.org/10.1111/soru.12208.

Rye, J.F., M.H. Slettebak and H. Bjørkhaug. 2018. 'From Family to Domestic and Global Labour? A Decade of Proletarisation of Labour in the Norwegian Horticulture Industry.' *European Countryside* 10(4): 528–542. DOI: 10.2478/euco-2018-0030.

Scott, J.C. 1985. *Weapons of the Weak. Everyday Forms of Peasant Resistance*. New Haven, CT: Yale University Press. https://doi.org/10.2478/euco-2018-0030.

Van der Ploeg, J.D. 2008. *The New Peasantries. Struggles for Autonomy and Sustainability in an Era of Empire and Globalization*. London: Earthscan.

Waldinger, R. and M.I. Lichter. 2003. *How the Other Half Work: Immigration and the Social Organisation of Labour*. Berkeley, CA: University of California Press.

Chapter 6

Temporary farmworkers and migration transition

On a changing role of the agricultural sector in international labour migration to Poland

Agata Górny and Paweł Kaczmarczyk

Introduction

Poland has traditionally been perceived as a net emigration country (Okólski 2012). Following the post-1989 political transition and 2004 accession to the European Union, Poland came to figure as a main sending country of intra-European migrants. In total, around 2.5 million Poles have emigrated to western European countries in last three decades.

However, recently Poland has also become a magnet for international migrants, mainly Ukrainian temporary workers (Górny *et al.* 2018), and currently appears as the European leader in terms of first residence permits given to foreigners (OECD 2019). The underlying factors of this include the outbreak of the Russian-Ukrainian conflict, resulting in a high supply of Ukrainian workers, the presence of liberal legal regulations regarding labour migration (especially for seasonal work) to Poland and, last but not least, the growing activity of employment agencies in the recruitment of foreign labour to Poland (Górny *et al.* 2018). At the same time, the Polish labour markets' demand for migrant workers has changed. While the agricultural sector's recruitment of foreign farm workers initially constituted the main driver for labour migration from Ukraine to Poland, the relative importance of this sector has been on the decline in recent years, despite a dynamic growth of labour migration to Poland in other sectors (Górny and Kaczmarczyk 2018).

Against this background, the goal of this chapter is to evaluate the competitive strength of the rural sector in attracting foreign workers. This will be achieved by examining the selection of Ukrainian farm workers and patterns of their recruitment in the context of the progressive opening up of new labour market sectors for foreign labour in Poland (Górny *et al.* 2018). The latter is a consequence of both exceptionally high supply of Ukrainian workers and unmet demand for workers in selected sectors of the Polish labour market, such as services and industry, and especially the food processing industry (Work Service 2019). Consequently, the low attractiveness of agriculture for incoming migrants in terms of relatively low wages and high workload might constitute a challenge for Polish farmers who want to attract foreign workers, as has been observed in most agricultural sectors in high-income countries (Rye and Scott 2018, Taylor 2010). In the Polish context, such a scenario might be particularly problematic for these rural areas which have already become highly dependent on a foreign labour force.

We address two research questions. What are the wages, work arrangements, and individual socio-demographic characteristics of Ukrainian farm workers in comparison to the characteristics of Ukrainian labour migrants employed in other sectors of the Polish labour market? What are the differences between the patterns of recruitment of Ukrainian farm workers and the rest of Ukrainian migrants working in Poland?

In responding to these questions, we differentiate between the Mazovian region, representing the key agricultural centre in Poland, particularly for horticulture production, and where employment of foreign workers has already become the norm (Górny and Kaczmarczyk 2018), and other Polish regions which by and large represent newer destination areas with a shorter history of migrant labour (Górny and Śleszyński 2019). The Mazovian region, as used in this chapter, refers to the Mazowieckie voivodeship which is an administrative unit at the NUTS2 level (in total, there are 16 voivodeships in Poland). It includes Warsaw, Poland's capital. In methodological terms, we analyse unique quantitative data sets on foreign employment in Poland, including a nationwide survey of employers and a survey of their international migrant employees conducted in 2017.

The first two sections below provide the context for our analysis by demonstrating the recent dynamic changes in migration flows to Poland and the structural composition of the foreign workforce in the Polish labour market, with a focus on the agriculture sector and Ukrainian migrants. The following section examines the rural sector versus other sectors of the Polish labour market that employ foreigners. The analysis identifies the features of selected jobs, the individual characteristics of Ukrainian workers, and their recruitment patterns. The results provide for an assessment of the competitive strength of agriculture in attracting foreign workers.

From labour exporter to labour importer

Until recently, it would have been difficult to present the inflow of migrants to Poland as a mass population process, although, as a consequence of the post-1989 political transition, different types of migrants arrived in Poland. These movements had several specific features, however, such as low or very low scale, a narrow spectrum of countries of origin (mainly the former Soviet Union and selected Asian countries), the predominance of temporary and circular mobility, a largely irregular character, and strong regional concentration, with Warsaw and the surrounding areas of the Mazovian region as key migration destinations (Górny and Kaczmarczyk 2019, Górny *et al.* 2010). The accession of Poland to the European Union in 2004 did not change the above picture considerably. Although it induced a massive outflow of Polish workers to the European Union countries, it did not result in a growth of migration into Poland (Górny and Kaczmarczyk 2019).

The year 2014 brought about a major increase in migration to Poland, mainly from Ukraine. This date is not accidental: it is the moment of the outbreak of the armed conflict in the eastern part of Ukraine, resulting in a deterioration of the Ukrainian economy. One of its consequences has been massive labour migration of Ukrainian nationals (Drbohlav and Jaroszewicz 2016). However, a dynamic increase in migration to Poland would not be possible without the progressively liberal regulations regarding the employment of foreigners. Among them, the so-called 'simplified procedure' has played a special role. This allows employers to hire labour from six specific countries, including Ukraine, for up to six months during a 12-month period based on a simple procedure whereby employers make a declaration of consent to employ a foreigner.

Originally, this procedure was designed for employment in agriculture in 2006. Since then, it has been modified several times, including its extension to all sectors of the Polish labour market in 2007 (Szulecka 2016). The most recent reform, in 2018, introduced a special permit for seasonal work which applies to all non-EU nationals, allowing employment for nine months during a 12-month period. Among other signs of regulatory liberalisation was an extension of the list of almost 300 professions for which the employment of foreigners do not require a labour market test (where employers prove that the labour demand cannot be met by inland workers), and the relaxation of access to the Polish labour market for foreign students and graduates of Polish universities (Okólski and Wach 2020).

Growth of international migration to Poland after 2014 is documented by registry data pertaining to foreigners (Górny *et al.* 2018). The most numerous category is migrants employed based on the 'simplified procedure.' While the number of registered declarations was 160,000–240,000 per year until 2013, it has risen to around 800,000 in 2015, around 1.3 million in 2016, and around 1.6 million in 2018. By comparison, in 2018, the number of issued work permits reached 'only' 329,000 in 2018. The 'simplified procedure' is unambiguously dominated by Ukrainian employees for whom 91–95 per cent of all registered declarations were issued in recent years (Górny and Śleszyński 2019). These numbers position Poland as the most important recipient of a seasonal workforce worldwide, well ahead of the United States, the traditional destination of temporary foreign workers (OECD 2019).

According to an estimate by the Polish Central Statistical Office (CSO), the number of foreigners aged 18 and over residing on the territory of Poland reached approximately 744,000 in 2016. Men (66 per cent) and people of working age (96 per cent) clearly dominated. Ukrainians constituted 61 per cent of all migrants. The majority of foreigners stayed in Poland temporarily (over 70 per cent up to 12 months) and were employed (67 per cent).

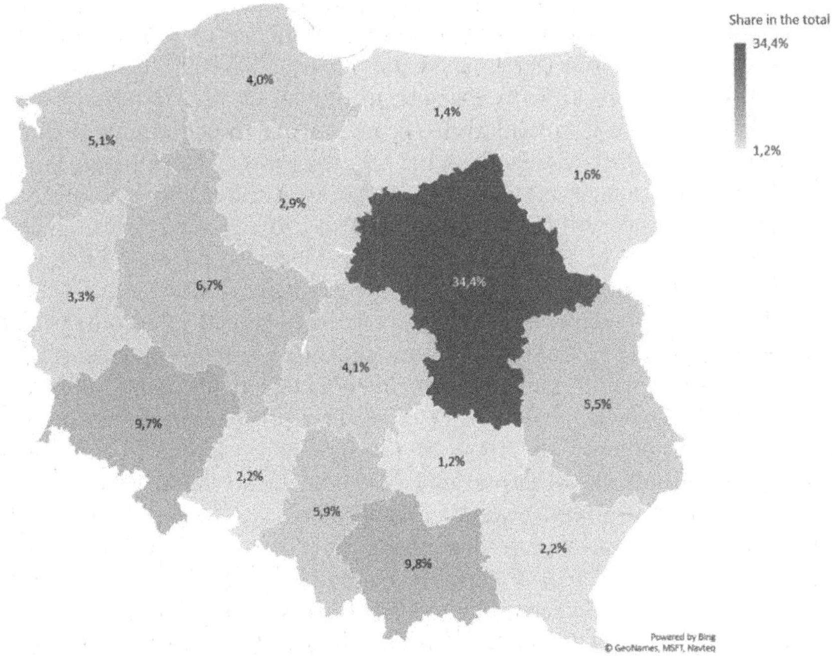

Figure 6.1 Foreigners aged 18 years and more residing in Poland, by regions, 2016
Source: Own elaboration based on the CSO 2018.

The key receiving area was the Mazovian region, with 34 per cent, and in particular the city of Warsaw, with 22 per cent of all foreigners (see Figure 6.1, CSO 2018). This clearly points to the very important role of the Mazovian region in international labour migration to Poland. However, its relative significance has been on the decline in recent years (Górny and Śleszyński 2019). This signifies the spreading of labour migration to new destination areas in Poland outside the Mazovian region.

Rural sector and dynamics of international migration

A gradual decline in the importance of the rural sector in the Polish economy has been observed since the post-1989 political transition. However, in terms of employment, the change has been much slower than expected. In 2004, at the time of Poland's accession to the European Union, the share of individuals employed in agriculture still exceeded 17 per cent but fell to 12 per cent in 2012. In comparison, the EU15 average was three per cent in 2012) (Górny and Kaczmarczyk 2018). The process continued as the number of persons employed in agriculture dropped to less than 1.6 million in 2018 (9–10 per cent, depending on the quarter). At the same time, however, agriculture has been lagging behind other sectors in terms of its input into the national economy, especially in relation to the level of employment in this sector (Eurostat). In fact, an excess of workers in Polish agriculture has been estimated at as many as 500,000–900,000 persons (Wiśniewski and Rudnicki 2016), which clearly signals the need for further modernisation of this sector, particularly as the majority of those working on farms are members of farmers' families and not salaried workers. Nonetheless, Polish agriculture is becoming increasingly heterogeneous in spatial and sectoral terms (Wąs and Małażewska 2012). The growing role of a foreign workforce on Polish farms in some areas of Poland, especially the Mazovian region, additionally contributes to this heterogeneity (Górny and Kaczmarczyk 2018).

At the same time, agriculture has played a very special role in the recent history of migration to Poland as labour shortages in this sector, especially in the Mazovian region, motivated the introduction of the 'simplified procedure' of employment of foreign workers. This procedure has become the most important channel of inflow of the foreign workforce to Poland in recent years (Górny and Kaczmarczyk 2019). Such shortages arose specifically in highly labour-intensive sub-sectors of the rural sector such as horticulture, especially fruit farming. In this respect, the Polish 'simplified procedure' resembles the Bracero programme in the United States and numerous recruitment programmes implemented by western European countries in the 1950s and 1960s (Martin 2002, Chapter 13 (this volume), Ruhs and Martin 2008).

During the first years after the introduction of the 'simplified procedure' in 2006, agriculture was the main recipient of foreign seasonal workers in Poland with a share exceeding 60 per cent. After 2014, however, its role has been clearly declining: the share of declarations registered by farm-owners dropped to 35 per cent in 2015 and to less than 20 per cent in 2017. Examining data that combine numbers on declarations and work permits issued in 2014–2018 (MRPiPS data 2019), it is also clear that the importance of other areas of the labour market has been growing, in particular the role of temporary work agencies or intermediaries which, as will be discussed below, primarily serves other sectors than agriculture.

The observed sectoral changes are attributable to a high supply of Ukrainian workers and to labour shortages in various sectors of the Polish economy (Górny *et al.* 2018), leading to the opening of new sectors of the Polish labour market to a foreign labour force. They are, however, also related to the evolution in the spatial distribution of migrants in Poland, and a diminishing role of the Mazovian labour market in the employment of foreign labour. While in 2013, the share of declarations registered in this region amounted to 56 per cent, it dropped to 40 per cent in 2015 and only 23 per cent in 2017. This spatial shift is important if we consider that the Mazovian region represents one of the major agricultural centres in Poland due to its horticulture production and is the main local labour market for foreign (mainly Ukrainian) farm workers (Górny and Śleszyński 2019). The two areas that employ the vast majority of migrant farm workers (Grójec and Płońsk) are just 50km away from the capital

(Górny and Kaczmarczyk 2018). This is in contrast to many other countries where foreign farm workers tend to concentrate in remote, peripheral areas (Fonseca 2008, Kasimis *et al.* 2003, McAreavey 2017, Rye and Scott 2018).

It should be stressed, however, while the agricultural sector's share of the declarations and work permits issued were declining, the numbers of agricultural migrant workers were still increasing in absolute numbers between 2013 and 2018. Their numbers equalled around 100,000 annually between 2010 and 2013, they started to grow rapidly after 2014 and reached almost 280,000 in 2015 and then 306,000 in 2017. However, the pace of this growth was clearly smaller than in other sectors, which experienced close to a fivefold increase during this period.

The same tendency has been observed in the Mazovian region, where numbers of declarations registered for agriculture 'only' more than doubled between 2013 and 2017. At the same time, however, the share of declarations registered for rural workers in the Mazovian region declined from 80 per cent of all Mazovian declarations in 2014 to less than 40 per cent in 2017. In other words, although numbers of foreign farm workers grew between 2013 and 2018, though moderately when compared with other sectors, the role of agriculture in the employment of foreigners has also been decreasing in the Mazovian labour market.

In the following we will discuss this development from the hypothesis that it reflects a weakening competitive strength of the farm sector relative to other sectors in attracting foreign workers. This implies that the farm owners may demand migrant hired workers to replace family labour, however, they are outcompeted by employers in other sectors. In order to analyse the diminishing relative importance of Polish agriculture in foreign employment in recent years, the next section therefore focuses on the competitive strength of agriculture in attracting foreign workers by looking at the characteristics of the sector, as well as at the selection and recruitment processes of Ukrainian workers to this sector.

Theoretically, the declining share of migrant workers in the agricultural sector may also indicate a limited demand for a foreign workforce in Polish agriculture, for instance due to overall modernisation and other structural changes. As mentioned above, Wiśniewski and Rudnicki (2016) estimated a surplus of 500,000–900,000 persons in the farming sector. However, the evaluation of such a hypothesis is problematic due to the high importance of informal modes of agricultural production (e.g. very large scale of informal employment of family members) and its progressive modernisation, which impacts patterns of employment in this sector (Strzelecki 2010, Wąs and Małażewska 2012).

Towards an understanding of the competitive position of the agricultural sector

To assess the competitive position of Polish agriculture in attracting foreign workers analytically, we propose two complementary lines of reasoning: the first one is linked to the attractiveness of the sector (in terms of work conditions) and the second to the modes of selection of foreign workers (their characteristics) and the recruitment processes that are in place. We differentiate between the Mazovian region and the rest of Poland. The former deserves a separate analysis for at least two reasons. First, it still attracts the majority of foreigners coming to Poland in general, and to the rural sector in particular. Second, high demand for foreign farm workers on the one hand and strong pulling forces on the neighbouring Warsaw labour market on the other, contribute to the specificity of the Mazovian labour market in the Polish context.

The analysis presented in this section is based on data derived from a project devoted to the 'simplified procedure' of employing foreigners in Poland carried out by the Centre of Migration Research (University of Warsaw) in 2016–2018. The project delivered a countrywide survey of Polish employers (N=3598) and their foreign workers employed through the 'simplified procedure' (N=1349, for Ukrainians N=1288). The sampling method involved quotas for given voivodeships and the number of declarations registered by an employer. While the sample of employers can be tentatively treated as representative for the studied population, the same should not be assumed for migrants interviewed in the surveyed companies. However, weights correcting for the distribution of declarations according to voivodeship were applied to the sample of migrants to improve its representativeness.

Other data collected within the project (including an additional sub-sample of 181 recruitment agencies and 250 in-depth interviews with various actors engaged in the 'simplified procedure') are treated as complementary. The studied sample of foreigners covers the largest group of migrants in Poland – Ukrainians employed within the 'simplified procedure.' They are also usually the most recent and temporary migrants given the specificity of the procedure. This can be treated as an advantage in the context of this chapter which aims to formulate conclusions regarding developments in the migration process.

The attractiveness of Polish agriculture for foreign workers

It can be argued that the agricultural sector plays a specific role in the recent dynamic inflow of foreign labour to Poland due to the strong demand for foreign workers and also due to its structural characteristics. These include relatively low hourly wages, relatively high workload, and low-skilled jobs offered to foreigners (Górny *et al.* 2018). Thus, conditions offered by this sector may not be attractive for all migrants (not to mention the local workforce), which is commonly presented as a major developmental barrier (Taylor 2010). Namely, both in the Mazovian region and the rest of Poland, the hourly wage in agriculture earned by Ukrainians was around 25 per cent smaller compared with the industry, construction, and other services, which were the sectors where Ukrainians' mean hourly wages were the highest in 2017 (Table 6.1). At the same time, the weekly workload of farm workers was exceptionally high especially in the Mazovian region, amounting to over 64 hours, which could be translated into almost 11 hours of work per day, assuming six days of work per week. Although the workload in agriculture was smaller in regions other than the Mazovian region, it was still always 10 hours more than in other sectors (except for domestic services). This means that it is only through a very high intensity of work that foreigners employed in agriculture were able to achieve relatively high monthly incomes (yet still below the average).

A specific feature of the agricultural sector is that it offers predominantly low-skilled jobs. In 2017, around 90 per cent of all Ukrainian farm workers were employed as unskilled blue-collar workers and this share was undoubtedly the highest among all analysed sectors. Additionally, the share of skilled blue-collar workers was very low (seven per cent in the Mazovian region and 11 per cent respectively). This is in sharp contrast to the structure of employment in Mazovian industry, construction, and other services where the share of skilled blue-collar workers exceeded 30 per cent (and amounted to 53 per cent in the case of construction). These sectoral differences are even more visible in other regions of Poland, where the majority of jobs offered in construction and industry constituted skilled blue-collar posts. From the presented data, it follows that Ukrainian migrants in Poland have only limited chances of achieving a high-skilled position in the labour market (one per cent in Mazowieckie, five per cent in the rest of Poland). However, agriculture presents an extreme case with a highly skewed occupational distribution, not only because of the characteristics of the agricultural sector as such, but also because migrant workers are strongly concentrated in its labour-intensive sub-sectors (e.g. horticulture).

Additionally, agriculture is the only sector in the Mazovian region where Ukrainians happened to be employed solely on the basis of an oral agreement (one per cent), and also where engagement based on a written contract of employment was particularly infrequent (five per cent). In other sectors, the share of persons with written contracts varied between 30 and 45 per cent (apart from very specific domestic services). Interestingly, the formal basis of employment was more favourable for foreign workers outside the Mazovian region. For example, in construction and services, the share of Ukrainians employed according to a written contract of employment varied between 56 per cent (industry) and 72 per cent (construction) and even in the case of agriculture was as high as 19 per cent. At the same time, however, eight per cent of Ukrainian farm workers were employed based on an oral agreement only, which is several times more than in the Mazovian region (one per cent). In all Polish regions, the share of contracts that contains description of specific tasks to be performed by the employee was exceptionally high in the case of agriculture (88 per cent in the Mazovian region and 58 per cent in other regions). This particular form of employment is not very well suited for agricultural production and its usage could be seen as an attempt to circumvent labour law (and to pay lower taxes). A high degree of informal employment practices is common for farm sectors in different countries (Rye and Scott 2018), but it clearly contributes to relatively low attractiveness of employment in this sector.

Table 6.1 Selected job characteristics of Ukrainian migrants by sector of employment, 2017

Variable	*Total*	*Agriculture*	*Industry*	*Construction*	*Domestic services*	*Other services*
Mazovian region						
Mean monthly net income (PLN)	2,538.4	**2,453.0**	2,663.2	2,853.8	2,234.5	2,775.2
Mean hourly wage (PLN)	10.5	**9.6**	12.5	12.2	10.4	12.7
Weekly workload (hours)	61.2	**64.2**	52.4	54.3	49.3	54.6
Employed on:						
written contract of empl. (%)	11.8	**4.5**	30.2	44.4	19.0	29.8
free-for-task agreement (%)	8.6	**6.1**	25.4	20.3	57.1	3.2
contract for spec. task (with material outcome (%)	78.6	**88.0**	44.4	35.3	23.8	67.0
oral agreement (%)	1.0	**1.4**	0.0	0.0	0.0	0.0
Type of occupation:						
unskilled blue-collar workers (%)	79.6	**93.1**	57.1	46.6	72.7	55.0
skilled blue-collar workers (%)	17.5	**6.9**	36.5	53.4	0.0	33.4
sellers and service workers (%)	1.7	**0.0**	0.0	0.0	27.3	5.3
white-collar workers (%)	1.2	**0.0**	6.3	0.0	0.0	6.4
N (unweighted) – Mazovian region	*627*	***431***	*15*	*56*	*22*	*88*
Other regions						
Mean monthly net income (PLN)	2,181.6	**2,148.5**	2,331.4	2,222.0	1,865.0	2,147.2
Mean hourly wage (PLN)	11.3	**9.8**	13.5	12.2	9.8	12.3
Weekly workload (hours)	50.3	**55.4**	44.9	50.4	62.4	45.5

Employed on:						
written contract of empl. (%)	46.6	**18.6**	55.7	72.0	3.9	67.1
free-for-task agreement (%)	24.0	**15.0**	35.4	19.8	71.2	25.1
contract for specific task (with material outcome (%)	25.9	**58.2**	8.9	8.2	21.1	6.6
oral agreement (%)	3.5	**8.1**	0.0	0.0	3.8	1.2
Type of occupation:						
unskilled blue-collar workers (%)	47.2	**88.6**	16.9	22.8	49.1	23.2
skilled blue-collar workers (%)	38.2	**11.4**	77.4	67.8	2.5	41.8
sellers and service workers (%)	9.6	**0.0**	4.3	4.4	38.4	22.6
white-collar workers (%)	5.0	**0.0**	1.4	4.9	0.0	12.4
N (unweighted) – Other regions	*667*	**223**	*74*	*74*	*20*	*178*

Notes: *Results for Mazovian region:* results for 'industry' and 'domestic services' should be treated with care due to a small number of cases. Additionally, for 'domestic services' the share of missing data on information of earnings equals as much as 50%; *Results for other regions*: results regarding earnings in the other services sector should be treated with care due to high share of missing data in this category exceeding 40%. *Independent variables:* The category 'sellers and service workers' also includes care workers, who usually work in private houses.

Source: Poland-wide survey on Ukrainian migrants 2017.

Attractive for whom? Socio-demographic characteristics of Ukrainian workers in Poland

If, as shown above, the agriculture sector does not offer attractive working conditions nor occupational positions for Ukrainian workers, then the question must be: what are the characteristics of those migrants who are still employed in this particular sector and are there any observable selectivity patterns? The key socio-demographic characteristics, as well as selected features of workers' migration careers, are summarised in Tables 6.2 and 6.3. Ukrainians employed in different sectors of the Polish labour market differ in several characteristics, some specific to agriculture. In the Mazovian region, the 2017 survey shows that women were in a minority among Ukrainian workers, except for the rural sector where the gender structure was balanced, and domestic services, which were monopolised by female migrants. The share of women in other Polish regions was significantly smaller but this does not refer to agriculture with around 44 per cent of female workers. The mean age of migrants was around 35 years with negligible differences between sectors. Regarding the differences between the Mazovian region and other parts of Poland, migrants originating from rural areas of Ukraine predominated in Warsaw and its surroundings (66 per cent) but were in a minority elsewhere (35 per cent). This

Table 6.2 Selected characteristics of Ukrainian migrants by sector of employment, 2017. Mazonvian region

Variable	*Total*	*Agri-culture*	*Indu-stry*	*Con-struc-tion*	*Dom-estic services*	*Other services*
Women (%)	34.9	**55.5**	34.1	20.6	95.5	35.1
Mean age	35.1	**34.5**	35.8	35.6	37.1	36.1
Originating from countryside (%)	65.6	**72.9**	44.4	41.0	45.5	61.7
Education:						
primary or lower (%)	18.7	**24.2**	12.7	5.7	0.0	10.6
vocational (%)	62.6	**59.1**	87.3	71.4	45.5	70.9
secondary (%)	12.6	**13.2**	0.0	1.1	40.9	14.9
higher (%)	6.1	**3.5**	0.0	21.7	13.6	3.6
Good writing skills in Polish (%)	18.8	**20.5**	34.1	6.9	18.2	19.1
Occupational situation prior to migration:						
working (%)	52.8	**44.9**	65.9	69.4	54.5	72.0
unemployed (%)	32.9	**39.6**	19.0	11.2	45.5	19.4
other (%)	14.3	**15.5**	15.1	19.4	0.0	8.6
Mean migration experience (in months)	23.2	**20.9**	26.3	36.6	19.6	23.4
First-timers (%)	43.4	**44.5**	40.5	49.0	59.1	29.1
N (unweighted) – Mazovian region	*627*	***431***	*15*	*56*	*22*	*88*

Note: Results for industry and domestic services should be treated with care due to a small number of cases in the sample.

Source: Poland-wide survey on Ukrainian migrants 2017

Table 6.3 Selected characteristics of Ukrainian migrants by sector of employment, 2017. Other regions than the Mazovian region

Variable	*Total*	*Agri-culture*	*Indu-stry*	*Con-struc-tion*	*Dom-estic services*	*Other services*
Women (%)	36.4	**44.1**	16.0	14.7	100.0	41.9
Mean age	36.3	**35.9**	35.9	37.0	38.4	35.2
Originating from countryside (%)	35.1	**54.6**	13.7	14.3	25.6	25.5
Education:						
primary or lower (%)	5.7	**6.2**	4.3	11.0	2.7	6.3
vocational (%)	57.1	**61.7**	50.8	68.0	57.2	55.2
secondary (%)	20.6	**21.5**	25.0	7.9	26.2	15.1
higher (%)	16.7	**10.6**	19.8	13.1	13.9	23.3
Good writing skills in Polish (%)	40.9	**24.5**	47.8	44.4	81.0	53.6
Occupational situation prior to migration:						
working (%)	58.7	**47.2**	73.4	73.3	66.6	67.8
unemployed (%)	30.8	**36.1**	21.2	24.9	28.0	21.8
other (%)	10.5	**16.7**	5.4	1.8	5.4	10.4
Mean migration experience (in months)	33.3	**38.5**	20.9	41.8	51.1	29.1
First-timers (%)	65.2	**57.5**	71.9	53.8	55.7	80.2
N (unweighted) – other regions	*667*	***223***	*74*	*74*	*20*	*178*

Note: Results for domestic services should be treated with care due to a small number of cases in the sample.

Source: Poland-wide survey on Ukrainian migrants 2017

reflects the growing participation of inhabitants of Ukrainian cities (also those more distant) in migration to Poland which is most visible in new Polish destination areas, i.e. those outside of the Mazovian region (Górny *et al.* 2019). Not surprisingly, inhabitants of the Ukrainian countryside were overrepresented among farm workers in Poland and they constituted almost 73 per cent of the total in the Mazovian region and 55 per cent in the rest of the country.

Overall, Ukrainian migrants working in Poland represent a selective group with regard to human capital: over 19 per cent of those working in the Mazovian region and 37 per cent employed in other areas had at least secondary education (Tables 6.2 and 6.3). International migrants with vocational education predominated everywhere (almost two thirds). Additionally, 19 per cent of those working in Warsaw and its surrounding areas and 41 per cent in other regions reported good writing skills in Polish. This demonstrates that 'new' migrants, i.e. those coming to other areas than the already well-trodden Mazovian region, are on average better educated and, interestingly, better prepared for work in Poland with respect to language skills.

In contrast, there is a clear overrepresentation of poorly skilled persons among Ukrainian workers employed in agriculture. The share of persons with only primary education was as high as 24 per cent in the Mazovian region and six per cent in other regions. Respective shares of persons with vocational or lower education amounted to 83 per cent and 68 per cent and were substantially higher than the average (with some regional and sectoral variations). One could thus conclude that Polish agriculture, and, in particular, the Mazovian agriculture, is attractive, first of all, for poorly skilled persons.

In general, more than 50 per cent of all migrants were working before emigrating (and this share was slightly higher outside the Mazovian region), while the proportion of previously unemployed persons was around 30 per cent. These results are in line with other studies conducted in various Polish cities and can be indicative of a changing character of Ukrainian labour migration to Poland encompassing more and more workers seeking not only 'any' job, but rather a better-paid job in Poland, in new destination areas (Górny *et al.* 2019). However, there are clear differences between sectors in this regard. In agriculture in the Mazovian region, the share of persons who had suffered unemployment before arriving in Poland was very high at 40 per cent, and comparable only to those (women) working in domestic services. In other Polish regions, the representation of previously unemployed persons was also remarkable (36 per cent as compared with 22–24 per cent in other sectors excluding domestic services). Additionally, agriculture, more often than other sectors, especially outside the Mazovian region, attracts persons who had been economically inactive before arriving in Poland.

What might seem counterintuitive is that Ukrainian migrants working in the Warsaw agglomeration and its surroundings had a shorter experience with migration to Poland (measuring the time since the first arrival in Poland) than those in other regions. The migration experience of Mazovian farm workers is, on average, two times shorter than that of migrants in the rest of Poland. This can stem, however, from the fact that foreigners employed within the 'simplified procedure' represent, in general, the most recent and temporary migrants in the Mazovian region. Percentages of first-timers among farm workers did not deviate substantially from other groups of Ukrainian workers, being higher outside Warsaw and its surroundings (45 per cent in the Mazovian region and 58 per cent elsewhere). In the case of the whole country, services and industrial production were the sectors with particularly high proportions of first-timers (80 per cent and 72 per cent, respectively) which is line with the growing role of these sectors in the employment of foreigners in Poland (Górny *et al.* 2018). The picture for the Mazovian labour market demonstrates its distinctiveness on the map of Poland. The well-established niches in construction and domestic services (Brunarska *et al.* 2016) are apparently much stronger magnets for first-timers than in other regions.

The role of modes of recruitment

As shown by Górny and Kaczmarczyk (2018), the attractiveness of given sectors for migrants is a crucial factor in the allocation of the foreign labour force in the Polish labour market. However, one should take into account also the role of recruitment practices, especially given that, in recent years, recruitment agencies became important actors in the employment of foreigners in the Polish labour market (Górny *et al.* 2018). Their activities impact not only the inflow of foreign workers to Poland but also the allocation to different sectors. Nevertheless, Figure 6.2 shows that most Ukrainians working in Poland within the 'simplified procedure' in 2017 still found their work with the help of their social networks, i.e. family or friends in Poland and Ukraine (over 80 per cent in all sectors). This was particularly common in the case of the rural sector, which can be explained by the relative importance of informal employment practices in this sector in general (Corrado *et al.* 2016, Kasimis *et al.* 2003, Rye and Scott 2018). In fact, informal intermediaries were also a quite important channel of recruitment to the rural sector outside the Mazovian region.

Overall, Figure 6.2 also shows that recruitment agencies play only a marginal role in the case of Polish agriculture. The share of Ukrainians recruited that way was only 4 per cent in the Mazovian region and less than 3 per cent in other Polish regions. These are the lowest shares recorded (except for the Mazovian construction sector). This observation seems important given that in the case of industry and other services, that is, sectors attracting the biggest numbers of newly arriving Ukrainian migrants (Górny and Kaczmarczyk 2018), the role of recruitment agencies was most clearly visible.

The secondary role of recruitment agencies in agriculture has also been portrayed in the declarations of farmers employing foreigners within the 'simplified procedure' (based on the 2017 survey), which sheds additional light on the mechanisms behind the recruitment process. Only 6 per cent of farmers found their workers with the help of recruitment agencies, while 17 per cent turned to informal intermediaries. At the same time, only 14 per cent of the surveyed recruitment agencies admitted helping farmers in hiring foreign workers, while as many as 50 per cent of workers recruited to the service sector and 40 per cent to construction (Górny *et al.* 2018). Furthermore, qualitative interviews with Polish farmers employing foreigners within the 'simplified procedure,' showed they are reluctant to use the services of recruitment agencies due to their high cost. They also claimed that the search for foreign workers via informal intermediaries had not been very effective. Farmers often complained that awaited workers had not arrived and that they have to initiate recruitment for more workers than they need (Górny *et al.* 2018). Consequently, the rural sector lagged behind other sectors in terms of the effectiveness of recruiting foreign workers, especially in taking advantage of activities of recruitment agencies that recently became an important vehicle for the inflow of foreign workers to Poland and that are shaping the sectoral composition of foreigners' employment.

Conclusions

The analysis presented in this chapter demonstrates substantial heterogeneity of Polish agriculture and, in particular, the distinct local character of

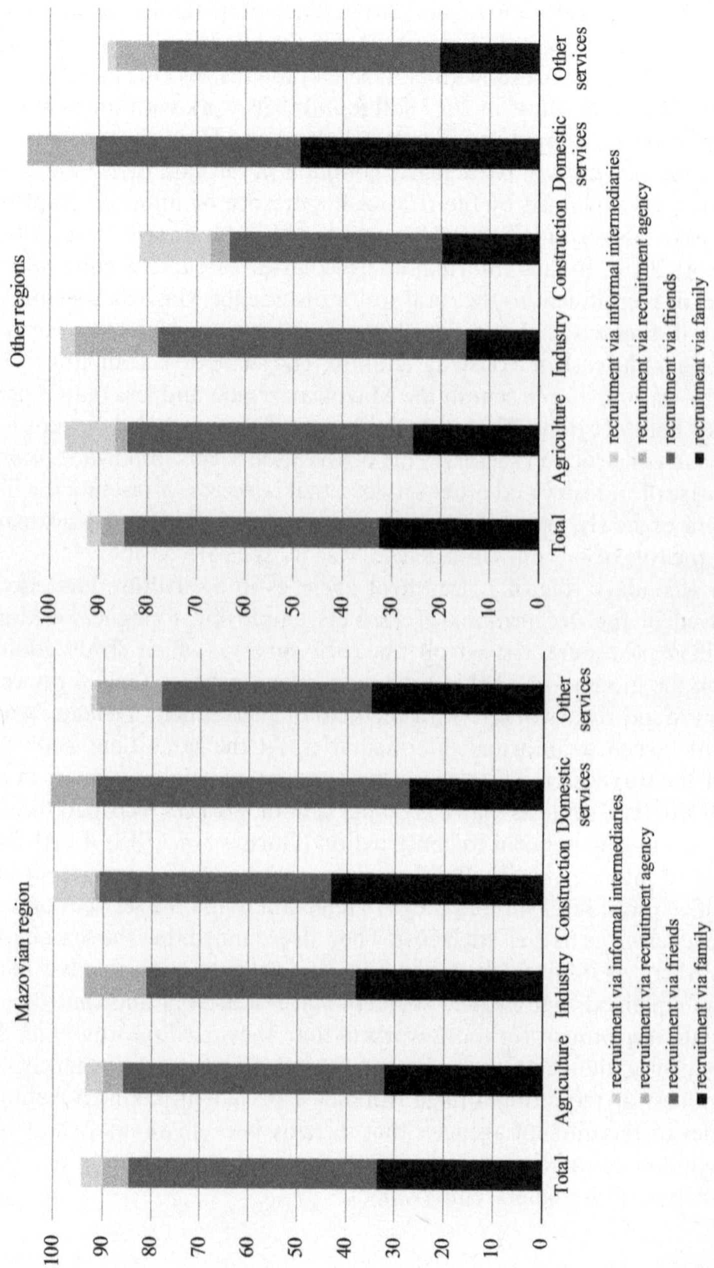

Figure 6.2 Selected modes of recruitment of Ukrainian workers in various sectors of the Polish economy. Percentages. 2017

the demand for foreign workers in the Mazovian region, and specifically in the direct surroundings of Warsaw. This is a region with relatively strong and market-oriented horticulture sector that has employed temporary migrant workers on a massive scale for over a decade (Górny and Kaczmarczyk 2018). Nevertheless, the continuation of this process is not obvious, and neither is the growing importance of foreign labour in the rural sector in other Polish regions.

The results of the study presented in this chapter suggest that the competitive strength of the rural sector in attracting foreign workers has been weakened given the opening of other sectors of the Polish labour market for employment of foreigners. Work conditions – in terms of wages and workload – are not competitive, which is a common feature of the rural sector worldwide (Taylor 2010, Rye and Scott 2018). Further, an examination of the individual characteristics of Ukrainian farm workers suggests that they are pre-selected on important variables. For instance, this is visible in relatively high shares of low-skilled persons among Ukrainian farm workers, a comparatively high share originating from the countryside and, additionally, with previously negative experiences in the labour market, such as unemployment.

Moreover, a shift in the structure of migration to Poland, that is, a decrease in the share of persons originating from rural areas (and thus accustomed to hard farm work) and an increase in shares of better educated Ukrainian migrants, might result in a relatively low propensity of recent cohorts of migrants to seek employment in agriculture. Although the shares of first timers among farm workers do not deviate substantially from other sectors, what deserves attention is the relatively short migration experience of Ukrainian workers in Mazovian agriculture. This might signify that it is treated by migrants only as an entry to the broader Mazovian or Polish labour market (compare also Górny and Kaczmarczyk 2018). In other regions of Poland, this tendency is less apparent and Ukrainian farm workers encompass more experienced migrants. However, sectoral competition for workers could be even more important in other regions of Poland – usually new destination areas for migrants where various sectors, next to agriculture, have just opened up to the employment of foreigners.

Consequently, the active role that recruitment agencies play in the process of facilitating migration to Poland in recent years can constitute an important force that might hinder the employment of foreign workers in Polish agriculture. It is not only due to the fact that the agencies' activities are directed to other sectors of the Polish labour market, mainly the food-processing industry and construction, but it is also an outcome of the general approach of Polish farmers to the recruitment of foreigners. As discussed above, Polish farmers are reluctant to take advantage of formal recruitment services and rely predominantly on migrant networks and informal intermediaries. These methods worked particularly well in the case of the Mazovian region in the past, but their effectiveness became smaller as migration from Ukraine intensified and began to include more and more persons without prior migration experience nor developed migrant networks.

A shrinking pool of foreign labour that can be attracted to Polish agriculture is commonly presented as one of the major future challenges for the sector and particularly for its labour-intensive sub-sectors such as horticulture. The medium- and long-term consequences of a massive inflow of temporary foreign workforce to Poland are less obvious. In particular, it is still to be seen whether a high supply of Ukrainian workers in the Polish labour market will act as a factor to reshape work relations in the Polish countryside and fostering structural change in rural areas, as has happened in the Mazovian region.

Acknowledgements

The authors wish to thank the anonymous reviewers for their comments on the manuscript. Analyses presented in this article were supported by the National Science Centre in Poland under the research project: 'The economic integration of immigrants in a country in the intermediate phase of the migration cycle – Poland versus selected EU countries' (grant no. 2014/14/E/HS4/00387).

References

Brunarska, Z., M. Kindler, M. Szulecka and S. Toruńczyk-Ruiz. 2016. 'Ukrainian Migration to Poland: A "Local Mobility"?' In *Ukrainian Migration to the European Union: Lessons for Migration Studies,* edited by O. Fedyuk and M. Kindler, 115–131. Berlin: Springer.

Corrado, A., C. de Castro and D. Perrotta, eds. 2016. *Migration and Agriculture: Mobility and Change in the Mediterranean Area.* Abingdon: Routledge.

CSO. 2018. Informacja o rozmiarach i kierunkach czasowej emigracji z Polski w latach 2004–2017 (Information on the Scale and Destinations of Temporary Migrants from Poland, 2004–2017). Warsaw: Central Statistical Office.

Drbohlav D. and M. Jaroszewicz, eds. 2016. *Ukrainian Migration in Times of Crisis: Forced and Labour Migration.* Prague: Charles University Press.

Fonseca, M.L. 2008. 'New Waves of Immigration to Small Towns and Rural Areas in Portugal.' *Population, Space and Place* 14(6): 525–535.

Górny, A. 2017. 'All Circular but Different: Variation in Patterns of Ukraine-to-Poland Migration.' *Population Space and Place* 23(8), https://doi.org/10.1002/psp.2074.

Górny, A. and P. Kaczmarczyk. 2018. 'A Known but Uncertain Path: The Role of Foreign Labour in Polish Agriculture.' *Journal of Rural Studies* 64: 177–188. https://doi.org/10.1016/j.jrurstud.2017.12.015.

Górny, A. and P. Kaczmarczyk. 2019. 'European Migration Transition in the Context of Post-enlargement Migration from and into Central and Eastern Europe.' In *The Sage Handbook of International Migration,* edited by Ch. Inglis, W. Li and B. Khadira, 358–375. London: Sage.

Górny, A. and P. Śleszyński. 2019. 'Exploring the Spatial Concentration of Foreign Employment in Poland Under the Simplified Procedure.' *Geographia Polonica* 91(3): 331–346.

Górny, A., I. Grabowska-Lusińska, M. Lesińska and M. Okólski, eds. 2010. *Immigration to Poland: Policy, Employment, Integration.* Warsaw: Wydawnictwo Naukowe Scholar.

Górny, A., K. Kołodziejczyk, K. Madej and P. Kaczmarczyk. 2019, 'Nowe obszary docelowe w imigracji z Ukrainy do Polski. Przypadek Bydgoszczy i Wrocławia na tle innych miast (New Target Areas for Ukrainian Migrants in Poland: The Case of Bydgoszcz and Wrocław vs. other Polish Cities).' *CMR Working Papers 118/176*. Warsaw: Centre of Migration Research.

Górny, A., P. Kaczmarczyk, M. Szulecka, M. Bitner, M. Okólski, U. Siedlecka and A. Stefańczyk. 2018. *Imigranci w Polsce w kontekście uproszczonej procedury zatrudniania cudzoziemców (Immigrants in Poland in the Context of the Simplified Procedure)*. Warsaw: OBM/WISE EUROPA. www.migracje.uw.edu.pl/wp-content/uploads/2016/11/raport-power.pdf.Kasimis, C., A. Papadopoulos and E. Zacopoulou. 2003. 'Migrants in rural Greece.' *Sociologia Ruralis* 43(2): 167–184.

Martin, P. 2002. 'Mexican Workers and U.S. Agriculture: The Revolving Door.' *International Migration Review* 36(4): 1124–1142.

McAreavey, R. 2017. *New Immigration Destinations: Migrating to Rural and Peripheral Areas*. London: Routledge (Routledge Advances in Sociology).

MRPiPS. 2019. Informacja o zatrudnieniu cudzoziemców w Polsce (Information on the Employment of Foreigners in Poland). Warsaw: MRPiPS, Departament Rynku Pracy.

Okólski, M. and D. Wach. 2020. 'Immigration and integration policies in the absence of immigrants. A case study of Poland.' *In Relations between Immigration and Integration Policies in Europe,* edited by M. Duszczyk, M. Pachocka and D. Pszczółkowska, 146–172. London: Routledge.

OECD. 2019. *International Migration Outlook 2019*. Paris: OECD.

Okólski, M. 2012. 'Transition From Emigration to Immigration. Is it the Destiny of Modern European Societies?' In *European Immigrations. Trends, Structures and Policy Implications,* edited by M. Okólski, 23–44. Amsterdam: Amsterdam University Press.

Ruhs, M. and P. Martin. 2008. 'Numbers vs. Rights: Trade-Offs and Guest Worker Programs.' *International Migration Review* 42, 249–265. DOI:10.1111/j.1747-7379.2007.00120.x.

Rye, J.F. and S. Scott. 2018. 'International Labour Migration and Food Production in Rural Europe: A Review of the Evidence.' *Sociologia Ruralis* 58(4).

Strzelecki, P. 2010. Projekcja liczby pracujących w rolnictwie indywidulanym w Polsce w latach 2008-2035.' Institute of Statistics and Demography Working Papers 31. Warsaw: Warsaw School of Economics.

Szulecka, M. 2016. 'Paradoxes of Formal Social Control. Criminological Aspects of Foreigners' Access to the Polish Territory and Labour Market.' *Biuletyn Polskiego Towarzystwa Kryminologicznego*, 23, 79–95.

Taylor, J.E. 2010. 'Agricultural Labor and Migration Policy.' *Annual Review of Resource Economics* 2, 369–93.

Wąs A. and S. Małażewska. 2012. 'Przemiany strukturalne w rolnictwie w wybranych krajach europejskich (Structural Changes in Agriculture in Selected European Countries).' *Roczniki Ekonomii Rolnictwa i Rozwoju Obszarów Wiejskich* 99(4): 75–88.

Wiśniewski Ł. and R. Rudnicki. 2016. 'Labour Input in Polish Agriculture Against Size of Agricultural Holdings – Spatial Analysis.' *Journal of Agribusiness and Rural Development* 3(41): 413–424.

Work Service (2019). *Migracje zarobkowe cudzoziemców z Ukrainy i Azji do Polski (Labour migration from Ukraine and Asia to Poland)*. Warsaw: Work Service.

Chapter 7

'Living on the edge'?

A comparative study of processes of marginalisation among Polish migrants in rural Germany and Norway

Jakub Stachowski and Kamila Fiałkowska

International migrants in rural areas

A growing geographical dispersion of intra-European migrants and their increasing presence in rural areas have become distinguishing features of migratory patterns in recent years (McAreavey 2017). Scholarly concern with this phenomenon is becoming extensive and has resulted in a rich body of empirical evidence illustrating the substantial national and regional diversity of receiving contexts (Górny and Kaczmarczyk 2018, McAreavey and Argent 2018, Rye and Scott 2018). The context and character of migration, its pace, and volume differently affect the degree of social change in the receiving areas and variously shape the pathways of accommodation and positions of migrants within social hierarchies of receiving rural communities (Jentsch and Simard 2009). Related to this is the observation made by Bock *et al.* (2016, 81), that rural 'integration and exclusion (…) is a matter of degree and dimension, and depends on the extent to which exclusion accumulates or eliminates in the intersection of legal, market and civil integration at different levels.'

The goal of this chapter is to study the processes by which migrants are marginalised in rural areas through a comparative analysis of two cases of labour migration from Poland to rural Germany and Norway, demonstrating two types of occupational concentration: in agriculture and in fish production respectively. We draw on ethnographic data gathered independently by the authors in two different research settings. While acknowledging the multifaceted character of marginalisation processes (Vasas 2005, Bernt and Colini 2013), we limit our analysis to the intersecting dimensions of migration regimes, sectoral concentration of the migrants within local industries, and the materiality and settlement structure of the hosting areas. We pay attention to temporal dimensions, and analyse marginalisation not as an achieved state, but as developing within specific structural conditions. The comparison of the two cases enables us to view patterns of international migration to rural areas not as isolated phenomena, but as entangled within wider global and international interconnections (Woods 2007) which mould into specific *glocalised* forms (Robertson 1994).

The first case is the once widely popular seasonal migration from Poland to German agriculture, the other, a more recent non-seasonal migration from Poland to Norwegian salmon production. The German case is an example of a seasonal, temporary labour migration from Poland that stretches back to the mid-nineteenth century and remains popular (Kępińska and Stark 2013, Wagner *et al.* 2013). The Norwegian case is of relatively recent origin and has been prompted by Poland's accession to the EU in 2004. It has also been highly intensive in terms of numbers and cross-border mobility, and within its short duration developed traits of permanence (Friberg 2012).

Our intention is to demonstrate what forces are at play in two quite distinct receiving contexts and how migrants accommodate themselves to them. We illustrate that the marginalisation of migrants manifests itself differently in these contexts due to their position in rural labour markets and within material rural space. At the same time, migrants are not simply victims of oppressive structural forces, but also display an array of agentic competences, making sense of their situation, achieving a degree of control over their lives and being able to pursue their life plans (O'Reilly 2012a). As such, they are able to compensate for and to somewhat mitigate the effects of marginalisation.

At the margins of what? Marginalisation, migration, and rural areas

In a broad sense, the notion of marginalisation invokes connotations of periphery and denotes a restricted or underprivileged position of an individual or a group within a given social hierarchy (Vasas 2005). It is closely related to the notion of exclusion and integration and designates limitations in political, social, and cultural rights as well as various forms of social disadvantage such as poverty, discrimination, or inequality (Bernt and Colini 2013, Mowat 2015). Marginalisation is not a static condition but a process that involves complex mechanisms depriving people of access to resources or participation in various domains of social life (Vasas 2005). While keeping in mind this multifaceted character of the processes of marginalisation, in this chapter we focus on selected aspects. One central dimension is the migrants' location in the labour market, work arrangements, and how these shape the outcomes and strategies inscribed in the process of migration and/or settlement in rural areas. Conventionally, labour migrants have been depicted as occupying an underprivileged position in hosting societies (Piore 1979, Standing 2011). Concentration of migrants within particular occupational sectors often leads to the development of 'immigrant niches' adding to their marginal position in receiving contexts (Waldinger and Lichter 2003). Research has shown how such occupational concentration of migrants within low-skill sectors is augmented by the employers' explicit targeting and selection among groups that lack power, a perception of migrants as particularly suited for certain jobs or exhibiting an exceptional work ethic (MacKenzie and Forde 2009, Holmes 2013).

The interplay between marginalisation and place is important for this analysis. While literature on the intentions of settlement in the immigration country informs us that contact with the natives is crucial in forming a place attachment and making settlement decisions (Søholt *et al.* 2012, Brunarska and Toruńczyk-Ruiz 2019), the scholarship on international rural migration illustrates how problematic it may be. Lever and Milbourne (2017) have demonstrated how the intersection of labour market and spatial positioning renders migrants invisible in the local community. Similarly, Wagner *et al.* (2013), based on the case of labour migration from Poland to German agricultural production, showed how such conditions result in an ambiguous self-perception among migrants. On the one hand, they view themselves as occupying a marginal position in the social structures of the receiving communities, on the other, they are conscious of their pivotal role in the industry. Andrzejewska and Rye (2012), who researched seasonal workers in Norway, found that the geographical isolation of the farms and the long work hours suppress the possibility to engage in the local community and develop social relationships with the local Norwegian population.

Polish migration to Germany and Norway – two contexts, two stories

Polish intra-European migration eludes a single conceptualisation and has been shaped throughout the years by changing policies regulating the cross-border movements, access to jobs and settlement of Polish migrants abroad. In the aftermath of the collapse of communism, migration from Poland was an important livelihood strategy and has been labelled 'incomplete' (Jaźwińska and Okólski 2001) due to its largely temporary and circular character. Poland's accession to the European Union in 2004 granted a larger degree of freedom of movement for Polish citizens. Similar to their earlier migration movements, the post-2004 migratory processes were also largely analysed as temporal, and their transnational and 'liquid' (Engbersen and Snel 2013), or 'intentionally unpredictable' (Eade *et al.* 2007), character was emphasised. At the same time, treating intra-European Polish migration as in a state of constant flux would be an oversimplification, as evidence from major receiving countries clearly reveals patterns of permanence. In the case of Germany, the circular migration for many became a lifelong project to the extent that one can talk about 'permanent temporariness' (*cf.* Martin 2001). In the case of Norway, settlement is clearly observed, for instance in the transnational rearrangements of family lives (Friberg 2012).

The 1989 collapse of the iron curtain opened new avenues for migration from Poland to Germany (*cf.* Cyrus and Vogel 2006). A high number of irregular Polish migrants in Germany and the labour demand of the

German farmers resulted in a bilateral agreement legalising the access of Poles to seasonal employment in Germany, signed as early as December 1990 (Okólski 2004). It became one of the few possibilities for legal employment in the west for the growing numbers of Polish citizens. The number of seasonal workers grew steadily, reaching nearly 300,000 workers on the eve of Poland's EU accession in 2004 (Kępińska 2013, 539). While the inclusion of Poland in the EU granted a greater degree of freedom of movement to its citizens, Germany decided to introduce and maintain the transitional period for a maximum length of seven years (as regulated in the Accession Treaty). In practice, this restricted the freedom of movement of workers from the acceding countries until 2011, apart from those working on the basis of the seasonal work agreement. While the country hosts a substantial Polish diaspora numbering between 1.5 million to 2 million people (Nowosielski 2016), many of whom are settled but living transnational lives (Barglowski 2019), it is also evident that thousands of workers continue to circulate between the countries (Wagner *et al.* 2013).

While not a regular member of the EU, through its membership in the European Economic Association (EEA), Norway participates in the policy of a cross-border flow of people, capital, services, and goods. This fact has had far-reaching implications for the patterns of migration in the country. While Polish migrants were no strangers to Norwegian society before 2004 (Godzimirski 2005), as a result of the opening of the Norwegian labour market, they have soon become the biggest group of migrants in the country, totalling today approximately 100,000 registered persons (Statistics Norway 2019). Similarly to Germany, Norway upheld the transitional period, but only for a period of five years. Between 2004 and 2009, the conditions for obtaining a residence permit demanded a full-time work offer from the employer and a guarantee of wages following Norwegian standards. However, a bulk of migration has been organised as posted workers and through recruitment agencies, which has been an effective way of avoiding collective agreements such as equal wages (Friberg 2013). In May 2009, the transitional period ended and, from this time on, holding a part-time contract was sufficient for obtaining permission to stay and work (Friberg *et al.* 2013). The reports of 'social dumping' from labour intensive sectors in which many Polish migrants concentrate, for instance construction, agriculture, or manufacturing, have led to state intervention and the implementation of measures such as a generalisation of wages and greater control in several sectors (Friberg 2013). From 2018, the generalisation of wages also includes the fish industry.

Researching migrants in rural areas – methods and challenges

The data used in this chapter come from two independently conducted projects. In both cases, the researchers were guided by the logic of an ethnographic approach, combining in-depth interviews and participant observation. The common objective was to gain an understanding of Polish migration as a process developing in time and space, and the consequences it generates for the migrants.

The German case comes from multi-sited fieldwork in Poland and Germany lasting for eight months and stretching between 2010 and 2012. Fieldwork was conducted in the local community in Poland, where seasonal migration was a widely popular livelihood strategy, and in Germany, at the place of work for the seasonal migrants (see Wagner *et al.* 2013). Data collection comprised covert and overt participant observation, including five weeks of employment as a strawberry picker in Germany. The author was thus able to live and work with the migrants, and observe the daily work-life rhythm at the farm, which employed over 200 people in the high season. Importantly, due to mistreatment and malpractices in the work and living spaces of the migrants, some of the findings were only able to be obtained if the identity of the researcher was concealed. Such a method of data collection inevitably raises ethical concerns due to the workers' lack of awareness of the aim of her seasonal employment. Thus, the questions of protecting the identity and privacy of the participants were of crucial importance and had to be handled with a great level of reflexivity and care for the co-workers, all of which were addressed by the author in her work and the institution in which she was based. Towards the end of the fieldwork, Fiałkowska disclosed the aim of her seasonal employment to trusted co-workers, with whom she discussed the observations, and she acquired their consent to use the data in her work. These touched upon topics that were important parts of the migrants' experiences and workers' discussions (for instance, arrangements related to living in Poland and working in Germany, accommodation and working conditions, and the general wellbeing of the migrant workers). This was combined with 40 semi-structured in-depth interviews conducted in Poland with the seasonal workers. Altogether, this allowed for a discussion regarding the observations and to inter-subjectively reinforce the accuracy of the interpretations. To protect the co-workers and interviewees, their names and the place of the fieldwork have been anonymised.

In the case of Norway, the fieldwork has been conducted among Polish migrants who live and work in one of the rural municipalities located by the Norwegian coast. From 2004 onwards, the area has attracted a substantial number of east and central European labour migrants who found employment at the local fish-processing plant. Today, the share of the migrant population in the municipality is over 25 per cent and the Polish local population numbers approximately 200 persons. The fieldwork was divided into a series of ethnographic stays conducted between May 2016 and May 2018. It combined formal and informal interviews, participant observation, visits to the fish-processing plant where the majority of the migrants worked, and visits to migrants' houses. During the fieldwork, 30 in-depth interviews with

36 Polish migrants were conducted. They included 19 men and 17 women ranging from their early 20s to early 60s. Twenty-three of the participants were in their late 20s or 30s. An average time the interviewees had lived in the locality was six and a half years. The approach to the interviews was biographical (Roberts 2002). Its aim was to understand how the situation of the migrants in the locality changes with time. The themes discussed were their living and working conditions, social relationships, rationale for arriving and staying, their everyday concerns, and experiences and practices. All the interviews were conducted in the informants' first language, most of them in the setting of the migrants' private living spaces. The conducted fieldwork was entirely overt.

Due to obstacles encountered, the recruitment of the informants combined purposive and opportunistic sampling (O'Reilly 2012b). Two gatekeepers have been central for establishing contact with the participants and aiding the recruitment process. An important issue that emerged during the fieldwork was the social visibility of the local Polish community. This prompted the researcher to reflect upon issues of ethics, and to anonymise the identity of the participants and the name of the locality.

Living on the edge(s) of rural societies

In this chapter, we analyse and compare two domains of migrants' lives across the two contexts: work arrangements and spatial aspects of their lives in the community and beyond. We illustrate their impact on migrants' overall position in the receiving context and how migrants respond to them.

At the edge of the local labour market

Unskilled labour in German agriculture and Norwegian fish production have been largely abandoned by local workers and gradually replaced by international migrant workers. As a result, the continuous flow of migration over the years has led to an occupational concentration of workers with a foreign background.

The migration trajectory from Poland to Germany built around circularity and concentration in agriculture has been a result of the above mentioned bilateral agreement in 1990, which continued after 2004 and up to 2011, independently of restrictions following from Germany's transitional arrangements. Access to this form of employment was organised through informal networks, on which workers were dependent. At the time of the fieldwork (2010–2012), many of Fiałkowska's respondents were expected to pay an informal fee of 20 up to as much as 100 euros to a senior employee, who often also acted as a middleman for such an arrangement.

Faced with limited options for other kinds of employment, migrants had to be resilient and obedient at work in order to secure employment for the next season. Often unclear employment conditions caused an intensification of work (Smith 2006) and competition among the workers, breaking down loyalties and cooperation. This was critically addressed by one of the interviewees, Iza. She worked alongside her cousin and friend, forming a team, for which the cousin was made responsible. The work was arranged by her cousin, who had to earn the trust of the employer to be allowed to 'bring' someone else to work. In the interview, Iza explained how this happened:

> *[...] they slept for five hours, there was a lot of work [...]. The German stood and watched them in the field. Something's not right and he kicked the box with strawberries and made you start over from the beginning of the row. So, from what she said, it was just terrible. But as it turned out later, it was about choosing the best workers, who later could recruit others.*

Insecurity related to future employment translates into an intensification of work and self-exploitation, which also emerges from Iza's account: 'she said that once I decided to come to work, I have to endure as long as the boss wants, and not to quit after a week.' As she explained, this would negatively affect her cousin's situation, who depended on this form of employment. This adds to the burden of the employees, who realise that their position and relationship with the employer is determined not only by the quality of their work but also by those whom they recruited. Yet they learned to rationalise and to adapt to such situations. While work in agriculture and the circulation between the two countries was not simply a matter of choosing but often a necessity due to financial difficulties in the home country, the seasonal migration was often referred to as inscribed into their lives, or as a desire to go 'when the spring comes and you will smell the soil' (cf. Wagner *et al.* 2013, 46).

Yet migrants were acutely aware that they do the jobs locals will not do. 'They laughed at us, *Polnishe Maschine* they say' is what another respondent overheard from a few locals employed on higher positions on the farm. Such attitudes unveil their dehumanising approach towards the employees, which legitimises foreign workers' exploitation, all of which they are aware of.

Negotiating their marginal social and labour market position, the interviewees referred to what Morawska (2001) called a 'cultural kit,' a combination of features such as reliability or diligence inextricably linked with national identity. This is evident in the narrative of Grzegorz, who has been a permanent seasonal migrant for the last 20 years. In a conversation that took place just before his forthcoming apple-picking season, he stressed the reliability of Polish workers and their high work ethic.

> *The boss tries to be fair because he knows that who else would come here to work, right? He will not turn to Germans, because they won't come. They won't come to work in the field, and not for this money [...]*
>
> (Grzegorz, mid 50s)

Constructing the figure of an 'ideal worker' (MacKenzie and Forde 2009) and contrasting it with the locals' approach to work, Grzegorz's statement also points to how migrants rationalise, normalise, and narrate the story of their migration. Paradoxically though, by becoming an 'ideal worker' and enhancing their employability by appealing to their 'cultural kit,' migrant workers contribute to their marginalisation by becoming exactly the kind of workers the employers need – hardworking, flexible, and with few demands. Their marginal labour market positioning as well as social invisibility resembles in some aspects the situation of Polish migrants in Norway.

In the Norwegian case, migrants cluster predominantly within the local salmon industry. After 2004, the industry started to rely increasingly on the recruitment of migrant workers and experienced a rapid growth in its share of foreign labour force. As a result, the company that employs most of the migrant workers in the study locality has gradually become ethnically segmented. With only a few exceptions, the physical tasks of fish processing, such as slaughtering, cutting, filleting, and packing, were performed by workers with a foreign background. Increasing migration to the locality prompted competition between the migrant workers, creating a pressure to improve performance and resulting in an overall intensification of work. In addition, the workers over time experienced a worsening of their working conditions. From the full-time permanent contracts offered to them during the first years after the EU-extension, the employment policy changed to an offer of 80 per cent permanent contract, preluded by a lengthy trial period. This change contributed to the internal segmentation of the foreign workforce, with more recent arrivals experiencing an increased insecurity in their work situation. Dariusz shared his thoughts on this issue:

> *They don't give us the rights we deserve. If I was Norwegian, I think they would give me a 100 per cent contract (…) This system makes you insecure. It gives people the feeling that if they don't work hard, they are not good enough. They squeeze them like lemons for two years, and then people can't work properly after they get the permanent contract. They are too exhausted after the two-year struggle for the contract.*
>
> (Dariusz, early 30s)

The narratives of the migrants concerning the working conditions were often framed as exploitation and instrumental treatment. They reflected the awareness of being treated as a flexible and disposable labour force, and not as long-term assets.

The occupational concentration of the Polish migrants has wider implications for their marginalisation. The organisation of work in the fish industry severely limited possibilities for the acquisition of the Norwegian language, as migrants socialised almost exclusively with other migrants. Some have spent years performing menial, physically demanding tasks in the fish industry, prioritising financial gains but at the same time risking a deterioration of their health and wellbeing, and limiting the opportunities for inclusion in other spheres of the local community. While some have managed to find other jobs in the local labour market, for most, changing jobs was a risky venture that may put strain on an otherwise fragile life. As one of the female informants, Krystyna confessed:

INTERVIEWER: *What are the pros and cons of your job?*

KRYSTYNA: *Salary is a positive side. The negative side is that my health deteriorates. Your joints, back, and psyche are worn-out. But when it comes to the salary, it is ok.*

INTERVIEWER: *Do you consider changing this job?*

KRYSTYNA: *Yes, I do.*

INTERVIEWER: *What are the real chances for making it come through?*

KRYSTYNA: *I think that chances are good but there is... I don't have courage. You think, what is going to happen, right? (...) there is this waiting time in the job office. Two months [waiting time before one is entitled to benefits in case of voluntarily quitting job]. And what then? What about finances, then? So, I refrain from doing that for the time being.*

(Krystyna, mid 40s)

The above story illustrates sentiments that are characteristic for many migrants. The prolonged stay in the locality is a form of sacrifice. It involves an improvement of their financial situation and gradual settlement, but at the same time offers very few perspectives on mobility in the local labour market, and may in turn result in consolidating migrants' position within the second sector of the labour market (Piore 1979).

Spatial edges

In this section, we discuss how migrants' marginalisation is related to their spatial distribution within the respective localities, and how this reflects their overall position within the hosting communities.

Becker (2010, 7) has metaphorically conceived seasonal migrant workers in Germany as an 'army of goblins': fairylike creatures, whose role is reduced to performing a certain job and then vanishing. The workers arrive, do the job and return home largely unnoticed by the mainstream society. Their invisibility, also experienced by the researcher during the fieldwork, is strengthened by a clear spatial separation, as migrants are accommodated in remote areas where work is performed. Accommodation must be provided by the employer in case of seasonal work in agriculture (for which migrants are usually charged). Often it is a cellar or the attic in an outbuilding – in the analysed case, approximately 200 co-workers were accommodated in containers and caravans, forming a sort of ethnic colony on the side of a little-used road at the margins of the village, in the vicinity of the farmlands.

The minimum conditions set in the law for accommodation are: a minimum of six square meters per person, a maximum of six persons in a room – women and men separately, bed and a cupboard should be provided for every person, as well as a chair and place by the table, and there should be a place to prepare food – minimum one kitchen stove per two persons, access to the fridge, one toilet per eight persons, and one shower per 10, access to a washing machine and access to a first aid kit. These were suggestions for newly built accommodations. A departure from these norms has been tolerated over time and in practice.

In the analysed case, the containers were too small to host six people, not to mention their belongings, which were stored under the beds since there was no cupboard (see Figure 7.1 for an example). The number of showers or toilets was below the required amount, there was a lack of hot water and limited access to the washing machine. Facing frequent power cuts, workers used candles, but no fire extinguishers were provided. Interviews with other seasonal workers confirm that these observations from the field are still frequently experienced problems, while there is a limited awareness of the workers' rights regarding the minimum standards of accommodation (Wagner *et al.* 2013).

Intersecting with the structural dimensions, most notably with the mentioned earlier sectoral concentration and type of work, migrants are practically excluded from the life of the host community. They spend most

Figure 7.1 Accommodation of seasonal migrant workers in Germany, 2010 (Photo credit: Kamila Fialkowska)

of their time working and then resting, which limits their opportunities to have outside contacts or relationships, or to seek help or advice when needed. Moreover, working and living alongside their compatriots, they hardly ever have a chance to learn or practice the local language. The host community usually means the farm, so the most important issue here is what kind of relation they have with their co-workers, employer, or their employer's representatives. 'We came here to work, not to take a rest' was an oft-repeated phrase, which helped to build resilience in the face of poor accommodation, a demanding job, and the demeaning treatment of workers. The temporality of this arrangement made it easier to consent to it. Regular seasonal workers on the farm would return to the same container every other year. As such, they could live with their former colleagues, which increased their sense of comfort as well as the ability to adjust the containers to their needs, domesticating the unhomely space (Boccagni 2014).

In the Norwegian case, the local spatial distribution of Polish migrants and their living arrangements were different. Unlike the German case, the occupational concentration did not transcend into specific housing patterns. One of the reasons was the fact that Norwegian employers are not obliged to provide accommodation for the migrant workers. Migrants are thus responsible for finding and arranging their own living places in the local housing market. During the fieldwork, no specific area in the local housing and settlement structure where migrants would concentrate was identified. The non-seasonal character of the work in the fish industry has facilitated a longer-term stay of many migrants and invited them to invest in better housing arrangements. Despite the sparsely distributed population and frequently experienced isolation caused by considerable distances between villages in the locality, and the fact that 90 per cent of the housing structure consists of detached houses, migrants belonged to the 'natural' existing settlement structure (see Figure 7.2 for an example). Nevertheless, the material and geographical conditions of the locality were experienced by many as burdensome, as they imposed geographical barriers which needed to be traversed on a daily basis. Radek, in his late 20s, was among those who reflected upon this:

> *There is not so much motivation to be (participate) everywhere, let's say play basketball, because everything is far away. Everything is so spread out here (…) During the weekends… in Poland when we used to go out with our peers to a restaurant or a pub, it was easy to get back because there was public transportation. Here you have to drive.*
>
> (Radek, late 20s)

The material structure of the location necessitated migrants to relate to it and to domesticate it. As Radek's experiences indicate, long distances could effectively limit migrants' participation in spare-time activities and socialisation with other inhabitants in the locality (Cass *et al.* 2005). As such, the experiences of the locality were often described as an ambivalent mixture of rural idyll and the drudgery of everyday material obstacles (Woods 2011). At the same time, such experiences have not refrained many from reuniting with their families in Norway and purchasing properties. Both are tangible signs of an intention to stay longer term. Ela, who together with her child joined her husband in Norway, reflected upon this:

> *I don't want to move anywhere else (outside this particular location in the area) (…) We're looking for a house here, but we can't find one (…) It has to be here. We're close to the doctor's office and to school … and the shop is close… (…). We want to buy a house because we want to have something that is ours. I want to feel that this is my place, I want to feel that I am coming back home, not to a soulless apartment.*
>
> (Ela, early 40s)

The quotation illustrates place-attachment and the development of a feeling of being at home. For house owners or those considering buying property, this was often an important life stage associated with stability and a 'grounding' of life (Bygnes and Erdal 2016).

Figure 7.2 An example of migrants' housing in the Norwegian case (Photo credit: Jakub Stachowski)

Thriving on the edges of rural communities – final thoughts

In this chapter, we have compared two cases of international migration from Poland to different rural contexts in Germany and Norway respectively. We placed our analysis within a wider context of migration regimes but paid particular attention to industrial and material aspects of receiving local contexts. As the initially quoted observation by Bock *et al.* (2016) suggests, exclusion and integration, but also marginalisation, work intersectionally and are the results of interaction and overlap between various factors.

The role of working conditions, migrants' position in the local labour market, and the fact that they are largely contracted to perform certain types of physical, unskilled tasks were central factors in this analysis. These conditions have proved central in grasping the workings of the marginalisation processes, as they illustrate how the disadvantaged position of the migrants is impacted by their work arrangements. While, in both cases, a combination of recruitment strategies and the volume of migration has led to the formation of ethnic niches (Waldinger and Lichter 2003), their existence intersects differently with another dimension emphasised in the analysis, namely the rural place. In the case of the German agriculture, the combination of spatial and physical emplacement of work in the fields and seclusion through camp accommodation pushes migrants drastically to the edge of, and out-of-sight in, the local community. In Norway, however, despite the high occupational concentration of the migrants, the workings of spatial marginalisation differ. Despite the frequently experienced social isolation as a result of the material attributes of the place, migrants are spatially distributed within the 'naturally' existing settlement structure of the location.

While the German case features seasonal production and, as such, presupposes largely circular migration, throughout its duration over many years, the migration has evolved into a recurring circuit. One of the reasons the seasonal migration of Poles to Germany developed as a life-long project for some of the migrants has been long-lasting limitations inscribed in the migration regime that supported circulation rather than settlement. By contrast, through its membership in the EEA, Norway grants EU-migrants a higher degree of freedom to seek employment and settle down. In addition, the non-seasonal character of the work in fish production invites and facilitates some of the Polish migrants to establish long-term roots in the locality. These factors affected the ways in which the respective streams of migration developed.

As the German case showed, the circular seasonal migration turned into a permanent phenomenon in the researched case, with profound implications for migrants' personal life trajectories, as well as their families and local communities (*cf.* Fiałkowska 2019). In this case, the continuous treatment of the home country by migrants as a primary point of reference may facilitate rationalisations of their marginal positions. Furthermore, a belief in the good reputation of the Polish migrant workers who are vital in the success of the harvesting season in Germany may be also a compensatory strategy. In Norway, on the other hand, there is a tendency towards a more permanent settlement, visible through the acquisition of properties in the locality, family reunifications, and place attachment. Creating a home and focusing on constructing familiarity in the relative social isolation and relatively low labour-market position is how they exercise their agency.

As such, these examples are manifestations of migrants' agentic capabilities. Narratives of the migrants and concrete practices reveal various ways of making sense of their situation, rationalising and, in consequence, mitigating the experience of marginalisation experienced otherwise. Considerations of migrants' agency, viewing them as reflexive and able to exercise some control over their actions, and as negotiating the asymmetrical social relations they experience, enables us to better comprehend and problematise the processes of marginalisation in receiving rural areas.

One of the final reflections emerging from the analysis is the importance of keeping scholarly pace with the dynamically changing character of rural international migration. Migrant positionalities in rural contexts are not constant but rather continuously evolving as a result of cross-cutting mechanisms of exclusion/inclusion within respective migration regimes and the ways of negotiating these conditions by the migrants.

Acknowledgements

The chapter is result of the 2017–2022 Global Labour in Rural Societies research project financed by the Norwegian Research Council (grant no. 261854/F10). The authors wish to thank the external reviewers for their comments on the manuscript. Funding from the Norwegian University of Science and Technology has made possible open access publishing of the chapter.

References

Andrzejewska, J. and J.F. Rye. 2012. 'Lost in Transantional Space? Migrant Farm Workers in Rural Districts.' *Mobilities* 7(2): 247–268. DOI:10.1080/17450101.2012.654996.

Barglowski, K. 2019. *Cultures of Transnationality in European Migration: Subjectivity, Family and Inequality*. Abingdon: Routledge.

Becker, J. 2010. *Erdbeerpflücker, Spargelstecher, Erntehelfer: Polnische Saisonarbeiter in Deutschland, temporäre Arbeitsmigration im neuen Europa*. Bielefeld: Transcript Verlag.

Bernt, M. and L. Colini. 2013. 'Exclusion, Marginalization and Peripheralization. Conceptual Concerns in the Study of Urban Inequalities.' Working Paper. Leibniz Institute for Regional Development and Structural Planning.

Boccagni, P. 2014. 'What's in a (Migrant) House? Changing Domestic Spaces, the Negotiation of Belonging and Home-making in Ecuadorian Migration.' *Housing, Theory and Society* 31(3): 277–293. DOI:10.1080/14036096.2013.867280.

Bock, B.B., G. Osti and F. Ventura. 2016. 'Rural Migration and New Patterns of Exclusion and Integration in Europe.' In *Routledge International Handbook of Rural Studies*, edited by M. Shucksmith and D. Brown, 71–84. Oxon, New York: Routledge.

Brunarska, Z. and S. Toruńczyk-Ruiz. 2019. 'Through Attachment to Settlement: Social and Psychological Determinants of Migrants' Intentions to Stay." *Journal of Ethnic and Migration Studies*: 1–19. DOI:10.1080/1369183X.2018.1554429.

Bygnes, S. and M.B. Erdal. 2016. 'Liquid Migration, Grounded Lives: Considerations about Future Mobility and Settlement among Polish and Spanish Migrants in Norway.' *Journal of Ethnic and Migration Studies* 43(1): 102–118. DOI:10.1080/1369183X.2016.1211004.

Cass, N.E. Shove and J. Urry. 2005. 'Social Exclusion, Mobility and Access.' *The Sociological Review* 53: 539–555. DOI:10.1111/j.1467-954X.2005.00565.x.

Cyrus, N. and D. Vogel. 2006. 'Managing Access to the German Labour Market: How Polish (Im)migrants Relate to German Opportunities and Restrictions.' In *Illegal Immigration in Europe: Beyond Control?*, edited by F. Düvell, 75–105. London: Palgrave Macmillan UK.

Eade, J., S. Drinkwater and M. Garapich. 2007. *Class and Ethnicity: Polish Migrant Workers in London: Full Research Report. ESRC End of Award Report*. RES-000-22-1294. Swindon: ESRC.

Engbersen, G. and E. Snel. 2013. 'Liquid Migration: Dynamic and Fluid Patterns of Post-accession Migration Flows.' In *Mobility in Transition: Migration Patterns after EU Enlargement*, edited by B. Glorius, I. Grabowska-Lusińska and A. Kuvik, 21–40. Amsterdam: Amsterdam University Press.

Fiałkowska, K. 2019. 'Remote Fatherhood and Visiting Husbands: Seasonal Migration and Men's Position within Families.' *Comparative Migration Studies* 7(1): 2. DOI:10.1186/s40878-018-0106-2.

Friberg, J.H. 2012. 'The Stages of Migration. From Going Abroad to Settling Down: Post-accession Polish Migrant Workers in Norway.' *Journal of Ethnic and Migration Studies* 38(10): 1589–1605. DOI:10.1080/1369183X.2012.711055.

Friberg, J.H. 2013. *The Polish Worker in Norway. Emerging Patterns of Migration, Employment and Incorporation after EU's Eastern Enlargement.* Ph.D. Diss., University of Oslo.

Friberg, J.H., J.E. Dølvik and L. Eldring. 2013. *Arbeidsmigrasjon til Norge fra Øst- og Sentral-Europa.* Temanotat. Oslo. Fafo.

Godzimirski, J.M. 2005. *Tackling Welfare Gaps: The East European Transition and New Patterns of Migration to Norway*. NUPI.

Górny, A. and P. Kaczmarczyk. 2018. 'A Known but Uncertain Path: The Role of Foreign Labour in Polish Agriculture.' *Journal of Rural Studies* 64: 177–188. DOI:10.1016/j.jrurstud.2017.12.015.

Holmes, S.M. 2013. *Fresh Fruits, Broken Bodies. Migrant Farmworkers in the United States.* Berkeley: California Series in Public Anthropology.

Jaźwińska, E. and M. Okólski. 2001. *Ludzie na huśtawce: Migracje między peryferiami Polski i Zachodu.* Warszawa: Wydawnictwo Naukowe Scholar.

Jentsch B. and M. Simard. 2009. 'Conclusion: Comparative Perspectives on Rural Immigrants' Integration.' In *International Migration and Rural Areas,* edited by B. Jentsch and M. Simard, 179–196. Farnham and Burlington: Ashgate.

Kępińska, E. 2013. 'Gender Differentiation in Seasonal Migration: The Case of Poland.' *Journal of Ethnic and Migration Studies* 39(4): 535–555. DOI:10.1080/1369183X.2013.745231.

Kępińska, E. and O. Stark. 2013. 'The Evolution and Sustainability of Seasonal Migration from Poland to Germany: From the Dusk of the 19th Century to the Dawn of the 21st century.' *International Review of Economics and Finance* 28: 3–18. DOI:10.1016/j.iref.2013.05.003.

Lever, J. and P. Milbourne. 2017. 'The Structural Invisibility of Outsiders: The Role of Migrant Labour in the Meat-processing Industry.' *Sociology* 51(2): 306–322. DOI:10.1177/0038038515616354.

MacKenzie, R. and C. Forde. 2009. 'The Rhetoric of the "Good Worker" versus the Realities of Employers' Use and the Experiences of Migrant Workers.' *Work, Employment and Society* 23(1): 142–159. DOI:10.1177/0950017008099783.

Martin, P. 2001. *There is Nothing More Permanent than Temporary Foreign Workers. Backgrounder*. Center for Immigration Studies. https://cis.org/Report/There-Nothing-More-Permanent-Temporary-Foreign-Workers.

McAreavey, R. 2017. *New Immigration Destinations: Migrating to Rural and Peripheral Areas.* New York: Routledge.

McAreavey, R. and N. Argent. 2018. 'New Immigrant Destinations (NID) Unravelling the Challenges and Opportunities for Migrants and for Host Communities.' *Journal of Rural Studies* 64: 148–152. DOI:10.1016/j.jrurstud.2018.09.006.

Morawska, E. 2001. 'Structuring Migration: The Case of Polish Income-seeking Travelers to the West.' *Theory and Society* 30(1): 47–80. DOI:10.1023/A:1011081228016.

Mowat, J.G. 2015. 'Towards a New Conceptualization of Marginalization.' *European Educational Research Journal* 14(5): 454–476. DOI:10.1177/1474904115589864.

Nowosielski, M. 2016. *Polskie organizacje w Niemczech. Stan i uwarunkowania.* Poznań: Instytut Zachodni im. Zygmunta Wojciechowskiego, Poznań.

Okólski, M. 2004. *Seasonal Labour Migration in the Light of the German-Polish Bilateral Agreement*. OECD. DOI:10.1787/9789264108684-en.

O'Reilly, K. 2012a. *International Migration and Social Theory*. London: Palgrave Macmillan.

O'Reilly, K. 2012b. *Ethnographic Methods.* London: Routledge.

Piore, M.J. 1979. *Birds of Passage: Migrant Labor and Industrial Societies*. Cambridge University Press.

Roberts, B. 2002. *Biographical Research.* Maidenhead Berkshire: Open University Press.

Robertson, R. 1994. 'Globalisation or Glocalisation?' *The Journal of International Communication* 1(1): 33–52. DOI:10.1080/13216597.1994.9751780.

Rye J.F. and S. Scott. 2018. 'International Labour Migration and Food Production in Rural Europe: A Review of Evidence.' *Sociologia Ruralis* 58(4): 929- 952. DOI:10.1111/soru.12208.

Smith, C. 2006. 'The Double Indeterminacy of Labour Power: Labour Effort and Labour Mobility.' *Work, Employment and Society* 20(2): 389–402. DOI:10.1177/0950017006065109.

Standing, G. 2011. *The Precariat. The New Dangerous Class*. London: Bloomsbury Academic.

Statistics Norway. 2019. *Fakta om innvandring.* www.ssb.no/innvandring-og-innvandrere/faktaside/innvandring.

Søholt, S., A. Aasland, K. Onsager and G.M. Vestby. 2012. *'Derfor blir vi her' innvandrere i Distrikts Norge.* NIBR-rapport 2012: 5.

Vasas, E.B. 2005. 'Examining the Margins: A Concept Analysis of Marginalization.' *Advances in Nursing Science*, 28(3): 194–202. DOI:10.1097/00012272-200507000-00002.

Waldinger, R. and M.I. Lichter. 2003. *How Other Half Works. Immigration and the Social Organization of Labour*. Berkeley: University of California Press.

Wagner, M., K. Fiałkowska, M. Piechowska, M. and W. Łukowski. 2013. *Deutsches Waschpulver und polnische Wirtschaft. Die Lebenswelt polnischer Saisonarbeiter. Ethnographische Beobachtungen.* Bielefeld: Transcript Verlag.

Woods, M. 2007. 'Engaging the Global Countryside: Globalization, Hybridity and the Reconstitution of Rural Place.' *Progress in Human Geography,* 31: 485–508. DOI:10.1177/0309132507079503.

Woods M. 2011. *Rural*. New York: Routledge.

Chapter 8

Changing labour standards and 'subordinated inclusion'

Thai migrant workers in the Swedish forest berry industry

Aina Tollefsen, Charlotta Hedberg, Madeleine Eriksson and Linn Axelsson

Thai migrant workers in the Swedish forest berry industry

The forest berry industry in the north of Sweden operates within a highly competitive global market for nutritious wild berries and is heavily dependent on seasonal migrant workers. Based on unique survey material with Thai berry pickers, this chapter analyses the actual wage levels and costs of these workers after a series of changing laws and regulations surrounding migration and labour standards in Sweden. Labour standards improved in Sweden in 2010 with the implementation of collective agreements and work contracts for non-European Economic Area (EEA) wild berry pickers, the only country employing such standards within this type of industry. We examine how, despite these improvements, Thai migrant berry pickers continue to be exploited in a process that we theorise as *subordinated inclusion*. The concept, as advanced by Mulinari and Neergaard (2004), captures a migrant position with formal inclusion and right to negotiated wages 'on paper,' while in actual practice the migrant workers' position on the Swedish labour market remains subordinated. Our focus is on outcomes in terms of actual wages and costs, while we also place our analysis in a context of an industry characterised by peripherality and changing geographies of production and consumption. We found that one third of the workers in the survey reported earnings below the level of income they are entitled to according to the collective agreement. The results also showed that the earnings were substantially lower than what was given in some of our previous interview studies. One reason for this might be that, in semi-structured interview situations, informants want to highlight their earnings in a more positive light by referring to their most successful years in Sweden. We also found that the costs for migrants surrounding berry picking are high given the short period the pickers work in Sweden. The concept of subordinated inclusion is useful for understanding the outcome of our data analyses: workers are included with formal work contracts and a collective agreement, but subordinated in terms of actual earnings and protections. The result of the survey, given that one third of the workers earned less than the guaranteed wage, showed that this formal inclusion of the workers has not worked out in practice.

The changes in the globalising labour markets and the varying forms of conditions and access to rights granted to different groups of migrant workers in relation to national systems provide examples of severe employment inequalities worldwide (ILO 2014, Keeley 2015). Conditions around employment differentiate rights and protections in complex ways, which lead to insecure everyday life situations, in particular for temporary migrant workers. Work in rural economic sectors such as agriculture, forestry, or industries of non-timber forest products (NTFP) links increasingly to global value chains and their institutional, ideological, and economic dynamics. Groups of workers in these businesses find themselves in insecure situations and are exposed to unpredictable risks. There are nevertheless important examples where there have been improvements in labour standards in previously unregulated rural sectors such as NTFP industries. One such example is, as mentioned, the new regulations established in 2010 in the Swedish forest berry industry, subsequent to a turbulent berry season in 2009 (Axelsson and Hedberg 2018, Wingborg 2011). Negotiations and a government decision led to a new standard for this industry, stipulating that non-EEA temporary labour migrants working as berry pickers are entitled to a work contract and wage levels according to union bargaining and collective agreements. The collective agreement applied to the sector – after years of non-commitment from Swedish unions – was finally negotiated between the Swedish Municipal Workers union and the Federation of Swedish Forestry and Agricultural Employers in 2009 and came into practice from 2010 and onwards (Hedberg 2016).

Our previous research on this sector (Axelsson and Hedberg 2018, Eriksson and Tollefsen 2013, 2015, 2018, Hedberg 2013, 2014) indicates successive regulatory improvements and proclaimed ambitions to come to terms with irregularities in the forest berry industry. Nevertheless, it proves difficult to find evidence of sustainable forms of organisation and assumed responsibility for labour conditions in the sector (see also Wingborg 2019). A strike performed in 2013 by 150 berry pickers in front of the Swedish Municipal Workers' office in the city of Umeå demonstrated how the berry pickers used their formal work contracts to claim their rights when the employer did not pay them (Eriksson and Tollefsen 2015). Even though the capacity and resources of the union were insufficient to handle the situation and the pickers lost the battle in the end, the strike nevertheless illustrated the potential power of unionisation and the importance of placing the protests in a strategically visible location. This particular case revealed an alarming weakness of Swedish institutions and labour unions in protecting migrant workers in a situation when work contracts and collective agreements already were in place. Our analysis showed how most of the organised resistance against the maltreatment took place outside of conventional Swedish unionism, involving a Thai NGO, a Thai trade union, and International Labour Organization representatives. Yet, despite deploying varying forms of resistance, the pickers lacked social and cultural capital to negotiate and defend their wage-labour jobs and were disassociated from 'ordinary' Swedish labour struggles (*ibid.*). Following Neergaard and Mulinari (2004), in our 2015 study we theorised their position as *subordinated inclusion* given that on paper they had full access to rights and protections, were represented as 'usable for low-skilled work' (Neergaard 2009, 218), and had legitimate claims to the wage through collective bargaining. In practice, however, their inclusion proved subordinated and their contracted wages were lost. In the present chapter, we explore a new set of empirical data to analyse the effects of the 2010 labour standard regulation, with specific focus on actual wages and the nature/extent of inclusion under collective agreements. We found that the concept of subordinated inclusion was again useful for understanding the outcomes. In previous research we have also analysed the situation of migrant workers as being linked to the transnational employment relations that prerequisite Thai berry picking in Sweden, since transnational construction enables the firms to circumvent national regulations (Axelsson and Hedberg 2018).

Since 2011, based on qualitative interview material, we have documented how the level of open conflicts has decreased in the sector, despite remaining structural issues (see also Wingborg 2015, 2019). Industry actors now consider the situation for temporary migrant workers in Sweden as improved and for the most part largely solved. Firms, trade unions, and the government agencies recognise that there have been problems but repeatedly state that labour protection now works well because the necessary steps have been taken. In their argumentation, they refer to the work contracts and the collective agreement. However, while the employer side argues that Sweden's 2008 policy on labour migration, which is enshrined in the Aliens Act (2005, 716), now functions as intended, the Swedish Trade Union Confederation (Sw. LO) maintains that the law needs to be reformed as systematic exploitations and irregularities persist (LO 2013, 2018). The Swedish Trade Union Confederation and other unions are worried about the situation for temporary migrant workers in the urban service and construction sectors (LO 2013, HRF 2012). However, they agree with the employer side that the berry sector situation is largely solved. In fact, both the employer and the union sides frequently exclude the berry pickers in their argumentation when they debate the functioning of the 2008 law, despite them being the largest group of temporary migrant workers (Migrationsverket 2014, 2015). The employer side focuses on the skilled temporary migrants to the IT sector, while the union highlights unskilled temporary migrants in urban sectors (LO 2013). Swedish media debates in 2019 illustrate the polarised positions. 'Labor immigration works better than ever,' argue Rehbinder and Svanborg-Sjövall (2019) from the market liberal think-tank Timbro, while Wingborg (2019) writing for the progressive news platform *Dagens Arena* states, 'Increasingly harsh conditions for Thai berry pickers'

(Wingborg 2019). As we will see below, these different positions connect to the unique construction enshrined in amendments of the Aliens Act in December 2008, under which all temporary migrants (skilled or unskilled, in shortage or non-shortage economic sectors) are subject to the same employer-driven regulations (Emilsson 2014). The aim of this chapter is to analyse the conditions of temporary migrants working in the berry industry, with specific focus on their wages, in the wake of the changing laws and regulations surrounding migration and labour standards described above.

Following on our previous work, this study builds upon several interview studies and original survey data with 165 Thai berry pickers regarding their actual income from the berry industry. We analyse the outcome theoretically, drawing on scholarship on subordinated inclusion and building on our previous use of this concept in analysing the 2013 strike (Eriksson and Tollefsen 2015). After presenting the results, we conclude by discussing the interconnections between this industry and the subordinated inclusion of rural migrant workers within the spatial context of a neoliberal Swedish migration regime.

Methodology

The present study is based on unique, original survey data with Thai berry pickers in combination with our previously performed interview studies with various actors in the berry business. The survey was performed in order to complement our previous knowledge on Thai berry pickers with extensive data in order to get a comprehensive picture of their costs and earnings from work in Sweden (see Hedberg *et al.* 2019). The survey gives a detailed and standardised picture of a relatively large number of workers. In addition, we have performed multi-sited ethnographic studies in both Thailand and Sweden, which includes interviews with a range of actors.

The survey consists of standardised interviews with 165 berry pickers. It was performed in 2016 in the home villages of the respondents by a locally based interview team, who could speak the local dialect. The respondents were selected based on geographical criteria and then snowballed through the informants' networks, a methodology that is valid due to the fact that the berry pickers arrive from geographically concentrated areas. The main cohort of informants were interviewed in the province Chaiyiaphum, primarily the district Kaeng Khro, which is known to be the 'cradle' for Thai berry pickers travelling to Sweden. The snowballing selection closely reflects the networking strategies that the industry is using in the recruitment of workers, however, it also means that the material is skewed in the sense that one transnational recruitment chain is overrepresented. The prerequisite for taking part in the survey was that the respondents had been active as berry pickers in Sweden at any time, and the questions regarded the last time they had been in Sweden. For the majority of the informants, 82 per cent, that year represented the previous season (2015). Almost all respondents (95 per cent) had been active after 2010, which is the year of the collective agreement.

The qualitative interview material consists of various sets of ethnographic studies, mainly based on interviews that have been performed from 2011 to 2019. The studies concern interviews with Thai berry pickers, Thai and Swedish authorities, Thai and Swedish berry companies, and Swedish trade unions. For the analysis of this chapter, most of these interviews serve to give a general knowledge of the berry industry. Two major sets of interviews with the berry pickers, however, more directly inform the interpretation of the results. The first set of interviews consist of semi-structured interviews with around 40 berry pickers, who mainly were selected through geographical snowballing in their home villages. Some of them were also found on recommendation from the Swedish berry companies. The interviews concerned their work as berry pickers, including earnings from work, and were performed with interpreters who could speak the local dialect, and then translated to English. The second set of interviews was gathered during and after a strike by Thai berry pickers in Sweden in 2013. It consists of brief participant observation of the events during the strike, and 10 interviews with strikers and other Thai labour migrants in Thailand and in Sweden in 2016. The interviewees were all men between the ages of 30 and 70. They all came from the Manchakiri district in Isan, which is one of the areas from which many of the pickers come (Wingborg 2011); most were even from the same area in the district and were thus family and friends who knew each other before coming to Sweden. All interviews were semi-structured with thematic questions that covered the interviewees' thoughts on work, earnings, working conditions, labour rights, and employers. We have published elsewhere broader analyses of these interviews (Axelsson and Hedberg 2018, Eriksson and Tollefsen 2015). Here, we draw mainly on information regarding wages and working conditions. While the material was rich and multifaceted, there were themes that recurred and provided narratives of importance for understanding the berry industry (Gubrium and Holstein 2003).

Subordinated inclusion

Several theoretical concepts have been developed in order to capture the differentiated ways migrant workers are treated in national labour markets and in order to distinguish between varying forms of inclusion and exclusion. Feminist and migration scholars have theorised how states in a differentiated manner can simultaneously include and exclude groups of people, for example migrant workers (Anthias and Yuval-Davis 1992, Hall 1986, Castles 1995, Knocke 2003, Ålund and Schierup 1991, McCall 2001, Neergaard 2009). The concept of differential inclusion (Mezzadra and Neilson 2012, De Genova *et al.* 2014) captures how labour migrants may be physically present within a nation-state and yet at the same time excluded from labour market rights and protections (see also Allen and Axelsson 2019). Baban *et al.* (2016) use the concept of differential inclusion in their research on Syrian refugees in Turkey to bring to the forefront 'links that produce different gradations of precarity and status such as when access to social citizenship rights opens and closes' (49). The authors point out how the ambiguous status granted to Syrians in Turkey place them in a context where they experience subordination and exploitation, which contributes to their differential inclusion. In line with De Genova *et al.* (2014), Baban *et al.* argue that differential inclusion can lead to marginalisation of certain groups of migrants and to new social divisions, including encouragement of pathways to certain types of subordinated migrant statuses. Allen and Axelsson (2019) contribute to this theorising by providing a temporal dimension and advancing a topological reading of two forms of regulated time-spaces which simultaneously include and exclude migrant workers. The more precise ways that migrant workers are included and/or excluded in national labour markets have not been subject so often to extensive empirical studies, examining for instance how formal rights in many cases may be lacking in practice due to contemporary border management practices.

In our previous work (Eriksson and Tollefsen 2015), as well as in the present chapter, we use the concept of subordinated inclusion as advanced by Mulinari and Neergaard (2004) in their research on immigrant unionists in Sweden. They showed the historical and contemporary difficulty workers with migrant backgrounds have in gaining legitimacy and recognition as part of the Swedish working class, or in being seen as 'Swedish workers.' Subordinated inclusion is a concept that captures the phenomenon of recognition of the strengthening of labour standards and access to negotiated collective agreements (inclusion), but in practice not being able to fully enjoy those rights (subordination). We found the concept useful for understanding how the entitled collective agreement and work contracts work out in practice in our case. Thai migrant workers in the Swedish forest berry industry are legally present in Sweden, entitled to wages according to collective agreements, are seen as legitimate workers 'usable for low-skilled work' (Neergaard 2009, 218) (inclusion), and therefore secured in terms of formal wages and labour standards. The analysis of the data showed, however, that actual fulfilment of the collective agreement is lacking (subordination). While inclusion/exclusion has many dimensions, we see fair wages under collective agreements as particularly important as a concrete measurement/indication of inclusion in the Swedish workforce. Here we put emphasis on entitlements to negotiated wages by the parties under collective bargaining, as it is a cornerstone of the Swedish/Nordic labour market model (as opposed to models with state legislated minimum wages). Building on Mulinari and Neergaard (2004), we also argue for the importance of discourses of peripherality and global industry actors in the production and processes of migrant positions and subordinated inclusion of workers within nation-states. Other researchers have used the concept of subordinated inclusion to capture restricted access to a number of welfare benefits such as housing or social services, but also how labour market rights and protections are differentially granted (Castles 1995, McCall 2001).

A new Swedish migration regime

We contribute to research on temporary rural labour migration, access to rights and protections and globalising labour markets. In processes of mobility across borders for work in rural sectors, typically dependent on a migrant workforce, there has been a change in the shape and composition of citizenship towards precariousness, as analysed by scholars in various fields (Mezzadra and Neilson 2012, Schierup *et al.* 2006, Neergaard ed. 2009). Mezzadra and Neilson (2012) discuss the changes in terms of a new social composition of the workforce and a new constitution of labour markets – which they describe as changes in 'the production and reproduction of the very fabric of citizenship' (61). In their analysis, they go back to what they call the dyadic figure of the citizen-worker, from Marshall (1950), assuming social rights of citizenship intimately connected to the dynamics of the national labour market. In contemporary capitalism, the nexus of citizenship and labour is fundamentally challenged, but Mezzadra and Neilson argue, nevertheless, that the nexus is not fully ruptured. Scandinavian social democratic welfare states, in particular Sweden, long rejected as politically unacceptable EU proposals for extending models of temporary contract labour (Castles *et al.* 2006). While the citizen-worker nexus historically has been particularly strong in the Swedish labour market system, in previous research we have argued, following many other scholars, that contemporary developments have undermined previous labour protective regulations, in favour of neoliberal deregulations (Thörnqvist and Woolfson 2012, Herzfeld Olsson 2018, Schierup and Åhlund 2011). Nevertheless, scholars also point out the persistent existence of situations with 'paths to citizenship that pass coercively through the labor contract' (Mezzandra and Neilson 2012, 61). In this sense, the 2010 new migrant labour standards for the wild berry industry is particularly interesting. It is a case of newly introduced labour contracts, where they did not exist previously in a previously unregulated NTFP sector. It is questionable, however, whether these labour contracts in any way resemble a path towards full access to rights of citizenship, entitled to workers on pair with national labour market standards.

In fact, 'both citizens and workers have been invested by diffuse processes of division and multiplication, and migration has played crucial roles within these processes' (*ibid*, 62). This is a development that Tsing (2009) has theorised as the emergence of new figurations of labour under supply chain capitalism, the Swedish wild berry industry is a topical example (see further Eriksson *et al.* 2019). Tsing argues that diversity is structurally central to contemporary capitalism, and sector-specific supply chains produce relevant figurations of the capital–labour relationship, and thus changing forms of inclusion. Legally admitted temporary migrant workers in the berry industry are 'included through specific labor practices' (Allen and Axelsson 2019, 118) formed under a new Swedish migration regime.

High costs and insecure earnings for temporary migrants

We put the survey results in dialogue with our previous studies and qualitative data from interviews. After analysing the effects of the 2010 collective agreements on actual wages, we use the concept of subordinated inclusion to understand the outcomes. In their subordinated position in the transnational employment setting, the workers may either be unaware of their rights due to their disempowered position in the recruitment chain, as was the case in the first set of interviews (Hedberg *et al.* 2019) or they may be unable to defend and negotiate their rights (Eriksson and Tollefsen 2015). The latter is shown in our second set of interviews with workers who went on strike in 2013, where substandard living and working conditions were confirmed, and where their sense of powerlessness was expressed towards the industry as well as towards labour standard regulations. Yet, the quotation below may also illustrate these workers' resistance and agency.

> *They took our car keys, they were afraid we should join the others and go on strike. [One of the pickers] needed to go to the hospital, he was beaten by a Thai who work for them. In the end, we were also threatened by the Swedes in Hällnäs, we simply needed to leave, they would never pay us.*
>
> (Somchai, a man in his 50s, interviewed 2016 in Sweden)

One of the key issues that has been debated in relation to rural migrant workers in Sweden (Andersson *et al.* 2013, Rydman and Hökerberg 2009, Wingborg 2011, 2014), and also internationally (Yimprasert 2010, 2014, Saltmarsh 2010, *Economist* 2012), is how much the workers are earning, and if the earnings are substantial or not. In the Norwegian context, Rye and Andrzejewska (2010) found that eastern European migrant farm workers experienced far poorer wages and working conditions than prescribed by regulations on minimum standard for migrants in Norway, following EU enlargement. Whereas some of our previous studies have given a relatively positive view on the earnings as an alternative source of income for Thai migrant workers (Hedberg 2013, Hedberg 2015), other studies have shown how the subordination of the workers have resulted in low and insecure earnings (Eriksson and Tollefsen 2018, Vogiazides and Hedberg 2013). While both of these latter studies may contain parts of the explanation for the low earnings of many Thai berry pickers, the results from our present survey show that the earnings often are

Table 8.1 Costs and earnings of Thai berry pickers (per season)

	Mean (USD)	*Median (USD)*	*Standard deviation (USD)*
Total costs	3,955	3,902	568
Total earnings	5,915	5,621	1,704
Earnings after deductions	1,960	1,719	1,136
Earnings after deductions per month	840	737	487

Source: Thai-Swedish survey 2016 (Hedberg *et al.* 2019)

substantially lower than what was given in some of the previously performed interview studies. We think that one reason for this might be that, in semi-structured interview situations, informants want to highlight their earnings in a more positive light by referring to their most successful years in Sweden.

The analysis of the survey shows that the earnings for Thai berry pickers many times were considerably lower than the collective agreement had stipulated. Whereas the total costs, which included both a fee paid to the Thai staffing agency and costs for accommodation and food in Sweden, were rather homogeneous, the earnings varied significantly among the workers (Table 8.1; Figure 8.1). The high standard deviation signals that there is a wide distribution of earnings, which varied between 7,645 USD and -971 USD for one season. Accordingly, there are both 'top pickers,' who earn an extra annual income while working in Sweden, and a few workers who returned indebted. The firm with the highest number of workers, which was overrepresented in the study, had mainly workers in the middle categories of earnings. Accordingly, this skewness of the sample does not explain the high variation in earnings. When the total costs had been deducted, the mean earnings were 1,960 USD. This is the sum that the worker receives in his (or sometimes her) hand, which is why earnings after deductions is the calculation that the workers themselves are considering. When comparing the mean earnings with the guaranteed wage in the work contract, the earnings were slightly higher. The guaranteed wage was 2,340 USD/month, and in order to compare this with earnings after deductions, we have deducted the total costs also from the guaranteed wage, which explains why the equivalent guaranteed wage is 645 USD/month.

However, the wide distribution of earnings is central to understand that behind the mean value a high number of workers actually earned less than the guaranteed wage. In fact, one third of the workers belonged to this category. A clue to why this may be the case can be found in the interviews where the workers describe how their car keys may be confiscated for a couple of days or weeks during some seasons, hence they are forbidden to pick berries during this time and are not getting paid. The firms refer to 'full fridges,'

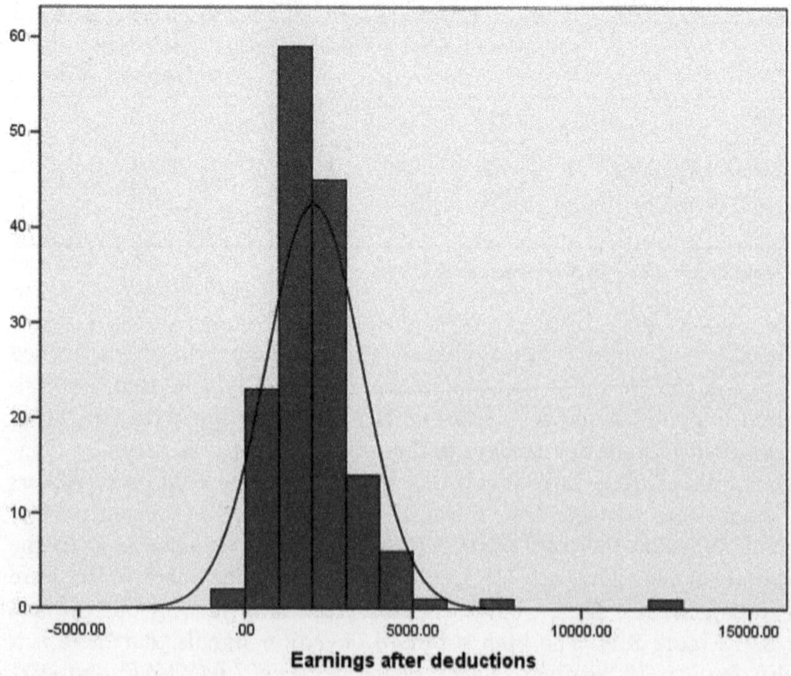

Figure 8.1 The distribution of reported earnings (USD) after deductions (n=152)

this stands for a sudden mismatch in export and import, demand and supply. This indicates how the global character of the industry contributes to the subordinated inclusion to which the Thai workers are subject.

> *We have been paying back on our loans, and right now we are about to start to earn money. We don't understand why we have to stop working now. The only explanations we got was that the fridges in the storehouse are already full of berries.*
>
> (Interview with male berry picker in Fredrika, Sweden 2016)

This incongruence between actually received earnings and the entitled guaranteed wage may have its roots in the parallel system of payment which exits in the berry business. Since the beginning of Thai berry picking in Sweden, which started on an informal, networked basis in the 1980s (Hedberg 2016), the praxis has been to pay the workers on a piece rate. The earnings hence were directly related to the number of kilos the workers had picked. This system is explained by the history of the berry-picking activity, which for a long time was not viewed as an industry but as an opportunity for poor people living in deprived sparsely populated areas, often in northern Sweden, to earn an extra income (Eriksson and Tollefsen 2018).

Before 2010, when the workers had no collective agreement to lean against, this comprised a quite fortunate system for the business, which took small economic risks, but put the workers in a precarious position without a safety net. This also explains the unfortunate season 2009, when a lack of berries in Sweden and an all-time high number of international workers in the country made a substantial number of them return home indebted (Yimprasert 2010). The problematic season of 2009 also explains the timing of the introduction of the collective agreement in the berry business, which was in 2010, when Swedish authorities realised the unbearable situation (Axelsson and Hedberg 2018). According to the berry business, after 2010 the payment would be a combination of the old system with the guaranteed wage. That is, the workers would still be paid on a piece rate, but they would at the very least be guaranteed the wage that was stipulated in the collective agreement. The idea behind this system, which never has been formalised in a document, was that the incitement of the piece rate would be combined with an economic safety net.

The result of the survey, given that one third of the workers earned less than the guaranteed wage, shows that this formal inclusion of the workers has not worked out in practice. This can also be seen in the light of how the informants themselves responded that their payment had been made. According to table 1.2, only 18 per cent responded that they were paid according to the parallel system of payment as outlined above. Instead, 28 per cent say that they were in fact paid on a piece rate, and the majority responded that their payment was the guaranteed wage only. That the latter is a direct falsity is a matter of fact for anyone who has been in contact with the berry business, and is confirmed in interviews with all parties, including the trade union, since piece rate is the dominant payment system. Our qualitative interviews also tell us that the motivation of the workers is to earn as much as possible, to be 'a number-one picker,' and the guaranteed wage would not suffice these expectations.

The informal knowledge that came out in the performance of the survey, however, gives important guidance for interpreting the result. The survey

Table 8.2 Distribution of berry pickers by system of payment

	Number of workers	*Per cent of total number of workers*
Payment per kilo berries picked	46	27.9
Guaranteed wage	89	53.9
Payment per kilo and guaranteed minimum wage	30	18.2
Total	165	100.0

Source: Thai-Swedish survey 2016 (Hedberg *et al.* 2019)

interviewer explained to us that in fact the staffing agencies had informed many of the workers that they were entitled to a guaranteed wage, but that they had to choose between one of the two ways of payment. This is also information that we have received in other interview studies with berry pickers.

Since the workers were motivated to earn substantially more than what was stipulated in the collective agreement, they signed the formal contract with the guaranteed wage, which they knew that they had to sign in order to be accepted to work in Sweden. Simultaneously, however, they agreed with the staffing agency to work on a piece rate. According to the survey interviewer, 'they're fine with this arrangement, [...since] they believed that they would earn more money by having "payment per kilo of berries picked."' But in our interviews the workers also address what they view as a great injustice; that the prices of berries any time may drop due to world market prices. The above is an example of how the process of negotiation works, and how interdependent migrants and brokers are in the actual practices and production of migration routes, which differs greatly from the view that governments have on migrants (Deshingkar 2019).

Based on this information, we interpret that the majority responding that they were paid the guaranteed wage did so because they knew that this was expected with respect to their signed contract. The lowest interpretation of Table 8.2 hence would be that 28 per cent would not have received the guaranteed wage if they had been entitled to it, whereas the highest interpretation would be that as many as four out of five of the respondents would not have received this wage.

If we combine this with the result of the earnings, we can nonetheless conclude that the attempted inclusion of the workers into the Swedish labour market system of negotiated guaranteed wages, to a high degree, did not work out. Since one third of the workers earned less than the guaranteed wage, a substantial part of the workers would have been de facto better off economically with the guaranteed wage than with payment on piece rate.

Conclusions

The results point to a continued subordinated inclusion of temporary migrant workers. They are included in terms of the formal access to rights and protections, but it is a subordinated inclusion since, despite a collective agreement on wages and a labour contract, and a recognition of being 'usable low-wage workers' in the Swedish labour market, the fulfilment of the rights is lacking in practice. In contrast to migrant workers recruited to urban service sectors, where there is no labour shortage and workers arrive on false premises and often based on illegal trade in work contracts, the recruitment of temporary workers to the wild berry industry is usually legitimised in public discourses. They are included given a presumed shortage of workers in a remote NTFP sector, in which unemployment statistics never have been registered. The fact that this NTFP sector was previously completely unregulated is important in this context because it stands out as a 'special case' with its newly introduced regulations. Most other labour market sectors in the Swedish welfare state historically have to a high degree been monitored and regulated by trade unions, employer organisations, and work authorities, but are currently instead undergoing deregulation or reregulation under neoliberal conditions. These differences between sectors regarding migrant workers connect to the contrasting views referred to above on whether the 2008 law 'works well' or not. As mentioned before, under the Aliens Act of 2008, all temporary migrants (skilled or unskilled, in shortage or non-shortage economic sectors) are subject to the same employer-driven regulations (Emilsson 2014), regardless of their varying historical and geographical contexts.

We thus argue that the non-fulfilment of the negotiated wages, and therefore subordination in the labour market of legally admitted temporary migrant workers, also has to do with the sector's characteristics as rural, peripheral, and natural resource base, as well as the transnational construction of employment relations (Axelsson and Hedberg 2018). The berry pickers are thus 'included through specific labour practices' (Allen and Axelsson 2019, 118) but in practice subordinated in terms of access to stipulated wages and protections.

Land-based, peripheral, and natural resource dependent industries seem particularly problematic in terms of how labour issues are handled and resolved. Workers are needed on a regular basis, the sectors are usually labour intensive, and markets are often relatively established, with end products in demand on local, regional, and global markets. Nevertheless, there is often an ad hoc, erratic, preliminary, and random organisation of work in these sectors, where each season is largely confronted as if happening for the first time. Parts of the picture are also unpredictable aspects such as the weather and the changing rules set out by governments, in our case Sweden and Thailand. There is a mix of continuity and novelty in the wild berry industry, with workers arriving in Sweden repeated times and a few large actors who have managed a system of logistics for decades, on the one hand, combined with new companies, new workers, and new logistic solutions, on the other hand. Another aspect of the subordinate inclusion of temporary workers in the berry industry has to do with the changing geographies of production and consumption in the industry (Eriksson and Tollefsen 2018, Axelsson and Hedberg 2019). The berry pickers' earnings are dependent on the fluctuating demand of berries on the world market and big actors are able to put pressure on smaller ones to reduce their costs often at the expense of workers' salaries. Researchers on global markets and sourcing of non-timber forest products (NTFP), of which forest berries is a part, have pointed out how these products usually lack forms of governing or management in legal terms (Laird *et al.* 2010). This chapter also points specifically at the informality of the parallel payment system, which all actors know exist, but which has never been formalised in a document. Hence, it is easy for the Thai staffing agencies to urge the workers to 'choose' between a traditional system of payment and a formally stated and negotiated system of payment. It is typical that workers within NTFP sectors belong to already marginalised groups in society and that there are high risks of illegal harvesting, logging, and fraudulent economic behavior, as well as maltreatment of the labour force.

Acknowledgements

The authors wish to thank the anonymous reviewers for their comments on the manuscript. This chapter was partly supported by the Swedish Research Council Formas under grant 2013–01457, the Swedish Research Council under grant 2017-01010 and the Migration Studies Delegation, Sweden. Funding from Umeå University (Sweden) has made possible open access publishing of the chapter.

References

Allen, J. and L. Axelsson. 2019. 'Border Topologies: The Time-spaces of Labour Migrant Regulation.' *Political Geography* 72: 116–123.

Aliens Act (2005: 716) www.government.se/49cf71/contentassets/784b3d7be3a54a0185f284bbb2683055/aliens-act-2005_716.pdf

Ålund, A. and C-U. Schierup. 1991. *Paradoxes of Multiculturalism. Essays on Swedish Society.* Aldershot: Avebury.

Andersson, L-F, M. Eriksson, A. Tollefsen and M. Wingborg. 2013. 'Arbetsgivarna har total makt över bärplockarnas situation.' *Dagens Nyheter*, 30 September 2013.

Anthias, F. and N. Yuval-Davis.1992. *Racialised Boundaries – Race, Nation, Gender, Color and Class and the Anti-Racist Struggle.* London: Routledge.

Axelsson, L. and C. Hedberg. 2018. 'Emerging Topologies of Transnational Work: Posting Thai Workers in Sweden's Wild Berry Industry Beyond Regulatory Reach.' *Geoforum.* 89: 1–10.

Baban, F., S. Ilcan and K. Rygiel. 2016. 'Syrian Refugees in Turkey: Pathways to Precarity, Differential Inclusion, and Negotiated Citizenship Rights.' *Journal of Ethnic and Migration Studies.* 43(1): 41–57.

Castles, S. 1995. 'How Nation-states Respond to Immigration and Ethnic Diversity.' *New Community*, 21(3) 293–308.

Castles, S. 2006. 'Guestworkers in Europe: A Resurrection?' *International Migration Review.* 40(4): 741–766.

De Genova, N., S. Mezzadra and J. Pickles, editors. 2014. 'New Keywords: Migration and Borders.' *Cultural Studies* 29(1): 55–87.

Deshingkar, P. 2019. 'The Making and Unmaking of Precarious, Ideal Subjects – Migration Brokerage in the Global South.' *Journal of Ethnic and Migration Studies*, 45(14): 2638–2654.

The Economist. 2012. 'Foreign Workers in Sweden. Berry Pickers, Unite!' 4 September 2012.

Emilsson, H. 2014. 'Who Gets in and Why: The Swedish Experience with Demand Driven Labour Migration, Some Preliminary Results.' *Nordic Journal of Migration Research* 4(3): 134–143.

Eriksson, M. and A. Tollefsen. 2013. 'Of Berries and Seasonal Work: The Swedish Berry Industry and Disciplining of Labour Migration from Thailand.' In *Disciplining the Transnational Mobility of People,* edited by M. Geiger and A. Pécoud. Palgrave Macmillan.

Eriksson, M. and A. Tollefsen. 2015. 'New Figurations of Labor in Gendered Global Circuits. Migrant Workers in the Forest Berry Industry in Norrland, Sweden.' In *Remapping Gender, Place and Mobility: Global Confluences and Local Particularities in Nordic Peripheries,* edited by S.T. Faber and H. Nielsen. Surrey: Ashgate.

Eriksson, M. and A. Tollefsen. 2018. 'The Production of the Rural Landscape and its Labour: The Development of Supply Chain Capitalism in the Swedish Berry Industry.' *Bulletin of Geography. Socio-economic Series* 40: 69–82.

Eriksson, M., A. Tollefsen and A.S. Lundgren. 2019. 'From Blueberry Cakes to Labor Strikes: Negotiating "Legitimate Labor" and "Ethical Food" in Supply Chains.' *Geoforum* 105: 43–53.

Gubrium, J. F. and J. A. Holstein. 2003. *Postmodern Interviewing*. London: Sage.

Hall, S. 1986. 'Gramsci's Relevance for the Study of Race and Ethnicity.' *Journal of Communication Inquiry* 10(2) 5–27.

Hedberg, C. 2013. 'Grapes of Wrath? Power Spatialities and Aspects of Labour in the Wild Berry Global Commodity Chain.' *Competition and Change.* 17(1): 57–74.

Hedberg, C. 2014. 'Restructuring Global Labor Markets: Recruitment Agencies and Work Relations in the Wild Berry Commodity Chain.' In *Labour Relations in Globalized Food,* edited by A. Bonanno and J.S.B. Cavalcanti, 33–56. Emerald Publishing.

Hedberg, C. 2015. 'Thailändska bärplockare – hushållsstrategier på en global arbetsmarknad. Arbetskraft från hela världen.' In *Arbetskraft från hela världen. Hur blev det med 2008 års reform? Delmi Rapport 2015:9*, edited by C. Calleman and P. Hertzfeld Olsson, 114–149. Stockholm: Delegationen för migrationsstudier.

Hedberg, C. 2016. 'Doing Gender in the Wild Berry Industry. Transforming the Role of Thai Women in Rural Sweden 1980–2012.' *European Journal of Women's Studies.* 23(2): 169–184.

Hedberg, C., L. Axelsson and M. Abella. 2019. *Thai Berry Pickers in Sweden – A Migration Corridor to a Low-wage Sector. Delmi Report* 2019:3. Stockholm: Delegationen för migrationsstudier.

Herzfeld Olsson, P. 2018. 'Towards Protection of Vulnerable Labour Migrants in Sweden: The Case of the Thai Berry Pickers.' In *Towards a Decent Labour Market for Low Waged Migrant Workers,* edited by C. Rijken and T. de Lang, 149–168. Amsterdam University Press.

HRF (Hotell och restaurangfacket). 2012. 'Till vilket pris som helst? En uppföljning av arbetskraftsmingranters villkor i hotell- och restaurangbranschen.' Stockholm: HRF.

ILO (International Labour Organization) 2014. *Fair migration: Setting an ILO agenda.* Report of the Director-General, Report I(B), International Labour Conference, 103rd Session, 2014. Geneva: International Labour Office.

Keeley, B. 2015. *Income Inequality: The Gap Between Rich and Poor*, OECD Insights, Paris: OECD Publishing. https://doi.org/10.1787/9789264246010-en.

Knocke, W. 2003. *Rekrytering för mångfald?* Norrköping: Integrationsverket.

Laird, S., A, R.J. McLain and R.P. Wynberg, editors. 2010. *Wild Product Governance: Finding Policies that Work for Non-Timber Forest Products*. London: Earthscan.

LO (Landsorganisationen) (Swedish Trade Union Confederation). 2013. *Fusk och utnyttjande – om avregleringen av arbetskraftsinvandringen.* Stockholm: LO.

LO (Landsorganisationen) (Swedish Trade Union Confederation). 2018. "Bra med begränsad arbetskraftsinvandring." *Landsorganisationen i Sverige*, 27/4/2018.

Marshall, T.H. 1950. *Citizenship and Social Class, and Other Essays*. Cambridge: Cambridge University Press.

McCall, L. 2001. *Complex Inequality. Gender, Race and Class in the New Economy.* New York: Routledge.

Mezzadra, S and B. Neilson. 2012. 'Between Inclusion and Exclusion: On the Topology of Global Space and Borders.' *Theory, Culture and Society* 29 (4/5): 58–75.

Migrationsverket (Swedish Migration Board). 2014. *Årsredovisning Migrationsverket 2014*. Norrköping, Sweden: Migrationsverket.

Migrationsverket (Swedish Migration Board). 2015. *Årsredovisning Migrationsverket 2015*. Norrköping, Sweden: Migrationsverket.

Mulinari, D. and A. Neergaard. 2004. *Den nya svenska arbetarklassen. Facket och de rasifierade arbetarna.* Umeå: Borea.

Neergaard, A, ed. 2009. *European Perspectives on Exclusion and Subordination: The Political Economy of Migration.* Maastricht: Shaker Publishing.

Rehbinder, C. and K. Svanborg. 2019. "Arbetskraftsinvandringen fungerar bättre än någonsin." *Dagens Nyheter*, 8/9/2019.

Rye, J.F. and J. Andrzejewska. 2010. 'The Structural Disempowerment of Eastern European Migrant Farm Workers in Norwegian Agriculture.' *Journal of Rural Studies* 26(1): 41–51.

Rydman, A. and J. Hökerberg, J. 2009. 'Uppror bland thailändska bärplockare i Norrland.' *Dagens Nyheter*, 25 August.

Saltmarsh, M. 2010. "Asian migrant workers see exploitation in Sweden." *New York Times*, 7/9/2010.

Schierup, C-U, P. Hansen and S Castles. 2006. *Migration, Citizenship, and the European Welfare State.* Oxford: Oxford University Press.

Schierup, C-U. and A. Åhlund. 2011. 'The End of Swedish Exceptionalism? Citizenship, Neoliberalism and the Politics of Exclusion.' *Race and Class* 53(1): 45–64.

Thörnqvist, C. and C. Woolfson. 2012. 'When Tender Turns Tough: Posted Workers and the Tendering Regime in the Swedish Construction Industry.' *Construction Management and Economics,* 30: 525–533.

Tsing, A. 2009. 'Supply Chains and the Human Condition.' *Rethinking Marxism* 21(2): 148–176.

Vogiazides, L. and C. Hedberg. 2013. 'Trafficking for Forced Labour and Labour Exploitation in Sweden.' In *Exploitation of Migrant Workers in Finland, Sweden, Estonia and Lithuania*, edited by N. Ollus, A. Jokinen and M. Joutsen, 171–237. European Institute for Crime Prevention and Control, affiliated with the United Nations.

Wingborg, M. 2011. *Mors lilla Olle. Så exploateras asiatiska bärplockare i de svenska skogarna.* Swedwatch Rapport 41. Peach and Love Foundation, Svenska kyrkan.

Wingborg, M. 2014. *Villkoren för utländska bärplockare säsongen 2014.* Arena Idé, 2014.

Wingborg, M. 2015. *Så var säsongen för utländska bärplockare* 2015. Arena Idé, 2015.

Wingborg, M. 2019. 'Allt hårdare villkor för thailändska bärplockare.' *Dagens Arena* 9 February 2019.

Yimprasert, J. 2010. *Labour Trafficking: The 2009 Billberry Fiasco in Sweden.* Bangkok: Network Against Trafficking and Exploitation of Migrant Workers, Thai Labour Campaign, Migrant Workers' Union.

Yimprasert, J. 2014. *Cruel Realities in the Swedish Forest-Berry Industry.* Accessed 25 July 2016. www.academia.edu/7016668/Cruel_realities_in_the_Swedish_forest-berry_industry.

Section II

Transforming Europe's rural societies

Chapter 9

Agricultural employers' representation and rationalisation of their work offer

The 'benevolent moderator'

Johan Fredrik Rye and Sam Scott

Farmers and precarious work: perpetrators or victims?

An abundant literature has detailed the precarious work and everyday living conditions experienced by migrant farm workers in the horticultural industries in Europe (Gertel and Sippel, eds. 2014, Corrado *et al.* 2016, Rye and Scott 2018) and the US (Wells 1996, Holmes 2013) and Canada (Bélanger and Candiz 2015). Extreme yet not exceptional cases include 'quasi slavery relations' (Bock *et al.* 2016), housing in 'ghettos' and slums (Perrotta 2017, 2015), exposure for sexual abuse (Andreu and Jiminez 2010, quoted in Lindner and Kathman 2014), racist treatment, discrimination (Papadopoulous and Fratsea 2017, Hellio 2017, McAreavey 2012), and other examples of de-humanising practices. Holmes (2007, 50–51) describes a 'hierarchy of suffering' in which different migrant groups are pitched against each other:

> *The further down the ladder one is positioned, the more degrading the treatment by supervisors, the more physically taxing the work, the more exposure to weather and pesticides, the stronger the fear of the government, and the less control one has over one's own time.*

In the literature, the prevalence of 'gruelling' working conditions (Guthman 2017a, 2014) is usually framed with reference to the structural drivers of the contemporary capitalist food production system (Farinella and Nori, Chapter 5). The global agri-business value chain – made up of producers, processors, distributers, marketers, financial institutions, retailers, and others – is driven by the dynamics of capitalism. Most obviously, productivity and efficiency are positioned as key to profitability and through this capitalist logic the (migrant) manual farm worker becomes more 'structurally vulnerable' (Quesada *et al.* 2011) than any other actors.

In this chapter, we explore this landscape from the intermediate level in the food value chain by examining the perspective of the employer/farmer. At the intersection between the interests of labour and capital, farm employers have first-hand knowledge of the everyday plight of the (migrant) workers they employ but are also aware of the larger demands of the food industry. In short, they are mediators and moderators, often in the apparently impossible position of acting ethically in relation to their employees, making a good living for themselves and their families, while responding to the demands of the market. Holmes (2013, 2007, 54), in his widely acknowledged work on the suffering of US migrant farm workers, therefore argues that we should conceptualise farmers '… as human beings trying to lead ethical, comfortable lives, committed to the family farm in the midst of an unequal, harsh system,' if we want to better understand their social practices as employers, even when these imply exploitative working arrangements.

It is outside the reach of the current research to evaluate farmers' 'objective' conditions or to discuss their social responsibilities for migrant farm workers' conditions, or capacities to alter these, which are all relevant research topics. This chapter rather examines the farmers' contradictory position between the interests of labour and capital by exploring how they develop discursive strategies to makes sense of their everyday practices as employers. We ask, specifically: *How do low-wage employers rationalise the pay and conditions they offer their (migrant) workers?* In posing this question the chapter responds to Holmes' (2013) and other (see Scott 2013a) calls for research to better conceptualise the perspectives of the employer.

Strawberries in the US, the UK, and Norway

To examine similarities and differences in the ways employers 'talk about' low-wage migrant labour, we conducted qualitative interviews with strawberry farmers in three locations: the US (California), the UK, and Norway. The strawberry industry offers an instructive case-study for international research and has many similar features irrespective of location. Most important are the biological properties of the berry (lat.: *Fragaria*). Strawberry production has a shorter time horizon than many agricultural products and investments can pay off over the course of a few years. Thus, even though profits can be volatile with weather, plant disease, and rapid changes in market demand playing a part, the strawberry has been called the 'red gold' of agriculture (Hellio 2008, i).

Over recent years, biological innovations (e.g. breeding programmes, genetics, pesticides), changes in production (e.g. variants of polytunnels/greenhouses), and organisational shifts (e.g. value chain integration, including on a global scale) have transformed the strawberry industry in many countries. At one extreme are the global corporations with involvements at all stages of the value chain, often backed by non-agricultural finance. At the other extreme is the family farmer cultivating a few hectares of berries and often relying on direct sales to the consumer. Calleja *et al.* (2012), studying the historical development of UK strawberry industry between 1920 and 2009, identifies the recent polarisation of the industry into two business models.

The first is 'productivism,' characterised by intensification, concentration, and specialisation. The second is 'post-productivism' which in essence refers to the remnants of a more traditional mixed-farming system, now threatened by competition from the 'super-productivist' farms specialising only in strawberries and making much larger investments in technology and innovation. The introduction of polytunnels, for instance, drastically extended the production season and quality of berries (Evans 2013) and favoured productivist and super-productivist growers in the early stages. In addition, there are often geographical clusters of these type of growers: Spain's 'sea of plastic' in the Huelva region and Greece's rural Manolada district (where about 20 farmers employ some 3,500 workers and produce 90 per cent of the country's strawberries) spring to mind (Gialis and Herod 2014).

Consistent across time and space is the labour-intensive character of strawberry production, although efficiency has increased over recent years particularly with the introduction of table-top growing. Wage costs account for about 50 per cent of total production expenses and constitute the key variable for the strawberry farm's profitability. Picking demands not only a high level of labour but also 'good' labour. The sensitive berry demands careful, considerate, and dedicated workers and what farmers call 'delicate hands' (Hellio 2008, vi). Also important is workers' ability and willingness to endure the work in the strawberry fields, which by nature is physically demanding, monotonous, and has little to offer in terms of personal fulfilment. While practical skills are required, the harvesters need no formal education, and the picking process is possible to acquire in the matter of days (though it can take much longer to get up to the top picking speeds). As in other agricultural production:

> *The most important reason for hiring migrants – instead of local/native workers – is their readiness to accept jobs for which vacancies have been difficult to fill; often this means jobs that are physically demanding, with unpredictable working schedules, long hours of work, offering poor pay and low social status.*
>
> (Bock *et al.* 2016, 76)

The strawberry industry – from the industrial, global agri-business to the small-scale family farmer – has come to rely on low-paid migrant farm labour. However, more than simply being low paid, the strawberry industry has been accused of being highly exploitative. According to Ivancheva (2007, 116), no other horticulture product line has been as frequently witness to sub-standard working conditions as the strawberry industry. Numerous other papers have been published detailing the exploitative labour conditions in the industry in Europe (e.g. Mannon *et al.* 2012, Hellio 2008, 2017) and particularly in the US (for instance, Schlosser 1995, Wells 1996, Sanchez 2013, Guthman 2017a, 2017b). Thus, while food production, more generally, has been associated with intensification and exploitation (Rogaly 2008, Scott 2017), it is a problem that appears particularly pronounced within the strawberry sector.

In this chapter, we draw on materials from a comparative study of the strawberry industries in three localities in the western world: The Watsonwille/Salinas district in California, US; west and southwest England in the UK; and Trøndelag in Norway. These are identified as interesting 'contrasting' cases (Yin 2009) as they represent three different societal contexts as well as agricultural systems.

California hosts one of the world's most industrialised agricultural production systems. Its strawberry industry accounts for 88 per cent of the total US production and 20 per cent of world production (Guthman 2017a). The production is centralised to a few locations along the Californian central coast with particularly good soils and superb climatic conditions. The population of farmers and their organisational structure are heterogeneous. Manual labour at the farms is exclusively provided by migrants originating in Mexico or other Latin-American countries. Some are recent arrivals in the US and had planned to return, in theory constituting circular migrants. However, recent changes to US immigration policy and implementation has made it more difficult to cross the US-Mexico border. In effect, many of today's workers are now long-term residents in the US, roughly split into two equal-sized groups of those with and those without legal papers (Martin 2019). The US labour market is less regulated than the UK and Norwegian labour markets, reflecting general differences in societal models. However, California has more progressive labour regulations than most other US states and, importantly, these also apply to the agricultural sector. Despite an interesting history of trade unionism (Mireles 2013), today there are no organised labour movements within the strawberry industry.

Norway's strawberry industry – relative to the Californian case – has a small-scale and highly seasonal character. Farms are few, small, and dispersed around the country; most are the only ones growing strawberries for miles around. Most are owned and operated by family farmers, exclusively of Norwegian ethnic origin, who also live on the farm and participate in daily operations. If California represents the 'super-productivist' business model (Calleja *et al.* 2012), Norway is the 'post-productivist' model, exclusively serving the domestic market. The Norwegian strawberry industry is, as the agricultural industry at large, strongly regulated by the state – however in an intimate interaction with industrial representatives, both from farmer associations and agri-business agents (Rye 2017). From this chapter's perspective, the (relatively) extensive and worker-friendly labour market regulations are of particular importance. After trends towards 'informalisation' of the farm migrant labour market around 2000, later years have been characterised by a process of 're-formalisation' of labour relations, with improving wages and working conditions (Rye 2017). While not present at the farm level, trade unions have a strong voice in labour market regulation and rights to bargain on behalf of workers, including non-union members. Starting in the 1990s, Norwegian strawberry farmers have increasingly come to rely on migrant labour from eastern, central, and southern Europe. Work is predominantly circular and seasonal.

The UK strawberry industry represents an interesting middle point between the US extreme of super-productivist and Norwegian post-productivist horticulture production, both in terms of production structure, technologies, and harvests. Almost all of the UK crop is for home consumption with very little export production (Defra 2018). There is some but limited geographical clustering of the industry. Since early 2000s, there has been a heavy dependency on Polish labour for strawberry harvesting but now it is largely Bulgarian and Romanian workers employed in seasonal roles. As in Norway, labour is often circular in nature (though the UK growing season is longer) and labour generally lives on-site rather than in the local community (as occurs in the US). In terms of labour market regulation, the UK represents a middle ground between the US and Norwegian models.

Researching employers' talk – materials and methods

The core research question for our study presented in this chapter was: how do low-wage employers rationalise the pay and conditions they offer their (migrant) workers? The material to inform our answer to this question comes from 15 in-depth interviews with strawberry producers in the three study localities: Watsonville in California, US; the west and southwest of England, UK; and Trøndelag, Norway. Given the nature of the research topic (farmers' talk around low-wage and seasonal labour), we sought to capture the dominant discourses that are constructed and reproduced, and we work to provide collective accounts of social practices, both descriptively and normatively. To this end, informants were approached as representatives of their social category ('strawberry farmers') and we were less interested in their unique personal histories. The enduring impression from the interview encounters was that informants willingly, and with confidence, took on the role as industry 'spokespersons.'

The sampling process sought to cover a variety of informants in terms of characteristics of farmer (age, gender, farming history) and farm (size, production technologies, conventional/ organic, value chain integration). The heterogeneity varied between study localities; higher in California, lowest in Norway. The objective was to include voices from different positions in the social landscape of strawberry farming in each of the localities, both to add nuance and to identify potential contrasting and/or contesting discourse. While further materials possibly would fortify the analysis, five interviews in each locality appeared enough to reach a 'saturation point' (Bloor and Wood 2006).

The interviews were semi-structured and covered topics of relevance to the farmers' labour recruitment and employment strategies past, present, and future. The interviews were flexible and allowed the informants to bring up topics they found relevant, and for the interviewer to follow up on these. Thus, the structure of interviews differed between individuals (e.g. due to personal experiences) and between localities (e.g. in Watsonville questions on immigration policy were salient, in west and southwest England questions on Brexit were salient, and in Norway experiences with trade unions were relevant). The farmers were not explicitly confronted with the academic literature's documentation of precarious living and working conditions for migrants on farms in advanced economies; however most did, through their own initiative, provide thoughts on the welfare and quality of work and life for migrants in the strawberry industry.

The data gathered through low-wage employer interviews is evidently one viewpoint on to the labour process. This partial approach was purposeful: we wanted to examine the presence of hegemonic low-wage employer discourses in the strawberry industry across different country contexts. In other words, we were interested in the stories that employers tell about the labour that they employ and how they rationalise the low-wage and seasonal opportunities they provide.

Interviews were conducted by the authors in the farmers' native language. Conversations lasted for about 60–80 minutes and were recorded. Interviews were transcribed by professional transcribers, and published testimony has been anonymised to protect interviewees' identities. Translations of the Norwegian quotes are by the authors. Further detail on the materials is provided in Scott and Rye (forthcoming). All interviewee names have been changed to pseudonyms.

Importantly, the chosen research strategy cannot capture the 'objective' realities of (migrant) farm work, which was never the intention. Tapping into employers' talk and rationalisations of their practices provides information about exactly that: their discursive representations. Other methodologies, preferably involving a mixed methods approach, are required to gain complementary accounts of employment relations and practices, as we have done in other papers (see for instance, Rye and Andrzejewska 2010).

Picking strawberries as 'tough but rewarding work'

Despite the numerous academic accounts of low wage and seasonal horticultural work being extremely tough, and by some accounts increasingly exploitative (Rye and Scott 2018, Scott 2017, Bock *et al.* 2016, Holmes 2013, Rogaly 2008), the employers we interviewed were universally prone to rationalise the pay, work, and living conditions they provided in a very positive manner. Migrants may constitute the archetypal 'good worker' (Baxter-Reid 2016, MacKenzie and Forde 2009, Tannock 2015) and this was also the case for the informants (Scott and Rye, forthcoming) but in our research we also uncovered a strong and consistent 'good farmer' discourse across the study localities. Specifically, while low-wage seasonal picking work is unquestionably tough and demanding, employers first and foremost positioned it as economically rewarding and, furthermore, also positioned themselves as socially responsible employers.

This positive rationalisation, which emerges despite the fact that employers occupy a constrained, and somewhat impossible, position between the demands of capital and labour, will now be examined in detail. We demonstrate how the farmers construct themselves as 'benevolent moderators,' despite a highly constrained structural context, and the presence of relatively harsh wage and working conditions. Moreover, this narrative appears consistent as the dominant story employers tell across diverse study locations and across farm types.

The good work narrative

Farmers' presentation of their work offer was underpinned by an apparently solid conviction that strawberry work is 'good work.' By offering employment largely to migrants from less affluent societies, farmers claimed to provide them with a much-needed source of income and allow them to improve their living conditions and quality of life in both the home and host countries. The income from farm work was argued to be good both in an absolute and relative sense. Farmers contended that strawberry picking paid well in comparison to other (farm) jobs available in the study locations (piece-rate bonuses – where workers are paid according to output – were often mentioned as a major advantage to the migrant workers employed). Moreover, they also argued that hard-working migrants could earn wages that were excellent when compared with wages in the migrants' home countries, i.e. when considered within a 'dual frame of reference' (Suárez-Orozco and Suárez-Orozco 1995, Waldinger and Lichter 2003). Californian informant Cole found the workers' affluence apparent to all, as evidenced by their cars: 'Go look at what my employees drive. They drive BMWs. They drive newer cars. Newer than mine.' Other informants would provide similar examples to demonstrate the good, or at least reasonable, material living standards of their workers.

None of the informants did at any time provide examples to the contrary; of migrant workers' poverty or failure to succeed. Insofar as stories of exploitation emerged in the interviews, they were explained by the exceptional 'bad egg' employer or intermediary and/or with reference to erroneous accounts constructed by (biased) urban media outlets. Certainly, the voluminous literature on workplace exploitation and job intensification in food production (for instance, Scott 2017, Rogaly 2008) has never found a receptive readership among agricultural employers.

Furthermore, in Norway and (at the time of interviews) pre-Brexit England, circular seasonal migration is legally and practically quite feasible for eastern and central European migrants. Particularly in the Norwegian case, workers would move back and forth and spend the larger part of the year 'at home.' In the UK, where thc growing season is longer, time spent back home was more limited but still significant. Against this circulatory context, farmers emphasised how their migrant workers would make their earnings pay on a transnational level. For instance, Norwegian farmer Eirik detailed how the younger migrants used the money earned to both boost their current living conditions and to invest in educational careers in their homelands.

> *The students, obviously, are here to finance their studies, some of those with good jobs… they spend what they make here on luxurious goods. To be straight. The money goes to luxury, to live some kind of luxurious life.*

The farmers emphasise the migrants' 'dual frame of reference' to underline that wages for them are even better within a transnational context. Interviewees would often provide specific comparisons between wage levels 'here' (host country) and 'there' (home country), and argue that middle-class migrants accept what might appear to domestic workers as low wages because of these different reference points. This is what Nieswand (2014) refers to as the 'status paradox of migration': poor pay abroad is still good at home. Thus, Anders (Norway) explained his workers' preference for piece rates – often introduced by farmers to intensify the work process (Rogaly 2008) – by the opportunity they provide relative to what is on offer back home:

> *Cause they see the potential, right? 'Wow – I may pick two boxes per hour, three boxes! I have those making 2,500–2,600 [about £235] a day. And that is more than a months' wage in Lithuania, on the minimum wage in Lithuania.*

Similarly, Trevor (UK) told how his workers '…can come, earn 11,000 GBP as quick as you can and then go and build your house for six months, that's quite a nice, quite a nice way of doing it, isn't it?' Such 'delayed gratification' (Scott 2013b) not only motivates migrants to endure the hardships of work, but also allows their employers to judge wages on standards other than those of the domestic economy.

In California, due to the recent tightening of border controls, workers are now less circular in their migration patterns. They also tend to live off-farm in the local communities (unlike in the UK and Norway). Their US wages are therefore spent largely in the US, and thus the 'dual frame of reference' and principle of 'delayed gratification' are of lesser relevance. However, strawberry picking may, according to employers, still function as a springboard for social mobility. Second generation strawberry farmer Eva (California), for example, detailed how laborious work may provide future prosperity, not just for the worker but also for his/her offspring:

> *My father started the farm in 1978 (...) He was still working for another employer at that time (...) and he started there with the mentality that 'one day I can do this myself and I'm gonna have my own farm.' He started there.*

In this way the employment of one migrant worker is, according to farmers, good for the many. Incomes from hard farm work provide opportunity for the larger migrant community. UK farmer Paul, in the context of a recent media scandal involving the food industry and migrant workers, criticised the media coverage for its one-sided perspective, ignoring the larger societal benefits of the industry's employment of migrants:

> *And we are employing people, these people are going back home, building houses and feeding families, yeah. You know, for everyone person we employ that's 10 people that we are actually feeding in one way or another. Why not look at that as positive?*

The informants also underlined that strawberry picking provided benefits other than remuneration. Many emphasised how many migrants used strawberry work for travelling and adventure, exploring the world, even as a 'holiday.' Again, this motive was more prominent in the UK and Norway. Norwegian farmer Eirik, for instance, talked about his female workers:

> *Well, for some of them, it is kind of a holiday. Particularly those mothers with smaller kids at home, almost... I did get it but more recently I have come to understand, that, they are friends [knowing each other since childhood] coming here, kind of housewife's holiday. Getting away from their husbands or kids for a period, and that is good.*

The farmers are able to corroborate their overwhelmingly positive account of strawberry picking via a number of discursive strategies. Most important is the 'workers voting by their feet' argument: the rewards of strawberry picking are evidenced by high number of returning workers, year after year. Eirik (Norway) described his female workers' obvious like of the work:

> *Most of them come back, and if they do not, they often send their mother, the sister, or a friend. And that would not be if they not were [satisfied]. (...) Some families have been her for three generations, and some have worked for 10-15 years.*

In other regards the workers appear satisfied. Most notably, farmers emphasised that they rarely received any complaints from the migrants they employed. However, many also admitted that if they were not happy with a migrant's work rate (which is constantly monitored) they would either be warned then eventually dismissed, or simply not invited back the following season.

In Norway and the UK (though not in the US), farmers emphasised how many of their workers held or hold good job positions back home; for instance as managers, teachers, and other professional occupations. For the farmer this works to confirm that the migrants they employ do not represent precarious workers. Victor (UK), for example, talked about the origins of his eastern European workforce:

> You know, I've had doctors, university faculty lecturers, you know, vets, all sorts of people work for me in, in the course of time. (…) I had – one guy was a university faculty lecturer and he had 12 lecturers under him and he could earn more money picking strawberries for six months in the UK, than he could in a year being, being a top lecturer, you know.

From the perspective of the farmers, the legal and ethical soundness of the labour arrangements they preside over are confirmed via the actions of external authorities. Wage levels are set by legislative bodies in all three localities. These are strictly observed, according to informants, both by themselves and the industry at large. If anything, employers argued that they exceeded the baseline regulations because of the opportunities provided to workers, for example through the piece-rate system and other bonus mechanisms (though see Rogaly 2008). Daniel emphasised that he paid out annual bonuses to his workers, and other informants similarly told about how they rewarded their better pickers more than was required by law.

In the opinion of the informants, wages and working conditions have improved over the years. UK farmer Rosalyn implicitly acknowledged the harsh work conditions of the past, but stated that farmers now have no choice but to follow rules and regulations: 'Gone are the days you can treat them like a slave (…). I have to be legal, I have to have health and safety, got to comply.'

In conclusion, the farmers emphasise their role as providers of 'good work,' which to them is an integral aspect of being a farmer; they do not only produce food but also provide careers and opportunities for the migrants they employ. Once again, we emphasise that these are discursive accounts presenting the employer perspective and not 'objective' descriptions of the realities of work. Nevertheless, these accounts provide insights into the ways that employers rationalise their position between capital and labour, and make sense of the low-wage migrant employment practices that they are engaged in.

The socially responsible employer

The employers we interviewed further expressed their benevolence by emphasising how their responsibilities towards the migrant workers extended beyond a pure economic and contractual relationship. Their workers were not just workers but part of a team and a family, with attendant social obligations and caring duties attached. For Californian small-scale strawberry farmer Eva, the workers were 'family':

> *With us, we treat them like family. Once a week, I will treat my employees. I will take them lunch, I will take them breakfast, coffee in the morning (…) …usually for Christmas, my mother will make dinner, family will get together and they'll come. All of our employees know all my brothers, all my family, my aunts, my uncles, they've all worked with us. Yeah, it's like a big party. (…). Actually, some of the employees have married my cousins.*

Most strawberry farms employ large numbers of migrant workers in the high season and so the farmer cannot nurture intimate social relationships with all employees, especially as many are temporary. Nonetheless, the narrative of the socially responsible farmer appeared strong across study locations. For instance, Cole, a US farmer with a larger workforce, described how his whole family were involved with the care for their workers. His dad:

> *… tries to, whenever he can, take a group of employees, as soon as he can, take them to Vegas or Reno to show them the different places, not just work. On their own, they won't go. Very few of them will go. If they do go out, they go to places that they know it's people like them around there.*

Similarly, Norwegian Daniel, recalled how they '…have a party every year, to mark the end of the strawberry season. And every year we do a hike in the mountains, for a weekend or so.' Other employers shared similar stories of facilitating social life on the farm.

Furthermore, the informants recalled how they regularly assisted workers in their often troublesome interactions with local bureaucracies. Rather than employers exploiting their workers, the informants placed themselves as allies of their workers in their encounters with officialdom.

In the US case, the US-Mexico border was a recurring theme. While the US farming community generally leans towards the Republican party, our informants – in line with other agricultural employers – were concerned about the current (Trump) administration's tightening of the border. They argued the policy reduces the availability of migrant workers and places many already in the US in a more vulnerable position. Adam (US) explained:

> *There came a point where it became increasingly difficult to pass through the border to get down to Mexico, and people stopped taking those breaks over winter. They essentially chose to stay here year round, so we felt somewhat obligated to provide more employment over winter, and we decided to do an, every other week, delivery on our produce boxes through the winter months, from November until March, and that's worked out well. It's provided more*

> *work for the crew during the wet, rainy months, and that was partially a concession to provide more hours for the people that were working for us.*

This emphasis on care and support for migrant workers was commonplace across study locations. Spencer (UK), for instance, emphasised how:

> *We try and care for them (...) they all know me and my main supervisor is very caring because I explained to him that they are the most important part of the farm and without them we'd give up. So, they need caring for and time spent caring for them.*

The informants present themselves as socially responsible and they see their role as good employers extending well beyond the narrow economics of the contractual wage relationship. They see themselves as decent people, following the adage: 'You know, I treat people as I would expect to be treated myself' (Trevor, UK).

Irrespective of the 'objective' reality of low-wage agricultural work, the informants appeared genuine as to their intentions of treating workers respectfully. They emphasised, for instance, how their consideration for workers' welfare can impact upon the very operation of the farm, and even incur economic costs. US informant Dennis stressed how he would never risk the health of his workers: 'We value a person's life over an hour of work.' To illustrate this, he told of a particularly hot day the year before, where temperatures reached 95 degrees Fahrenheit (35 degrees Celsius). Workers wanted to keep picking regardless but, in the end, Dennis had to force workers to leave the field:

> *I'd rather pay you an hour out of my pocket, you guys go home. It's just too hot. We're not gonna put somebody's life in danger because we want to produce an hour worth of labour.*

Anders, referring to a discussion with a representative of the shipping company, underscores that the welfare of workers is more important than profits. He adamantly stated that he would never consider lowering wages in order to enhance profits.

> *I told him, if that what it takes to make a surplus – reducing the wages of workers, or even go down below the legal minimum wage... If that what it takes to stop worrying for the farm, not sleeping at nights... Then I quit farming. End of story.*

None of the informants provided examples to the contrary, and appeared unaware of the extensive literature detailing work-based harm related to the hardships of manual farm work, such as strawberry picking (Holmes 2013, Scott 2017).

The informants in all three localities identified a relationship between the good treatment of workers and a productive and happy workforce. Employment intermediaries/agencies, for instance, were avoided by many because of the potential for exploitation. Trevor (UK) explained:

> *So we have our own recruitment team, which I'm responsible, so – and that's not, that's not really done for cost, it's more done for ethical reasons. There is, there is perhaps a, a better, a slightly better cost side of it, but it's more we've got the control.*

More broadly, many talked about the importance of recruitment and retention in a tight labour market, and how this translated into excellent living and working conditions. UK farmer Patrick explained:

> *To retain the people, as well, you know, they've left their families behind and they've come here. So, we try to offer them a home environment here so they can enjoy their life as well. Not just working so the leisure time – they can do many things because the campsite is really nice, they have a football ground there, a pool table is there just to make their life easier and more enjoyable.*

According to Trevor (UK) good-quality living and working conditions had become 'pretty industry standard' now. Particularly where labour shortage appears more prevalent in employers' discourses (in the US given Trump's border restrictions and in the UK given Brexit) the need to provide attractive work was seen as imperative. Rosalyn (UK), quoted above on the industry no longer treating workers as 'slaves,' openly stated that they had no other choice: they needed to compete for workers now and it was the worker who could decide where to pick, and the farmers were at their mercy.

The informants sought to establish a narrative of equality, where farmers and migrants – employers and employees – shared the same interest. Hard work and a good harvest are viewed as to the mutual benefit of both parties; they depend on each other to make the strawberry fields a source of shared profit. In this storyline, the undoubted hardship of migrant manual work in the fields is rendered invisible. More than anything, strawberry picking is presented as good work for good workers, provided by socially responsible and benevolent employers.

Integrating interests of labour and capital

Drawing on the strawberry industry in the US, Norway, and UK, this chapter set out to examine how low-wage agricultural employers rationalise the pay and conditions they offer their (largely migrant) workforce. Despite numerous accounts emphasising the exploitative nature of the strawberry industry, and indeed horticulture more generally (Rye and Scott 2018, Scott

2017, Bock *et al.* 2016, Holmes 2013, Rogaly 2008), the stories employers told us emphasised positive moral and ethical dimensions to migrant employment in labour markets that often appear harsh and unyielding to the outsider. As a consequence, one is presented with a 'good farmer' discourse that draws on the transnational frame of migrant employment (Suarez-Orozco and Suarez-Orozco 1995, Scott 2013b, Waldinger and Licther 2003) and also on the importance of the socially responsible employer. Resonant with Weber's ideal types of human action (1968 [1921]), low-wage employers claim to operate according to the logics of *both* economically rooted means-ends rationality and a value-oriented rationality. They act as *homo economicus* and *homo socius*, and seek to demonstrate how these rationalities are complementary rather than contradictory. In this respect, and given low-wage employers' location between capital and labour, one can conclude that farmers see themselves as 'benevolent moderators' who successfully manage to combine the economic necessities of the strawberry industry, providing 'good workers' with 'good jobs,' and doing so in socially responsible and ethically sound ways.

What is missing from farmers' rationalisation of their work offer is the critique of the structural context within which they are embedded and through which they must operate. The farmers do not openly question the 'natural' order of the contemporary world but accept it as given both in terms of their position in the food value chain and in terms of their migrant workers' position relative to the rest of society. The stories they tell contain an element of 'misrecognition' by taking reality for granted (Bourdieu 1990), or at best a public 'silence' with respect to the possibility for alternatives both for themselves and their workers. They are then, to an extent at least, captives of dominant discourses (Foucault 1972): whether through misrecognition or a more conscious and considered silence. This may not be purely incidental or contrary to their interests; the silence possibly works to bolster their relative privileged status vis-à-vis their workers, or at least uphold the status quo.

Another omission from the 'good work' discourse, and this relates to the structural silence noted above, is any real acknowledgement that the temporary, seasonal, and low-wage work offer is exploitative. The strawberry picker generates surplus value but is largely disenfranchised from this. There is a paradox, then, whereby employer exploitation and employer benevolence appear to be co-located at the bottom of the labour market across developed world horticulture. This is entirely feasible; most obviously employers (like most people) are prone to present their actions in a positive light. More than this, however, one gets the sense that the economic arguments (that work pays for migrants) and moral arguments (that employers are socially responsible) that farmers made were genuine rationalisations rather than cover stories. In short, farmers – in their own accounts – find themselves in a conflicted position between capital and labour and felt they did the best they could in the face of the competing pressures.

Overall, the chapter has emphasised striking similarities in strawberry farmers' representation and rationalisation of migrant workers' (relatively low) wages and (relatively tough) working conditions. The informants' accounts are largely uniform in their structure, both within and across study locations, and appears to reflect a dominant 'good work' discourse and the associated role of farmers as 'benevolent moderators' between capital and labour. Nevertheless, the materials do suggest some geographical nuances in farmers' representation and rationalisation. For instance, as briefly noted above, the US context of immigration policy reform, the UK context of Brexit, and the Norwegian trade union context are all noteworthy. In terms of future research, it would be interesting to explore these nuances in more detail. In addition, alternative methodologies could be used to challenge or corroborate the stories employers tell. For instance, the global leader of the strawberry industry, Driscoll's, details on its webpages how it retains a thriving workforce in phrases echoing the informants in this chapter: 'Treating the workforce with dignity isn't just the right thing to do, it's crucial to the future of our business' (Driscoll's 2020). Moving beyond the employer, it would also be interesting to examine workers' responses to the employer discourse identified. One could also examine whether the employer representations and rationalisations profiled above are reflected in other low-wage sectors of the economy (such as care work, cleaning, hospitality, food processing) or are farmers unique in their 'benevolent moderator' role?

Acknowledgements

The chapter is result of the 2017–2022 Global Labour in Rural Societies research project financed by the Norwegian Research Council (grant no. 261854/F10). The authors wish to thank the external reviewers for their comments on the manuscript. Funding from the Norwegian University of Science and Technology has made possible open access publishing of the chapter.

References

Baxter-Reid, H. 2016. 'Buying into the "Good Worker" Rhetoric or Being as Good as They Need To Be? The Effort Bargaining Process of New Migrant Workers.' *Human Resource Management Journal* 26: 337–350.

Bélanger, D. and G. Candiz. 2015. 'Fraises douces amères: territoire et précarité chez les travailleurs agricoles migrants de la région de Québec.' *Cahiers de géographie du Québec* 59(166): 7–28.

Bloor, M. and F. Wood. 2006. 'Theoretical Saturation.' In *Keywords in Qualitative Methods*, edited by M. Bloor and F. Woods, 156–166. London: Sage.

Bock, B., G. Osti and F. Ventura. 2016. 'Rural Migration and New Patterns of Exclusion and Integration in Europe.' In *The Routledge International Handbook of Rural Studies*, edited by M. Shucksmith and D. Brown, 71–84. New York: Routledge: 71–84.

Bourdieu, P. 1990. *In Other Words. Essays Towards a Reflexive Sociology*. Cambridge: Polity Press.

Calleja, E.J., B. Ilbery and P.R. Mills. 2012. 'Agricultural Change and the Rise of the British Strawberry Industry, 1920–2009.' *Journal of Rural Studies* 28(4): 603–611.

Corrado, A., C. de Castro and D. Perrotta, eds. 2016. *Migration and Agriculture Mobility and Change in the Mediterranean Area*. London: Routledge.

Defra (Department of Environment, Food and Rural Affairs. 2018.) 'Horticultural Statistics.' Accessed 5 May 2019. www.gov.uk/government/statistics/latest-horticulture-statistics.

Driscoll's. 2020. 'Thriving Workforce.' Online information brochure. Accessed 29 March 2020. www.driscolls.com/ about/thriving-workforce.

Evans, N. 2013. 'Strawberry Fields Forever? Conflict over Neo-productivist Spanish Polytunnel Technology in British Agriculture.' *Land Use Policy* 35: 61–72.

Foucault, M. 1972. *The Archaeology of Knowledge and the Discourse on Language*. New York: Phanteon Books.

Gertel, J. and S.R. Sippel, eds. 2014. *Seasonal Workers in Mediterranean Agriculture*. Abingdon: Routledge.

Gialis, S. and A. Herold. 2014. 'Of Steel and Strawberries: Greek Workers' Struggle Against Informal and Flexible Working Arrangements During the Crisis.' *Geoforum* 57: 138–149.

Guthman, J. 2014. *Agrarian Dreams: The Paradox of Organic Farming in California*. Oakland: California: University of California Press.

Guthman, J. 2017a. 'Paradoxes of the Border: Labour Shortages and Farmworker Minor Agency in Reworking California's Strawberry Fields.' *Economic Geography* 93(1): 24–43.

Guthman, J. 2017b. 'Life Itself Under Contract: Rent-seeking and Biopolitical Devolution Through Partnerships in California's Strawberry Industry.' *Journal of Peasant Studies* 44(1): 100–117.

Hellio, E. 2008. 'Importer des femmes pour exporter des fraises (Huelva).' *Etudes rurales* 182, 185–200.

Hellio, E. 2017. '"They Know That You'll Leave, Like a Dog Moving onto the Next Bin". Undocumented Male and Seasonal Contracted Female Workers in the Agricultural Labour market of Huelva, Spain.' In *Migration and Agriculture. Mobility and Change in the Mediterranean Area*, edited by A. Corrado, C. de Castro and D. Perrotta, 198–216. London: 6.

Holmes, S.M. 2007. '"Oaxacans Like to Work Bent Over": The Naturalization of Social Suffering Among Berry Farm Worker.' *International Migration* 45(3): 39–68.

Holmes, S.M. 2013. *Fresh Fruit, Broken Bodies: Migrant Farmworkers in the United States*, Berkeley: University of California Press.

Ivancheva, M. 2007. 'Strawberry Fields Forever? Bulgarian and Romanian Student Workers in the UK.' *Journal of Global and Historical Anthropology* 49: 110–117.

Lindner, K. and T. Kathmann. 2014. 'Mobility Partnershops and Circular Migration.' In *Seasonal Workers in Mediterranean Agriculture. The Social Costs of Eating Fresh*, edited by J. Gertel and S.R. Sippel, 121–129. London: Routledge.

MacKenzie, R. and Forde, C. (2009). 'The Rhetoric of the "Good Worker" versus the Realities of Employers' Use and the Experiences of Migrant Workers.' *Work, Employment and Society* 23: 142–159.

Mannon, S.E., P. Petrzelka, C.M. Glass and C. Radel. 2012. 'Keeping Them in Their Place: Migrant Women Workers in Spain's Strawberry Industry.' *International Journal of the Sociology of Agriculture and Food* 19: 83–110.

Martin, P. 2019. 'Trump, Migration, and Agriculture.' *Crossing Borders* 9: 9–27.

McAreavey, R. 2012. 'Resistance or Resilience? Tracking the Pathway of Recent Arrivals to a "New" Rural Destination.' *Sociologia Ruralis* 52(4): 488–507.

Mireles, G.F. 2013. *Continuing La Causa. Organizing Labor in California's Strawberry Fields*. Boulder, Colorado: FirstForumPress.

Nieswand, B. 2014. 'The Burgers' Paradox: Migration and the Transnationalization of Social Inequality in Southern Ghana.' *Ethnography* 15(4): 403–425.

Papadopoulos, A.G. and L-M. Fratsea. 2017. 'Migrant Labour and Intensive Agricultural Production in Greece. The Case of the Manolada Strawberry Industry.' In *Migration and Agriculture. Mobility and Change in the Mediterranean Area*, edited by A. Corrado, C. de Castro and D. Perotta, 128–144. London: Routledge.

Perrotta, D. 2015. 'Agricultural Day Laborers in Southern Italy: Forms of Mobility and Resistance.' *South Atlantic Quarterly* 114(1): 195–203.

Perrotta, D. 2017. 'Processing Tomatoes in the Era of the Retailing Revolution. Mechanization and Migrant Labour in Northern and Southern Italy.' In *Migration and Agriculture. Mobility and Change in the Mediterranean Area*, edited by A. Corrado, C. de Castro and D. Perrotta, 58–75. Abingdon: Routledge.

Quesada, J., L.K. Hart and P. Burgeoise. 2011. 'Structural Vulnerability and Health: Latino Migrant Laborers in the United States.' *Medical Anthropology* 30(4): 339–362.

Rogaly, B. 2008. 'Intensification of Workplace Regimes in British Horticulture: The Role of Migrant Workers.' *Population, Space and Place* 14(6): 497–510.

Rye, J.F. 2017. 'Negotiating Neoliberalism: Informalisation and Reformalisation of Industrial Relations in Norway's Agricultural Industry in the 21st Century.' *Population, Space and Place* 23(7): unpaginated. DOI:10.1002/psp.2042.

Rye, J.F. and J. Andrzejewska. 2010. 'The Structural Disempowerment of Eastern European Migrant Farm Workers in Norwegian Agriculture.' *Journal of Rural Studies* 26(1): 41–51.

Rye, J.F. and S. Scott. 2018. 'International Labour Migration to/in Rural Europe: A Review of the Evidence.' *Sociologia Ruralis* 8(4): 928–954.

Sanchez, T.F. 2013. 'Californian Strawberries: Mexican Immigrant Women Sharecroppers, Labor, and Discipline.' *Anthropology of Work Review* 34(1): 15–26.

Schlosser, E. 1995. 'In the Strawberry Fields.' *The Atlantic Monthly* 276(5): 80–108.

Scott, S. 2013a. 'Migration and the Employer Perspective: Pitfalls and Potentials for a Future Research Agenda.' *Population, Space and Place* 9(6): 703–713.

Scott, S. 2013b. 'Migrant–Local Hiring Queues in the UK Food Industry.' *Population, Space and Place* 19(5): 459–471.

Scott, S. 2017. *Labour Exploitation and Work-based Harm*. Bristol: Policy Press.

Scott, S. and Rye, J.F. Forthcoming. 'Praised, Prized, yet Penalised: A Critical Examination of Low-wage Hiring Queues in the Global Strawberry Industry.'

Suárez-Orozco, M. and C.E. Suárez-Orozco. 1995. 'The Cultural Patterning of Achievement Motivation: A Comparison of Mexican, Mexican Immigrant, Mexican American, and Non-Latino White American Students.' In *California's Immigrant Children: Theory, Research, and Implications for Educational Policy*, edited by R.G. Rumbaut and W.A. Cornelius, 161–190. San Diego, Center for U.S.-Mexican Studies: University of California.

Tannock, S. 2015. 'Bad Attitude? Migrant Workers, Meat Processing Work and the Local Unemployed in a Peripheral Region of the UK.' *European Urban and Regional Studies* 22: 416–430.

Waldinger, R. and M.I. Lichter 2003. *How the Other Half Works: Immigration and the Social Organization of Labor*. Berkeley: University of California Press.

Weber, M. [1921] 1968. *Economy and Society. An Outline of Interpretive Sociology*. Berkeley: University of California Press.

Wells, M. 1996. *Strawberry Fields. Politics, Class, and Work in California Agriculture*. Ithaca: Cornell University Press.

Yin, R.K. 2009. *Case Study Research. Design and Methods*. London: Sage.

Chapter 10

Emotions and community development after return migration in the rural Arctic

Marit Aure and Larissa Riabova

Emotions in return migration and rural development

Migration is highly emotional (Castles, de Haas, and Miller 2014) and often evokes strong feelings of optimism for human and economic development in societies of origin. In 1998, during a period of harsh economic and political transition in Russia, temporary labour migration started from Teriberka, a small, remote Russian village on the Barents Sea coast, to Båtsfjord, an equally small village in the Norwegian Arctic. The labour mobility programme brought about 40 villagers, mainly women, to work in the fish-processing industry in Båtsfjord. Most of the migrants were formerly employed at the kolkhoz in Teriberka – a fishing and fish-processing collective farm established in the Soviet era. The migration was designed to fit Norwegian regulations, which restricted the work to *two years* of *unskilled* jobs in the *fish-processing industry* in *northern* Norway for *Russian* workers (no families). The mobility programme was organised by Norwegian and Russian businessmen as part of a broader development project in Teriberka.

The migration organisers, most migrants, villagers, and politicians expected that the migration would improve the migrants' and their families' situation and catalyse economic activity and development in the declining Russian village. They hoped for a better life for migrants and the community, while fear, euphoria, joy, homesickness, disillusionment, and nostalgia for the Soviet past were other strong feelings. With extensions of the work permits, the migration ceased after three years and most migrants returned to Teriberka. Thus, return migration occurred, which refers to migrants returning to their countries of origin or later generations returning to their family's homeland (Kunoroglu *et al.* 2016). In Teriberka, the migrants returned after back-and-forth migration but the expected developmental outcomes of migration were not achieved. The extent of the emotional strain contained in people's stories drove us to acknowledge affectivity as a way of comprehending the world (Markussen 2006). This motivated our examination of the emotional underpinnings of this rural return migration and its lack of impact on the development of Teriberka.

Research on return migration has, since the 1960s, shown that few return migrants engage in cooperative or economic development efforts (King 1986, Christou 2006, Vathi and Duci 2015). King (1986, 20) also states that the belief that human capital improves after return migration has '[been] shown to be almost entirely fallacious,' highlighting that return migrants do not play the role as catalysts for economic development in their home communities, in opposition to expectations such as in Teriberka in this study. However, contrary to King (1986), we observed, and the migrants highlighted, improvements in their human capital during migration. Despite this, the expectations of rural development after the migrants' return went unmet in Teriberka.

Kunuroglu, Vijver, and Yagmur (2016, 10) point to return migration and its impact as a 'multi-layered phenomenon influenced by multiple interrelated factors' which neither economic perspectives, transnationalism, nor reacculturation theories explain. Cassarino (2004, 254) suggests that understanding 'the link between migration and development… requires revisiting approaches to return migration and distinguishing between different forms of migration.' Our focus on the role of emotions in explaining the lack of rural development after the return of temporary labour migrants in a post-Soviet context responds to these requests. While King (1986) and later writers reveal the lack of post-return migration development, we attempt to understand and explain why this is the case. Paraphrasing Ahmed (2004), we ask what emotions do during the migratory process and what analysing emotions does to the understanding of the development impact in societies of origin.

Examining migration requires investigating the situation before migration, the migration itself, the situation abroad, the return migration, and the situation after return (King 1986). We enquire about the role of emotions among individuals, social groups, and the community across these phases, with a particular focus on the (lack of) development in the origin community in the post-migration phase. We argue that emotions play a significant role in expectations and considerations in the migratory process. To support our contention, we explain how migrants use emotional experiences abroad in individual strategies, showing how emotion increases the post-return disappointment imposed by the lack of public policies for rural development. The positive migration experiences are to a lesser degree used at the community level as they are not being met by state or municipal strategies. Focus on emotions hence makes visible the impact of economic and political state policies on people's actions. This chapter adds to clarifying the ambiguity of international mobility in rural places (Aure, Førde, and Magnussen 2018) and the role of emotions in various migration phases.

Emotions in migration and development

During the past two decades, emotion has increasingly been used as a lens to (re)examine aspects of individual, group, organisational, and community life

(Tanner 2005, 122). There is also a growing interest in emotions in migrations studies (Carling and Collins 2018). However, although Castles, de Haas, and Miller (2014) find migration highly emotive, they and others have paid little attention to the role of emotions across different phases of migration and especially in the return phase. While Halfacree (2004) highlights the non-economic worlds of migration, the role of emotions seems missing in studies of return migration and rural development. We find that discussions on emotions in migration studies centre on emotional labour (Hochschild 1979), the emotional constitution of the migrant subject (Ahmed 2004), and transnational families, diasporas, and the emotional costs of migration (Svašek 2010, 865). There is rarely focus on emotions in studies of migrant labour markets (Aure 2013). Theoretically, there is a development towards understanding the role of social imaginaries of migration (Benson and Osbaldiston 2014), although the concept's relationship to the emotions remains unclear (O'Reilly 2014).

We see emotions as 'processes in which individuals experience, shape and interpret the world around them, anticipate future action and shape their subjectivities' (Svašek 2008, 218). Emotions may be social, as in shared experiences (Heady and Miller 2006); physical and 'culturally elaborated ..., socially and historically nuanced and thus variable'; and structured and structuring (Burkitt 1997, 39). Rather than seeing reason and passion as opposites, we consider them relational and complementary, with neither taking precedence over the other (Burkitt 1997).

Heady and Miller (2006) use the concept of 'emotional capital' to ascertain the role of emotions in rural development, arguing that economic activity requires not merely mental, physical, and rational efforts but also emotional orientations, as rational behaviour also rests on irrational premises. Emotional capital may be a form of social capital (Nowotny 1981) or cultural capital (Reay 2000); we apply emotional capital as an analytical tool that describes a set of resources inherent to individuals and useful for development through informing action (Gendron 2017, Voronov 2013), and also at the community level. This means that migration memories present in Teriberka '[seem like] individual knowledge of the past,' and shared memory (history) may work as 'the cognitive maps' of communities (Heady and Miller 2006, 34–35). Hence, emotional capital is accumulated stocks of emotional resources formed by positive and negative emotional experiences constituting a resource inherent to particular practices. These resources form relational skills, self-esteem, adaptability, and other emotional competencies (Gendron 2017). We highlight emotions to include what is often excluded as being non-rational – fear, joy, anger, and so forth – and show how this adds to the understanding of migration and the lack of post-return rural development.

A multi-sited study of organised labour migration

This analysis draws on longitudinal, connected community studies in Teriberka and Båtsfjord from 1996 to 2018, a suitable time span to discuss the intersection of return migration and rural development. The main study was carried out in Teriberka and Båtsfjord in 1998 to 2002, with follow-up studies in both villages in 2012 and in Teriberka in 2015. Preliminary material was collected in 1996 in Teriberka and since then the village has been monitored through visits, interviews, phone calls, documents, and register studies. This provides narratives before the migration, during the migration in Båtsfjord, upon migrants' return, and after the migration ended.

Although the migrants were employed as unskilled workers, many had backgrounds as engineers, economists, and administrators. Thirty-seven of the 40 migrants were women, from 22 to 46 years old, a distribution resulting from the Norwegian businessmen's requirements based on gendered work in the Norwegian fish processing industry (Aure 2011).

Our qualitative methods included interviews, ethnographic field talks, and notes from participant and non-participant observations. Altogether, 16 migrants were interviewed once or several times, individually or in focus groups. Information regarding other migrants was also obtained through interviews. We interviewed employers, managers, family members, co-workers, and political and administrative leaders in Russia and Norway. The main study involved 74 Russians and 74 Norwegians. Migrant interviews employed a 'life course' approach aimed at understanding migration experiences, everyday life, and the local context. The interviews lasted from one and half to two hours, discussing life at home and abroad, family, education, work, spare time, civil activities, networks, and opinions on the past, present, and future of Teriberka. In some interviews, emotions were an important theme, and in others they were present but not explicit – the analysis includes both. We believe the theme and the ambience produced in the long-term interactions inspired these discussions. Excerpts from the respondents' narratives and our observations support this argument and provide examples of people's expression of thoughts, practices, and emotions. As this regards a group of people from a small village, anonymity prevents us from expanding on the migrants' biographies, and to protect the co-workers and interviewees their names have been anonymised.

Cross-border labour migration: when emotional capital grows

Teriberka, the home of 900 people, stands on a windy coast 450km above the Arctic Circle. The nearest cities are Severomorsk, the naval base, and Murmansk, the capital of the region, which is a two- to three-hour drive through empty tundra. Teriberka is one of the oldest and, formerly, wealthiest fishing communities on the Kola Peninsula, inhabited for 500 years by Russians, Pomors, Sami, Norwegians, and Finns. Teriberka had strong international ties across the Barents, White, and Norwegian Seas until the Russian Revolution in 1917. In the Soviet era, Teriberka flourished, growing to about 5,000 inhabitants due to its fishing industry and shipyard. However, in the mid-1960s most industries were moved to Murmansk and the number of inhabitants had declined to 1,732 by 1997 (Riabova 2001, 123). Until 2009 , the village was under a military border regime with restricted access for foreigners. Market reforms in the early 1990s caused a deep socio-economic crisis, and local unemployment reached 40–50 per cent. The situation led to children coming to the village hospital to ask for bread (Riabova 2001). Many people were desperate and many of those who secured permission to leave for work did so.

Migration to Båtsfjord

By the late 1990s, the situation in Teriberka was more complicated than ever. Then, Russian businessmen who formerly worked in Teriberka and their Norwegian partners from Båtsfjord established a project with help from the government of the Murmansk region and local mayors. They invited villagers to train and work as unskilled filleters in the fish-processing industry in Norway (Aure 2008, Riabova and Ivanova 2009). Some of the migrants were among the first group recruited; others arrived in Båtsfjord later. The migrants and the migration organisers learned along the way that the regulated two-year term was counted day by day, and this decided their actual stay abroad. All migrants returned home for Christmas and several weeks in summer, while some had their families visit. As the migrants became familiar with the road, they drove between Teriberka and Båtsfjord in private cars (about 600km), although the roads were bad and regularly closed due to snowstorms. Yet other migrants stayed as long as possible to earn as much as possible, and saved time and money by not visiting home. A few were sent home due to problems we cannot expand on for reasons of anonymity, and some resigned. Most migrants lived in low-quality dormitories and had the rent deducted from their salaries. They were paid minimum wage without increases for seniority.

The following section presents the emotions inherent in the migration process, starting with the recruitment phase, followed by the experiences of life in Båtsfjord and migrants' hopes for the future. The next section focuses on the return and the post-return situation in Teriberka and migrants' imaginaries, emotions, and practices. In the conclusion, we discuss emotions in migration and their role in the lack of post-return rural development.

Recruitment, considerations, and migrant life in Båtsfjord

In 1998, rumours abounded about the prospects of migrating to Norway and created strong feelings in Teriberka: the migration organisers and most villagers saw work in Båtsfjord as a prize. Candidates were interviewed carefully before they were selected and completed the 15-hour drive to Båtsfjord in a chartered bus organised and prepaid by the businesses, with the travel costs later reimbursed by the migrants. Living in an isolated society, few migrants had previously been abroad or had international passports, and many feared the unknown. Pavel, a young migration organiser, explained:

> *The first group consisted of 16 people. Many did not believe it would be good for them to go, and several people withdrew right before departure. But those who went to Norway started to call home saying that things are good, and people began to ask to be allowed to go.*

All the interviewees said that before migration they were sad to separate from their families and felt guilty leaving their children. Young mothers were scared to abandon small children, as is the case in female migration elsewhere (Hochschild 1979). Older mothers asked for their children to be included in the migration, crying and begging if refused. The main and pressing factor behind the migration decisions was to improve personal standards of living, the most common motivation for migration (Castles, de Haas, and Miller 2014). Natalia, aged 23, a woman recently married at the time of migration, said:

> *It was the only chance to get money. My relatives promised to help with the child. Most women who went to Norway had grandmothers to take care of the kids. My husband and I thought I would make 300 USD per month, but it was more – about 1,100 USD!*

The hope to earn seven to eight times more than the average local salaries in a time when most people at home were almost starving mitigated other problems. Natalia continued: 'My husband did not like me leaving him. We quarrelled, but finally he let me go. He was satisfied with the prospect of the wages and the possibility to make savings.'

Most people in Teriberka stressed that the migration was motivated by poverty; however, some were adventurous, which aligns with Favell's (2008) argument about mixed motives for migration adding to simple cost-benefit calculations. Valeria, higher educated and in her mid-40s, was from the 'pioneer' group and stayed for three years. As she explained while living in Båtsfjord:

> It was so exciting. I was curious and wanted to stay in a foreign country. The kids had grown up, and their father could care for them. I really liked to go and felt almost forced to use the opportunity.

Some migrants also highlighted that they felt good about the personal advancement. Nadia, aged 40, also interviewed while working in Båtsfjord, expressed the following: 'Before coming here, I could not talk to people as freely as I do now. I thought I was too old to go to Norway. [In Norway] I became brave.'

Besides satisfaction with the Norwegian salary, life in Båtsfjord was mostly rewarding. The early period of migration was dominated by euphoria. Natalia recalled her arrival:

> *It was 'wow' and 'oh.' All the lights at night, Båtsfjord looked like a diamond! Civilization... Everything was sterile at the factory. In the kolkhoz [in Teriberka], everything smells fishy. The streets [in Båtsfjord] were clean. Nice houses, beauty everywhere. Work was much easier than in the kolkhoz.*

After a while, loneliness, disillusionment, and homesickness added to the positive emotions. These feelings related to limited contact with non-Russian people and the perception of sometimes being treated badly. Elena, aged 35, a trained engineer doing unskilled work in Båtsfjord, was not allowed to use her education and skills. She wanted a transfer to a skilled job, but the supervisor refused and told us what he also told Elena: 'Of course, she could not do those tasks. The equipment is expensive, and it requires experienced and skilled workers.' In addition to the migration regulation that permitted only unskilled work, in his view she did not possess the required skills and qualities, mostly held by men. Elena felt that 'Russians are the bottom of the pile. I, as a Russian, am not allowed this [opportunity].' Elena was frustrated by her subordination due to gender and nationality in Båtsfjord (Aure 2011), as well as homesickness and longing for her child left in Teriberka. As a single mother, she desperately needed money while also trying to prepare herself for a brighter future in the planned factory in Teriberka.

Norway became, for migrants and Russian organisers, a positive point of reference: everything was compared with how it was arranged in Norway, and, mostly, the Norwegian way was considered best – roads, houses, enterprises, salaries, people. One woman expressed the view of many while living in Båtsfjord:

> *It is clean here, nice, quiet, and there is a possibility to make big money. I like people – they are polite. In Russia, not all people are like that. Enterprises [in Norway] are better. It is like 'sky and earth' compared to Russia. Nothing is bad here.*

Despite disillusionment, the positive emotions caused by migration experiences prevailed and the (positive) emotional capital among the group grew in terms of increased knowledge, experience, self-development, and self-awareness, along with the feeling that the migration verified their expectations and choices and improved their lives.

Dreams about the future back home

Although there may be no direct links between the intentions, plans, and expectations of migration and the results after return (King 1986), migration phases, intentions, expectations, and outcomes are connected (see O'Reilly and Rye, Chapter 14). The Russian–Norwegian development plan for Teriberka included an export-oriented joint fish-processing plant, a water pipeline, maintenance, and improved electricity supply. The Norwegian partners claimed that they saw Teriberka as a model for building a fishing community in Russia while providing the Norwegian plant access to the scarce raw material (fish) and trained labour force. The Russian partners wanted to revive fisheries and make Teriberka a decent place to live and saw labour migration as a route to poverty reduction. They believed that the military control in Teriberka would be lifted, and it would become a zone of international economic development. Most migrants were 'home-oriented' and expected development in their village, based on the recovery of fisheries, internationalisation, and the development of new knowledge.

Valeria, 'home-oriented' with an education degree, highlighted the value of visits abroad, specifically learning new languages, working methods, and work organisation. She expected her new skills to benefit her and the planned plant, and thereby Teriberka's economic situation, leading to employment in a management position. She expected a new future for Teriberka, with international industries and modernisation of the Russian top-down management style. As another Russian woman explained: 'In Russia, the boss is The Boss. Most of our bosses are very… [bossy]; bosses and staff are not mixed. In Norway, after work, we can be equal.' Norway hence became a point of reference for the wished-for future in Teriberka. A manager in Teriberka said: 'If there could be any good investment programmes, we would imagine [Teriberka] as a village of the Norwegian type.' Another manager laughed at what he considered a collective naïve imaginary: 'We have a dream – to move with the entire village to Norway!' However, some migrants and villagers anticipated that nothing would change: the international project was established to 'earn on the Russian skin,' as Yuri, a migrant, put it:

> *Tales… The Teriberka project was established for other purposes. It is good to build a factory in Teriberka – cheap labour force, cheap energy—and have people with this certificate [from the Norwegian industry].*

Nevertheless, we found, that despite doubts, there was a shared dream among migrants, businessmen, and people in Teriberka – a dream of Teriberka as a comfortable, joyful, Norwegian-type fishing village with an unbiased community life and vivid economic development. As an image, this 'new Teriberka' was often on people's minds. We suggest that this collective dream, produced by the experiences of labour migration in Norway, shaped aspirations, or imaginaries, for some before migration even started but also increasingly during the migration (Benson and Osbaldiston 2014). This dream, including its hopes, became part of the positive community-level emotional capital in Teriberka.

Post-return: emotional capital devastation

In three years, the labour migration ceased and the plans for an export-oriented plant in Teriberka collapsed due to Teriberka's status as a 'closed' border-zone settlement and lack of investment. Most migrants returned to Teriberka. Return migration has many causes: home orientation and planned return, plans for innovation in the home country, retirement, and some sort of failure (Cerase 1974). In this case the migration was temporary, and most migrants planned to go back and continue their life in Teriberka, feeling that they belonged there. Others lacked the opportunity, money, or work to move away and hence stayed.

While this migration was triggered by the harsh socio-economic situation and channelled by the migration organisation, it ceased due to the Norwegian migration regime. Specific migration policies thus impact return migration and its outcomes. In this case, the policies on temporary migration made it resemble long-term commuting. This demonstrates the blurriness of migration types and processes. Both business partners and migrants regarded the return as too early and felt unprepared, which is an important factor for the developmental outcome of migrants' return (Cassarino 2004). Frustration of the abrupt return became an emotional impact of the migration.

In the return phase, in the early 2000s, the situation in Teriberka was typical for most rural Russian settlements. Russian pro-market policies, which neglected the human dimension, were coupled with an absent state in rural areas, making the effects of reforms especially destructive for small rural places (Kalugina 2000). According to Wegren (2016, 7): 'The main story in rural Russia during the 1990s was a struggle for survival amidst economic collapse.' The number of villages in Russia decreased from 142,200 in 1989 to 132,200 in 2002 (Wegren 2016). Teriberka survived but most people endured poor quality of life due to high unemployment, alcohol problems, lack of maintenance, and declining municipal budgets. Young people lacked money to leave for work or education. The unemployment grant was 120 roubles per month, less than five USD (a decent wage would be 10 times more). Some people lived on their 'mama's neck' until they were 30, as one woman told us.

In the following years, many former migrants used the money earned in Båtsfjord for everyday expenses and savings, or they bought cars. Some bought flats in Murmansk for their children to use while studying. Most stayed in Teriberka and used their new skills at the kolkhoz's fish factory. The main visible results from migration were, however, that former migrants paid more attention to home decoration. The women who had returned tried to make their homes look nice, putting effort into buying furniture in Murmansk and bringing it to Teriberka, traversing the 200km in hired cars on unpaved roads. This was not just an issue of decorating – this was making their everyday lives better, making themselves feel better. During our visit, they proudly showed us their efforts to make the best of their homes in a dilapidated environment. People with whom they shared the migration experience recognised and reinforced their efforts by supporting each other at an identity level. Appleyard (1989) describes this as 'conspicuous consumption' applying the expression in the migration context. This fails to acknowledge the importance of dignity in a situation of economic insecurity and depression.

Returning to life in Teriberka evoked pain and despair even worse than that before migration. The emotional experiences from Norway influenced migrants' views on Teriberka: 'Before, I did not notice that I live in ruins. When I came back home, it was like I saw my village for the first time: it looked like after the war' (Nadia). The experiences from the migration turned to shame and painful resignation, made the re-integration difficult, and triggered a downward spiral of positive emotional capital devastation. In a self-escalating cycle, negative emotions may escalate into negative externalities (Turner 1999) and produce a sense of paralysis (Gray 2008). In Teriberka people experienced sorrow: the place that former migrants called their own was now unable to provide them with the life they wanted. A villager said: 'How can people live in Teriberka after they lived in Norway? This is a big question…'

The previous glory of Teriberka, its continuous decline, and the emotions related to migration became unbearable. We saw the tears and despair of former migrants, and people talked about some villagers wanting to hurt themselves – those who could not bear the pain of the destruction of their home community. Households longed to move, and internal remigration occurred, which is common after return migration (Cassarino 2004) and emphasises the emotional strain and stress in return migration (Kunuroglu *et al.* 2016, Christou 2006). Both the self-confidence and money from migration contributed to such movements, while the Norwegian work experience also helped some people to obtain new jobs outside Teriberka. We found that, rather than inspiring positive development through the experience and emotional capital gained, return migration and the lack of state support for the exhausted village, produced negative feelings and increased negative emotional capital at the individual, group, and community levels, as Turner (1999) discusses. This produced a dichotomy between people who migrated and those who stayed in Teriberka. One of the kolkhoz leaders said: 'People went to Norway, earned easy money, and came back to poverty. We wanted to improve [the] situation here, at home.'

Studies on entrepreneurship in post-Soviet Russia reveal a legacy of the Soviet state in the form of people's negative attitudes to individual entrepreneurial activity (Petrovskaya, Zaverskiy, and Kiseleva 2017). In Teriberka, this legacy contributed to the failed effects of positive migration experiences. We saw almost no new private economic initiatives or investments of migration money into local businesses. An exception was the family of a woman who worked in Båtsfjord buying a boat and organising fishing tours, partly using migration money. We found no social initiatives from former migrants, though they met individually and celebrated holidays together. We explain this by the disillusionment following the migration and the deep depression in Teriberka. 'It looked like a village forgotten by the state, by businessmen, by everybody,' one of the migrants said. This made people indifferent, apathetic, and passive. People longed for the Soviet past when the state was responsible for many aspects of people's lives. A Russian businessman said: 'The problem is that depression in Teriberka influenced people in a negative way – they are not committed.' Apathy, as a state of indifference and the suppression or even absence of emotions (Marshall 2012), is destructive to people's minds. At the community level, apathy leads to the nullification of emotional capital. The absence of emotions such as concern, motivation, or passion, hinders positive activity and development; this characterised Teriberka after migration.

Twenty years later

After two decades, the experience of labour migration is still remembered in the continuously declining Teriberka. When interviewing Irina and Anna in 2015, we found that positive emotions still dominated their memories of Båtsfjord. Both women, now in their late 40s, smiled warmly when recalling migration. They were happy to host the Norwegian researcher and wished to return and work in fish processing. Irina dreamily said: 'I would love to go to Norway again.' Obviously, this wish was not only related to economic considerations; they were longing for their positive experiences and emotions during migration.

Sitting in Irina's flat, we saw the elegant furniture that greatly contrasted with the view from the window of the ruined buildings that are everywhere in contemporary Teriberka. Paintings of fishing boats on the wall and old souvenirs from Norway were visible. The women told us how groups of former migrants continue to meet as they did for years after returning, but lately more families are moving away and only a few of their fellow migrants still live in Teriberka. These two women gained skills in Båtsfjord that were useful at the factory in Teriberka, but the factory later closed and their skills lost value.

The movie *Leviathan*, a Golden Globe winner of 2015 and filmed in Teriberka, introduced a new era. Tourism is growing while the fisheries continue to decline. Large numbers of visitors arrive to see the coast and northern lights, but the consequent developments are not influencing the lives of former migrants or most local inhabitants. Some women said in the interviews that to start even a small business to provide food for tourists would be impossible for them: they did not believe that they would be able to sell their product, and they were afraid to run into problems regarding taxation or competition. They did not see themselves as entrepreneurs and the idea of undertaking any new activity seemed unrealistic and even exotic to them. Human capital increased during migration, but emotional capital did not appear to be a stable stock of resources to be drawn on – being relational, dynamic, and contextual.

However, the 'dream' of Teriberka as a Norwegian-type village is still alive and continues to circulate among people and in local and regional political debates. During our last talk with Irina and Anna, it became clear that the biggest chance to use the positive emotional capital gained by the migrants, at the community level, was immediately after their return. But this chance (and resource) was lost by not being addressed properly and in a timely manner; it might not even have been noticed at the community level.

Emotions in migration and post-return community development

The migration from Teriberka for work in the fish-processing industry in Båtsfjord involved emotions ranging from the deepest despair to the highest excitement for migrants, their families, and other people in the Russian community. While rational economic concerns are usually considered core motivations for labour migration, we have found that emotions strongly direct how migrants even recognise opportunities and formulate migration considerations. The focus on emotions revealed how difficult the insecurity and separation from children were. It highlighted how the desperate situation in Teriberka combined with the prospects of making 'big' money and dreams for positive outcomes of migration allowed migrants to negotiate the pain, guilt, and fear of separating from their children, families, and community. The joy of new experiences could grow, despite migrants' loneliness and disillusionment.

The focus on emotions helped us understand how the expectations and considerations before and during migration were mixed and yet important in forming migration experiences. The emotional aspects, including increasing knowledge, gaining experience, self-development, and the feeling that the migration eventually verified migrants' choices and improved their lives, are important factors in understanding migrants' increased human capital.

This chapter shows how migrants, after the return, used their experiences from abroad in individual everyday strategies but to a much lesser degree at the community level. It shows how new skills, self-awareness, and money made some migrants relocate in Russia after the migration ended, while others managed to secure their children's future. At the individual level, some migrants grew stronger and kept their pride and dignity in post-migration times by providing a more pleasant home environment for themselves and their families in the midst of the dilapidated ruin in which they live. We argue that the so-called 'conspicuous consumption' signals the strong emotions involved, such as shame, as well as self-esteem, and respect for human life, in a situation where these are threatened.

The migration experiences also caused collective frustration, by making the depressing situation in Teriberka more visible to migrants who returned, and fuelled a downward spiral of passivity and apathy. The positive emotional capital accumulated during migration was depleted by negative emotions in the post-return period. This capital was not used in a timely manner at the community level after migrants' return, and it did not catalyse development in the home village. It eventually vanished. The depletion of the community's positive emotional capital undermined motivation for actions that could produce development in the village. The lack of both local and state rural development policies, the Soviet state's legacy of scepticism of individual entrepreneurial activity, the vanished emotional capital, and apathy all worked in concert to hinder post-migration community development. Today, the remaining positive emotional experiences from migration exist mainly at the individual level. However, these memories and the dream of a Norwegian-type Teriberka actually became a part of the community's cognitive map, referred to and talked about 20 years later. This makes many people long for the former Soviet state.

Our study shows that emotions are highly important in migratory decisions, during migration, for the processes after return, and the outcomes of migration for the community of return. Focusing on emotions provides a new insight into post-migration community development and aids the understanding of how emotions are inherent in other structures and that lack of development after return migration relates to the depletion of the positive emotional capital gained during the migration. Emotional capital, which constitutes an important resource for positive action, may vanish through negative post-return emotions, strengthened by downward development of the home community in the absence of proper state rural public policies. Paradoxically, the focus on emotions highlights the importance of economy and politics but also reveals the significance of emotional aspects of these 'rational' structures. The chapter thus adds to the understanding of the ambiguity of international mobility in rural places, the role of emotions in migration, and the role of emotions in origin-community development after the migrants' return.

Acknowledgement

Riabova's work on the chapter was supported by the Ministry of Education and Science of the Russian Federation (project AAAA-A18-118051590115). The publication charges for this article have been funded by a grant from the publication fund of UiT The Arctic University of Norway. The authors wish to thank the external reviewers for their comments to the manuscript.

References

Ahmed, S. 2004. *The Cultural Politics of Emotion.* Edinburgh: Edinburgh University Press.

Appleyard, R.T. 1989. 'Migration and Development: Myths and Reality.' *International Migration Review* 23(3): 486–499. DOI:10.1177/019791838902300305.

Aure, M. 2008. 'Arbeidsmigrasjon fra Teriberka til Båtsfjord 1999–2002 [Labour Migration from Teriberka to Båtsfjord 1999–2002].' Ph.D. diss., University of Tromsø.

Aure, M. 2011. 'Borders of Understanding: Re-Making Frontiers in the Russian-Norwegian Contact Zone.' *Ethnopolitics* 10(2): 171–185. DOI:10.1080/17449057.2011.570981.

Aure, M. 2013. 'The Emotional Costs of Employment-Related Mobility.' *Norsk Geografisk Tidsskrift* 67(5): 284–294. DOI:10.1080/00291951.2013.847855.

Aure, M., A. Førde and T. Magnussen. 2018. 'Will Migrant Workers Rescue Rural Regions? Challenges of Creating Stability through Mobility.' *Journal of Rural Studies* 60: 52–59. DOI:10.1016/j.jrurstud.2018.03.005.

Benson, M. and N. Osbaldiston, 2014. *Understanding Lifestyle Migration.* London: Palgrave Macmillan.

Burkitt, I. 1997. 'Social Relationships and Emotions.' *Sociology* 31(1): 37–55. DOI:10.1177/0038038597031001004.

Carling, J. and F. Collins. 2018. 'Aspiration, Desire and Drivers of Migration.' *Journal of Ethnic and Migration Studies* 44(6): 909–926. DOI:10.1080/1369183X.2017.1384134.

Cassarino, J-P. 2004. 'Theorising Return Migration: The Conceptual Approach to Return Migrants Revisited.' *International Journal on Multicultural Societies* 6(2): 253–279.

Castles, S., H. de Haas and M.J. Miller. 2014. *The Age of Migration: International Population Movements in the Modern World.* New York: The Guildford Press.

Cerase, F.P. 1974. 'Expectations and Reality: A Case Study of Return Migration from the United States to Southern Italy.' *The International Migration Review* 8(2): 245–262.

Christou, A. 2006. *Narratives of Place, Culture and Identity: Second-Generation Greek-Americans Return 'Home.'* Amsterdam: Amsterdam University Press.

Favell, A. 2008. *Eurostars and Eurocities: Free Movement and Mobility in an Integrating Europe.* Oxford: Blackwell.

Gendron, B. 2017. 'Emotional Capital: The Set of Emotional Competencies as Professional and Vocational Skills in Emotional Works and Jobs.' *Revista espanola de educacion comparada* 29: 44–61. DOI:10.5944/reec.29.2017.17433.

Gray, B. 2008. 'Putting Emotion and Reflexivity to Work in Researching Migration.' *Sociology* 42(5): 935–952. DOI:10.1177/0038038508094571.

Halfacree, K. 2004. 'A Utopian Imagination in Migration's Terra Incognita? Acknowledging the Non-Economic Worlds of Migration Decision-Making.' *Population, Space and Place* 10(3): 239–253. DOI:10.1002/psp.326.

Heady, P. and L.L. Gambold Miller. 2006. 'Nostalgia and the Emotional Economy: A Comparative Look at Rural Russia.' In *Postsocialism: Politics and Emotions in Central and Eastern Europe*, edited by M. Svašek, 34–52. New York: Berghahn Books.

Hochschild, A.R. 1979. 'Emotion Work, Feeling Rules, and Social Structure.' *American Journal of Sociology* 85: 551–575. DOI:10.1086/227049.

Kalugina, Z.I. 2000. 'Survival Strategies of Enterprises and Families in the Contemporary Russian Countryside.' In *Russian Views of the Transition in the Rural Sector: Structure, Policy Outcomes, and Adaptive Responses*, edited by L.A. Norsworthy, 118–131. Washington, D.C.: The World Bank.

King, R. 1986. 'Return Migration and Regional Economic Development: An Overview.' In *Return Migration and Regional Economic Problems*, edited by R. King, 1–37. London: Routledge.

Kunuroglu, F., F. van de Vijver and K. Yagmur. 2016. 'Return Migration.' *Online Readings in Psychology and Culture* 8(2): 1–28. DOI:10.9707/2307-0919.1143.

Markussen, T. 2006. 'Moving Worlds. The Performativity of Affective Engagement.' *Feminist Theory* 7(3): 291–308. DOI:10.1177/1464700106069038.

Marshall, J.C. 2012. 'Apathy in Learning.' In *Encyclopedia of the Sciences of Learning*, edited by N.M. Seel, 275–276. Boston, MA: Springer US. DOI:10.1007/978-1-4419-1428-6_997.

Nowotny, H. 1981. 'Women in Public Life in Austria.' In *Access to Power: Cross-National Studies of Women and Elites*, edited by C.F. Epstein and R.L. Coser, 147–156. London: George Allen and Unwin.

O'Reilly, K. 2014. 'The Role of the Social Imaginary in Lifestyle Migration: Employing the Ontology of Practice Theory.' In *Understanding Lifestyle Migration*, edited by M. Benson and N. Osbaldiston, 211–234. London: Palgrave Macmillan.

Petrovskaya, I.A., S.M. Zaverskiy and E.S. Kiseleva. 2017. 'Attitude to Entrepreneurship in Russia: Three-Dimensional Institutional Approach.' *Advances in Systems Science and Applications* 2(17): 29–43. DOI:10.25728/assa.2017.17.2.483.

Reay, D. 2000. 'A Useful Extension of Bourdieu's Conceptual Framework? Emotional Capital as a Way of Understanding Mothers' Involvement in Their Children's Education?' *Sociological Review* 48(4): 568–585. DOI:10.1111/1467-954X.00233.

Riabova, L. 2001. 'Coping with Extinction: The Last Fishing Village on the Murman Coast.' In *The Reflexive North*, edited by N. Aarsæther and J.O. Bærenholdt, 115–138. Copenhagen: MOST and Nordic Council of Ministers.

Riabova, L. and L. Ivanova. 2009. 'Fishery Governance in Northwest Russia.' In *The Changing Governance of Renewable Natural Resources in Northwest Russia*, edited by S. Nysten-Haarala, 77–103. Farnham: Ashgate Publishing Limited.

Svašek, M. 2008. 'Who Cares? Families and Feelings in Movement.' *Journal of Intercultural Studies* 29(3): 213–230. DOI:10.1080/07256860802169170.

Svašek, M. 2010. 'On the Move: Emotions and Human Mobility.' *Journal of Ethnic and Migration Studies* 36(6): 865–880. DOI:10.1080/13691831003643322.

Tanner, K.J. 2005. 'Emotion, Gender and the Sustainability of Communities.' *The Journal of Community Informatics* 1(2): 121–139.

Turner, J.H. 1999. 'The Formation of Social Capital.' In *Social Capital: A Multifaceted Perspective*, edited by P. Dasgupta and I. Serageldin, 94–146. Washington, D.C.: World Bank.

Vathi, Z. and V. Duci. 2015. 'Making Other Dreams: The Impact of Migration on the Psychosocial Wellbeing of Albanian-origin Children and Young People upon Their Families' Return to Albania.' *Childhood*, 23(1): 53–68. DOI:10.1177/0907568214566078.

Voronov, M. 2013. 'Emotional Capital and Institutional Reproduction.' *Academy of Management Proceedings* 2013(1): 11152–11152. DOI:10.5465/ambpp.2013.11152abstract.

Wegren, S.K. 2016. 'The Quest for Rural Sustainability in Russia.' *Sustainability* 8(7). DOI:10.3390/su8070602.

Chapter 11

Does international labour migration affect internal mobility in rural Norway?

Marie Holm Slettebak

International and internal migration in the Norwegian countryside

During the last two decades, Norway has evolved from a relatively homogenous country to a more multicultural one with international migrants in all parts of the country. According to register data from Statistics Norway, the proportion that are international migrants has increased from 5.3 per cent in 2000 to 14.4 per cent in 2019 (Statistics Norway n.d.). In addition to the arrival of refugees, it is particularly the enlargement of the European Union (EU) to the east, starting in 2004, that sparked an unprecedented increase in migration to Norway. These 'new' labour migrants, originating in eastern Europe, have, to a larger degree than other migrants, settled outside Norway's urban regions (Rye and Slettebak 2020). Therefore, many rural areas previously unfamiliar with international migration have experienced a large influx of labour migrants.

The large body of academic literature discussing the impact of international migration on native-born workers is mostly focused on wages, employment and other outcomes related to *social* mobility (See, e.g. Blau and Kahn 2012, Card 2009, Hoen, Markussen and Røed 2018). Less attention has been paid to the effect on *geographic* mobility. Particularly in Europe, this is an under-researched field. Further, the extant research has little focus on rural areas.

This chapter offers an examination of whether international labour migration to rural areas has had any effect on the internal mobility patterns of 'natives,' that is: people born in Norway (note that the term 'native,' which is commonly used in the literature to refer to someone that is born in a particular country, does not refer to ethnicity). Are international migrants only adding to the population, or are they replacing other in-migrants and pushing out similarly skilled workers, or creating new inflows of internal migrants? These questions are interesting and important for three reasons.

First, answering these questions provides important insight into the role of eastern European labour migrants in rural labour markets and their effect on Norwegian-born workers. Although there seems to be agreement in the public discourse that international labour migration has been positive for the Norwegian economy in general, worries regarding low-wage competition, displacement effects, and increasing social inequality have been voiced, researched, and debated (Friberg 2016). Second, the questions are demographically interesting – particularly in rural areas. Many rural areas struggle with depopulation, and the literature abounds with research on how international migration can rescue rural regions that are struggling with diminishing and aging populations (see Aure, Førde and Magnussen 2018, Bayona-i-Carrasco and Gil-Alonso 2013). Hedberg and Haandrikman (2014) argue that international migrants are repopulating rural areas and can be seen as a rural 'demographic refill.' How international migration might also affect native-born inflows or outflows is an important part of this picture and of importance to rural communities' future demographic development. Third, these questions are methodologically interesting, as many studies use spatial variations in international migration to study the effects of migration on the labour market outcomes (wages, employment, etc.) of native-born workers. However, a potential weakness in previous studies is that labour markets are not closed, and people can selectively move in or out in response to the effects of migration from abroad. If so, the effects of international migration will be spread across the country and thus appear weaker (Borjas 2003). Although many researchers acknowledge this potential weakness, previous studies on the relationship between native-born internal mobility and international migration is limited. Most of the research has been conducted in the US, and only a few studies have focused on Europe.

The present analysis was conducted using Norwegian public register data from 2005 to 2015 at the municipality level. The Norwegian case is interesting due to the sudden increase in international labour migration. Further, the availability of high-quality register data at the municipality level provides an opportunity to examine the consequences of this increase in rural areas, which has been less explored, as international migration to western countries has, historically, been an urban phenomenon (see Rye and O'Reilly, Chapter 1).

Connecting international and internal migration: theoretical perspectives

According to King and Skeldon (2010), the field of migration studies has traditionally been split in two, as students of international and internal migration use different literatures, concepts, and methods. This chapter attempts to bridge this gap by discussing international and internal migration in interaction.

The effect of international migration on native internal mobility

According to Borjas (2003), the laws of supply and demand have clear implications for how international migration affects the labour market in the short run. The entry of international migrants into a certain area will create a supply shock that lowers the wages of competing workers, that is, workers who have the same types of skills. Workers with complementary skills, however, will experience increased wages as their skills become more valuable. Thus, according to classic economic theory, international migration should affect the wages and employment opportunities for native-born workers. However, a large number of studies have provided mixed and conflicting results (Blau and Kahn 2012, Card 2009, Borjas 2003). Many of these studies exploit the spatial variations in international migrants across the country to study the effect of international migration. The concern with this approach is that local labour markets are not closed – natives may respond to the impact of migration on the labour market by moving their labour or capital to another labour market, or they may avoid moving into a particular area. In this case, the effect of international migration is spread throughout the country, so that many towns and cities are affected – not just the places that received the international migrants (Borjas 2003). One of the most-cited examples in the literature is Card's (1990) analysis of the labour market in Miami, Florida, after the Mariel boatlift (the mass emigration of Cubans to the US in 1980), which increased Miami's labour force by seven per cent without affecting the wages or unemployment rates of native workers. Card suggests that one of the reasons for this wage stability was that the net migration of natives and earlier international migrants slowed considerably after the boatlift. This is considered a possible explanation for the mixed and conflicting results in the literature.

Despite the above, another possible explanation for the conflicting results is that the actual competition between labour migrants and natives is much more limited than classic economic theory would suggest. Within dual (or segmented) labour market theory, it is argued that the labour market has become increasingly divided into a primary and secondary sector (Doeringer and Piore 1971, Piore 1979). The jobs in the primary sector are secure and often high paying, and mainly reserved for natives. The jobs in the secondary sector are not secure, often low-paying and require few skills. Native workers are often unwilling to accept jobs in the secondary labour market, not just because of the low income they yield, as conventional economic theory would suggest, but because they signify or confer low status (Piore 1979). This might limit the competition between natives and labour migrants and explain why the effect on wages has been found to be small or non-existent in many studies.

Previous research on the connection between international migration and native-born internal mobility is limited, particularly in Europe. Much of the discussion also revolves around cities and metropolitan areas, while rural areas have not been in focus. In the US, where most of the empirical work on this topic is done, research has produced conflicting results. In 1996, demographer William Frey claimed that immigration was creating social and demographic divisions across the national landscape, which he labelled 'demographic balkanization in America.' Part of the reason for this division, according to Frey, is that 'there is a unique, accentuated outmigration of low-income, less-skilled domestic migrants from high immigration areas' (Frey 1996, 741). Wright, Ellis and Reibel (1997), however, argue that the cause of net migration's loss of natives in the large cities is more likely a result of industrial restructuring than of competition with international migrants. They found that the net migration of the native-born workers to metropolitan areas is either positively related or unrelated to international migration.

Labour economists have also presented contrasting results as they have entered the debate. Contrary to the demographic balkanisation hypothesis (that immigration leads to native out-migration), Card and DiNardo (2000) found that – if anything – increases of international migrants in specific skill groups lead to small *increases* in the population of native-born workers in the same skill group. Card (2001) found that intercity mobility rates of natives and earlier international migrants are insensitive to new inflows of international migrants. In other words, the effect of immigration was minimal, and, as a result, cities that received many international migrants expanded their labour markets. By contrast, Borjas, Freeman, and Katz (1997) found evidence that native migration flows respond to local influxes of international migrants. In a more recent study, Borjas (2006) found that international migration is associated with lower in-migration rates and higher out-migration rates of natives. At the metropolitan area level, he found that, for every 10 international migrants who choose to enter an area, between three and six natives will choose to not to live in that area.

In the few studies from Europe, the findings are less conflicting and suggest a clear connection between international migration and internal mobility. In the UK, Hatton and Tani (2005) finds consistently negative correlations between immigration to a region from abroad and in-migration from other regions. They conclude that these results suggest that internal migration is one of the mechanisms through which regional labour markets adjust to immigration shocks. In Italy, Brücker, Fachin, and Venturini (2011) have studied the effect of international migration on international mobility from poor to wealthy regions and found that the presence of international migrants significantly discourages internal mobility. Mocetti and Porello (2010) also investigated the relationship between native internal mobility and international migrants in Italy, but studied the differential impact by skill level. They found that international migration has a positive effect on inflows of highly educated natives, while displacing low-educated natives.

Summing up, though previous research is limited, the majority has found a connection between international migration and native-born workers' internal mobility. Although a few US studies find that immigration leads to increases in the native population, most of the studies find that higher rates of immigration are followed by fewer natives choosing to live in a particular area, either by moving out or avoiding moving in.

Relevant factors beyond the labour market

While this study's main argument is that the possible connection between international labour migration and native-born internal mobility is due to mechanisms in the labour market, there are also other factors beyond the labour market that are relevant to consider. First, the housing market can influence decisions about moving. An increasing number of labour migrants in a municipality often puts pressure on the housing market, leading to higher prices (Gonzalez and Ortega 2013, Saiz 2007). This might also affect native-born migration. Mocetti and Porello (2010) found a significant negative effect of higher housing prices on native net migration, which suggests that higher housing costs reduce labour mobility and deflate income prospects in a region.

Second, a large and diverse body of literature exists on the issue of residential segregation and international migrants' concentration in urban neighbourhoods. Several studies have found that the native-born population increasingly flees or/and avoids neighbourhoods with high proportions of international migrants (Brama 2006, Crowder, Hall, and Tolnay 2011, Wessel and Nordvik 2019). Although this strand of the literature cannot be ruled irrelevant for this study, it can be argued that the processes at the neighbourhood level in the cities are distinct from migration at the municipality level in rural areas, the topic with which this study is concerned. While attitudes toward international migrants or high-immigration areas might affect neighbourhood choices within cities, these are less likely to lead to migration patterns across greater distances.

The Norwegian case

While previous research has treated international migrants as one group, the focus in this chapter is on a specific group of international migrants, namely labour migrants from the newest EU countries. In 2005, approximately 2,600 labour migrants from post-communist EU countries (in this chapter referred to as 'EU11 labour migrants') were residing in Norway, compared with more than 115,000 in 2015. While previous labour migrants and refugees often settled in urban areas, the labour migrants from EU11 displayed a settlement pattern more representative of the general population. In 2015, 2.24 per cent of the population in the average rural municipality were EU11 labour migrants, compared with 2.10 per cent in urban municipalities. These people were, however, very unevenly distributed across rural Norway – some municipalities have received many, while others have received very few (Rye and Slettebak 2020).

The majority – more than 75 per cent – of EU11 labour migrants in Norway are registered as being employed in manual and low-skilled work. They are overrepresented in agriculture, fish processing, the shipyard industry, hotels, cleaning, construction work, and transportation. Only six per cent work in technical, administrative, or academic occupations, compared with 50 per cent of Norwegian-born workers (Friberg 2016). This means that Norwegian-born workers with higher levels of education face little competition from this group of migrants, while the low-skilled potentially do.

To this author's knowledge, no previous research has been conducted in Norway to study the connection between international migrants and Norwegian-born workers' internal mobility. However, some studies exist on the effects of international migration on native workers' wages and employment. Bratsberg and Raaum (2012) studied the construction industry and found that professions with high international labour migration experience significantly lower growth in wages. They also found that international labour migration increases the probability of low-skilled natives leaving the workforce. Bratsberg *et al.* (2014), looking at the entire Norwegian labour market, found that migration from low-income countries affects the income and employment of international migrants already in Norway, but has less of an effect on Norwegian-born workers. More recently, Hoen, Markussen and Røed (2018) found that migration from low-income countries has steepened the social gradient in natives' labour market outcomes. While exposure to migrants from low-income countries lowers wages and employment for lower-class natives, it affects natives in the higher classes by raising their expected earnings. Similarly, Slettebak (in-press) found that labour migration increases income inequality within the native population in rural areas.

Although the findings are somewhat mixed, previous research suggests that international labour migration has affected the wages and employment of Norwegian-born workers. The question to be answered in this chapter is whether these effects affect settlement decisions. An important question in this regard is whether employment/job opportunities are important factors for explaining out- and in-migration in rural Norway. Sørlie (2009) argues that employment is actually a more important motivation for moving into or staying in the peripheral regions of Norway than in the country in general. Part of the reason for this phenomenon is that there are fewer available jobs in the periphery, which puts more focus on the necessity of employment. Similarly, Grimsrud (2011) found that work and family are the most important reasons for in-migration to rural areas, and that the 'counter-urbanisation story'– depicting urban to rural migration as motivated by anti-urban preferences – is not a good fit for rural Norway.

Assuming that low-skilled labour migrants have a negative effect on the employment and wages of less-ducated workers and a positive effect on the employment of highly educated ones, and assuming that this is relevant for their settlement decisions, the following hypotheses can be tested:

H1: Increasing international labour migration is followed by *higher out-migration* of *less-educated* Norwegian-born people.

H2: Increasing international labour migration is followed by *lower in-migration* of *less-educated* Norwegian-born people.
H3: Increasing international labour migration is followed by *higher in-migration* of *highly educated* Norwegian-born people.
H4: Increasing international labour migration is followed by *lower out-migration* of *highly educated* Norwegian-born people.

It is important to note that there is an essential difference among the hypotheses concerning out- and in-migration. For instance, H1 assumes that the weakened position of lower educated people in the labour market will increase their chance of leaving the particular municipality. H2, however, simply assumes that lower educated people, to a larger degree, will avoid the particular municipality. It is possible to argue that leaving a place is a much stronger statement than avoiding one place in favour of another.

Another relevant point in this regard is that Norway and the other Nordic countries are characterised by a large welfare state with universal benefits, including free education and health care. Being a part of what Esping-Andersen (1990) calls the 'social democratic welfare states regimes,' the dependence on the market is weaker in Norway than in other less de-commodifying welfare states, such as in the US, UK, or southern Europe. Such features of the Norwegian case could imply weaker incentives to relocate for economic reasons.

Lastly, Norway's geographic and demographic features have implications for the frequency of migration. In many western European countries, people move frequently and in all directions among populous regions with short distances between them. Large distances and relatively small populations, however, characterise the Nordic countries. This has implications for mobility patterns. In Norway, relocation often implies moving to another part of the country and across a great distance. Therefore, it is natural, according to Sørlie (2010), that, compared with the populations of many other western European countries, Norwegians move less often.

Researching movements in rural municipalities

The analysis is based on municipal level register data from 2005 to 2015. All data were obtained or ordered from Statistics Norway or Microdata.no, a service that gives researchers access to microdata from Statistics Norway.

Defining the 'rural'

This analysis focuses on rural municipalities. When defining what constitutes a rural or urban municipality, a conventional approach, building on Almås and Elden (1997) and Farstad, Rye, and Almås (2009), has been applied to define rural municipalities according to three criteria:

1) *Centrality*: this refers to the number of jobs and service functions that can be reached by car in 90 minutes for thc average inhabitant in the municipality. A scale from one to six is constructed, where 'six' is the least central (Statistics Norway's centrality scale, see Høydahl 2017). Municipalities at levels five and six (238 municipalities) are defined as 'rural.' These are the municipalities described as least and second-least central by Statistics Norway.
2) *Settlement density*: this refers to the percentage of the population residing in 'sparsely populated areas' (settlements with more than 200 people in houses less than 50 meters apart are *not* sparsely populated). Municipalities are defined as 'rural' according to this criterion if more than 50 per cent of the population resided in a sparsely populated area in 2016.
3) *Labour markets*: this is the percentage of the working population employed in the primary sector (agriculture, fisheries, forestry). Municipalities are defined as 'rural' according to this criterion if more than seven per cent of the working population was employed in the primary sector in 2016.

A municipality is categorised as rural if at least one of these criteria are met; this yielded 271 'rural' municipalities in Norway, out of 426. Roughly 18 per cent of the Norwegian population resides in a rural municipality. The other remaining municipalities are neither peripheral nor characterised by a dispersed settlement structure or strong primary industries; they are defined as 'urban.'

Measuring internal mobility among Norwegian-born people

The dependent variables measure the municipal out- and in-migration of high and low educated Norwegian-born people. The dependent variables were constructed using Microdata.no. Due to confidentiality concerns, the output from this platform is noise inflicted. However, no counts (numbers) are noise inflicted by more than +/-5 and the noise is random and should not affect the conclusion of this analysis.

Out-migration is defined as being registered as settled in the municipality in year *t*, but registered in a different municipality in year t+1 (1 January). In-migration is defined as being registered as settled in the municipality in year *t*, but registered in a different municipality in year t-1. Only internal mobility is included. Compared with internal mobility, the frequency of international in- and out-migration is very low among Norwegians, thus the exclusion of this type of mobility is not expected to affect the results.

A distinction is made between less and highly educated people to look for patterns in mobility based on educational level. In- and out-migrants over the age of 25 are categorised as 'highly educated' if they have education to the college or university level, and as 'less educated' if they do not have such an education. The age limit of 25 was set to avoid including too many children and young adults who have not yet finished their education.

This resulted in six dependent variables: out-migration (all), out-migration of the highly educated, out-migration of the less educated, in-migration (all), in-migration of the highly educated and in-migration of the less educated. The variables are measured as proportions, that is, what per cent moved out or in during a specific year (number/total number in group*100).

Independent variables

In this chapter, 'international migrants' are defined as people born in a foreign country with two foreign-born parents. International migrants are only registered as settled in a municipality if they have lived in Norway for at least six months. This means that migrants on shorter stays, for example seasonal workers staying only for the summer, are not included in the data. This is due to theoretical considerations and lack of data for this group over time.

The main independent variable measures the proportion of EU11 labour migrants in a municipality each year. EU11 refers to migrants from the (post-communist) countries that joined the EU after 2004. This includes migrants from Poland, Lithuania, Latvia, Estonia, Czech Republic, Slovakia, Hungary, Slovenia, Romania, Croatia, and Bulgaria. The term '*labour* migrant' refers to their main reason for migration and has been used in Norwegian registries since 1989. This includes those who have been granted a work permit or, in the case of EU/EEA (European Economic Area) citizens, who are registered via the EEA registration (Dzamarija 2013). All EU/EEA citizens who intend to stay in Norway for more than three months need to register.

In addition, the study controls for *refugees,* a term that includes all migrants who have a residence permit in Norway and where refugee status has been given as the reason for their residence application. This includes asylum seekers who have been granted residence, those who have been granted residence on humanitarian grounds and quota refugees (UN refugees) (Dzamarija 2013).

Unemployment measures the proportion of the labour force (workers 15–74 years) who are registered as unemployed. Monthly data were obtained from Statistics Norway for 2005 through 2014. The variable was constructed by calculating the average for each year.

Median income measures the median income for households after tax each year. The numbers have been adjusted for inflation using 2015 as the base. The numbers are divided by 100,000 to obtain larger units. Descriptive statistics for all variables are presented in Table 11.1.

Testing the connection between international labour migration and natives' internal mobility patterns

The analysis uses fixed effects linear regression models, which explore the relationship between the independent and dependent variables within a given entity, municipalities in this case. Fixed effects models remove the effect of all time-invariant variables, which means that only variables that have changed between 2005 and 2015 can affect the results. All models are also controlled for year, making them time and entity fixed effects regression models.

Table 11.1 displays the results of a fixed effects linear regression with two dependent variables, the out- and in-migration of Norwegian-born people in rural municipalities. Starting with out-migration, we see that the effect is close to zero and not statistically significant. Controlling for changes in the proportion of refugees, unemployment, and median income (adjusted for inflation) does not alter this result, but clearly shows that increasing unemployment and median income are followed by higher levels of out-migration. Moving on to the in-migration models, we see that, when the proportion of EU11 labour migrants increases, the in-migration rate increases, but again the results are not significant.

Overall, Table 11.2 depicts a very weak and insignificant relationship between the arrival of EU11 labour migrants and the general moving patterns of Norwegian-born people in rural regions.

In Table 11.3, however, the dependent variables distinguish between the out- and in-migration of people with lower and higher education, and a pattern emerges between EU11 labour migrants and the moving patterns of higher educated Norwegian-born people. When the proportion of EU11 labour migrants increases with one per cent, the out-migration of higher educated people decreases, and the rate of in-migration increases. The effect on the less educated is close to zero and not significant.

Table 11.1 Descriptive statistics (variables used in Tables 11.2 and 11.3)

	Min	*Max*	*Mean*	*SD*
Out-migration	1.10	9.20	3.39	1.01
In-migration	0	9.2	2.90	1.02
Out-migration, low educated	0	8.79	2.04	0.83
Out-migration, high educated	0	26.67	5.40	3.01
In-migration, low educated	0	8.15	2.08	0.89
In-migration, high educated	0	69.51	4.26	3.15
EU11 labour migrants	0	14.52	1.01	1.55
Refugees	0	9.60	0.88	1.01
Unemployment	0.27	10.31	2.43	1.30
Median income (100,000 NOK) – adjusted	3.03	6.57	4.39	0.55

Source: Statistics Norway and Microdata.no

Table 11.2 Fixed effects linear regression, out-migration and in-migration of Norwegian-born

	Out-migration		*In-migration*	
EU11 labour migrants, t-1	-0.009 (0.016)	-0.008 (0.017)	0.012 (0.017)	0.005 (0.017)
Refugees t-1		-0.028 (0.033)		-0.043 (0.033)
Unemployment t-1		**0.087***** (0.023)		-0.022 (0.024)
Median income t-1 (adjusted)		**0.350**** (0.119)		-0.220 (0.121)
Constant	3.524*** (0.041)	1.902*** (0.477)	2.776*** (0.041)	3.726*** (0.486)
R2within	0.025	0.034	0.023	0.025
N	2,710	2,710	2,710	2,710
Year control	Yes	Yes	Yes	Yes

Standard errors in parenthesis

***Sig<=0.001, **Sig<=0.01, *Sig<=0.05

Source: Statistics Norway and Microdata.no

Two issues can be raised concerning these models. First, changes in the proportion of labour migrants can be affected – particularly in smaller municipalities – by the dependent variables. For instance, the *number* of labour migrants may remain unchanged, but the *proportion* may increase due to the out-migration of Norwegian-born people. Second, it could be problematic to study proportions in the smallest municipalities, as they have only a few hundred inhabitants. In the descriptive statistics in Table 11.1, it is clear that relative measures, particularly of the in- and out-migration of highly educated people, are problematic when the original numbers are too small.

Neither of these weaknesses is present in models with frequencies instead of proportions. Further, both weaknesses are mainly related to the smallest municipalities. Additional analyses have been conducted to test the robustness of the models presented; first by running the analysis from Table 11.3, but without the smallest municipalities included, and, second, by running the analyses using frequencies instead of proportions.

Only the coefficient for EU11 migrants is presented in Table 11.4, but all control variables used in Table 11.3 were also used in these analyses. The first row shows the results from the models, which are identical to the models in Table 11.3, though the smallest municipalities (those with fewer than 900 inhabitants) are excluded. The effect of EU11 labour migration on out- and in-migration of Norwegian-born people is strongly reduced and no longer significant, which suggests that a few very small municipalities affected the regression and might have overestimated the effect.

Table 11.3 Fixed effects linear regression, out- and in-migration of low- and high-educated Norwegian-born

	Out-migration, low educated		*Out-migration, high educated*		*In-migration, low educated*		*In-migration, high educated*	
EU11 labour migrants, t-1	-0.020	-0.018	**-0.148***	**-0.159***	0.013	0.015	**0.155***	**0.154***
	(0.016)	(0.017)	(0.062)	(0.065)	(0.016)	(0.017)	(0.072)	(0.075)
Refugees t-1		-0.021		-0.117		-0.030		-0.062
		(0.033)		(0.124)		(0.032)		(0.143)
Unemployment t-1		**0.063****		0.142		0.021		**-0.323****
		(0.023)		(0.088)		(0.023)		(0.101)
Median income t-1		**0.306***		0.285		0.191		-0.997
		(0.119)		(0.454)		(0.118)		(0.523)
Constant	2.109***	0.736	6.808***	5.309**	2.021***	1.237**	4.291***	9.269***
	(0.041)	(0.478)	(0.154)	(1.818)	(0.040)	(0.472)	(0.178)	(2.091)
R2within	0.015	0.021	0.068	0.070	0.017	0.019	0.007	0.012
N	2,710	2,710	2,710	2,710	2,710	2,710	2,710	2,710
Year control	Yes	Yes	Yes	Yes	Yes	Yes	Yes	Yes

Standard errors in parenthesis

***Sig<=0.001, **Sig<=0.01, *Sig<=0.05

Source: Statistics Norway and Microdata.no

Table 11.4 Sensitivity analysis. Fixed effects linear regression with different model specifications

	Out-migration, low educated	*Out-migration, high educated*	*In-migration, low educated*	*In-migration, high educated*
EU11 labour migrants, t-1 N=2,550 (excluding small municipalities) **Proportions**	-0.023 (0.016)	-0.054 (0.055)	0.006 (0.016)	0.060 (0.060)
EU11 labour migrants, t-1 N=2710 **Frequencies**	**0.012**** (0.004)	**0.009**** (0.003)	**0.012**** (0.004)	0.005 (0.004)
EU11 labour migrants, t-1 N=2,550 (excluding large municipalities) **Frequencies**	-0.010 (0.006)	-0.004 (0.004)	0.008 (0.006)	**0.010*** (0.005)

(Standard errors in parenthesis)

***Sig<=0.001, **Sig<=0.01, *Sig<=0.05.

Source: Statistics Norway and Microdata.no

The second row depicts the results from models that are identical to those in Table 11.3, except that all variables are measuring frequencies, instead of proportions. The results are drastically different; for instance, the results display a significant positive relationship between EU11 migrants and out-migration. The reason is that Norway's rural municipalities are of very different sizes, which means that the larger rural municipalities will have an extremely strong effect in a model with frequencies. Because a few of the larger municipalities (with roughly 18,000 inhabitants) experienced an increase in out-migration that was relatively small, but very high in absolute numbers, the results changed.

In the third row, the 16 largest rural municipalities (which have more than 8,000 inhabitants) have been removed from the analysis. The results from these regressions are similar to the results in Table 11.3, thus strengthening the conclusion that the connection between international labour migration and Norwegian-born internal migration is weak and insignificant. When the number of EU11 labour migrants increases with one per cent, out-migration decreases and in-migration increases, but the coefficients are close to zero and not significant, except for the in-migration of more highly educated people.

Models with control for housing prices (based on the price per square meter) were tested as well, but about half of the rural municipalities have missing values for this variable, so it is therefore not included in the presented analyses. The results were not altered after controlling for housing prices, which had no significant effect on internal migration in rural municipalities.

My overall interpretation of the results is that there is no significant systematic connection between international labour migration and Norwegian-born internal mobility patterns. There is a tendency for higher international labour migration to attract more highly educated natives, but this correlation is weak and not robust enough to argue that there is any clear connection between these two phenomena.

International labour migration as demographic refill and expansion of the rural labour market: discussion and conclusion

Norway's rural areas have experienced an unprecedented increase in labour-related migration in the years since the enlargement of the EU. The present analyses show that, overall, the internal migration of Norwegian-born people in rural areas is unaffected by international labour migration. This has several important implications.

First, the results suggest that, overall, the migrant's role in the rural labour market is mainly an expansion – new jobs are created and filled by migrants. There are no signs of a displacement of less-educated Norwegian-born people. Municipalities that, over time, have received many labour migrants have seen no significant change in the in- and out-migration of their less-educated workers. The hypotheses claiming there should be visible changes rest on two main assumptions. First, that the less-educated workers would, to some degree, compete with the migrants and that their wages and employment opportunities are negatively affected by the migrants' presence. Second, it was assumed that these effects are relevant and important enough to affect workers' settlement decisions. We can speculate that both assumptions, to some degree, are invalid. Although an analysis of settlement decisions cannot say anything directly about labour market outcomes for natives, the results suggest that the effect of international labour migration on natives' wages and employment cannot be particularly strong in rural areas. If it was, we would likely see some change, if not in out-migration (which could be counteracted by a de-commodifying welfare state or strong place attachment), at least in in-migration of the less educated. If increasing international labour migration has no effect on the in-migration of Norwegian-born people without a higher education, it likely means that their employment opportunities are not negatively affected in any major way. Rather than labour migrants and less-educated Norwegian-born workers being in competition, it seems more likely that they are often operating in different segments of the labour market (Piore 1979). Further, even if international labour migration has a significant effect on natives' wages and employment opportunities, which some Norwegian studies have indicated (Bratsberg and Raaum 2012, Hoen, Markussen, and Roed 2018, Slettebak in press) these effects might not be sufficient to affect the settlement decisions of Norwegian-born workers. Strong place attachment to the rural area, or a strongly de-commodifying welfare state, could counteract the economic incentives and perhaps explain why the (rural) Norwegian case is different from the British, Italian, or American cases.

Despite the above, an alternative explanation, one that involves the economic climate of the times, should also be discussed. It is possible to argue that, although we cannot observe any systematic effects of international labour migration on internal migration, we do not know what would have happened in a counterfactual scenario where rural industries experienced booms (such as the fish-farming industry in Norway, which has also occurred during the period under study), but without the option of recruiting labour migrants. One possibility is perhaps the higher in-migration of natives to the booming industry. In this scenario, international labour migrants have cancelled out the in-migration of natives. In other words, the results suggest that labour migrants' roles in the rural labour market are mainly an expansion, but they might have replaced (some) natives who would otherwise have migrated to the municipalities with booming industries. However, it is unlikely that employers within, for instance, the fish-processing industry, would have managed to recruit enough native workers, at least not without improving wages and working conditions. Without cheap and flexible labour, higher capital investments (such as investments in machines) might have been a more likely development.

Further, it is interesting that this expansion, both in the labour market and in the population in general, has not resulted in a higher demand for more highly educated native workers. In many cases, international migration has led to a significantly higher number of inhabitants, which in theory would require increasing numbers of doctors, nurses, teachers, and other professions that require strong Norwegian language skills and higher education. Although there is a tendency toward a lower net-loss of highly educated workers in municipalities with larger labour migrant populations, this correlation is weak and not systematic. A possible explanation could be that, in many peripheral municipalities, labour migrants (or other migrants) themselves help to fill these high-competence jobs. Although the majority of EU11 labour migrants work in manual and low-skilled jobs (Friberg 2016), not all of them do. In a study of the regions of western Norway, Båtevik and Grimsrud (2017) found that the peripheral regions receive relatively more high-competence workers, such as those in the academic professions, through international labour migration than the central regions do, thus reducing the traditional 'peripheral disadvantages.' They also, however, note that there are big differences among the peripheral regions. Some receive many highly skilled migrants, while others receive very few, which might help explain the weak and unsystematic results emerging from this analysis.

Second, the results clearly show that international labour migration benefits rural municipalities that are otherwise struggling with depopulation. While many studies reviewed in this chapter found that international migration is associated with increasing rates of out-migration among natives, no such effects are found in the case of rural Norway. Labour migrants from EU11 are mainly adding to the population, giving a much-needed 'demographic refill' to many rural areas (Hedberg and Haandrikman 2014).

Third, the results of these analyses show that it is unlikely that the results from spatial correlation exercises on the effect of international migration on native wages and employment are biased, due to the selective out-migration of natives in rural Norway. Further research is required to determine whether these results are more generally representative for rural areas in western Europe.

Acknowledgements

The chapter is result of the 2017–2022 Global Labour in Rural Societies research project financed by the Norwegian Research Council (grant no. 261854/F10). The author wishes to thank the external reviewers for their comments on the manuscript. Funding from the Norwegian University of Science and Technology has made possible open access publishing of the chapter.

References

Almås, R and K.M. Elden. 1997. *Den rurale dimensjonen. En teoretisk og geografisk avgrensning,* Trondheim: Centre for Rural Research.

Aure, M., A. Førde and T. Magnussen. 2018. 'Will Migrant Workers Rescue Rural Regions? Challenges of Creating Stability through Mobility.' *Journal of Rural Studies* 60: 52–59. doi.org/10.1016/j.jrurstud.2018.03.005.

Bayona-i-Carrasco, J. and F. Gil-Alonso. 2013. 'Is Foreign Immigration the Solution to Rural Depopulation? The Case of Catalonia (1996–2009).' *Sociologia Ruralis* 53(1): 26–51. doi.org/10.1111/j.1467-9523.2012.00577.x.

Blau, F. and L. Kahn. 2012. 'Immigration and the Distribution of Incomes.' *NBER Working Paper Series*: 18515. doi.org/10.3386/w18515.

Borjas, G. 2003. 'The Labor Demand Curve is Downward Sloping: Reexamining the Impact of Immigration on the Labor Market.' *Quarterly Journal of Economics* cxviii(4): 1335–1374.

Borjas, G. 2006. 'Native Internal Migration and the Labor Market Impact of Immigration.' *The Journal of Human Resources* 41(2): 221–258.

Borjas, G., R.B. Freeman and L.F. Katz. 1997. 'How Much do Immigration and Trade Affect Labor Market Outcomes?' *Brookings Papers on Economic Activity* 1997(1): 1–90. doi.org/10.2307/2534701.

Brama, A. 2006. '"White flight"? The production and reproduction of immigrant concentration areas in Swedish cities, 1990–2000.' *Urban Studies* 43(7): 1127. doi.org/10.1080/00420980500406736.

Bratsberg, B. and O. Raaum. 2012. 'Immigration and Wages: Evidence from Construction.' *Economic Journal* 122(565): 1177–1205. doi.org/10.1111/j.1468-0297.2012.02540.x.

Bratsberg, B., O. Raaum, M. Røed and P. Schøne. 2014. 'Immigration Wage Effects by Origin.' *Scandinavian Journal of Economics* 116(2): 356–393. doi.org/10.1111/sjoe.12053.

Brücker, H., S. Fachin and A. Venturini. 2011. 'Do Foreigners Replace Native Immigrants? A Panel Cointegration Analysis of Internal Migration in Italy.' *Economic Modelling* 28(3): 1078–1089. doi.org/10.1016/j.econmod.2010.11.020.

Båtevik, F.O. and G.M. Grimsrud. 2017. 'Kapittel 3: Nye sentrum–periferi-mønster.' In *Immateriell kapital*, edited by J.R. Andersen, E. Bjørhusdal, J.G. Nesse, T. Årethun, 49–68. Oslo: Universitetsforlaget.

Card, D. 1990. 'The Impact of the Mariel Boatlift on the Miami Labor Market.' *Industrial and Labor Relations Review* 43(2): 245–257. doi.org/10.1177/001979399004300205.

Card, D. 2001. 'Immigrant Inflows, Native Outflows, and the Local Labor Market Impacts of Higher Immigration.' *Journal of Labor Economics* 19(1): 22–64. doi.org/10.1086/209979.

Card, D. 2009. 'Immigration and Inequality.' *American Economic Review* 99(2): 1–21. doi.org/10.1257/aer.99.2.1.

Card, D. and J. DiNardo. 2000. 'Do Immigrant Inflows Lead to Native Outflows?' *American Economic Review* 90(2): 360–367. doi.org/10.1257/aer.90.2.360.

Crowder, K., M. Hall and S.E. Tolnay. 2011. 'Neighborhood Immigration and Native Out-Migration.' *American Sociological Review* 76(1): 25–47. doi.org/10.1177/0003122410396197.

Doeringer, P.B. and M. Piore. 1971. *Internal Labor Markets and Manpower Analysis*. New York: D.C Heath and Company.

Dzamarija M.T. 2013. *Innvandringsgrunn 1990–2011, hva vet vi og hvordan kan statistikken utnyttes?* Oslo: Statistisk sentralbyrå.

Esping-Andersen, G. 1990. *The Three Worlds of Welfare Capitalism*. Cambridge: Polity Press.

Farstad, M., J.F. Rye and R. Almås. 2009. *By, bygd og fritidsboliger 2008. Kommentert frekvensrapport,* Trondheim: Centre for Rural Research.

Frey, W. 1996. 'Immigration, Domestic Migration, and Demographic Balkanization in America: New Evidence for the 1990s.' *Population and Development Review* 22(4): 741–763. doi.org/10.2307/2137808.

Friberg, J.H. 2016. *Arbeidsmigrasjon. Hva vet vi om konsekvensene for norsk arbeidsliv, samfunn og økonomi?* Oslo: Fafo.

Gonzalez, L. and F. Ortega. 2013. 'Immigration and Housing Booms: Evidence from Apain*.' *Journal of Regional Science* 53(1): 37–59. doi.org/10.1111/jors.12010.

Grimsrud, G.M. 2011. 'How Well Does the "Counter-urbanisation Story" Travel to Other Countries? The Case of Norway.' *Population, Space and Place* 17(5): 642–655. doi.org/10.1002/psp.655.

Hatton, T.J. and M. Tani. 2005. 'Immigration and Inter-Regional Mobility in the UK, 1982–2000.' *Economic Journal* 115 (507): F342-F358. doi.org/10.1111/j.1468-0297.2005.01039.x.

Hedberg, C. and K. Haandrikman. 2014. 'Repopulation of the Swedish Countryside: Globalisation by International Migration.' *Journal of Rural Studies 34:* 128–138.

Hoen, M., S. Markussen and K. Røed. 2018. 'Immigration and Social Mobility.' *IDEAS Working Paper Series from RePEc*.

Høydahl, E. 2017. 'Ny sentralitetsindeks for kommunene.' *Statistics Norway.* Document 40.

King, R. and R. Skeldon. 2010. ' "Mind the Gap!" Integrating Approaches to Internal and International Migration.' *Journal of Ethnic and Migration Studies* 36(10): 1619–1646. doi.org/10.1080/1369183X.2010.489380.

Mocetti, S. and C. Porello. 2010. 'How Does Immigration Affect Native Internal Mobility? New Evidence from Italy.' *Regional Science and Urban Economics* 40(6): 427–439. doi.org/10.1016/j.regsciurbeco.2010.05.004.

Piore, M.J. 1979. *Birds of Passage. Migrant Labor and Industrial Societies*. New York: Cambridge University Press.

Rye, J.F. and M.H. Slettebak. 2020. 'The New Geography of Labour Migration: EU11 Migrants in Rural Norway.' *Journal of Rural Studies* 75: 125–131.

Saiz, A. 2007. 'Immigration and Housing Rents in American cities.' *Journal of Urban Economics* 61(2): 345–371. doi.org/10.1016/j.jue.2006.07.004.

Sørlie, K. 2009. *Bolyst og stedsattraktivitet: motiver for å flytte og bo i distriktene*. Oslo: Norsk institutt for by- og regionforskning.

Sørlie, K. 2010. 'Bosetting, flytting og regional utvikling.' In *Det norske samfunn*, edited by I. Frønes and L. Kjølsrød, 457–478. Oslo: Gyldendal akademisk.

Statistics Norway (n.d.) 'Innvandrere og norskfødte med innvandrerforeldre'. https://www.ssb.no/statbank/table/07110/.

Wessel, T. and V. Nordvik. 2019. 'Mixed Neighbourhoods and Native Out-mobility in the Oslo Region: The Importance of Parenthood.' *Urban Studies* 56(5): 885–905. doi.org/10.1177/0042098018768452.

Wright, R.A., M. Ellis and M. Reibel. 1997. 'The Linkage between Immigration and Internal Migration in Large Metropolitan Areas in the United States.' *Economic Geography* 73(2): 234–254. doi.org/10.1111/j.1944-8287.1997.tb00069.x.

Chapter 12

'If we do not have the pickers, we do not have the industry'

Rural UK under a Brexit shadow

Keith Halfacree

Introducing Brexit

The United Kingdom officially joined the European Economic Community (EEC) on 1 January 1973, a decision ratified in 1975 by a two-thirds majority in a referendum (Bailey and Budd 2019). While never one of the most Euro-enthusiastic of the 28 countries which, in January 2016, comprised what had by then become the European Union (EU), few commentators were ready for the political upheaval to come. In response to mounting anti-EU pressures within his Conservative Party and the success of the anti-EU UK Independence Party in the 2014 European elections, Prime Minister David Cameron tabled an 'in-out' referendum on UK EU membership for 23 June 2016. This poll involved voters responding 'yes' or 'no' to the simple question: 'Should the United Kingdom remain a member of the European Union or leave the European Union?' (Electoral Commission n.d.).

Cameron and many political commentators expected the referendum result to back the UK remaining in the EU, although surveys consistently showed the situation to be very tight. However, from the 72 per cent turnout (unexceptional in size if compared with General Election turnouts from 1945 until a 59 per cent nadir in 2001; Dempsey and Loft 2019), the result was: 51.9 per cent to leave, 48.1 per cent to remain, 0.08 per cent votes invalid (Bailey and Budd 2019, Electoral Commission n.d.). Supporters of what was termed Brexit (British exit) had won the day.

Notwithstanding much continuing uncertainty within what Bailey and Budd (2019, 157) sharply labelled 'a constitutional imbroglio moving towards a crisis,' this chapter explores some potential consequences of Brexit for the rural UK, a spatial focus underdeveloped to date. These are considered under four headings. First, withdrawal from the Common Agricultural Policy and other EU forms of economic support for rural businesses is evaluated. Second, implications of Brexit for EU-originating migrant labour, mostly involved in agriculture, are drawn out. Third, staying with international labour migrants, attention is focused on how the everyday lives of those who come in the future and those who live in the UK now may be changing with Brexit. Fourth, and drawing on all three previous consequences plus the electoral geography of the pro-Brexit vote, the chapter suggests that a 'revanchist rural' expressive representation has emerged, challenging the countryside's status as a diverse, welcoming and modern space, not least for international labour migrants.

Agricultural and other economic support

The most significant immediate economic consequence for the UK rural from Brexit is the withdrawal from the EU's Common Agricultural Policy (CAP). This prominent range of farming subsidies still absorbs around 38 per cent of the EU budget (Shucksmith 2019). Although a consistent net CAP budget contributor (Browne *et al.* 2016), in 2015, for example, the UK received over €4 billion from the CAP, of which 76 per cent comprised direct payments to farmers (Institute for Government 2020). Unsurprisingly, therefore, loss of this huge subsidy is of high prominence and concern for farmers' groups such as the National Farmers' Union (2019).

A strong clue to government thinking on how such substantial support to farmers may be (partly) replaced after Brexit comes from the 'Health and Harmony' consultation paper (Defra 2018, Downing and Coe 2018). This document, overseen by leading Brexiteer (as supporters of Brexit are labelled) and, at the time, the Environment Secretary, Michael Gove, emphasised in particular negative environmental impacts of modern agriculture. Outlining these helped politically to underpin the paper's proposals for a post-Brexit public support system for farmers prioritising grants not for agricultural production but for provision of 'public goods,' such as wildlife habitats and biodiversity, flood risk, climate change, air quality, public health, and access. In CAP terminology, it suggested an almost total shift from Pillar 1 (direct income support) to Pillar 2 (rural development support). Such an impression was consolidated by subsequent publication of the Agricultural Bill 2018 for England. This proposes an 'agricultural transition' that will phase out (land-based) Basic Payments (Pillar 1) by 2027, the long transition period required to work out the details. Further complexity comes from the suggestion that more-or-less different agricultural support measures will be rolled out in Wales, Scotland, and Northern Ireland (Downing and Coe 2018, Dwyer 2018, Messenger 2018).

Elsewhere, much work is required to engage with the 6,256 World Trade Organisation (WTO) tariff lines for agriculture and fisheries (Shucksmith 2019), which will come into play if no new trade deal with the EU is agreed. Although adopting WTO tariffs is a solution preferred by some Brexiteers, these tariffs on agricultural goods are typically high, with the intention of protecting domestic markets, and if the UK's agricultural trade with the EU becomes so ruled then exports could be hit very hard (House of Commons 2018). For example, over 95 per cent of exported UK sheep meat by volume is destined for the EU but, with a likely tariff of at least 50 per cent, this would become uncompetitive. The Agriculture and Horticulture Development Board argued that it would 'devastating' for the sector (House of Commons 2018).

Besides CAP funding supporting direct agricultural employment, rural regions of the UK also receive project funding and, hence, employment support from the EU's Structural Funds (Browne *et al.* 2016). Through the European Regional Development Fund (ERDF), there is support for innovation and research, small businesses, digital infrastructure provision, and decarbonising the economy. The European Social Fund (ESF) further supports labour mobility and development of education, skills, and institutional capacity. Although the UK is not a prime recipient of such funds, it still contains two Less Developed Regions (west Wales, Cornwall, and the Isles of Scilly) and 11 intermediate Transition Regions (Browne *et al.* 2016). Loss of ERDF support would clearly have negative consequences for their development and employment (Shucksmith 2019).

Although current figures may immediately suggest massive economic consequences of loss of EU support after Brexit, some commentators are more sanguine. For example, Browne and colleagues from the Institute for Fiscal Studies not only note how the 'UK's gross contribution to the EU Budget represents about 2% of total public spending… the net contribution about 1%' (Browne *et al.* 2016, 48) but also observe how, in total:

> *The UK benefits* relatively little *from the two largest [EU] budget items. It is too rich to benefit significantly from structural and cohesion funds… [and a] relatively small agricultural sector and large amount of unimproved agricultural land… attract little subsidy [which] mean[s] that it receives less per person than most other EU member states from the CAP.*
>
> (Browne *et al.* 2016, 36, my emphasis)

Nonetheless, if assessment shifts from such a macro-scale overview to the individual farmer or rural business, the loss of support can be potentially financially devastating. For example, it is estimated that around 80 per cent of Welsh farm income comes from subsidies (compared with 55 per cent for the UK overall), not least directed at 'less favoured' sheep farms on often steep ground with thin soils and heavy rainfall (Messenger 2018, Morris 2019). Elsewhere, the National Farmers' Union (NFU) have warned of potential rises in farmer suicides over, at least in part, worries about the impacts of Brexit on already challenging livelihoods (Case 2019, Parveen 2019).

This more discriminating focus on individual cases and situations becomes more pertinent still when other areas of potentially significant change and challenge across the entire post-Brexit agri-food sector are taken into account (Lawrence 2017, Maye *et al.* 2018, 270). These include changes to: overseas trade; food security, food standards, health and environmental regulations; wage rises in the sector that may lead to higher food costs; and other changes in the rural labour market. One must anticipate all the upheavals of a 'major new phase of agrarian change and regulation' (Maye *et al.* 2018, 271; Lawrence 2017), while recognising Brexit as already active across the rural UK, as indicated in the next section.

Seasonal and migrant labour

It is widely noted that concern about 'migrants' coming to the UK was a major stimulus to the 2016 pro-Brexit vote (Clarke *et al.* 2017). During the referendum campaign it appears that 'a reservoir of latent racism was activated,' the Leave campaign frequently bringing to the surface 'pre-existing community sentiments that migrants were "a drain on local resources"' (Lumsden *et al.* 2019, 172, 179–180), blamed for things from housing shortages to pressure on the National Health Service. From a specifically EU perspective, critics noted the openness of labour movement and recruitment through the whole Union under European Freedom of Movement (EFM): 'a fundamental principle... enshrined in Article 45 of the Treaty on the Functioning of the European Union' (European Commission 2019).

Freedom of EU nationals to migrate to the UK contrasted markedly with the situation for non-EU residents wishing to work in the country. For such nationals, a five-tier Points Based System (PBS) since 2008 has sought only to welcome the 'brightest and best' and emphasises their need for 'self-sufficiency' (Kilkey 2017, 805) via a prioritising of wealth and income. It seems increasingly likely that EU citizens will become entangled in a similar PBS-type scheme after Brexit, possibly one modelled on that used in Australia (Sumption 2019). Indeed, it is suggested that freedom of EU nationals to move to the UK will be curtailed immediately on Brexit if no agreement on this issue has been reached (Abboud 2019).

Such change to the legal labour migrant framework for the UK has major potential implications for rural economies (Lawrence 2017). This is because the UK agri-food (and beyond) sector is highly dependent on EU migrant labour (House of Lords 2017). Moreover, within this labour force there is 'no easy distinction... between skilled and unskilled labour (House of Lords 2017, para. 259),' strongly suggestive of how loss of such hard to categorise workers may not be easily replaced.

UK agriculture's high reliance on EU migrant labour is especially expressed by horticulture's 80,000 seasonal workforce, where 90–98 per cent presently come from the rest of the EU, especially the eastern countries (House of Lords 2017, FLEX 2018). Moreover, it is not just peak demands of seasonal employment that rely on EU migrants. It is important to distinguish here between migrants who respond to the high labour demands of planting, harvesting, and Christmas sales, and those who are more permanently employed. Some 60 per cent of workers employed to produce poultry meat, 50 per cent of egg-packers, and 40 per cent of egg farm workers are from outside the UK, 20 per cent of pig farms employ migrant labour, and 11 per cent of UK dairy processing workers are migrants (House of Lords 2017). Very many of these people are long-established in the UK. Broadening the perspective still further, 48 per cent of newly registered vets in the UK in 2016 qualified elsewhere in the EU or European Economic Area (House of Lords 2017).

That Brexit is already very active in the rural UK (Maye *et al.* 2018) is very clear from consequences stemming from a lack of this agri-food migrant labour, especially seasonal workers. As the Chair of the British Soft Fruits Industry put it in 2017: 'If we do not have the pickers, we do not have a soft fruit industry' (quoted in Butler 2017, np). This fear was soon being realised. The NFU's website features the challenge of recruiting labour prominently (www.nfuonline.com) and their survey of UK horticulture in 2017 found over 4,000 (12.5 per cent) unfilled labour vacancies (rising to 29 per cent for the September harvest) (Carrington 2018). This expressed, in part, a decline in the proportion of international workers returning for the harvest from 41 per cent in 2016 to 29 per cent in 2017, a trend that mirrored the large overall decline in EU migration to the UK since 2016 (Vargas-Silva and Fernández-Reino 2019). Reasons given for this decline were a rise in xenophobia and racism, the weak Pound and a general sense of uncertain employment futures (Carrington 2018), all relatable to the wider Brexit atmosphere explored in the next two sections.

A first consequence of this employment shortage situation, which has been repeated and worsened since 2017, was a shift by farmers to production overseas (Butler 2017, O'Carroll 2018a), a trend which, if accelerated, would have major implications for UK horticulture (and other farm sectors). Second, and still more immediately, the press soon picked up on foods such as strawberries or apples being left to rot in the fields (Carrington 2018, Ennals 2019). Third, and in part reflecting how just 0.06 per cent of the seasonal workers covered in the NFU survey were UK nationals (Carrington 2018), there grew a call, articulated by the government in their 'Health and Harmony' consultation paper, 'to help attract more of our graduates and domestic workforce into this vibrant industry' (Defra 2018, 10). How immediately realistic this prospect is can be doubted, given the physical and other challenges of much of the work which is, nonetheless, often paid only minimum wage plus bonuses (Abboud 2019).

In response to these labour concerns, the UK government in July 2019 launched a two-year pilot scheme involving issuing 2,500 visas to non-EU nationals, although it was argued that at least 10,000 are needed (O'Carroll 2018b). If deemed to be successful, this scheme might revisit the Seasonal Agricultural Workers Scheme (SAWS) scrapped in 2013 after EU expansion. This would reinforce the point noted earlier that international (labour) migration to the UK is being sharpened towards guest-worker style schemes. These assume the overwhelming predominance of 'single, temporary workers without family members (Kilkey 2017, 800),' thereby reinforcing the position of seasonal workers as compared with more permanent labour migrants. This is in stark contrast to rights and practices under the existing EFM, which 'does not reduce migrants to individual units of labour' (Kilkey 2017, 798). Instead, it allows family migration/reunion and the sense of home place-making discussed in the next section. SAWS-type schemes have also attracted specific criticisms (FLEX 2018), not least in terms of how they can restrict workers' ability to escape abusive relationships through being so strongly tied to a specific employer.

Futures: settlement undermined?

The anticipated and ongoing major shifts in state support for agriculture and migrant labour practices clearly have significant implications for UK rural futures. The details are hard to pin down yet, and predictions may be unwise because Brexit is still very much an emerging experience. However, a wider sense of futures is engaged in this section and the next in respect of Brexit's potential impact on the everyday cultural and socio-political experience and place of the twenty-first century UK rural. This is examined in this section through noting Brexit-related changes in the everyday lives of international labour migrants in rural places. The significance of such changes will be broadened in the next section and shown as both congruent with and feeding into a 'revanchist rural.'

Debates and news coverage of Brexit to date have seen a notable 'absence of migrant workers' voices (Maye *et al.* 2018, 283).' This reflects a broader lack of recognition of such people's place in today's UK rural (Green *et al.* 2009). Although many migrant workers have settled in rural locations, their presence within the diversity of people brought together within the broader academic concept of counterurbanisation, for example, has still to be fully recognised (Halfacree 2008). Consequently, it pays here to move away from emphasising the 'temporariness' within the rural UK of many of these people – 'seasonal workers' – and instead to note settlement processes and often broader family projects. All migrant workers into rural areas now comprise a key component of the twenty-first century UK countryside. In some locations they are critical to reversing still-dominant out-migration and population decline, such as in parts of rural Scotland (Green *et al.* 2009, Scott and Brindley 2012). This makes international labour migrants' rural occurrence, relatively at least, still more significant than their more fully recognised urban presence.

In their study of central and eastern European labour migrants resident in rural Scotland, Flynn, and Kay (2017) emphasised how such people, just as much as the non-migrant population, need material and emotional security for the playing out of 'a present and future life to be imagined in rural Scotland' (p.56). Overwhelmingly, while employment reasons explain their arrival in these remote places, the importance of 'settlement' soon emerges and develops within their life course (also Lumsden *et al.* 2019 on labour migrants in Boston, England). This broader appreciation is helped conceptually by taking a more temporal or event perspective on migration, rather than just seeing it as snapshot in time (Halfacree and Rivera 2012).

Within this post-relocation life course evolution, Flynn and Kay (2017) went on to note how migrants' development of an emplaced emotional security drew relationally (also Botterill 2018) from numerous sources. These ranged from the destination's recognised scenic beauty to the building of social connections in what was perceived as a safe, quiet, friendly context. Settlement ultimately encompasses the whole 'lived experience.' And an official part of this experience is a legal 'right to remain,' which has been thrown into doubt by the Brexit issue.

Research by both Botterill (2018) on Poles in Scotland and MacKrell and Pemberton (2018) on eastern Europeans in rural England are among other studies that reinforce Flynn and Kay's (2017) findings. For example, challenging any overly unique Anglo-centric cultural affiliation to the concept, MacKrell and Pemberton (2018) argued for an often strong fit to be recognised between the migrants and versions of a 'rural idyll.' This is expressed through newcomers' rural settlement being reinforced and 'normalised' (p. 55) by them exhibiting characteristics which conform to noted aspects of the idyllic representation (Bunce 2003, Halfacree 1993). These include a generally strong work ethic and record of getting jobs done, a large degree of self-sufficiency, relatively high 'community' involvement, and their whiteness of skin. However, following the 2016 Brexit vote, change was noted in this settlement fit. Migrants were feeling less comfortable, even 're-assessing their options… [on] whether to stay in the English countryside or to leave England' (MacKrell and Pemberton 2018, 56; also Lumsden *et al.* 2019). Or, if not 'going home,' Botterill (2018, 546) showed how Poles' feeling of rejection and alienation post-referendum often resulted in withdrawal 'from cosmopolitan modes of belonging towards the familiar, comforting national frames of belonging.'

These changing migrant experiences in respect of belonging suggest that, irrespective of what arrangements are made to meet rural labour requirements after Brexit, those providing this labour may struggle to settle. This is clearly likely to push rural migrant experiences and lives towards the 'anywhereness' of 'simply' being an inherently fluid and transient atomised individual and away from the 'somewhereness' of a more entangled, emplaced, and caught-up social person (Goodhart 2017). Such existential change has clear implications not only for the migrants but also for the whole socio-cultural and experiential character of UK rural places. It is likely to reinforce a highly divisive sense of 'us' (established population) versus 'them' (labour migrants). Thus, Boston in England, a noted location for both European labour migrants (Scott and Brindley 2012) and the strongest pro-Brexit vote (76 per cent leave; BBC 2016), has also witnessed migrants' post-referendum withdrawal from community and public spaces and a retreat into the private space of the home (Lumsden *et al.* 2019). Thoughts of return migration are also developing, expressed powerfully by this migrant:

> *I was getting used to local life, people, rules making it more my home. Since the referendum I don't feel this can be my home ever. I wasn't given the right to decide about my future here, while the others did. I cannot plan my future in this uncertainty. I can't see my future here.*
>
> (Migrants' Rights Network 2017: 7)

Brexit, in short, thus promotes the rural UK as *not* a place for international labour migrant settlement. Instead, it promotes the kind of rural place introduced next.

Futures: a revanchist rural?

Reinforcing and developing divisions between settled populations and migrants is not just of immediate concern for the lives of both groups in the rural UK today but also serves to undermine other positive labour and community trends that have been emerging in part through migrant settlement. For example, Flynn and Kay (2017, 58) observed how EU8 migrants were taking up 'devalued work,' while Green *et al.* (2009) earlier noted an increase in migrant workers to rural England in areas such as health, hotels, and catering. In other words, rural labour migrants are not only employed in agriculture but have begun to build links with and may ultimately underpin other key elements of twenty-first century UK rural economy and society, not least related to hospitality and caring. While such employees could also be 'reduced' to contracted 'anywhere,' labour migrants post-Brexit, a greater sense of their achieving settlement would surely reinforce and add value to their inherently social and emplaced activities.

The rural UK as a place for overseas labour migrants to regard more as an 'anywhere,' evaluated purely on its ability to provide waged work, rather than as a 'somewhere' suitable for more permanent settlement does little to promote it as a space of diversity and difference. Instead, it links to noted concerns within the broader academic literature of the rural evolving into a selective space of increasing socio-economic homogeneity (Woods 2011). This is often expressed via rural population turnover, whereby – crudely speaking – in-migrating middle-class counterurbanisers replace ever-declining numbers of out-migrating working class 'locals' (Woods 2011). However, the present chapter's perspective cuts across this class emphasis by drawing attention to the differing lives of settled residents and migrants, suggesting rural selectivity and exclusivity is also being potentially reinforced in population terms by Brexit-related overseas labour in-migration changes.

Moreover, enhanced rural selectivity and exclusivity, especially in how the rural is represented (Halfacree 1993), is arguably also a more central feature of the whole Brexit experience. This can be approached through consideration of the electoral geography of the Brexit vote. Although by no means unanimous or conclusive – very many rural UK people voted remain and are very supportive of the EU – this vote begins to suggest the rural in certain configurations as a key pro-Brexit player.

The Brexit referendum saw two cross-cutting voting patterns stand out (Hennig 2017). First, there was clearly a 'regional' distinction, with London and many of its surrounding areas, Northern Ireland and Scotland favouring remain. Second, there was a rural-urban contrast, albeit inconsistent, with the Brexit vote favouring more rural areas. Analysis of this geography soon recognised a complex range of divisions within both the pro-EU and, most especially, the pro-Brexit vote. An urban-rural distinction was again drawn out by numerous commentators, paralleling analysis of the equally surprising pro-Trump 2016 US presidential vote (Beckett 2016, Halfacree 2018; Jennings and Stoker 2018). For example, while a leave vote was quickly 'associated with the politics of the urban [rustbelt] "left behinds"' (Boyle *et al.* 2018, 101), it was particularly strong in many affluent rural areas. An urban-rural angle was also apparent in Burn-Murdoch's (2017) 'six tribes of Brexit.' All three of his 'remainer' groups were largely urban. Of the three 'leaver' groups, however, while young, anti-establishment 'working-class leavers' were urban, both lower education 'moderate leavers' and anti-immigrant, older, and well-off 'British values leavers' had a strong rural edge. Rural voters, it might thus be observed, had electorally outwitted the urban 'elite' with Brexit. Certainly, cultural factors, as much as economic and political concerns, all rooted in place, together mapped Brexit geographies (Bailey and Budd 2019, Clarke *et al.* 2017).

To begin to understand the rural-Brexit affiliation, one can first note the economic hopes of groups such as farmers and fishers for a more prosperous post-Brexit future, notwithstanding the post-CAP uncertainties for the former noted earlier. However, while most people in these 'traditional rural' groups supposedly did vote to leave (Clarke 2017, Wollaston 2018), their relatively small numbers alone do not explain adequately the rural-Brexit link. Instead, the voting of the rural population more generally must be considered, including people who have moved into rural areas. Indeed, this latter group is held responsible by geographer Danny Dorling for Wales voting overall to leave the EU, expressed specifically in terms of pro-Brexit votes by English migrants to rural and small town Wales (Perraudin 2019).

To understand more of the rural-Brexit link it helps to note how the world seemingly desired by much pro-Brexit discourse has a strong conservative to reactionary imagination that chimes strongly with similarly backward-looking rural representations. Regarding the former, Dorling and Tomlinson (2019) firmly and thoroughly link the pro-Brexit vote to the last gasps of colonial attitudes and imperial nostalgia. Similarly, Boyle *et al.* (2018, 102) were suspicious that 'imperial mentalities lurk deep in the dark recesses of the British mind' and that this came through in Brexiteers' invocation of a supposed Second World War (1939–1945) spirit, the 'Little England(er)' being able to survive alone in a hostile Europe (*sic.*). Likewise, Bailey and Budd (2019, 169) argued that 'Brexit appears to have created a nostalgia for an imagined imperium that never existed.' Crucially, these 'end of Empire' (Dorling and Tomlinson 2019) perceptions underpinning the Brexit vote can also invoke reference and connection to an equally 'besieged rural,' as articulated in long-noted powerful cultural constructs such as Wright's (1985) 'Deep England.' In other words, overall there was some specific rural 'emplacement' of nostalgic pro-Brexit sympathies and hopes for the future, albeit within a rural also represented as a very conservative and besieged spatiality. Or, adapting slightly Calhoun's (2016, 56) words, voters 'went to sleep in Great Britain and woke up in Little [rural] England.'

Projecting a rural nostalgia as a future hope did not just sit passively in the cultural political imagination but emerged more actively via the pro-Brexit vote as 'revenge' by a group seeing themselves as (geographically) marginalised by urban elites, especially from London (Calhoun 2016). It forms part of what Rodríguez-Pose (2018) more widely recognised as '[t]he revenge of places that don't matter' (also Halfacree 2018, Jennings and Stoker 2018). For example, the millennial discourse associated with the Countryside Alliance, a rural pressure group, of the need to 'listen to the countryside,' appeared reinvigorated after its earlier failure to prevent the outlawing of hunting with hounds (Woods 2005). Furthermore, and critically, this time many urban residents seemingly bought into a discourse favouring a quasi-Countryside Alliance UK over a more cosmopolitan European Union component state.

The net result of these cultural trends and the changing settlement experiences of international labour migrants noted in the previous sections mirrors for the rural UK a political process long-noted for many cities across the global north. Specifically, there seem to be parallels between the UK's pro-Brexit rural and the 'revanchist city' (Smith 1996). In short, a 'revanchist rural' has emerged.

The revanchist city expresses 'a broad, vengeful right-wing reaction against both… "liberalism"… *and* the predations of capital' (Smith 1996, 43, my emphasis). In other words, it seeks not only to challenge efforts to make the city more inclusive and diverse but also takes issue with certain trends within capitalism's engagement with the city. From the first perspective:

> *The revanchist city expresses a race/class/gender terror felt by middle- and ruling-class whites who are suddenly stuck in place by a ravaged property market, the threat and reality of unemployment, the decimation of social services, and the emergence of minority and immigrant groups, as well as women, as powerful urban actors.*
>
> (Smith 1996, 207)

From the second perspective, revanchism also takes issue with certain capitalist interests in the city, not least in terms of expressions ranging from extreme speculation to promotion of alternative economic actors.

For Smith (1996: 43–44), revanchism had both 'overtaken gentrification as a script for the urban future' but nonetheless kept 'gentrification… an integral part of the revanchist city.' In other words, upper middle class-based (re-) appropriation of the city remained the dominant trend but was not complacently simply 'going on.' Instead, it had also to engage critically with other urban experiences that could be seen as threatening to itself.

Such a tension over emerging futures is also arguably apparent for the UK rural and has been made more so via 2016's pro-Brexit vote. A proposed 'revanchist rural' expresses a highly selective rural spatiality that is seeking 'revenge' on forces perceived as seeking to undermine its hegemony. Crucially, this expression, although helping to explain the rural-Brexit link introduced above, is not restricted to rural residents but is articulated, albeit again unevenly, across the pro-Brexit population. Just as urban revanchism goes beyond (urban) gentrification, so too does rural revanchism not just involve rural lives and experiences. Put differently, in contrast to rural narratives always being transformed and thereby reduced by the urban, making rural an increasingly residual category, within Brexit the rural revanchist discourse has come to exert influence on the urban.

Turning directly to the proposed revanchist rural, the liberal 'terror' (Smith 1996, 207) is here represented by a perception of metropolitan (urban) elites, immigrants, liberal reformers, and others – all, in a Brexit context, associated with the EU project – not so much directly challenging the UK rural as it exists 'on the ground' but as undermining its status as the 'ideal type' geography of how the UK supposedly used to be and, in utopian terms, could be again (post-Brexit). And, as with urban revanchism, some currents within capitalism are also not seen as helping. The EU economic system, in particular, it is suggested, is regarded as more aligned with the priorities and logics of a multi-national, even global, capitalism than with the nationally emplaced interests of the UK. Rural revanchism, in short, seeks to 'take back control' for the UK through resisting the forces of both liberal and neo-liberal 'threat.'

Where now, post-Brexit rural UK?

Although Brexit at the time of writing still has to occur formally, a consistent message through this chapter has been that the UK's imminent departure from the EU speaks of a considerable number of likely disruptions for its rural areas and people. These were introduced through four themes, each of which will now be briefly revisited.

First, loss of agricultural support through the Common Agricultural Policy will undoubtedly have a major impact on UK farming. This need not be ultimately negative, however, as it throws up the potential to make UK agriculture 'greener,' suggested by the government's 'Health and Harmony' paper (Defra 2018). As Lawrence (2017, np, my emphasis) argues, 'departure from the EU represents both an existential risk to our food and farming system *and* a once-in-a-generation chance to reform it.' Nevertheless, while this potential may seem hopeful from a sustainability perspective, how change plays out in terms of farming incomes, marginal at best in some locations, and of the survival of the present farming diversity found across the UK raises strong concerns. And what is the future more generally for UK rural employment if other forms of economic support now obtained from the EU are also not (fully) replaced (Shucksmith 2019)?

From the second theme, international seasonal and migrant labour, the uncertain 'replacement' of present-day largely eastern Europeans has severe implications not only for the economic survival of many agricultural enterprises but also for the diversity of the UK rural population. More than this, however, and moving into the third theme of migrants' everyday rural experiences, any switch to migration for specific work demands only, as in a new SAWS scheme, has the potential to reinforce rural population instability through undermining settlement and inter-personal and place connections. This will not meet rising demands for workers in the growing rural hospitality industry and in healthcare, especially noteworthy given rural population ageing (Milbourne and Doheny 2012). Need for such workers seems poorly acknowledged now, as they are a group that often stays 'under the radar' of popular consciousness, but clearly requires urgent post-Brexit consideration.

The fourth theme built on the undermining of migrant workers' settlement in the rural UK to suggest that such lack of place within the country, except as passing-through transient workers, is in line with the Brexit discourse's reinvigoration of a reactionary rural imaginary. This representation has become a quasi-utopian statement in some Brexiteers' hoped for 'new' UK. While certainly taken up by all rural residents and, indeed, is to be associated as much with urban residents as rural, as a representation little attuned to the late twentieth century, let alone the twenty-first century, it articulates a rural revanchism rooted in political currents increasingly marginalised in the cosmopolitan world of the European Union. Yet, now having been taken up not just by conservative rural voters in 2016 but more generally within pro-Brexit discourse, it is a rural imaginary reinvigorated, with clear negative implications for those striving to recognise and make the rural UK a more diverse and inclusive place.

To end on two positive observations. First, Brexit has clearly drawn more than just academic attention to the neglected place and significance of international labour migrants, in particular, in the rural UK and their complex entanglements with farming systems and rural places. International labour migration can certainly no longer be seen as something largely irrelevant to the rural. Second, just as the revanchist city is never completely 'closed,' so will any UK 'revanchist rural' still have to deal with various presences, practices, and flows implicating rural places and people who challenge its representation in diverse ways. Struggles from within economy, society, culture, and/or politics will all feature prominently in the production of a post-Brexit rural UK that is never completely preordained. Letting in enough pickers to keep UK horticulture going will only be the start…

Acknowledgements

The author wishes to thank the anonymous reviewers for their comments on the manuscript.

References

All websites accessed January 2020.

Abboud, L. 2019. 'UK Farmers Struggle to Hire Overseas Workers for Harvest.' *Financial Times,* 25 August, www.ft.com/content/5127a0de-c4ee-11e9-a8e9-296ca66511c9.

Bailey, D. and L. Budd. 2019. 'Brexit and Beyond: A Pandora's Box?' *Contemporary Social Science* 14(2): 157–173.

BBC. 2016. 'Lincolnshire Records UK's Highest Brexit Vote.' www.bbc.co.uk/news/uk-politics-eu-referendum-36616740.

Beckett, A. 2016. 'From Trump to Brexit, Power has Leaked from Cities to the Countryside.' *The Guardian,* 12 December. www.theguardian.com/commentisfree/2016/dec/12/trump-brexit-cities-countryside-rural-voters.

Botterill, K. 2018. 'Rethinking "Community" Relationally: Polish Communities in Scotland Before and after Brexit.' *Transactions of the Institute of British Geographers* 43(4): 540–554.

Boyle, M., R. Paddison and P. Shirlow. 2018. 'Introducing "Brexit Geographies": Five Provocations.' *Space and Polity* 22(2): 97–110.

Browne, J., P. Johnson and D. Phillips. 2016. *The Budget of the European Union: A Guide.* Institute for Fiscal Studies Briefing Note BN181, www.ifs.org.uk/publications/8225.

Bunce, M. 2003. 'Reproducing Rural Idylls.' In *Country Visions,* edited by P. Cloke, 14–30. Harlow: Pearson.

Burn-Murdoch, J. 2017. 'The Six Tribes of Brexit.' *Financial Times,* 18 October. www.ft.com/content/61c12868-b350-11e7-a398-73d59db9e399.

Butler, S. 2017. 'British Farmers Warn Loss of EU Workers will see Strawberry Prices Soar.' *The Guardian,* 22 June. www.theguardian.com/business/2017/jun/22/british-farmers-warn-loss-of-eu-workers-will-see-strawberry-prices-soar.

Calhoun, C. 2016. 'Brexit is a Mutiny Against the Cosmopolitan Elite.' *New Perspectives Quarterly* 33(3): 50–58.

Carrington, D. 2018. 'Lack of Migrant Workers Left Food Rotting in UK Fields Last Year, Data Reveals.' *The Guardian*, 9 February. www.theguardian.com/environment/2018/feb/09/lack-of-migrant-workers-left-food-rotting-in-uk-fields-last-year-data-reveals.

Case, P. 2019. 'Lonely Farmer Took his Own Life amid Brexit Concerns.' *Farmers' Weekly,* 6 August. www.fwi.co.uk/news/lonely-farmer-took-his-own-life-amid-brexit-concerns.

Clarke, P. (2017) 'Farmer Support for Brexit as Strong as Ever, FW Poll Reveals.' *Farmers' Weekly,* 22 December. www.fwi.co.uk/news/farmer-support-brexit-strong-ever-fw-poll-reveals.

Clarke, H., M. Goodwin and P. Whiteley. 2017. *Brexit*. Cambridge: Cambridge University Press.

Defra [Department for Environment, Food and Rural Affairs]. 2018. *Health and Harmony: The Future for Food, Farming and the Environment in a Green Brexit*. Policy Paper. https://assets.publishing.service.gov.uk/government/uploads/system/uploads/attachment_data/file/684003/future-farming-environment-consult-document.pdf.

Dempsey, N. and P. Loft. 2019. 'Turnout at Elections.' House of Commons Library. https://researchbriefings.parliament.uk/ResearchBriefing/Summary/CBP-8060%23fullreport#fullreport.

Dorling, D. and S. Tomlinson. 2019. *Rule Britannia. Brexit and the End of Empire*. London: Biteback.

Downing, E. and S. Coe. 2018. *Brexit: Future UK Agriculture Policy*. House of Commons Library Briefing Paper 8218. www.parliament.uk/documents/commons-library/Brexit-UK-agriculture-policy-CBP-8218.pdf.

Dwyer, J. 2018. *The Implications of Brexit for Agriculture, Rural Areas and Land Use in Wales*. Public Policy Institute for Wales report. www.wcpp.org.uk/wp-content/uploads/2018/04/The-Implications-of-Brexit-for-Agriculture-Rural-Areas-and-Land-Use-in-Wales-1.pdf.

Electoral Commission. No date. 'EU Referendum.' www.electoralcommission.org.uk/who-we-are-and-what-we-do/elections-and-referendums/past-elections-and-referendums/eu-referendum.

Ennals, E. 2019. 'Millions of Apples Left to Rot as EU Pickers Stay Away.' *The Times*, 21 October. www.thetimes.co.uk/article/brexit-woes-millions-of-apples-left-to-rot-as-eu-pickers-stay-away-ctsdvtbsw.

European Commission. 2019. 'Free Movement – EU Nationals.' https://ec.europa.eu/social/main.jsp?catId=457.

FLEX [Focus on Labour Exploitation]. 2018. 'Preventing Exploitation in the Shadow of Brexit.' *FLEX Briefing*. www.labourexploitation.org/publications/preventing-exploitation-shadow-brexit-risks-temporary-migration-programmes.

Flynn, M. and R. Kay. 2017. 'Migrants' Experiences of Material and Emotional Security in Rural Scotland: Implications for Longer-term Settlement.' *Journal of Rural Studies* 52: 56–65.

Goodhart, D. 2017. *The Road to Somewhere: The Populist Revolt and the Future of Politics*. London: C. Hurst and Co.

Green, A., M. De Hoyos, P. Jones and D. Owen. 2009. 'Rural Development and Labour Supply Challenges in the UK: The Role of Non-UK migrants.' *Regional Studies* 43(10): 1261–1273.

Halfacree, K. 1993. 'Locality and Social Representation: Space, Discourse and Alternative Definitions of the Rural.' *Journal of Rural Studies* 9: 23–37.

Halfacree, K. 2008. 'To Revitalise Counterurbanisation Research? Recognising an International and Fuller Picture.' *Population, Space and Place* 14: 479–495.

Halfacree, K. 2018. 'Hope and Repair within the Western Skyline? Americana Music's Rural Heterotopia.' *Journal of Rural Studies* 63(1): 1–14.

Halfacree, K. and M.J. Rivera. 2012. 'Moving to the Countryside… and Staying: Lives Beyond Representation.' *Sociologia Ruralis* 52: 92–114.

Hennig, B. 2017. 'Cartogram Special – Brexit.' *Geographical*. https://geographical.co.uk/places/mapping/item/1805-cartogram-special-brexit.

House of Commons. 2018. *Brexit: Trade in Food.* Environment, Food and Rural Affairs Committee 3rd Report of Session 2017–19, HC348. https://publications.parliament.uk/pa/cm201719/cmselect/cmenvfru/348/348.pdf.

House of Lords. 2017. *Brexit: Agriculture.* European Union Committee, 20th Report of Session 2016–17, HL Paper 169. https://publications.parliament.uk/pa/ld201617/ldselect/ldeucom/169/169.pdf.

Institute for Government. 2020. 'Common Agricultural Policy.' www.instituteforgovernment.org.uk/explainers/common-agricultural-policy.

Jennings, W. and G. Stoker. (2018). 'The Divergent Dynamics of Cities and Towns: Geographical Polarisation after Brexit.' *Political Quarterly* 90: 155–166.

Kilkey, M. 2017. 'Conditioning Family-life at the Intersection of Migration and Welfare: The Implications for "Brexit families."' *Journal of Social Policy* 46(4): 797–814.

Lawrence, F. 2017. 'Brexit Could Destroy the UK's Food and Farming Industry – or be the Making of It.' *The Guardian.* 26 June. www.theguardian.com/commentisfree/2017/jun/26/brexit-watershed-farming-food-industry-michael-gove.

Lumsden, K., J. Goode and A. Black. 2019. '"I Will Not be Thrown Out of the Country Because I'm an Immigrant": Eastern European Migrants' Responses to Hate Crime in a Semi-rural Context in the Wake of Brexit.' *Sociological Research Online* 24(2): 167–184.

MacKrell, P. and S. Pemberton. 2018. 'New Representations of Rural Space: Eastern European Migrants and the Denial of Poverty and Deprivation in the English Countryside.' *Journal of Rural Studies* 59: 49–57.

Maye, D., H. Chiswell, M. Vigani and J. Kirwan. 2018 '"Present Realities" and the Need for a "lived experience" Perspective in Brexit Agri-food Governance.' *Space and Polity* 22(2): 270–286.

Messenger, S. 2018. 'Post-Brexit Farm Subsidy Shake-up for Wales Proposed.' *BBC News.* www.bbc.co.uk/news/uk-wales-44768077.

Morris, S. 2019 '"No Deal Would be Horrific": Welsh Farmers Brace Themselves for Brexit.' *The Guardian,* 24 January. www.theguardian.com/politics/2019/jan/24/no-deal-horrific-welsh-farmers-brexit-meat-eu-countries.

Migrants' Rights Network. 2017, *Migrants' Perspectives on Brexit and UK Immigration Policies.* London: Migrants' Rights Network. https://migrantsrights.org.uk/wp-content/uploads/2017/02/Migrants-Perspectives-on-Brexit-and-UK-Immigration-Policies.pdf.

Milbourne, P. and S. Doheny. 2012. 'Older People and Poverty in Rural Britain: Material Hardships, Cultural Denials and Social Inclusions.' *Journal of Rural Studies* 28: 389–97.

National Farmers' Union. 2019. *NFU Yearbook 2018–2019.* Stoneleigh Park: NFU. www.nfuonline.com/nfu-online/news/nfu-yearbook-2018–2019.

O'Carroll, L. 2018a. 'British Farmer Moves Fruit-growing to China over Brexit Uncertainty.' *The Guardian,* 11 February. www.theguardian.com/politics/2018/feb/11/british-farmer-moves-fruit-growing-to-china-over-brexit-uncertainty.

O'Carroll, L. 2018b. 'Brexit: Farmers Criticise Temporary Agricultural Worker Visa Scheme.' *The Guardian,* 6 September. www.theguardian.com/environment/2018/sep/06/government-to-issue-temporary-work-visas-to-help-uk-fruit-farmers.

Parveen, N. 2019. 'Brexit and Bad Weather Puts UK Farmers at Risk of Suicide, say Charities.' *The Guardian,* 3 March. www.theguardian.com/environment/2019/mar/03/brexit-and-bad-weather-puts-uk-farmers-at-risk-of-suicide-say-charities.

Perraudin, F. 2019. 'English People Living in Wales Tilted it Towards Brexit, Research Finds.' *The Guardian,* 22 September. www.theguardian.com/uk-news/2019/sep/22/english-people-wales-brexit-research.

Rodríguez-Pose, A. 2018. 'The Revenge of the Places that Don't Matter (and What to do About It).' *Cambridge Journal of Regions, Economy and Society* 11(1): 189–209.

Scott, S. and P. Brindley. 2012 'New Geographies of Migrant Settlement in the UK.' *Geography* 97(1): 29–38.

Shucksmith, M. 2019. 'Rural Policy after Brexit.' *Contemporary Social Science* 14(2): 312–326.

Smith, N. 1996. *The New Urban Frontier: Gentrification and the Revanchist City.* London: Routledge.

Sumption, M. 2019. 'The Australian Points-based System: What is it and What Would its Impact be in the UK?' *Migration Observatory Report.* COMPAS, University of Oxford.

Vargas-Silva, C. and M. Fernández-Reino. 2019. 'EU Migration to and from the UK.' *Migration Observatory Briefing.* COMPAS, University of Oxford.

Wollaston, S. 2018. 'Why did the Fishing Industry Vote for Brexit?' *The Guardian,* 26 November. www.theguardian.com/news/audio/2018/nov/26/why-did-the-fishing-industry-vote-for-brexit.

Woods, M. 2005. *Contesting Rurality. Politics in the British Countryside,* Aldershot: Ashgate.

Woods, M. 2011. *Rural,* London: Routledge.

Wright, P. 1985. *On Living in an Old Country,* London: Verso.

Section III

Concluding remarks

Chapter 13

Farm labour in California and some implications for Europe

Philip Martin

Introduction

Agriculture was once the largest employer in every society, making most of human history the history of agriculture. The industrial revolution in the mid-eighteenth century accelerated outmigration from agriculture and prompted governments to regulate wages and working conditions in the nonfarm industries that soon employed a majority of workers. Over time, industrial workers gained protections such as the right to form unions and the right to expect at least minimum wages, overtime pay, and pension and other work-related benefits.

Agriculture was often partially or fully exempted from these labour laws to protect and preserve family farmers. Many governments believed that small farmers could not cope with the complex labour laws that protected employees in factories, and that some hired workers want to become farmers, making them more interested in crop prices than in minimum wages. Even though few hired farm workers are able to climb the agricultural ladder from hired hand to farmer, the notion that many hired workers are farmers in waiting continues to be used to justify incomplete labour law protections for farm workers.

The reason why farm workers become more vulnerable as countries get richer is straightforward: the most capable workers get out of agriculture first, and the 'people left behind' to fill seasonal farm jobs usually lack the education, skills, and connections to get non-farm jobs (President's National Advisory Commission on Rural Poverty 1967). There are many reasons why farm workers find it hard to move up the job ladder and become farmers, including lack of land and capital. Local farm workers are often joined by legal and unauthorised migrants from other areas and countries.

This chapter explains the farm labour prosperity paradox, namely, why hired farm workers become more important and vulnerable as the share of labour employed in agriculture declines. Hired workers do a larger share of work on the fewer and larger farms that produce most farm commodities in richer countries, and they include local workers unable to find non-farm jobs and internal and international migrants away from their usual homes. The paradox is discussed by reference to the US, focusing particularly on the Californian agricultural industry, which has the world's most intensive farm system and provides one vision of a future that could emerge in Europe, namely, large and specialised farms that depend on a mix of vulnerable local and foreign workers who have few other job opportunities.

Farmers versus workers

There is a fundamental difference between farmers and farm workers in most industrial countries. Farmers and their families are businesses whose incomes are the difference between what they receive for the commodities they sell and the cost of producing them. Farm incomes fluctuate with weather, disease, consumer demand, and many other factors, which is why many governments intervene in agriculture to protect the incomes of farmers (Beckman *et al.* 2017).

Hired farm workers are paid for their work, so they receive wages whether farm prices and incomes are high or low. However, agriculture's biological production process means that most farm workers are employed seasonally, often less than the standard 2,000 hours a year from 40 hours a week for 50 weeks of work. Because farm work is an easy-entry occupation, farm wages are generally lower than non-farm wages, and this combination of lower wages and fewer hours of work translates into lower incomes. In the US, the median hourly earnings of private sector workers are $25 an hour, so a full-time worker earns $50,000 a year. Seasonal farm workers are often employed 1,000 hours a year and earn $12,500, a quarter as much.

Farmers and farm workers also differ in demographics and political clout. In the US, farmers tend to be older than non-farm workers, are often the third, fourth, or fifth generation to farm, and usually belong to associations that maintain support for agricultural subsidies. Farm workers, on the other hand, tend to be younger than non-farm workers, are often the first generation to do farm work in the country, and are not well represented by unions or other organisations that could protect their interests. A familiar US saying is that it is hard to find a farmer under 40 because of the capital required to operate a farm, and hard to find a farm worker over 40 because of the physical demands of the job.

Vulnerable farm workers

Despite massive past and ongoing current rural-urban migration, agriculture remains the world's major employer, employing 28 per cent of the world's 3.6 billion workers in 2019 and two thirds of all workers in low-income developing countries (World Bank 2019). All countries with more than 50 per cent of their workforces employed in agriculture are poor, and all countries with fewer than five per cent of their workers employed in agriculture are rich or considered to be high income by the World Bank (World Bank 2019).

The share of a country's workers employed in agriculture declines as incomes rise, while the share of farm work done by hired workers increases. There are several reasons why hired workers become more important in richer countries, including the fact that farm production becomes concentrated on fewer and larger farms. The total number of farms may remain stable, as with the roughly two million farms in the US over the past three decades, but an ever-smaller number of farms account for most farm output and employment. For example, in 2017, the largest 10,000 US farms with expenses for farm labour accounted for over half of total farm labour expenditures.

The workers employed on these 'factories in the fields' tend to be more vulnerable than hired farm workers in the past for three reasons. First, the farm workers most capable of protecting themselves are the first to leave agriculture: their ambition, education, and contacts help them to find better non-farm jobs rather than remain in agriculture and try to achieve higher wages. Second, as the domestic supply of farm workers decreases, farmers look further afield for workers, recruiting minorities left behind by economic growth, lawful guest workers, and unauthorised migrants. Hard-to-regulate contractors are often involved in the recruitment, transport, and housing of local minorities and foreign workers, increasing the vulnerability of the workers they bring to farms.

Third, as a competitive industry with many small producers, agriculture is often exempted from or treated differently from other sectors under labour laws and social welfare programmes. Children may be allowed to work on farms. US guidelines from the Department of Labor state that 'minors of any age may be employed by their parents at any time in any occupation on a farm owned or operated by his or her parent(s)' (US Department of Labor 2020) and 'children as young as 12 may be employed outside school hours for wages with parental consent or on farms where their parents are employed' (US Department of Labor 2016), and there may be a separate and lower minimum wage for farm workers. Farm workers may not be eligible for or earn access to employment-linked social insurance programmes such as unemployment insurance and workers compensation or some means-tested welfare programmes for poor residents.

This combination of more vulnerable workers, intermediaries, and the incomplete farm labour regulatory and social safety net coverage widens the gap between farm and non-farm labour markets as per capita income rises. Take education. In 1979, the average US hired farm worker aged 25 and older had 10 years of schooling, while the average American adult had 12 years, a two-year gap (Whitener and Coltrane 1981, 6). Today the National Agricultural Workers Survey (NAWS) reports that US crop workers have an average eight years of schooling, six years less than the average 14 years of all US workers (US Department of Labor n.d.). The reason for this widening education gap is straightforward: over the past four decades, Mexican-born workers have replaced US-born workers in the farm workforce.

When farm workers are found in poor housing, indebted to recruiters, or working under exploitative conditions, it may seem that agriculture has not broken links with a past that included slavery, serfdom, and other institutions that exploited farm workers.

Farmers often respond to reports of poor working conditions by emphasising that they are offering jobs to workers without other job options, and that the farm workers portrayed in media stories nonetheless return to work for them year after year. There is a widening gap between the often college-educated farm labour reformers who have never done farm work and sometimes see all manual labour as exploitative, and farmers who believe they are offering good jobs to low-skilled workers with few other options.

The best protection for all workers at all times is the power to say no to poor wages and exploitative working conditions. Workers can say no if they have better alternatives. However, empowering workers by providing them with alternative job options leaves unanswered the question of what to do until more development offers better options for farm workers.

Three US farm labour systems

The US farm labour system has been shaped by two centuries of history, and has produced distinct farm labour systems, each with their particular labour arrangements, including the roles of hired workers. In this section each of these are detailed, however, the focus is on the Californian agricultural system, which came to develop the most intensive agricultural industry in both the US and worldwide.

From the outset, family farms were praised as the ideal at a time when large plantations depended on slaves. The fact that most farms were family farms when labour protection laws were enacted allowed all of agriculture to be exempted, including the large farms that hired most farm workers. The first US Census of Population in 1790 found that 95 per cent of the four million Americans lived in rural areas, and almost all these rural residents were involved in agriculture. The number of people employed in agriculture rose with the westward expansion, but the share of US workers employed in agriculture fell with industrialisation, from 70 per cent in 1840 to 40 per cent in 1900 and to less than two per cent since the 1980s (USDA).

In the early 1800s, farmers obtained seasonal labour in three major ways (Martin 2003, ch. 2). First, large farm families in the east and midwest produced crops and livestock to satisfy their own needs, and relied on all members of the family to work at peak seasons; children went to school or had leisure time when there was little farm work. There was no reason for family farms in the northeastern states to expand and produce a surplus to sell in the early 1800s, since there were few cities and transport to them was very expensive. New York, the largest US city and the major market for farm commodities, had 60,000 residents in 1800.

Second, plantations in the south that produced cotton and tobacco for export needed more seasonal labour than even large farm families could provide. They relied on slaves who were owned by masters and were bought and sold. In a country that offered free land, free workers were unwilling to work for low wages on plantations, which needed workers for six to eight months. Plantations could justify the provision of food and housing for slaves year round to ensure that workers were available for planting and harvesting.

Before slavery ended with the Civil War in the 1860s, the prices of land used to grow cotton and the price of slaves to plant and harvest cotton were rising because cotton prices were increasing. There was little fertiliser used on cotton fields in the pre-Civil War south, so areas with older and less productive cotton land, such as Virginia, specialised in producing slaves for areas where cotton acreage was increasing, such as Louisiana and Texas. Conrad and Meyer (1958) conclude that slavery was profitable, as some areas specialised in producing slave labour and others in producing cotton.

Third, farms in the arid western states such as California developed differently. Spanish and Mexican land grants to a favoured elite and church missions created large ranches or ranchos of 50,000 acres or more that grazed cattle and produced wheat. Many large wheat farms were known as bonanza farms, owned by absentee owners who reaped a harvest and a bonanza if winter rains produced a crop. They were expected to be broken into family-sized units when the transcontinental railroad, completed on 10 May 1869, made it easier for small farmers to move west as the journey across the US was reduced from months to days, transforming California by integrating the state's economy into that of the other states. Further, the development of irrigation systems in the 1870s made the production of fruit profitable, which was first dried and canned and later sent to market packed in ice to be consumed fresh.

Since fruit production was labour intensive, it was assumed that large wheat farms would have to be broken into family-sized parcels in order to obtain seasonal workers. Contemporary observers expected the emergence of family farms to produce fruit for cooperatives that would market it for them. However, large California farms did not need to be sub-divided into family-sized units because workers with no other job options were available to be seasonal farm workers. Over 15,000 Chinese workers were imported from Guangdong to help to build the transcontinental railroad through the Sierra mountains for $1 a day. When the railroad was completed, the Chinese were laid off, and most moved to Sacramento, San Francisco, and other cities rather than returning to China.

The railroad brought cheaper manufactured goods to California from other states, prompting layoffs of white workers as the factories that had supplied goods for California residents closed. The Chinese were blamed for this recession, and many were driven out of Californian cities by jobless white workers who accused them of being willing to work for low wages. Farmers did not discriminate, but they also did not pay workers when there was no need for them. Many of the Chinese workers who had been laid off after the railroad was completed became seasonal farm workers. Contemporary observers described them as cheaper than slaves because they 'came with the wind and went with the dust,' that is, they were paid only when they worked (Fuller 1991).

Waves of other migrants without non-farm job options followed the Chinese into the fields and preserved the system of large farms inherited from Spain and Mexico. The Japanese government legalised emigration in 1886, and newcomers from Japan soon replaced aging Chinese workers on Californian farms until a 'Gentlemen's Agreement' between Japan and the US in 1907 stopped more Japanese arriving. Large farmers turned to Punjabis and Filipinos to fill the ranks of the expanding seasonal farm workforce early in the twentieth century. However, most immigration from Asia was halted by federal laws in the 1920s, prompting growers to encourage Mexicans to move north to become seasonal farm workers. Many Mexicans responded, but during the Depression of the early 1930s, some were 'repatriated' in order to open up jobs for Americans.

During 150 years of labour-intensive agriculture in California which began in the 1870s, there was only one period when most seasonal farm workers were white US citizens. The plains states such as Oklahoma were settled in the 1920s by small farmers who borrowed money to plough native grasses and plant wheat, setting the stage for a Dust Bowl in the 1930s when crops failed and drought whipped up dust storms. Millions of farmers were unable to repay their bank loans, and at least one and a half million people from Arkansas, Oklahoma, and other states moved to California to begin anew, as exemplified by the Joad family portrayed in John Steinbeck's 1939 novel, *The Grapes of Wrath*.

The US declared war on Germany and Japan in December 1941, and many Dust Bowl migrants were drafted or found jobs in non-farm defence industries. Farmers complained of labour shortages and won a Bracero programme, a series of agreements that admitted almost five million Mexicans between 1942 and 1964 as legal guest workers. Many Mexican Braceros returned year after year, but up to two million Mexicans gained experience working in US agriculture before the programme ended in 1964 as a form of civil rights for Hispanics, a way to put upward pressure on the wages of Mexican-Americans who worked alongside Braceros in the fields.

The availability of workers without options, from the Chinese to Dust Bowl farmers and Mexicans, provided an ample supply of labour that encouraged the preservation and expansion of large farms that were dependent on hired workers. Each new wave of migrants undercut established migrants, encouraging experienced farm workers to find non-farm jobs rather than seeking upward mobility in the farm labour market.

Farm worker unions

The increasing reliance on more farm workers, which on their side often have seen wages and working conditions worsening, has often generated conflicts between interests of capital and labour, both at farms and in society at large. This section outlines how trade unions since the end of the Bracero programme have sought to regulate labour practices, focusing on the California-based United Farm Workers.

Until the mid-1960s there were few successful self-help efforts to raise farm wages. However, the end of the Bracero programme ushered in a 15-year golden era for farm workers which ended in the 1980s with rising unauthorised Mexico-US migration. The United Farm Workers (UFW) union won a 40 per cent wage increase for grape harvesters employed by a subsidiary of liquor conglomerate Schenley Industries in 1966, raising the base wage for grape harvesters from $1.25 to $1.75 an hour at a time when the federal minimum wage was $1.25.

There were no government-supervised elections to determine if farm workers wanted to be represented by the UFW because farm workers were excluded from the National Labor Relations Act of 1935, the basic law granting workers the right to form or join a union or refrain from union activities. Organising in the 1960s meant that the UFW sent contracts to growers saying that their workers wanted UFW representation and asking growers to sign the contract or face a boycott of their commodity.

After many police interventions to break up disputes between growers and the UFW, state leaders agreed in the 1970s that farm labour disputes had to be moved from the streets into bargaining and court rooms. Governor Jerry Brown signed into law the Agricultural Labor Relations Act (ALRA) in 1975, making California the first state to grant farm workers the right to organise and bargain with farm employers. The ALRA and unions were expected to usher in a new era of farm labour, with most farm workers represented by unions and farm worker becoming an occupation akin to construction worker, offering high hourly wages when there was work and unemployment insurance benefits during the off season (Martin 2003).

However, the golden era for farm workers ended in the early 1980s, as unauthorised Mexico-US migration rose. The demise of the UFW since its high watermark in 1979 has been the subject of countless books and articles. There are four major explanations for why Cesar Chavez and the UFW failed to transform seasonal farm work from a job into a career (Martin 2003). The first centres on Chavez's flaws, explaining that he wanted to lead a poor people's movement rather than a union and was dismayed to realise that most farm workers wanted a middle-class lifestyle, not a perpetual struggle for a new society (Pawel 2009). The UFW lost most of its lawyers when Chavez insisted that they move from Salinas, the US salad bowl, to the UFW's mountain headquarters southeast of Bakersfield.

The second explanation for the UFW's demise focuses on state politics. The ALRA is one of the most pro-worker and pro-union laws in the US, with detailed election procedures that permit quick elections before seasonal workers move to other farms and providing extra remedies if employers fail to bargain with a certified union in good faith. The ALRA was enacted under Democrats, who also made the first appointments to the ALRB. When Republicans began to make ALRB appointments in the 1980s, the UFW charged that the state agency was biased against farm workers and refused to cooperate with it.

The third explanation for the demise of the UFW involves the changing structure of agriculture, that is, who owns farmland, who operates farms, and who hires workers. UFW boycotts were most effective against conglomerates with farming subsidiaries. For example, Schenley was a NY liquor firm based in the Empire State Building, one of the big four which also included Seagram, National Distillers, and Hiram Walker. UFW supporters picketed liquor stores selling Schenley whiskey during the Christmas buying season in 1965, reducing sales and prompting Schenley leadership to agree to a UFW table grape contract over the objections of Schenley's California farm managers.

UFW boycotts and the agricultural crisis of the 1980s, when commodity and land prices fell, prompted many conglomerates with agricultural operations to sell their farmland. Oil firms such as Shell and Tenneco, Hawaii land developer Amfac, and other conglomerates that earned most of their profits from non-farm businesses sold land to farmers who were not as susceptible to boycotts. These farmers, in turn, often relied on farm labour contractors to obtain workers, and farm labour contractors (FLCs) whose crews had pro-union leanings found it hard to find farmer clients.

Chavez anticipated that FLCs would compete with unions, and insisted that the ALRA make the farm operator the employer of workers brought to farms by FLCs for union purposes. The ALRA makes farmers, rather than FLCs, the employers of workers which FLCs bring to farms, so that an FLC employee who was employed on 10 farms could work under 10 different union contracts. However, Chavez did not anticipate that many FLCs would bring both equipment *and* workers to farms and thus be considered custom harvesters who were the sole employers of the workers they brought to farms under all labour laws, including tax, labour, and immigration. Employees of custom harvesters may work on 10 farms, but they would have only one union contract if their custom harvester employer was unionised.

The fourth explanation for the demise of the UFW was rising unauthorised Mexico-US migration. The UFW called a strike against lettuce growers in 1979, as its first contracts with vegetable growers – which were signed under the ALRA – were expiring, to support a demand for a 40 per cent wage increase, to raise the minimum wage in UFW contracts from $3.75 to $5.25 an hour. The late 1970s were a period of high inflation, and President Carter asked employers and unions not to raise wages more than seven per cent, the wage increase that was offered by farmers. The UFW feared that unauthorised Mexicans would enter the US and replace strikers in the fields, and so they mounted 'wet patrols' along the border which involved UFW supporters armed with bats trying to prevent unauthorised entries.

The UFW won, but at a high price. Sun-Harvest, the vegetable division of United Brands (Chiquita bananas), and other large vegetable farmers agreed to the UFW's demand for a $5.25 minimum wage in new contracts, but then went out of business, leaving workers without a contract as new owners changed commodities and farming methods. Pawel (2009) suggests that Chavez called the strike because of the UFW's inept handling of its health insurance plan, which made lettuce workers angry with the UFW when their health care bills were not paid. Chavez hoped that a large wage increase would stifle worker anger, but the strike boomeranged and helped growers who shipped lettuce. The strike reduced lettuce shipments from the Imperial Valley but, with less lettuce sent to market, the price tripled, and the winter lettuce crop was worth twice as much in 1979 as in normal years.

By the mid-1980s, the UFW had stopped trying to organise farm workers and had a dwindling number of contracts. Unauthorised newcomers from Mexico replaced aging Mexican-Americans who founded and marched with the UFW in the 1960s and 1970s. Mexican newcomers often associated Cesar Chavez with the famous Mexican boxer rather than the leader of a protective union. The UFW during the 1960s organised mostly US citizens. Today, over half of farm workers are unauthorised persons born in Mexico. As with previous newcomers who took farm jobs because they had no other US options, many of the unauthorised Mexicans would like to find non-farm jobs, and most who are parents of US-born children expect their children to complete high school and find non-farm jobs.

Mexico-US migration for farm work peaked in 2000, when a quarter of the hired workers employed on US crop farms were newcomers, defined as persons who were outside the US the year before they were interviewed. Unauthorised Mexico-US migration declined after the 2008–2009 recession, so that fewer than two per cent of crop workers today are unauthorised newcomers.

Contemporary US farm labour

There were two million US farms in 2017, according to the Census of Agriculture (COA). There were more farm producers, 3.4 million in 2017, than farms because the COA for the first time allowed respondents to designate more than one producer per farm. However, only two million of these producers were primary producers, and the average age of primary producers was 59. US farms are concentrated in the midwest and south: Texas had 12 per cent of all US farms in 2017.

The story of US agriculture involves the persistence of small farms despite the consolidation of farm production on fewer and larger farms. One measure of changing farm size is midpoint acreage, the acreage at which half of the production of a commodity is from larger farms and half is from smaller farms. For example, half of all cropland and harvested cropland was on farms with 1,200 or more acres in 2012, up from a midpoint of 600 acres in 1982 and 800 acres in 1997. Some 30,200 farms had more than 2,000 acres of harvested cropland (McDonald *et al.* 2018).

The consolidation of production on large and specialised farms increases the demand for hired farm labour. Rising labour costs may become another factor encouraging the concentration of production on fewer and larger farms, since large farms can spread the fixed costs of guest workers over more acres or workers, lowering per unit costs.

There are several measures of farm employment. The Bureau of Labor Statistics estimates the average employment of self-employed and wage and salary workers in agriculture. Average employment is derived from monthly or quarterly snapshots of employment, summed, and divided by 12 months or four quarters.

The US had an average of 850,000 self-employed farmers and family members in 2016, and an average of 1.5 million wage and salary farm workers (Table 13.1). The average self-employment of farmers and family members declined by five per cent between 2006 and 2016, and is projected to decline by another three per cent by 2026. In contrast, there was significant growth in the average employment of hired workers between 2006 and 2016, up 23 per cent, and BLS projects stable hired worker employment through 2026. This means that hired workers should account for two thirds of average employment in US agriculture by 2026.

Table 13.1 US agricultural employment (including forestry, fishing, and hunting), 2006–2026. 1,000s

	2006	*2016*	*2026*	*Change 2006–16*	*Change 2016–26*
Hired workers on (wage and salary)	1,219	1,501	1,518	23%	1%
Self-employed	893	850	828	-5%	-3%
Total employment in agriculture	2,112	2,351	2,346	11%	0%
Share hired workers	58%	64%	65%		

Source: US Bureau of Labor Statistics, table 1: employment by major industry sector, which is employment during the payroll period that includes the 12th of the month, summed, and divided by 12 months. Average employment is not a count of jobs or unique workers; both exceed average employment. (www.bls.gov/opub/mlr/2017/article/projections-overview-and-highlights-2016–26.htm.)

Crop agriculture employs three fourths of hired workers and offers many seasonal jobs, so there are peaks and troughs in hired worker employment. The total number of workers employed in agriculture over a year exceeds average employment, making the number of farm workers a multiple of average employment. In California, there are about two farm workers employed sometime during the year for each year-round equivalent job, a two-to-one worker-to-job ratio (Martin, Hooker, and Stockton 2018).

Some 16,150 California agricultural establishments (NAICS 11) hired an average 425,500 workers and paid them $13.7 billion in 2016. Average employment of 425,500 reflects hired worker employment on each farm for the payroll period that includes the 12th of the month; the monthly data are summed and divided by 12 months to generate average employment. Average employment misses workers who were employed sometime during the month, but not during the payroll period which includes the 12th. However, total wages of $13.7 billion were the wages paid to all workers, including those who were employed at other times of the month but not during the payroll period that includes the 12th (Martin, Hooker, and Stockton 2019).

All Social Security Numbers (SSNs) reported by agricultural employers when paying unemployment insurance taxes are considered farm workers. While some of those employed for wages on California farms are paid managers of corporate farms, office workers on such farms, and professionals including disease specialists, the large majority of those reported are manual workers. Their California jobs can be tabulated, so that workers with several employers can be assigned to the commodity or NAICS in which they had their highest earnings. This procedure identified 804,200 primary farm workers, and those with their highest wages from an agricultural employer were 81 per cent of the total 989,500 SSNs with at least one farm job. Primary farm workers had their highest earnings from an agricultural rather than a non-farm employer, while primary vegetable workers had their highest earning jobs with a vegetable farmer.

Analysis of the Quarterly Census of Employment and Wages data highlights three major items. First, the total farm workforce exceeds average employment in agriculture by at least two to one in California, which means that seasonal agriculture depends on a pool of workers who are employed only part of the year. There are many industries that offer seasonal jobs and assume workers will be available to fill them, from teaching to sports, and there are many occupations in which workers are employed full time but perform their job for only part time, from firefighting to the military. Agriculture is almost unique in assuming workers will be available when needed at roughly the minimum wage, which is why economist Varden Fuller (1991) asserted that crop agriculture depends on 'poverty at home and misery abroad' to assure itself a seasonal workforce.

Second, there is a gap between what a full-time worker would earn in a particular commodity and the average earnings of workers who were employed in

Table 13.2 Full time and actual average pay of California farm workers, 2016

		Employment (FTE) Percentages	*Pay($) (In full-time equivalents)*	*Pay($) (From primary empl.)*	*Primary/ FTE*	*Hourly wage ($)**
NAICS 11	All agriculture	100%	32,316	16,142	50%	15.54
NAICS 111	Crops	41%	34,411	20,540	60%	16.54
NAICS1112	Vegetables	8%	39,809	26,092	66%	19.14
NAICS1113	Fruits	23%	31,846	16,900	53%	15.31
NAICS1114	Nursery	6%	35,250	27,124	77%	16.95
NAICS 112	Animals	7%	37,372	30,989	83%	17.97
NAICS 112120	Dairy	4%	36,864	31,433	85%	17.72
NAICS 1151	Crop support	51%	29,956	12,297	41%	14.40
NAICS 115113	Machine harvesting	2%	35,457	17,571	50%	17.05
NAICS 115114	Other postharvest	10%	40,846	23,485	57%	19.64
NAICS 115115	FLCs	34%	24,589	9,026	37%	11.82

Notes. NAICS = North American industry classification system. FTE = full-time employment. FLCs = farm labour contractors. Hourly wage (last column) is calculated by dividing the estimated pay for full-time employment by 2080 (hours).

Source: Martin et *al.* 2019

that commodity (Table 13.2). The average pay of full-time equivalent workers whose maximum earnings were from agricultural employers in 2016 would have been $32,300. However, the actual average earnings of such primary farm workers were $16,100, half as much. A full-time worker is employed 40 hours a week for 52 weeks or 2,080 hours, so the implied hourly wage of a full-time worker in California agriculture was $15.54. However, most workers are employed fewer hours and/or at lower hourly earnings, which explains why they earn half as much or $16,100 (employers do not provide hours worked data).

Third, the gap between full-time equivalent and actual average earnings varies by commodity. Hired workers in animal agriculture earn over 80 per cent as much as full-time workers would earn because most are employed for long hours on one farm. Many large California vegetable farms operate in several areas to supply lettuce and other leafy green vegetables year round, and some of the workers they hire move with the harvest, explaining why the average directly hired vegetable worker earns two thirds as much as a full-time vegetable worker would earn.

The largest sector of employment, farm labour contractors, had the largest gap between full-time and actual average earnings. FLCs employed one third of all primary farm workers in 2016. A full-time worker hired by a FLC would have earned $24,600 in 2016, equivalent to $12 an hour. However, workers whose maximum earnings were with FLCs earned an average $9,000, or 37 per cent as much, equivalent to 900 hours of work at the then minimum wage of $10 an hour or 750 hours at $12 an hour. This gap between full-time equivalent and average actual pay reflects some combination of fewer hours and lower hourly earnings (Martin 2017a).

Responding to fewer unauthorised migrants

The combination of fewer unauthorised newcomers and state-mandated increases in minimum wages, federal health care insurance mandates and costs, and state requirements that employers pay overtime premium wages to farm workers has encouraged the subset of farmers who rely on hired workers to make adjustments to cope with rising labour costs. These farm employer adjustments embody 4-S strategies, namely, *satisfy* current workers, *stretch* current workers with mechanical aids that increase their productivity, *substitute* machines for workers where possible and switch to less labour-intensive crops, and *supplement* current workforces with H-2A guest workers.

Satisfying and stretching workers are short-term responses to rising labour costs. Mechanisation, crop switching, guest workers, and produce buyers turning to imports are longer-term responses. Farmers producing commodities where labour costs are 25 to 40 per cent of variable production costs are weighing their alternatives, including investing in machines to do work now done by hand, building housing for H-2A guest workers, and forming partnerships to produce in lower-wage countries.

The US farm workforce is becoming more Mexican and more legal, largely because the H-2A programme is expanding rapidly. Mexican-born workers are 70 per cent of all hired workers on US farms, and over 95 per cent of H-2A workers were born in Mexico. In 2019, half the Mexican-born workers employed on US farms are unauthorised and 15 per cent are legal guest workers (US Department of Labor n.d.).

Farm workers remain on the bottom rungs of the US job ladder, but over the past half century in US farm labour there has been a growing gap between the characteristics of farm and non-farm workers. Until the 1980s, most farm workers were US citizens. Today, with most farm workers being unauthorised Mexicans or legal Mexican guest workers, vulnerability has increased because unauthorised Mexicans can be removed by immigration authorities and legal Mexican guest workers must leave if they lose their US jobs.

The farm labour problem, and its solutions

The share of a country's workers employed in agriculture declines as a country's per capita income rises. As countries get richer, the production of farm commodities becomes concentrated on fewer and larger farms that rely on hired or wage workers to do most of their work. The farm labour problem, dealing with workers who occupy the bottom rungs of the job ladder, does not disappear as the share of labour in agriculture declines. Instead, protecting and assisting hired farm workers becomes more difficult because the composition of the workforce changes. Local or citizen workers who seek farm worker jobs are typically those who lack the skills and contacts to find non-farm jobs, and they are joined by migrants from other countries with a variety of legal statuses.

From farm jobs to farm work careers

One universal feature of farm work is that, for most workers, seasonal farm work is a job rather than a career. Most farm workers are looking for 'better jobs,' including jobs that offer higher wages, more hours of work, or respect from supervisors. Most seasonal farm workers hope that their children will not follow them into the fields. This makes the seasonal farm labour market akin to a revolving door, with local workers unable to find better jobs and newcomers from abroad entering the farm workforce, remaining for a decade or less, and exiting for non-farm jobs or because of the physical demands of farm work. There is an asymmetry between farmers, who often proudly proclaim that they are following in the footsteps of their parents and grandparents, and farm workers, who are usually the first generation to do farm work for wages in a rich country.

There have been many efforts to transform hired farm work from a job into a career, and there are some success stories. Many of the workers employed in animal agriculture are local citizens and legal migrants who prefer outdoor work and rural living to non-farm jobs. Employers often offer year-round workers housing and other benefits, and get to know the workers who live and work with the farmer and his/her family.

Converting seasonal farm work from a job into a career has proven to be much tougher. With the production of labour-intensive commodities concentrated on fewer and larger farms, many seasonal workers are hired as interchangeable members of crews that range in size from 20 to 60. Crews are often brought to farms by intermediaries such as contractors, and most workers do not work alongside or get to know the farm operator on the farm on which they work. Their employer is the intermediary and, since fields and orchards are similar, workers do not care too much who operates the particular farm on which they are working on a given day. There are exceptions, as with cases of workers employed alongside farmers and their families on smaller farms, but such farms account for a small share of production and employment.

Mechanisation, migrants, and imports

Rich countries face three major options in order to have fresh fruits and vegetables: mechanisation, migrants, and imports (Martin 2017b).

Mechanisation eliminates the demand for hired farm workers. Agricultural history is the story of machines replacing hand labour, and the declining cost of robotics promises a new wave of labour-saving innovations. For example, precision planting allows machines or sprayers to remove materials other than plants, since weeding machines know where plants are located. Similarly, planting and training dwarf fruit trees to develop fruiting walls expedites the machine picking of apples and other fruits. Soft fruits such as strawberries pose the toughest challenges, but forecasters predict that by 2030 half or more of fresh strawberries will be machine harvested.

The second major option is more migrant farm workers. Most rich countries have programmes that admit foreigners to fill farm jobs, with governments using a variety of techniques to determine how many guest workers to admit, what wages and work-related benefits must be provided to guest workers and any local workers who work alongside them, and what happens to guest workers when the season ends. The trend in most countries has been to give more power to employers to shape guest-worker programmes as the share of local farm workers declines.

The third option is to import more labour-intensive commodities from lower-cost countries. In order to supply fresh produce to consumers year round, most countries import fruits and vegetables when there is little or no local production. Investments in developing countries that have counter-seasonal climates and lower wages have extended what was previously only off-season production, so that countries such as Mexico which once exported fresh tomatoes seasonally now export tomatoes year round (Mexico is the world's largest tomato exporter).

Mechanisation, migrants, and imports are interdependent in the sense that faster rising labour costs give a boost to investment in machines and imports, while lower wages for guest workers encourage a continuation of labour-intensive production in the country where produce will be consumed. Over decades, most richer countries are likely to favour mechanisation and imports, but the speed at which they approach a more mechanised and more import-dependent agriculture depends in part on government trade and migration policies.

Implications for Europe

Agricultural production in both Europe and the US is being concentrated on fewer and larger farms which hire most of a country's farm workers. They have in common a larger than ever reliance on farm workers from poorer countries.

However, there are still four significant differences between US and EU agriculture that have implications for hired farm workers. The first is scale: the US has fewer and larger farms. The US has two million farms that produce farm commodities worth $400 billion a year, while the 10 million EU farmers produce a similar $400 billion worth of crops and livestock. The average farm is larger in the US and fewer than five per cent of the nation's two million farms account for two thirds of total farm production and employment. While it is hard to compare farm structure by commodity, Europe has few of the California-style factories in the fields that employ 5,000 to 10,000 workers during peak harvest periods, but has more production from small- and medium-sized farms, and more hired worker employment on such farms.

The second major transatlantic difference involves hired farm workers. Most of the newcomers to the US farm workforce over the past half century have been unauthorised foreigners. In Europe, the switch from local residents who worked seasonally and internal migrants occurred later and involved a much higher share of legal foreign workers. While most migrant farm workers on US farms are unauthorised Mexicans, most migrant workers on European farms are legal migrants from poorer EU countries who take advantage of freedom of movement regulations to earn higher wages in richer EU countries, such as eastern Europeans who moved to Britain, Germany, Italy, and Spain after the EU enlargements in 2004 and 2007 to fill farm jobs.

Third, on both sides of the Atlantic, intermediary contractors or gangmasters play key roles in organising and deploying crews of workers, which may limit direct communications between farm operators and hired farm workers. However, the US and especially California are ahead of Europe in relying on nonfarm intermediaries to bring more workers to farms. For the past decade, more farm workers have been brought to California farms by nonfarm intermediaries, mostly farm labour contractors, than were hired directly by farmers, so that a typical crew working in a field or orchard was not hired by the farm operator where the workers are employed. European experience with the exploitation of crews of eastern Europeans in the UK, or Africans in southern Italy, highlight the difficulty of protecting workers who are brought to farms by intermediaries. Worker abuse seems most prevalent in labour-intensive agriculture in countries with large informal labour markets, such as Greece, Italy, and Spain (Corrado *et al.* 2016).

Finally, most US labour-intensive agriculture is in metro rather than rural areas. The US has about 3,100 counties, and those with at least one urban area of 50,000 or more are considered metro counties; 80 per cent of Americans live in metro counties. The 384 metropolitan statistical areas that include groups of metro counties ranging from New York City with 20 million people to Carson City in Nevada with 55,000 people include almost all US labour-intensive fruit, vegetable, and greenhouse production and farm workers. US farm worker issues often raise urban rather than rural concerns, such as the high cost of housing.

Despite differences across the Atlantic, the US experience represents important insights for Europe's agricultural industries and their farm labour practices. California, which houses the world's most intensive farm system, provides one vision of a future that could emerge in Europe, namely, large and specialised farms that depend on a mix of vulnerable local and foreign workers, who have few other job opportunities.

Acknowledgements

The author wishes to thank the anonymous reviewers for their comments on the manuscript.

References

Beckman, J., J. Dyck and K.E.R. Herman. 2017. *The Global Landscape of Agricultural Trade, 1995–2014. Economic Information Bulletin Number 181*. Washington D.C.: United States Department of Agriculture.

Conrad, A. and J. Meyer. 1958. 'The Economics of Slavery in the Ante Bellum South.' *Journal of Political Economy* 66: 95–130.

Corrado, A., C. de Castro and D. Perrotta, eds. 2016. *Migration and Agriculture Mobility and Change in the Mediterranean Area*. London: Routledge.

Fuller, V. 1991. 'Hired Hands in California's Fields.' Giannini Foundation Special Report 91-1. http://giannini.ucop.edu/publications/historic/special-reports.

Martin, P. 2003. *Promise Unfulfilled: Unions*, Immigration, *and Farm Workers*. Ithaca: Cornell University Press.

Martin, P. 2017a. *Merchants of Labor: Recruiters and International Labor Migration*. Oxford University Press.

Martin, P. 2017b. 'The Race in the Fields: Imports, Machines and Migrants.' *California Agriculture* 72. No 2.

Martin, P., B. Hooker, M. Stockton. 2018. 'Employment and Earnings of California Farm Workers in 2015.' *California Agriculture* 72.

Martin, P.B. Hooker and M. Stockton. 2019. 'Ratio of Farmworkers to Farm Jobs in California Increased to 2.3 in 2016.' *California Agriculture* 73: 73–78.

Pawel, M. 2009. *The Union of Their Dreams: Power, Hope, and Struggle in Cesar Chavez's Farm Worker Movement*. Bloomsbury. http://miriampawel.com/

President's National Advisory Commission on Rural Poverty. 1967. 'The People Left Behind.'

US Department of Agriculture. (n.d.) Farm Labor. Economic Research Service. www.ers.usda.gov/topics/farm-economy/farm-labor/background.aspx.

US Department of Labor. 2020. Agricultural Employment. www.dol.gov/general/topic/ youthlabor/agriculturalemployment

US Department of Labor (2016) Child Labor Bulletin 102 Child Labor Requirements in Agricultural Occupations Under the Fair Labor Standards Act. www.dol.gov/sites/dolgov/files/ WHD/legacy/files/childlabor102.pdf.

US Department of Labor (n.d.) NAWS. National Agricultural Workers Survey. www.dol.gov/agencies/eta/national-agricultural-workers-survey.

Whitener, L. and R. Coltrane. 1981. 'Agricultural labour needs in the 1980s.' Report. UD Department of Labor. DOI:10.22004/ag.econ.276698

World Bank. 2019. Employment in Agriculture (% of Total Employment Modeled ILO Estimate) https://data.worldbank.org/indicator/SL.AGR.EMPL.ZS.

Chapter 14

The (re)production of the exploitative nature of rural migrant labour in Europe

Karen O'Reilly and Johan Fredrik Rye

Practice stories of international labour migration

This chapter draws across the major contributions of this edited volume to thread together a 'practice story' (O'Reilly 2012) of international labour migration to Europe's rural regions. Our starting point was our desire to explain the generally exploitative wage, working, and living conditions experienced by rural migrant workers, as described in several of the present volume's chapters as well as in the wider literature; conditions which appear to be perpetually reproduced irrespective of efforts of migrants or others to improve the situation (see for instance, Bock *et al.* 2016, Rye and Scott 2018, Corrado *et al.* 2016, Gertel and Sippel, eds. 2014). Our account in this chapter reveals how the daily practices of agency (of all agents involved in the process at whatever level) work to (re)produce the internal and external structural conditions that are well known to give rise to generally exploitative working conditions.

In Chapter 1 of this volume, we argued for a multiscalar and multidimensional approach to the field, where the ongoing outcomes of labour migration are understood to emerge out of the interaction between everyday practices of actors and the dynamics of local, regional, national, European, and global societal structures. To achieve coherence in this endeavour, in this chapter we employ the meta-theoretical framework of practice stories (O'Reilly 2012), informed by strong structuration theory (Stones 2005) to frame a substantive understanding of the processes involved in this phenomenon. Strong structuration theory understands the making of the social world as ongoing processes, both shaped by and shaping of general patterns, arrangements, and other external social structures. It explicates the ways in which cultures, behaviours, attitudes, institutions, and other sociological phenomena develop over time as norms, rules, organisational arrangements, and other internal structures are acted on and adapted by individuals through the performance of their daily lives, in the context of their communities, groups, networks, and families.

The discussion is organised in three sections. First, we outline our explanandum: the general conditions under which the migrants in this edited volume find themselves living and working. Second, we provide a necessarily brief account of the theoretical construct of *practice stories* and the structuration theory framework on which it builds. Third, we apply this conceptual framework to identify key elements in the making of the contemporary phenomenon of international labour migration to Europe's rural regions, in terms of structural forces, individual agency, practices, and outcomes. We illustrate how the social practices of the agents – migrants and others involved in the phenomenon – often lead to the reproduction of exploitative practices.

In conclusion, our analysis demonstrates how the rural labour migration phenomenon has developed from macro-level circumstances under which improved wage, working, and living conditions are difficult or impossible to achieve; meso-level developments continue to operationalise assumptions that labour migration is necessarily harsh and that employers need to be protected; employers and other powerful agents embody the normalisation of exploitative practices; and even the migrants themselves come to accommodate, or reproduce, their own marginalised, subordinated, and invisible status.

The explanandum: exploitative wage, working, and living conditions

The everyday life of labour migrants in Europe's rural regions is generally inscribed with exploitative wage, working, and living conditions. As noted in the review of the literature in the first chapter of the book, this follows from the very characteristics of the jobs they tend to perform. Work tasks are difficult, dirty, and often dangerous, and overall labour relations resemble those of the secondary labour market: low-paid and low-status jobs, substandard working conditions, including exposure to health hazards, high instability of employment, lack of promotion and training opportunities, and contracts between employers and employees that are too often based on informal and personal relationships (Doeringer and Piore 1971, Holmes 2013). Conditions at work are mirrored in migrants' marginal, subordinate, and often invisible positions in the various rural communities to which they arrive, even acknowledging that rural communities are themselves diverse, complex, and difficult to define, as we argue in the first chapter of this edited volume.

While the chapters in this edited volume add detail and depth to an understanding of the rural labour migrants' plight, they also emphasise common themes. These include: the vulnerable position of migrants and the continuous replacement of migrant labour with new arrivals and different ethnic groups (Farinella and Nori, Chapter 5), and the 'subordinated inclusion' of migrant workers, where rights with regards to wages and contracts are not implemented in practice despite collective agreements (Tollefsen *et al.*, Chapter 8). In Poland there is 'low attractiveness of agriculture for incoming migrants in terms of relatively low wages and high workload' (Górny and Kaczmarczyk, Chapter 6, 86). Şerban *et al.* (Chapter 2, 30) describe the work of Romanian strawberry pickers in Huelva as 'difficult and physically exhausting… supervision was tight and migrants shared a perception of "being watched"… the housing offered was isolated… sleeping three to seven in a room.' Brovia and Piro (Chapter 4) illustrate how isolation in camp and dormitory living means the worker is available at all times of day and night, with little privacy from other migrants or from the employer. These workers have little opportunity to improve their conditions or to go elsewhere, especially given their salaries can be held over until the end of the season. Thai berry pickers in Sweden (Tollefsen *et al.*, Chapter 8) are subject to diverse practices such as employers refusing to let them work once the fridges are full and confiscating car keys to ensure they can't go elsewhere. Farinella and Nori (Chapter 5) describe the dependency, subordination, isolation, and solitude that are typical features of life for immigrant shepherds, despite the fact they also have a great deal of autonomy and freedom in their work, managing much of their workday alone and unsupervised. And Stachowski and Fiałkowska (Chapter 7) describe the spatial separation of Polish migrants in Germany into an 'army of goblins,' invisible to local communities because they are housed close to where they work, often in cramped containers, rather than in proper housing in residential areas.

Our goal in this chapter is to attempt to explain this ongoing exploitation, the perpetual reproduction and augmentation of labour arrangements that are asymmetric in terms of power relations, working conditions, and outcomes. The rural labour migrants in the pages of this book move to new destinations in search of better employment conditions than they would have at home, and they arrive under conditions already set in favour of employers. Our task here is to ask: what are the processes that work to reproduce this ongoing cycle of exploitation?

Informing a practice story of rural labour migration

The goal of a practice story is to offer a substantive interpretation of a phenomenon that is faithful to understandings that structure and agency interact over time and space through the ongoing practice of everyday life. Our approach here owes a special debt to the work of Stones (2005) who developed a stronger version of structuration theory that builds on and develops the work of Giddens and Bourdieu and others (and see Greenhalgh *et al.* 2014 and Stones *et al.* 2019). This strong structuration theory (SST) was then specifically developed by O'Reilly (2012) for the study of migration. Employing practice stories to shape an understanding of a *substantive* phenomenon involves drawing attention to the following heuristically discrete elements that we will examine in more detail as we proceed:

i) *Upper structural, or macro-level, layers that frame actions* (O'Reilly 2012, 23–25).
ii) *The more proximate or meso-level structures* that may be somewhat malleable by the agents in focus (O'Reilly 2012, 23–25, and see Morawska 2009).

iii) *Habitus* (cf. Bourdieu 1990) and *internal structures* (O'Reilly 2012, 26–28).
iv) *Practice, active agency, and conjuncturally specific internal structures* (O'Reilly 2012, 26–28, and see Stones 2005), or the ways in which people adapt their habitus in daily life, within their relevant communities of practice (Lave and Wenger 1991).
v) *Outcomes or newly (re)formed external and internal structures* (O'Reilly 2012, 28–32, Emirbayer and Mische 1998).

We also use the concept of *agent in focus* (Stones 2005) to mean the given set of individuals and groups who are the main concern of the present analysis. In this chapter, as in most of the chapters in the present volume, the 'agents in focus' are the international labour migrants in Europe's rural regions. There is a fuller, in-depth discussion of the role of practice stories and strong structuration theory (SST) in migration research in Benson and O'Reilly (2018), O'Reilly (2012), and Stones *et al.* (2019).

Crucially, SST draws attention to social life as a process, and therefore seeks to frame interpretations of change, or transformations, over time and space. Practice stories, in their turn, offer narrative accounts of the empirical data to explicate these processes. In this chapter we use this approach to provide a coherent and integrated understanding of the continuous reproduction of rural migrants' poor wage and working conditions which goes beyond pure descriptions of social practices and structural forces. Importantly, the following analysis represents a coherent interpretation of the materials provided in the edited volume's individual chapters, and thus represents our perspective but not necessarily those of chapter authors.

i) Broad structural particularities of international rural labour migration

Here we examine the upper structural, or macro-level, layers that have shaped the current phenomenon of international migration in Europe's rural regions. These refer to deeply held assumptions, ideological frames, institutional arrangements, and geographical and material features, over which the current agents in focus (the migrants in the chapters here) had no direct control at the time they began their migration journey. While the structural context is far more complex than we possibly could account for here, the chapters in this volume offer important insights into key structural conditions such as general processes of globalisation, enhanced mobility patterns, and geopolitical events at the European level, such as the downfall of communist regimes and the EU enlargements, which we introduced in the first chapter of the volume. However, we find in the chapters in this edited volume three structural aspects especially important for understanding the distinctive features of the phenomenon of labour migration in Europe's rural areas and rural industries.

The first of these is the *changing fabric of state borders*, in which an increasing reliance on (temporary) migrant labour has become an integral and taken-for-granted characteristic of rural industries in western societies (Chapter 1). More than most industries, food production has come to rely on a migratory labour force as much as migrant workers have come to rely on work mobility as a strategy for achieving a sustainable livelihood. This reliance is often ideologically framed in a positive vein, such as the 'triple win' approach (Şerban *et al.*, Chapter 2, 23–24) which has become 'the most widespread argument for legitimising the initiation of new temporary, circular initiatives.' This approach assumes that circularity is beneficial for countries of origin, destinations, and for the migrants themselves. The latter, it is presupposed, prefer eventually to be able to return to their home countries and their families. Şerban *et al.*'s analysis in this volume (Chapter 2) is somewhat less optimistic. The institutionalisation of such a reliance on migrant labour has in turn informed regulatory efforts and governance regimes such as the EU's inner labour market with 'free' movement of workers, and a 'resurrection' of guest-worker schemes for citizens from non-EU countries (Castles 2006). The volume also provides other examples of how national borders have become porous, either as result of very direct, specific, and intentional policy measures to ease migration flows – for instance how east/west political collaboration steered Russian migrants to Norway's fish-processing industry around the turn of the century (Aure and Riabova, Chapter 10) – or as aggregate effects of less rigid border controls.

Second, a general *process of restructuring in Europe's rural industries*, most evident in the agricultural industry, has led to increasing levels of polarisation, competition, and exploitation of workers. In Europe, as in the US, agricultural production 'is being concentrated on fewer and larger farms, that hire most of a country's farm workers… (with) a larger than ever reliance on farm workers from poorer countries' (Martin, Chapter 13). This edited volume presents several examples of how the gradual disappearance of small farms in favour of land concentration, monoculture, and intensive agriculture provides an important backdrop for the unfolding rural labour migration phenomenon. These developments are most evident in the labour-intensive horticulture industries in the Mediterranean countries but are also observed in other parts of Europe. For instance, Farinella and Nori (Chapter 5) describe how these processes of agricultural modernisation and the global integration of the agri-food chains also have led to an increasing demand for low-waged workers and the growing exploitation of migrants in the agro-pastorial segments of Mediterranean agriculture. Another example is how Poland's farms have increasingly turned to Ukrainian farm workers (Górny and Kaczmarczyk, Chapter 6). However, the picture includes important nuances, and in Europe there still exists a substantial share of smaller-scale economic entities and farms that are family run. For instance, Rye and Scott

(Chapter 9, 142) note the extent of polarisation of the strawberry industry in western countries, in which:

> At one extreme are the global corporations with involvements at all stages of the value chain, often backed by non-agricultural finance. At the other extreme is the family farmer cultivating a few hectares of berries and relying on direct sales to the consumer.

Third, distinctive *characteristics of rural society* tend to be invoked to justify the exploitation and marginalisation of migrant workers. Most important, work in rural industries tends to be seasonal and/or fluctuating, as is particularly evident in land-based, peripheral, or natural resource-based industries like the berry industry in Sweden (see Tollefsen *et al.*, Chapter 8) and in the labour-intensive character of horticulture (Rye and Scott, Chapter 9). As a result, there seems to be a persistent exemption of rural migrant workers from rights granted to most other industries; as Martin (Chapter 13, 211) states, agriculture has historically been 'often exempted from or treated differently from other sectors under labour laws and social welfare programs.' The European case provides further examples where efforts to regulate conditions for migrant workers sometimes meet success (Rye 2017), but where formal regulations are often not realised by changes on the ground (Rye and Andrzejewska, 2010, Tollefsen *et al.*, Chapter 8). Relatedly, the volume's chapters suggest that rural society itself has features that work to ascribe the labour migrants social and spatial marginalised positions in the host localities. This is most evidently described in relation to housing in chapters by Stachowski and Fiałkowska (Chapter 7) and Brovia and Piro (Chapter 4). The often circular pattern of rural labour migration in Europe (in contrast to the US, Martin, Chapter 13) adds to their social detachment from the rural communities. This is further enhanced by the spatial structure of much of the labour the migrants perform, which tends to take place out of sight of, and at a physical distance from, the local community (Chapter 1).

Finally, it is important to note that these structural properties – the characteristics of rural work, the availability of circular or temporary labour, and the features of rural society that work to marginalise migrants – also take shape in the form of deep-seated assumptions about the nature of work in rural areas on the part of government agents, migration bodies, and even sometimes in academic work, such as in the 'triple win' approach. Here we are talking about ideological frames that are so taken for granted they are barely expressed. The chapters in this edited volume have revealed how manual work in the rural industries is 'normalised' as more precarious than is presumed to be the case in other industries; it is therefore argued to be more difficult to ensure workers' rights. These assumptions inform decision-making on behalf of those with the power to effect change, as they tend to be invoked to justify the exploitation of migrant workers.

In summary, as the chapters in this edited volume have shown, there are distinctive structural features that are unique to our understanding of the experiences, practices, and outcomes of international labour migration to Europe's rural regions, and as such, sets it apart from other migration phenomena.

ii) Specific localised features of rural labour migration

Next we look at more proximate or meso-level structural conditions that shape practices of rural labour migration: opportunities, limits, constraints, and pertinent ideological frames which pertain to a given situation, country, or locality (Morawska 1996). Several chapters in this volume refer to more localised or idiomatic conditions that have led (directly or indirectly) to increased international migration to rural areas, and thereafter continue to influence the experiences of the international labour migrants. Also, here we draw attention to three meso-level structures of particular interest for understanding the nature of international labour migration in rural Europe. These echo the macro structures discussed in the previous section and are decisive in understanding the heterogeneity of the phenomenon.

First, there is a diversity of *labour migration regimes* across the European continent that directly condition the migrants' access to Europe's rural regions. These are largely the domain of state level regulations, and thus raise concerns pertinent to national socio-political contexts. They are also constantly changing, despite efforts at the EU level to standardise this field of legislation, for instance through the seasonal worker directive. Nevertheless, one commonality across the various migration streams covered in this volume is that regimes and governance tend to be demand-driven, addressing employers' assumed need for labour in their provision of poor working conditions.

Second, there is diversity in *labour market regulations and practices* as enacted at the level of the nation-state, but a common trait is how authorities consistently overlook or ignore rural labour migrants' poor working and living conditions. Even when legislative intentions are good, or inscribed into law, it appears that state authorities are in many cases incapable of *de facto* regulating migrant labour for the actual improvement of the position of migrants. This is expressly argued in the chapter by Tollefsen *et al.* (Chapter 8), where they discuss migrants' 'subordinated inclusion.'

Related to the above, recruitment agencies also act as localised (proximate) structures shaping these migrations and contributing to their continued poor conditions. As Stachowski and Fiałkowska (Chapter 7, 107) argue, 'a bulk of migration has been organised as posted workers and through recruitment agencies, which was an effective way of avoiding collective agreements such as equal wages.' For others, much recruitment is by word of mouth, and through friends and relatives (Farinella and Nori, Chapter 5). Intimating our argument below, we note here how migrants' agency in turn consolidates the formation of ethnic niches and exclusion.

Third, there are a variety of local-specific *features of rural societies* that are explicitly connected to the hardships migrants experience. Europe's rural regions are dependent on employment in rural industries, either in agriculture or other industries that is likely to recruit migrant workers to low-skilled, manual jobs in global competitive branches. They also share processes of demographic decline, generation renewal problems and land abandonment. Furthermore, as in the case of Mediterranean agro-pastoralism described by Farinella and Nori (Chapter 5), it appears that the vulnerable conditions of migrants are furthered by the scarce presence of public control and trade unions in rural areas and the constant presence of a 'reserve army swelled by new migratory waves [that] consolidates exploitative conditions, as evidenced by the continuous replacement of migrant labour with new arrivals and different ethnic groups' (Farinella and Nori, Chapter 5, 71). However, these are processes that vary greatly across rural spaces and thus influence the everyday conditions for workers in different ways; the rural labour migration phenomenon unfolds uniquely across what we are here calling rural space (see Chapter 1 for an explanation of the use of this term in this way).

Nonetheless, a common trait of the proximate structures in the case of the rural labour migration phenomenon appears to be their existence independent of our agents in focus, the migrants. For the migrant worker, the migration regimes, labour conditions, and local community is experienced as a given; they are the ones least able within this labour context to modify and change these conditions but have to adjust to them as they are; that is, as they have been formed by other and more powerful agents in the localities.

In many cases, these structures are supported by cultural and ideological frames that work to fortify them. For instance, employers of migrant workers may internalise the ideas above and, despite numerous accounts of the exploitative nature of the work they provide, emphasise the positive aspects of their relationship to their workers. Examining such 'hegemonic discourses' in the strawberry industry in the US, UK, and Norway, Rye and Scott (Chapter 9) note how employers refer to migrants' 'dual frames of reference' and invoke what the migrants could earn at home to justify what are poor wages in the host country. These employers believe themselves to provide 'good work' for the migrants and, for instance, emphasise how the benefits are taken home to ensure 'future prosperity' rather than problematise their relatively deprived position in the host community. In this way they conceptualise migrant workers as genuinely different, and thus both in need of and less deserving of the working and living standards they take for granted for themselves and other 'locals.'

The employers in Farinella's and Nori's chapter are more explicit in their construction of a hierarchy between employers and workers, and they talk of the backwardness of their immigrant shepherds, which is an 'imagined backwardness' [that] serves the stockowner to assert a sort of moral, cultural, and technical superiority over the immigrant worker, which legitimises the low wage demand for obedience (Chapter 5, 80).

Other ideological frames include assumptions held on the part of some employers, migrants, and locals alike that local people will not do the work migrants do in these rural areas. This functions as a self-fulfilling prophecy *par excellence*. For example, as a result of Brexit, the British government announced it would like to encourage the local workforce. However, the only actual policy suggested so far to help replace recruitment is a seasonal and temporary scheme similar to the former Seasonal Agricultural Workers Scheme. This sort of scheme is known to lead to instability, exclusion, and marginalisation (Halfacree, Chapter 12). Contrary to the above, there are also some deeply held assumptions on the part of local populations that migrants are a drain on local resources, taking jobs locals could do, and requiring schooling and other services that might be in high demand (Halfacree, Chapter 12).

In summary, there are distinctive and more proximate structural features which are unique to our understanding of the experiences, practices, and outcomes of international labour migration to Europe's rural areas. First, despite the diversity of *labour migration regimes,* they are generally demand-driven, addressing employers' assumed need for labour as opposed to addressing workers' need for good working conditions. Second, labour migration regulations and practices consistently overlook (and work to consolidate) rural labour migrants' poor working and living conditions. Third, specific features of rural societies, such as demographic decline, generation renewal problems, land abandonment, and harsh territories, as discussed in many of the chapters, are related to the hardships migrants experience. Crucially, these localised structural features are internalised, enacted, and performed by a range of actors, including local employers, local people, and even the migrants themselves, to produce marginalisation and subordination. Thus, as with wider structures and despite their spatial heterogeneity, proximate structures generally appear to contribute to the shaping of poor work and life conditions.

iii) Migrants' aspirations, expectations, and accommodations

Internal structures are those taken-for-granted ways of doing things, ways of thinking, deeply held normative assumptions, and even embodied habits that shape all our lives and that, in turn, have been shaped by past experiences. Bourdieu's (1990, 53) term 'habitus' is one of the clearest ways to think about internal structures, as 'systems of durable, transposable dispositions, structured structures predisposed to function as structuring structures.' The migrants that feature in the chapters here are not homogeneous: their lives have been moulded by education, class, gender, age, diverse cultural orientations, and experiences, into deeply embodied dispositions, or habitus.

Their experiences after migration are, in turn, influenced and shaped by these internal structures in a variety of ways as they confront the new fields of their host societies (Stones *et al.* 2019), and especially the structural conditions outlined in the previous sections. For migrants, internalised structures include assumptions about the destination, the work one is moving for, the way of life assumed to be achievable, and even the plans for the future that have been shaped by prior migrants and their recreated experiences, as well as by other media of communication. Again, we outline, from the material in this edited volume, three features we find of particular relevance in the analysis of the rural labour migration phenomenon in Europe.

First, our agents in focus, the migrants in these chapters, have hopes, dreams and aspirations that are forged over time and tempered by the realities of those who have gone before, or their own experiences, and knowledge. Despite conditions pointing to the contrary, many migrants are hopeful for better futures, and for settled and good lives. Aure's and Riabova's chapter (Chapter 10) is especially rich in examples of such internalised structures. The migration from Teriberka, in Russia, to Båtsfjord, in Norway, was inscribed with tropes promising a better future from the outset. The 'candidate' migrants were 'interviewed and carefully selected,' which in itself must have raised hopes that this would be a positive experience. Furthermore, migration can be a very emotional experience; while 'they hoped for a better life' and 'it was so exciting,' Aure's and Riabova's migrants also experienced fear and apprehension. For some migrants, let's remember, there is optimism for the future, despite the fact migrants often leave family behind, and often have uncertain futures. This points to the importance of understanding migrants' actions as much more complex than a purely rational and instrumental interpretation might suggest. Their hopes for an imagined future can outweigh their factual knowledge about other migrants' hardships, and they therefore 'willingly' enter into migration trajectories despite knowing about the likely challenges, including exploitative work and life conditions, which are lying ahead.

Second, there are some populations for whom we could talk of a *migration habitus:* the migrants' prior internalisation of migration as a potential strategy, and their embodied and tacit adjustment to the parameters of action in their social contexts. As Bourdieu (1990) reminds us, objective constraints tend to shape what people aspire to. They follow routes laid down by earlier migrants, pursuing established networks and paths (and of course some pursue new routes they hear of through different media). In other words, where migrants go, their choices, and how they assume life will be when they get there, how long they expect to stay and so on, is shaped by their own and others' prior experiences, and the stories and discourses that frame those experiences.

Stachowski and Fiałkowska, for example, illustrate how Polish migration to Norway, in this case, is marked by high levels of cross-border mobility, probably because some Polish people have by now developed the habit of migrating (inscribed into the habitus, if not yet into practice) and, because Poland is not too distant from Norway, the habit of regular return visits. Yet, these Polish migrants also dreamed of settling and making a new home. Alternatively, the German case they speak of is 'an example of a seasonal, temporary labour migration from Poland that stretches back to the mid-nineteenth century.' Originating from an area in Poland where 'seasonal migration was a widely popular livelihood strategy,' it too has indubitably acquired the sense of a habit, with 'traits of permanence' (Stachowski and Fiałkowska, Chapter 7, 105). Similarly, as demonstrated in many of the chapters, and as a result of the regimes outlined above, many migrants develop transnational social practices spanning state borders that work to mitigate the negative experiences abroad.

Third, as result of their migration practices and experiences, migrants come to accommodate to the demanding nature of their working and home lives. In other words, they develop identities that are coherent with, and even reinforce, the 'normalisation' of the conditions within which they find themselves. Most of the migrants in the pages of this volume internalise the fact that work is often hard, and that life is challenging. Irrespective of dreams of settlement, some learn that in reality their migration needs to be cyclical, for example in Saluzzo, Italy, where the 'local administration systematically has closed the formal camp and dismantled the informal settlements at the end of each agricultural season' (Brovia and Piro, Chapter 4, 63). They are aware they are being exploited, and of course this will affect how they behave when they arrive. As Stachowski and Fiałkowska tell us, migrants often see themselves as marginal in the rural communities, although they are sometimes 'also conscious of their pivotal role' in the local economy, which may of course empower them at some stage. Similarly, the migrants in this book often share the assumptions discussed above that they are doing work that it is believed locals will not do.

In summary, our agents in focus, our migrants in these chapters, have hopes, dreams, and aspirations that are forged over time and tempered by the realities of those who have gone before, or their own experiences and knowledge. Many of these had already acquired a *migration habitus*, internalising and embodying migration as a potential strategy, transnationalism as a social practice, and other tacit adjustments to the parameters of action in their social contexts. Finally, we also note that despite any initial hopes or expectations to the contrary, as a result of their migration practices and experiences, migrants begin to accommodate to the demanding nature of their working and home lives.

iv) Rural migrants' agency

We now turn to what the ongoing practice of migration is like for the migrant workers in the pages of this book. This section is about the here and now, the constantly changing present – the *present continuous* – in which our migrants live and act. In a framework informed by strong structuration theory, active agency takes the shape of individual reflexive reactions to specific circumstances, which are always to some extent circumscribed by previous events and experiences, and by ongoing contingencies. As Morawska (2009) reminds us, migration is an unsettling experience, causing people to reconsider options and re-evaluate resources. Furthermore, we should not forget that habituses (or otherwise conceptualised internal structures) are malleable, transposable, and open to be amended in the practice of daily life. Stones (2005) developed the ontological concept of conjuncturally specific internal structures (CJS) as a means for better comprehending the daily interaction of structure and agency. CJS become relevant at the point of action, when agents confront specific sets of circumstances, or are in the position to make certain choices, shaped by their imagination of how things could be different. In turn, CJS are shaped in the everyday by the fact that all agents are at any time located within sets of relationships, or communities of practice (Wenger 1998).

The volume's chapters demonstrate how migrants are sometimes able to take advantage of conditions that arise to enable improvement in their lives: they are certainly not passive subjects of structural forces. Fratsea and Papadopoulos (Chapter 3) focus expressly on the agency of Romanians in Greece, who developed individual and family strategies to improve their quality of life and their social situation, offering them some resilience during the economic crisis in Greece. Some Romanians, despite difficult conditions, have been able to open Romanian restaurants, transport companies, and Airbnb businesses. Interestingly, the authors argue that much of the resilience shown by these migrants arrives through earlier coping mechanisms, including building strong social networks. These new businesses may not amount to wholescale structural change for Romanian migrants as a whole, but it still implies new outcomes for future migrants who can build on the contacts, knowledge, expertise, and aspirations of those who have been able to exercise agency to effect positive change (and see O'Reilly 2018).

Similarly, Stachowski and Fiałkowska (Chapter 7, 105) say the Polish migrants they studied 'are not simply victims of oppressive structural forces, but also display an array of agentic competences, making sense of their situation, achieving a degree of control over their lives, and being able to pursue their life plans.' Some are able to aspire to stay longer, to settle, and then to work towards achieving that, especially in Norway: the average time living in the community for Stachowski's participants was six and a half years. Farinella and Nori's (Chapter 5, 76) shepherds were able to demonstrate 'high degrees of mobility, often moving from one farm to another' in pursuit of better conditions. Some engage in practices such as selling products from a vegetable garden and earning a little on the side by fixing things.

However, agency amounts to more than actors' strategic actions. At times, it is exactly what our agents in focus do that contributes, over time and space, to the reproduction of their own marginalisation and subordination. For example, once Romania joined the EU and gained the right to freedom of movement, the recruitment processes of Romanians to Spain were informalised, relying on migrants' own networks. Yet these migrants themselves reproduced the former practices of temporary, circular migration, by continuing to assume this was the way to migrate in this context and repeating the patterns of earlier trends. Şerban *et al.* (Chapter 2, 34) argue this was the result of 'the power of social networks made up of migrants who learned to embody and enact employers' demands.'

To return to the examples above, while some Romanians in Greece have opened new businesses and broken away from exploitative rural labour, others continue to engage in temporary migration as a household support strategy or survival strategy. These migrations continue to support exploitative practices. Similarly, Stachowski and Fiałkowska (Chapter 7, 109–110) talk of how Polish migrants learn to be 'ideal' workers, to be resilient and obedient at work, 'we came here to work, not to take a rest' was an oft-repeated phrase, which helped to build resilience in the face of poor accommodation, a demanding job, the demeaning treatment of workers, and 'insecurity related to future employment translates into an intensification of work and self-exploitation.'

In Halfacree's chapter, migrants in the UK exhibit characteristics expected of them in line with notions of the good rural worker, including: 'a generally strong work ethic and record of getting jobs done, a large degree of self-sufficiency.' And Farinella and Nori (Chapter 5) admit that the shepherds' strategies, discussed above, in fact amount to little more than what Scott (1985) referred to as 'weapons of the weak,' everyday forms of resistance that work more as coping mechanisms than providing real structural change. The shepherding migrants learn to be the good migrants their employers want, and these everyday practices – while designed to limit subordination – in fact serve to legitimate their exploitation and lack of power to effect profound change. In what amounts to an excellent analysis of the interaction of structure and agency over time, Farinella and Nori (Chapter 5, 82) argue:

> The shepherd is a 'good worker' only as long as he is docile, obedient, and willing to accept low wages. The migratory paths remain circular and international migrants move from one farm to another, from one territory to another; they cannot think of shepherding as a 'career' with opportunities for social mobility, but only as a precarious and uncertain employment and temporary source of income.

The Thai berry pickers in Tollefsen *et al.* (Chapter 8) were told they were legally entitled to a guaranteed wage, but were then asked to choose between that or a piece rate which, though it promised to offer more, often meant in practice migrants ended up with less than the guaranteed wage. So, while they may have overtly *chosen* to be paid per kilo, they did it with the hope of earning more, while ending up with less.

In conclusion, many of the chapters in this edited volume are able to offer examples in which labour migrants in Europe's rural regions are sometimes able to take advantage of conditions that arise to enable improvement of their conditions. It is not our intention here to strip our agents in focus of their strategic agency. Nevertheless, it is clear that it is often through their own small, daily practices that they also contribute to the reproduction of the conditions under which they are marginalised, exploited, and subordinated. This is because their own agency, as with all agents involved in rural labour migration, is shaped by what has gone before through the constraints of external and internalised (and learned) structures.

v) The outcomes: newly (re)formed external and internal structures

What people do and the ways in which they interact will have an effect for subsequent perceptions, expectations, habits, ways of doing things, and agency. In turn, these shape communities of practice (networks, groups, relationships), and both local and broader structures are reproduced or transformed, to varying degrees, over space and time. Outcomes of structuration processes can be intended or unintended and can lead to innovation or consolidation. Outcomes, as we shall see here, take the shape of external and internal structures, of practices, and communities.

The chapters in this edited volume have sometimes been able to draw attention to small acts of agency that have led to new patterns or arrangements. We witness a few, minor positive changes for our agents in focus, the migrants. For instance, some of the Polish migrants in Norway settle more permanently, are joined by their families, and see an improved financial situation. Nevertheless, their opportunities for further enhancement, for example by moving into other work, appears limited. In the UK, some migrants put into practice their imaginings of the rural idyll and achieve some sense of settlement. However, since the 2016 Brexit referendum, migrants are apparently feeling less comfortable, less settled, and less accepted (Halfacree, Chapter 12).

However, very little of this change is transformational and the overwhelming emphasis in the chapters is on subordination and marginalisation of migrants. As Şerban *et al.* (Chapter 2) argue, employers and other decision-makers often relate to migrants as *labour* rather than as human beings. They mask exploitation, even to themselves, with a rhetoric of good work, invoking the 'good migrant.' In Chapter 10 by Rye and Scott, despite their recognition of the harsh nature of work in the strawberry industry, the employers first and foremost emphasised the positive aspects of the work and their role, talking of how good the work they provide is, and how working well and producing good harvests is to the benefit of employers and workers alike. This paternalistic attitude in which they view themselves as good and socially responsible employers, functions to reproduce, and also mask, labour arrangements that foster marginalisation and exploitation. Similarly, the way in which food and accommodation are provided 'in kind' as a way of offering savings for immigrant shepherds (Farinella and Nori, Chapter 5, 78) could instead be interpreted as 'a governmental power on migrant life' (Foucault 1975), in which 'the farmer's family establishes what and when to eat, how and when to sleep, how to dress, and when to wash.'

In some cases, what appeared to be a transformative form of agency was indeed conjuncturally specific internalised structures reproducing or causing negative outcomes. Stachowski and Fiałkowska talk of the awful conditions Polish migrants suffer in Germany, including seclusion in camp accommodation, frequent power cuts, and restricted access to storage, water, and washing facilities. But these migrants themselves continually compare their lives with home and this serves to enable them to rationalise their own marginality. In other words, they are somewhat complicit in their own marginalisation. This is a form of what Bourdieu has called symbolic violence, which:

> *Represents the way in which people play a role in reproducing their own subordination through the gradual internalisation and acceptance of those ideas and structures that tend to subordinate them. It is an act of violence precisely because it leads to the constraint and subordination of individuals, but it is also symbolic in the sense that this is achieved indirectly and without overt and explicit acts of force or coercion.*
>
> (Connolly and Healy 2004, 15)

In the end, what these migrants work towards changing is minimal, with the focus more on making things easier to bear than on actually shaping and acting on desires (see Stones 2009). As Fratsea and Papadopoulos (Chapter 3, 40) acknowledge, migrants always have to fit agency to conditions: their 'repertoire of strategies and practices,' their aspirations, hopes and dreams, are always shaped over time and space by the opportunity structures they confront.

Conclusion: the reproduction of the exploitative nature of rural labour

In this chapter we have outlined a practice story of international labour migration to Europe's rural regions which provides unique insights into the perpetual reproduction of exploitative wage, working, and living conditions of migrant workers. This, we argue, is the outcome of the dynamic interplay between structural properties of the rural labour migration phenomenon and the agency of migrants, and other agents involved in the making of the phenomenon, as practices that take place over space and time. In other words, our account reveals how the daily practices of agency (of all agents involved in the process) work to (re)produce generally exploitative working conditions.

There are three distinctive (upper level/macro) structural features that are unique to our understanding of the experiences, practices, and outcomes of international labour migration to Europe's rural areas. These are: an increasing reliance on migrant labour as part of *the changing fabric of state borders*; increasing levels of polarisation, competition, and exploitation in the context of a general *process of industrial restructuring in Europe's rural industries*; and the distinctive *characteristics of rural society* that tend to be invoked to justify the exploitation and marginalisation of migrant workers. Furthermore, farm work, agricultural work, and land-based work are 'normalised,' or unquestioningly deemed, as more precarious than work in other industries. The very nature of seasonal and land-based work as temporary and precarious is itself used to justify exploitation. This normalisation affects decisions made on the part of agents with power to effect change, for example, it is considered more difficult to ensure workers' rights in these areas.

There are three further distinctive (more proximate /meso-level) structural features that are unique to our understanding of the experiences, practices, and outcomes of international labour migration to Europe's rural areas. First, *labour migration regimes* are generally demand-driven, addressing employers' assumed need for labour as opposed to addressing workers' need for good working conditions. Second, *labour migration regulations and practices* consistently overlook rural labour migrants' poor working and living conditions. Third, *specific features of rural societies*, such as the nature of rural work, depopulation, land abandonment, and harsh territories, are viewed as inimical to improved conditions for migrants. Crucially, these localised structural features are internalised, enacted, and performed by a range of actors, including local employers, local people, and even the migrants themselves, to produce social and spatial marginalisation, and subordination.

The migrants in these chapters have aspirations for their migration that are tempered by the realities of those who have gone before and their own experiences, but still can be ambitious, hopeful, and emotional. Some had acquired a *migration habitus*, internalising and embodying temporary or seasonal migration as a potential strategy, transnationalism as a social practice, and other tacit adjustments to the parameters of action in their social contexts. Others dreamed of settlement and new lives in new destinations. But, over time, migrants begin to accommodate to the demanding nature of their working and home lives.

Several of the chapters in this edited volume offer examples in which labour migrants in Europe's rural regions take advantage of conditions that arise to enable improvement of their conditions. Nevertheless, as the chapters in this edited volume have indubitably shown, it is also clear that it is often through their own small, daily practices that they come to unwittingly contribute to the reproduction of the conditions under which they are marginalised, exploited, and subordinated.

In the end, the chapters in this edited volume have shown that migrants are only able to effect minimal change, with the focus more on making things easier to bear than on actually having the power to shape or act on desires (see Stones 2009). As Fratsea and Papadopoulos (Chapter 3) acknowledge, migrants always have to fit agency to conditions, their 'repertoire of strategies and practices,' their aspirations, hopes, and dreams, are always shaped over time and space by the opportunity structures they confront in their daily lives, communities, and practices.

Our practice story of international labour migration to Europe's rural regions concludes thus: macro-level conditions have developed under which change for the better, for migrants, is difficult or impossible to achieve; meso-level developments continue to operationalise assumptions that labour migration is necessarily harsh and that employers need to be protected; employers and other powerful agents embody the normalisation of practices; and even the migrants themselves come to accommodate or reproduce through their daily practices the conditions for their own marginalised and subordinated status.

Acknowledgements

The chapter project, is the result of the 2017–2022 Global Labour in Rural Societies research project financed by the Norwegian Research Council (grant no. 261854/F10). The authors wish to thank the external reviewers for their constructive comments on the manuscript.

References

Benson, M. and K. O'Reilly. 2018. *Lifestyle Migration and Colonial Traces in Malaysia and Panama*. Basingstoke: Palgrave Macmillan.

Bock, B., G. Osti and F. Ventura. 2016. 'Rural Migration and New Patterns of Exclusion and Integration in Europe.' In *The Routledge International Handbook of Rural Studies*, edited by M. Shucksmith and D. Brown, 71–84. New York, Routledge.

Bourdieu, P. 1990. *The Logic of Practice*. Cambridge: Polity.

Castles, S. 2006. 'Guestworkers in Europe: A Resurrection?' *International Migration Review*, 40(4): 741–766.

Connolly, P. and J. Healy. 2004. 'Symbolic Violence, Locality and Social Class: The Educational and Career Aspirations of 10-11-year-old Boys in Belfast.' *Pedagogy, Culture and Society* 12(1): 15–34.

Corrado, A., C. de Castro and D. Perrotta, eds. 2016. *Migration and Agriculture Mobility and Change in the Mediterranean Area*. London, Routledge.

Doeringer, P.B. and M. Piore. 1971. *Internal Labor Markets and Manpower Analysis*. New York: D.C Heath and Company.

Emirbayer, M. and A. Mische. 1998. 'What is Agency?' *American Journal of Sociology* 103(4): 962–1023.

Foucault, M. 1975. *Surveiller et Punir* [Discipline and Punish]. Paris: Gallimard.

Gertel, J. and S.R. Sippel, eds. 2014. *Seasonal Workers in Mediterranean Agriculture*. Abingdon, Routledge.

Greenhalgh, T., R. Stones, R. and D. Swinglehurst. 2014. 'Choose and Book: A Sociological Analysis of Resistance to an Expert System.' *Social Science and Medicine* 104: 210–219.

Holmes, S.M. 2013. *Fresh Fruits, Broken Bodies. Migrant Farmworkers in the United States*. Berkeley: California Series in Public Anthropology.

Lave, J. and Wenger, E. 1991. *Situated Learning: Legitimate Peripheral Participation*. Cambridge: Cambridge University Press.

Morawska, E. 1996. *Insecure Prosperity: Small-town Jews in Industrial America. 1890–1940*. Princeton, NJ: Princeton University Press.

Morawska, E. 2009. *A Sociology of Immigration: (Re)making Multifaceted America*. Basingstoke: Palgrave.

O'Reilly, K. 2012. *International Migration and Social Theory*. Basingstoke: Palgrave.

O'Reilly, K. 2018. 'The British on the Costa Del Sol Twenty Years On: A Story of Liquids and Sediments.' *Nordic Journal of Migration Research* 7(3): 139–147.

Rye, J.F. 2017. 'Negotiating Neoliberalism: Informalisation and Reformalisation of Industrial Relations in Norway's Agricultural Industry in the 21st Century.' *Population, Space and Place* 23(7): unpaginated. DOI:10.1002/psp.2042.

Rye, J.F. and J. Andrzejewska. 2010. 'The Structural Disempowerment of Eastern European Migrant Farm Workers in Norwegian Agriculture.' *Journal of Rural Studies* 26(1): 41–51.

Rye, J.F. and S. Scott. 2018. 'International Labour Migration to/in rural Europe: A Review of the Evidence.' Sociologia Ruralis 8(4): 928–954.

Scott, J.C. 1985. *Weapons of the Weak. Everyday Forms of Peasant Resistance*. New Haven, CT: Yale University Press.

Stones, R. 2005. *Structuration Theory*. Basingstoke: Palgrave Macmillan.

Stones, R. 2009. 'Power and Structuration Theory.' In *The Sage Handbook of Power*, edited by S. Clegg and M.Haugaard, 89–107. London: Sage.

Stones, R., K. Botterill, M. Lee and K. O'Reilly. 2019. 'One World is not Enough: The Structured Phenomenology of Lifestyle Migrants in East Asia.' *British Journal of Sociology* 70(1): 44–69.

Wenger, E. 1998. *Communities of Practice: Learning, Meaning, and Identity*. Cambridge: Cambridge University Press.

Index

Note: agriculture as a general term has not been indexed as it appears throughout the text.

abuse 226; *see also* sexual abuse and harassment
accommodation 236–8; minimum standards of 112–14; provision of by employer 77, 242; Romanian migrants in Spain 30 (*see also* living and housing conditions)
adaptability 161
adventure, migration as chance for 164
affectivity 159
agency 13–18, 228–30, 235, 238–42, 244; agro-pastoralism in Greece, Spain and Italy 72, 78, 81–2; Polish migrants in Germany and Norway 117; Romanian migrants in Greece 38–40, 47; Thai migrants in Sweden 128; transformative form of 242
agents 86, 144, 231; *see also* recruitment procedures
agro-pastoralism in Greece, Spain and Italy 14, 70–82, 235; agro-ecological and socio-cultural diversity 73; cheesemaking (high skilled) 74, 76, 77; dairy production 72; extensive agricultural systems 70–4; farm closure or restructuring 73; Greece 70, 73; herd expansion 73–4, 81; Indian migrants 75–6, 81; intensification 73; international competition 72; Italy 70, 76; land and labour reorganisation 73; Latin-American migrants 76; Macedonian migrants 73, 75–6; meat production 72, 74, 76; migrant shepherds and 'good workers' rhetoric 70–82, 240–1; mobility, reduced 74; Moroccan migrants 75–6; Pakistani migrants 75; price volatility 72; production costs 74; productivity rates 74; semi-extensive systems 73–4; semi-intensive systems 73; Spain 70; training 76; transhumant systems 73–6; Ukrainian migrants 76; wildlife predation 75–6
Albanian migrants in Greece 41, 43, 44, 75; in Spain and Italy 75
alienation 199
anonymity of participants; living conditions in enclaves of industrial agriculture in Italy 53; Polish migrants in Germany and Norway 108, 109; Romanian migrants in Greece 43; Russian migrants in Norway 162–3; strawberry pickers in USA, UK and Norway 146
anti-immigration discourses 6
apathy 169, 171
arrivals and length of stay, differences in 57–8
Asian migrants in Poland 87
aspirations, hopes and dreams 12, 15, 166–7, 237–9, 242–4
asylum seekers 57, 62, 66
autonomy 66, 72, 78, 81, 230

Bangladeshi migrants in Greece 43
bargaining power 55
belonging, sense of 11
bilateral agreements 23, 25, 27, 33–4, 107, 109

board and lodging provided by employer 77
bonuses 150, 197
Bourdieu, P. 236, 237, 242
Bulgaria 5
Bulgarian migrants; in Greece 41, 46, 75–6; in Italy 75–6; in Spain 75–6; in UK 145

Canada 54, 141
care and support by employers 151–2
Caritas 62, 63
charities, migrants' reliance on 59
Chavez, C. 217–19
children/minors working on farms 213
China 55
Chinese migrants in United States 216
circularity 5, 9, 14, 232, 233, 240; agro-pastoralism in Greece, Spain and Italy 82; Polish migrants in Germany and Norway 106, 109, 116; Romanian migrants in Greece 45–6; Romanian migrants in Huelva, Spain 26–7, 32; strawberry pickers in USA, UK and Norway 145, 147–8; Ukrainian migrants in Poland 87
citizenship 41, 126–7
co-development 22, 23, 35
Coldiretti trade union (Italy) 63
collateral tasks (non-contracted extra work) 60, 77
collective agreements/bargaining 121–3, 125–6, 128–9, 131–2, 217, 229
Common Agricultural Policy (CAP) 74–5, 193–5, 203
community development *see* Russian migrants in Norway: emotions, community development and return migration in fish processing industry
competition among workers 110
competitive advantage 81
complementary activities 78
conflict 12; *see also* resistance strategies; strikes and organised resistance
conspicuous consumption 168, 171
construction sector; Polish migrants in Germany and Norway 107; Romanian migrants in Greece 37, 41, 43–5; Thai migrants in Sweden 123; Ukrainian migrants in Poland 93, 99, 100*f*, 101
contact with host society 30
context of rural migration 7–9
contracts; and associated rights 26; eighty per cent permanent 111; formal 121, 122, 132; full-time 111; nominal 26; for non-EEA migrants 121; part-time 107; Romanian migrants in Spain 26; Thai migrants in Sweden 26, 122, 123, 132 (*see also* informal contractual arrangements)
control over migrants; agro-pastoralism in Greece, Spain and Italy 72, 77, 79, 82; industrial agriculture in Italy 55, 65
conventional and non-conventional strategies 47
conviviality between ethnic groups 12
coping mechanisms 39, 46, 239, 240
cosmopolitanism 3
Countryside Alliance 202
Covid-19 pandemic and 'new normal' 3–4, 7, 18
creative strategies 39
cultural capital 161
cultural kit 110–11

de-humanising practices 110, 141
delayed gratification 148
demeaning treatment 114
demographic characteristics 7–8, 18, 37
demographic decline 81
demographic regression 70
demographic sustainability 12
departure times to benefit employer 29
dependency 230; perceived 30
depression 169
differential inclusion 125–6
dignity 168, 170
diligence 110; *see also* 'good worker' rhetoric
discrimination 12, 105, 141; *see also* race, racialisation and ethnicity; racism and xenophobia
disempowerment 10
disillusionment 159, 165, 169–70
domestic service and Ukrainian migrants in Poland 93, 96, 98, 100*f*
domesticity sphere and loss of intimacy 53, 59, 65
dual frame of reference 71, 147–8, 235

earnings *see* wages
eastern European migrants in UK 199
education of migrants (Norway) 184*t*, 185–6, 188, 189

emotional capital 161, 165, 167–71
emotional experiences, positive and negative 161
emotional labour 161
emotional resources 161
emotional security 199
emotions of migrants 8, 12, 15, 237; absence of 169; anger 161; considerations 170; culturally elaborated 161; euphoria 165; excitement 170; expectations 170; fear (of the unknown) 161, 237; joy 161, 170; negative 168, 171; non-rational 161; painful resignation 168; physical 161; positive 165; pride 170; socially and historically nuanced 161; sorrow 168; structuring 161; suppression of 169
employability enhancement 111
employer/worker horizontal and direct working relationships 77
employer/worker separation 76
employers' interests and legislation requirements interplay 61
employers' point of view *see* strawberry picking in the USA, UK and Norway from employers' point of view
employment inequalities 122
employment opportunities combined with quality of life 42
empowerment 238
equality 18
essentialised characteristics 81–2
ethical issues 108–9, 142, 150, 153–4
ethnicity *see* race, racialisation and ethnicity
ethnographic approach; agro-pastoralism in Greece, Spain and Italy 70; Polish migrants in Germany and Norway 104, 108; Russian migrants in Norway 162; Thai migrants in Sweden 124–5
EURES network (Spain) 27
European Commission 24; emergency notice on critical occupations 3–4
European Migration Network (EMN) 23–4
European Regional Development Fund (ERDF) 195
European Social Fund (ESF) 195
European Union Structural Funds 195
everyday concerns, experiences and practices 109
exclusion 235, 236; Polish migrants in Germany and Norway 104, 105, 113–14, 116, 117; Thai migrants in Sweden 125
expectations 236–8
exploitative practices 15–16, 18, 228–44; agency 238–41; agro-pastoralism in Greece, Spain and Italy 71–2, 77, 81; aspirations, expectations and accommodations 236–8; external and internal structural conditions 228, 241–2; farm labour in California 214; Polish migrants in Germany and Norway 110, 111; practice stories of international labour migration 228–9; Romanian migrants in Greece 39; specific localised features of migration 234–6; strawberry pickers in USA, UK and Norway 142–4, 146–7, 153, 154; structural particularities of migration 231–4; Thai migrants in Sweden 121, 123 (*see also* self-exploitation)

family lives, transnational rearrangements of 106
farmer associations 144
farm labour contractors (FLCs) (United States) 218, 222–3
farm labour in California 211–27; Bracero programme (Mexican migrants as guest workers) 16, 216; Chinese migrants 215–16; contemporary farm labour 219–23; education 213–14; employment 220*t*; family farms 214–15; farmers *vs.* workers 212; from farm jobs to farm work careers 224; guest workers 223, 225; implications for Europe 225–7; large farms 216; mechanisation and imports 224–5; Mexican and Latin-American migrants 16; problems and solutions 223–5; prosperity paradox 211; railroad, effects of 215–16; response to fewer unauthorised migrants 223; rural migrants residing in metropolitan areas 8; Spanish and Mexican land grants 215; unions 217–19; vulnerable farm workers 212–14; wages 222*t*
Federation of Swedish Forestry and Agricultural Employers 122

Filipino migrants in United States 216
fish-processing *see* Russian migrants in Norway: emotions, community development and return migration in fish-processing industry
fitness of migrant 28
flexible grounded theory approach in data coding and analysis 43
flexible work arrangements 34
focus groups 162
food processing industry 3, 8; Romanian migrants in Greece 42, 43; Ukrainian migrants in Poland 86, 101
food production 4, 7; intensive 5
food, provision of by employer 77, 242
forced work reduction and unpaid days off 58
forestry 8, 122
formal economic activities 45
former experiences with migration 18
former migrants as recruiting intermediaries 27
Foucault, M. 78
freedom of movement 23, 226, 232, 240; Polish migrants in Germany and Norway 106–7; Romanian migrants in Greece 46; Romanian migrants in Huelva, Spain 27; UK and migrant pickers post-Brexit 196, 198
freedom, spaces of 72, 78, 230
futures of labour migration 16–18

gangmasters 226
gender factors; industrial agriculture in Italy 57, 62; Romanian migrants in Greece 41, 44; Russian migrants in Norway 162, 165; Ukrainian migrants in Poland 96
generational renewal problems 81
geopolitical changes 6, 57, 231
Germany 40, 226; *see also* Polish migrants and marginalisation in Germany and Norway
Global Forum on Migration and Development (GFMD) 23
good practice 22
'good worker' rhetoric 70, 71–81, 82, 240–1
Greece 14, 143, 226; Albanian migrants 41, 43, 44, 75; Bangladeshi migrants 43; Bulgarian migrants 41, 46, 75–6 (*see also* agro-pastoralism in Greece, Spain and Italy; Romanian migrants in Greece: social and spatial mobility strategies)
guaranteed wage 129–32, 131*t*, 240
guest-worker schemes 9, 197, 232; *see also* Romanian migrants in Huelva, Spain: guest-worker programme
guilt and fear at separating from children and families 164, 170

health and safety 150
'Health and Harmony' consultation paper (UK) 194, 197, 203–4
health insurance 219, 223
health of migrant 32
health sector 5
hierarchical labour relations 71, 76
historical sedimentation of practices and assumptions 10
holidays/time off 77
homesickness 165
horizontal interactions 14, 81
horticulture industry 3, 10–11, 14, 18, 42, 233; Poland 87, 89–93, 96–8, 100*f*, 99, 101–2
hospitality industry 5
household support strategy 46
housing conditions *see* living and housing conditions
human capital 34, 97, 160, 170
humanitarian residence permit 62
hygiene conditions, poor 65

ideal worker 111; *see also* 'good worker' rhetoric
illegality of migrant status 76
imaginaries of mobility 47
immigrant niches 105
immobilisation of migrants 55
inclusion 117; differential 125–6; formal 122
income *see* wages
indebtedness to recruiters 214
in-depth interviews; Polish migrants in Germany and Norway 108–9; strawberry pickers in USA, UK and Norway 145; Ukrainian migrants in Poland 92
Indian migrants; and agro-pastoralism in Greece, Spain and Italy 75–6, 81; in United States 216

individual and family attitudes, aspirations, perceptions and experiences 43
individual and/or family strategies 39
informal contractual arrangements 45, 75–7, 80–1, 91, 93, 109, 144, 229
informal networks 109
insecurity related to present and future employment 110, 111, 170; *see also* precarious status of employment
institutionalisation 232; of informal settlements 66
instrumental treatment 111
integration 12; economic 45; Polish migrants in Germany and Norway 104, 105, 116; Romanian migrants in Greece 37; social 28, 45
intensification of work 18, 110–11, 144, 147, 240
interconnectedness/interdependence 4
intermediaries 28; agro-pastoralism in Greece, Spain and Italy 71, 76; farm labour in California 213, 224, 226; industrial agriculture in Italy 56, 61; strawberry pickers in USA, UK and Norway 153; Ukrainian migrants in Poland 90, 99, 101
internal mobility in rural Norway 175–90; connection between labour migration and internal mobility patterns 184–8; de-commodifying welfare state 188; defining 'rural' 181–2; demographic refill 190; dependent variables 184, 185; descriptive statistics 184*t*; education of migrants 184*t*, 185–6, 188, 189; effect of international migration on native internal mobility 176–8; employment opportunities 188; fixed effects linear regression 184, 185*t*, 186*t*, 187*t*; high-competence workers 189; housing prices 187; in-migration 184*t*, 185*t*, 186*t*, 187*t*, 188, 189; independent variables 183, 184; international and internal migration 175–6; measurement among Norwegian-born people 182–3; out-migration 184*t*, 185*t*, 186*t*, 187*t*, 188, 190; place attachment 188–9; refugees 184*t*, 185*t*, 186*t*; relevant factors beyond labour market 179; theoretical perspectives 176–81; unemployment 184*t*, 185*t*, 186*t*; wages 184*t*, 185*t*, 186*t*, 188
International Labour Organisation (ILO) 123
International Organisation for Migration (IOM) 4, 23
intimacy, loss of due to workplace and domestic sphere overlap 53, 59, 65
invisibility 11, 15, 17, 18, 229, 230; Polish migrants in Germany and Norway 106, 111, 112
irregular status 25
isolation from local populations and nearest towns 8, 53, 54, 74, 77, 114, 116, 230
IT sector 123
Italy 14, 37, 40, 46, 226, 238; Albanian migrants 75; Bulgarian migrants 75–6; right-wing populism 6; Tunisian migrants 57, 58, 66 (*see also* agro-pastoralism in Greece, Spain and Italy; living conditions in enclaves of industrial agriculture in Italy)

Japanese migrants in United States 216

knowledge acquisition 16–17, 170, 239

labour laws (USA) 213
labour-market focused analytical perspectives 54–5
labour market niches 44–5
labour standards 26
Latin-American migrants and agro-pastoralism in Greece, Spain and Italy 76
lay-offs 3
legal status 66
life course approach 43, 162
life situation/conditions 7, 14, 18
lifestyle migrants 8
linguistic barriers 11
living conditions in enclaves of industrial agriculture in Italy 52–67; access to drinking water and services 63; access to health and legal assistance 63; *anti-caporalato* law (informal brokers) 60–1, 66; container camps 63; Foro Boario camp 63; *Grand ghetto di Rignano* (Apulia) 52; guardians and social workers 63; individual company

56; informal settlements 52, 63, 66; inter-ministerial agreement 61; living arrangements 54–5; living inside the companies 58–61; living inside labour camps 62–5; Saluzzo (Piedmont) 61–7; settlements 52–3; small and medium-sized enterprises 56; Transformed Littoral Strip (TLS) (Sicily) and greenhouse agriculture 14, 52–3, 56–61, 66; water riot 63
living and housing conditions 17–18, 28, 228–30, 233–7, 242–3; agro-pastoralism in Greece, Spain and Italy 74, 76, 81; container housing 230; dormitory labour regime 55, 163; farm labour in California 213, 214; ghetto and slum housing 71, 141; overcrowding 65; Polish migrants in Germany and Norway 108–9, 114; Romanian migrants in Greece 38; shanty towns 54; strawberry pickers in USA, UK and Norway 146–8, 153; temporary accommodation 66; Thai migrants in Sweden 128 (*see also* living conditions in enclaves of industrial agriculture in Italy)
loneliness 165, 170
long-term roots in locality 116–17
Luxemburg 5

Macedonian (north) migrants and agro-pastoralism in Greece, Spain and Italy 75–6
managed migration *see* guest-worker schemes
manufacturing sector 107
marginalisation 10–11, 14–18, 229, 233, 236, 239, 241–4; agro-pastoralism in Greece, Spain and Italy 81; Thai migrants in Sweden 126 (*see also* Polish migrants and marginalisation in Germany and Norway)
market failures 3
Marx, K. 77
means-ends rationality 154
meatpacking sector 10
mental and physical health issues 65
Mexican encampments 54
Mexican migrants in United States 216–19, 223, 226
Middle Eastern migrants 6, 8
migration habitus 236–9, 243
minimum wage; farm labour in California 211, 213, 219, 221, 223; UK and migrant pickers post-Brexit 197
mixed methods approach 146
mobility 3; agro-pastoralism in Greece, Spain and Italy 76; industrial agriculture in Italy 52, 60, 61; Romanian migrants in Greece 38–40, 42; social 13, 58, 148 (*see also* freedom of movement)
modes of belonging 199
Moroccan migrants and agro-pastoralism in Greece, Spain and Italy 75–6
Morocco and Plain of Sousse shanty town 54
multidimensional approach 228
multifunctionality 81
multiscalar spatial phenomenon, migration as 4–7, 19, 228

National Agency for Employment (Spain) 27
National Agricultural Workers Survey (NAWS) 213
National Farmers' Union (NFU) (UK) 194, 195, 197
national identity 11, 110
National Institute for Social Service (INPS) (Italy) 57
National Labor Relations Act (1935) (United States) 217
nationality 57; as a proxy 12
nativism 6
networking strategies 124; *see also* social networks
new communication technologies, virtual and physical 5
new migration and labour market policies 17–18
new mobilities paradigm 39
non-participant observation 162
non-timber forest products (NTFP) 122, 127, 132–4
normalisation of practices 243–4
Norway; emotions and community development (*see* Russian migrants in Norway: emotions, community development and return migration in fish-processing industry); internal mobility (*see* internal mobility in rural Norway); marginalisation (*see*

Polish migrants and marginalisation in Germany and Norway; Russian migrants in Norway: emotions, community development and return migration in fish-processing industry); strawberry picking (*see* strawberry picking in the USA, UK and Norway from employers' point of view)

obedience 109, 236, 240
Office for Labour Migration Abroad (OLMA) 26–7
oppression 39
organisation of production 53
origin and return obligations 28
'others', migrants perceived as 9, 12, 17
overtime pay 30, 211, 223
ownership structures 4

Pakistani migrants and agro-pastoralism in Greece, Spain and Italy 75
parallel payment system 130–1, 133–4
participant observation; living conditions in enclaves of industrial agriculture in Italy 53, 58; Polish migrants in Germany and Norway 108; Russian migrants in Norway 162; Thai migrants in Sweden 125
part-time contracts 107
passivity 169, 171
paternalist and authoritarian approach 65, 241–2
pensions 211
peripherality 8, 121
permanent employment 14
permanent migrants 9, 25, 40, 106
permanent temporariness 106
personal advancement 164–5
personal characteristics and migration regimes 7, 18
personal life trajectories 116
personal relations 71–2
personal style 78
piece rates 130–2, 148, 150, 240
pig farms (UK) 196
place-attachment, stability and grounding of life 115–17, 188–9
Points Based System (PBS) 196
Poland 229; Asian migrants 87; Central Statistical Office (CSO) 88 (*see also* Polish migrants and marginalisation in Germany and Norway; Ukrainian migrants in Poland)
polarisation 233, 243
policy-focused analytical perspectives 54–5
Polish migrants and marginalisation in Germany and Norway 11, 14, 104–17, 139, 230, 237–8, 240–2; Accession Treaty 107; at the edge of the local labour market 109–12; EEA membership 107; Germany 104–5, 109–11, 112–14, 116; glocalised forms 104; marginalisation 105–6, 116; materiality and settlement structure of hosting areas 104; methodology and challenges 107–9; Norway 104–5, 108–9, 111–12, 114, 116; sectoral concentration 104; spatial edges 112–15; structural conditions 104; temporal dimensions 104
Polish migrants in UK 12, 145, 199
political reconfigurations in EU 6
political, social and cultural rights 105
Portugal 37
Portuguese migrants and agro-pastoralism in Greece, Spain and Italy 76
poultry meat (UK) 196
poverty 16; Polish migrants in Germany and Norway 105; Russian migrants in Norway 164
powerlessness, sense of 128
precarious status of employment 14, 18; agro-pastoralism in Greece, Spain and Italy 81, 82; Romanian migrants in Greece 38; Thai migrants in Sweden 126, 127
prejudice 12; *see also* discrimination
pressure to improve performance 111
privacy, lack of 230
proximity to areas of production 55
pseudonimisation (for purposes of survey) 53, 146
Public Employment Office (Italy) 62

qualitative approach; agro-pastoralism in Greece, Spain and Italy 70; living conditions in enclaves of industrial agriculture in Italy 53; Romanian migrants in Spain: guest-worker programme 24; Russian migrants in Norway 162; strawberry pickers

in USA, UK and Norway 142; Thai migrants in Sweden 123, 125, 128, 131; Ukrainian migrants in Poland 101
quality of life 147, 167
quantitative approach 87
quasi-slavery relations 141
quitting without notice 80–1

race, racialisation and ethnicity 10, 12, 17; ethnic essentialisation mechanisms 79; ethnic hierarchy 44; ethnic niches 116; ethnic strategies 40
racism and xenophobia 7, 141, 197
rationale for arriving and staying 109
reception centres 54
recruitment procedures 5, 90, 98–99, 100*f*, 234; agro-pastoralism in Greece, Spain and Italy 76; campaigns 28; farm labour in California 213; industrial agriculture in Italy 53, 55, 56, 61, 66; Polish migrants in Germany and Norway 107, 116; private 27; recruiting newcomers to enable competition 58; Romanian migrants in Spain 26, 34; Russian migrants in Norway 163–5; strawberry pickers in USA, UK and Norway 153; Thai migrants in Sweden 124; Ukrainian migrants in Poland 90–2, 98–9, 101, 100*f* (*see also* intermediaries; word of mouth recruitment)
re-formalisation 144
refugees 5, 6, 8, 57, 66, 184*t*, 185*t*, 186*t*; *see also* Syrian refugees
regulatory procedures 3, 10, 53
relational skills 161
reliability of migrant worker 110
rent deduction from salary 163
repeaters-Romanian migrants in Spain 26
residence permits 86, 107
resilience and reworking strategies 39, 44, 46, 109, 114, 239, 240
resistance strategies 39, 123, 128, 240; *see also* strikes and organised resistance
restriction in accessing hospitals, schools and trade unions 54
retention of migrants 153
retirees 5
right to remain 199
rights, limited 76
Romania 5
Romanian migrants; agro-pastoralism in Greece, Spain and Italy 75–6, 77–81; Greece (*see* Romanian migrants in Greece: social and spatial mobility strategies); industrial agriculture in Italy 52, 57, 58, 59–60, 61, 66; Spain (*see* Romanian migrants in Spain: guest-worker programme pattern of migration); UK and migrant pickers post-Brexit 145
Romanian migrants in Greece: social and spatial mobility strategies 6, 13, 37–47, 143, 239; agency and mobility 38–40; austerity measures 41; citizenship 41; devising spatial mobility strategies 45–6; economic adjustment programmes 41; economic crisis (2008) 37, 40–2, 47; GDP 41; Ilia and Achaia regions 42–3; internal migration 40; mobility strategies 44; regularisation laws 41; transnational entrepreneurship 44–5; unemployment 41–2
Romanian migrants in Huelva, Spain: guest-worker programme 13, 22–35, 229–30, 240; agri-food industry 25; bilateral agreements 23, 25, 27, 33–4; bottom-up perspective 28–33; constant capital 25; Moroccan and Sub-Saharan Africans already in Spain with irregular status 25; permanent workers and trainees 25; private phase of migration 23, 25, 27–8, 34; public phase of migration 23, 25, 27, 34; regulated conditions 26; top-down perspective 25–7; triple-win approach 22, 23–4, 33, 35; variable capital 25; year of first departure 24
rural cosmopolitanism 12
rural idyll 199
rural translocalism 12
Russian migrants in Norway: emotions, community development and return migration in fish-processing industry 11, 14, 15, 18, 159–71, 232, 237; collective dream 166–7; considerations in migration process 160, 163–5; dreams about the future back home

166–7; emotional capital devastation 167–70; emotional capital, growth of 162–7; euphoria 159; expectations 160, 166; fear 159; home environment improvement 167–8, 170–1; homesickness 159; intentions 166; joy 159; migration phases 166; mobility programme 159; multi-sited study or organised migration 161–2; nostalgia 159; outcomes 166; plans 166; post-return community development 170–1; post-return re-integration problems 160, 167–70; recruitment 163–5; return migration and rural development 159–60; two years of unskilled jobs 159 (*see also* emotions of migrants)
Russian migrants in Poland 87

salary *see* wages
sampling, purposive and opportunistic 109
Seasonal Agricultural Workers Scheme (SAWS) (UK) 197–8, 204
Seasonal Reception Centre (PAS) 63
seasonal worker directive 234
seclusion 54, 55, 116, 242
secondary labour market 10, 41
segmentation, internal 111
segmented market theory 71
segregation 71
selection processes; Romanian migrants in Spain 26, 28, 29; Ukrainian migrants in Poland 90–2 (*see also* intermediaries; recruitment)
self-development 170
self-employment 71, 220, 220*t*
self-esteem 161, 171
self-exploitation 71, 77, 110, 240
self-perception 106
self-sufficiency 199, 240
self-tailored mobility strategies 53
semi-structured interviews; agro-pastoralism in Greece, Spain and Italy 70; living conditions in enclaves of industrial agriculture in Italy 53; Polish migrants in Germany and Norway 108; Romanian migrants in Greece 43; strawberry pickers in USA, UK and Norway 145–6; Thai migrants in Sweden 121, 125, 129
service sector 5, 10; Romanian migrants in Greece 41; Thai migrants in Sweden 123, 132; Ukrainian migrants in Poland 86, 99
settlement and housing structure 14
settlement structures, scattered 8
sexual abuse and harassment 60, 141
shame 168, 171
shut-downs 3
snowballing selection 124–5
social capital 161
social citizenship rights 126–7
social divisions 126
social dumping 107
social insurance 76
social mobility 13, 58, 148
social networks 234, 239, 240; agro-pastoralism in Greece, Spain and Italy 76; Romanian migrants in Greece 45; Romanian migrants in Spain 27, 34; Ukrainian migrants in Poland 99, 101
social relationships 109
Social Security Numbers (SSNs) 221
social and spatial mobility strategies *see* Romanian migrants in Greece: social and spatial mobility strategies
social status 38, 47
social upgrading 46
social welfare programmes (USA) 213
socio-economic status 44, 47
sociological perspectives 12, 18
sociopolitical characteristics 7
solitude 77, 230
Spain 10–11, 14, 37, 40, 46, 226; Albanian migrants 75; Bulgarian migrants 75–6; ghettos of Sicilia 11; shanty town (Andalusia) 54 (*see also* agro-pastoralism in Greece, Spain and Italy; Romanian migrants in Huelva, Spain: guest-worker programme)
spare time 77
staffing agencies 132, 134
standardised interviews 124
standards of living improvement 164
status 126
status paradox of migration 148
strawberry picking in the USA, UK and Norway from employers' point of view 15, 141–55, 235; 'benevolent moderators' 147, 150, 154–5; economic arguments 154; employer representations and rationalisations

155; 'good farmer' discourse 154–5; 'good work' discourse 155, 235; moral arguments 154; Norway 144–51, 155; post-productivism 143; productivism 143; social responsibility 154; super-productivism 143; UK 142–3, 145–50, 152–3, 155; USA 141, 143–5, 147, 151–2, 155
strawberry-picking-Romanian migrants in Greece 42, 46
strikes and organised resistance 122, 124, 125, 128
strong structuration theory (SST) 230–1, 238
structural factors; Polish migrants in Germany and Norway 113; Romanian migrants in Greece 37; Ukrainian migrants in Poland 90–2
structural forces 229
structural silence 154
structural vulnerability 10, 141
structuration processes 241
structuration theory 228–9, 230
students as migrant workers 5
Sub-Saharan African migrants 6; agro-pastoralism in Greece, Spain and Italy 75–6, 81; in Italy 53, 57, 62–3, 66–7, 226; in Mediterranean horticulture 11
subjection 78
subordinated inclusion *see* Thai migrants in Swedish forest berry industry: subordinated inclusion
subordination 15, 18, 229–30, 239–44; agro-pastoralism in Greece, Spain and Italy 72, 77, 79, 82; Russian migrants in Norway 165
subsidies 195, 212
substantive phenomenon 230
substantive rationality 47
super-diverse phenomenon 16
supply chain capitalism 127–8
survival strategies 46, 78
Sweden; Aliens Act 123–4, 133; Municipal Workers union 122; Trade Union Confederation 123 (*see also* Thai migrants in Swedish forest berry industry: subordinated inclusion)
switching employment 81
symbolic violence 242
Syrian refugees; in Myrsini Open Reception Centre (Greece) 43; in Turkey 126
targeting and selection by employers among groups that lack power 105
temporality of employment 52
Thai migrants in Swedish forest berry industry: subordinated inclusion 11, 14, 18, 121–34, 230, 233, 240; high costs and insecure earnings for temporary migrants 128–32; methodology 124–5; new migration regime 127–8; protections 122; strikes and organised resistance 122–5, 128; Thai NGO 122; Thai trade union 122–3
think-tanks 23, 123
tourism sector 5, 10, 37, 42
trade unions 122; farm labour in California 211; industrial agriculture in Italy 64 (*see also* collective agreements/bargaining)
transitional arrangements 107, 109
transnational entrepreneurship 44–5
travel cost reimbursement 29, 164
Treaty on the Functioning of the European Union 196
trial period 111
triple-win approach 13, 22–4, 33, 35, 232–3
Tunisian migrants in Italy 57, 58, 66
turnover rates 60

Ukrainian migrants and agro-pastoralism in Greece, Spain and Italy 76
Ukrainian migrants in Poland 5–6, 14, 86–102, 232; accession of Poland to EU 87–8; age of migrants 96*t*, 96, 97*t*; attractiveness of Polish agriculture for foreign workers 92–5; competitive position of agricultural sector 92–8; declaration of consent 88, 90–2, 99; education of migrants 96*t*, 97*t*, 97–8, 101; first-timers 96*t*, 97*t*, 98, 101; fruit farming 90; gender 96*t*, 96, 97*t*; horticulture 90, 93, 101; job characteristics 94*t*; labour exporter/labour importer transition 87–9; liberal legal regulations 86, 88; Mazovian region and horticulture production 87, 89–3, 93, 96–8, 100*f*, 99, 101–2; Mazowieckie voivodeship administrative unit 87; migration experience 96*t*, 97*t*; occupational

situation prior to migration 96*t*, 97*t*, 97; originating from countryside 96*t*, 97*t*; quotas 92; recruitment practices 91, 92, 98–9, 100*f*, 100–1; rural sector and dynamics of migration 89–91; 'simplified procedure' 88, 90, 92, 98, 99; socio-demographic characteristics 87, 96–8, 96*t*, 97*t*; Warsaw labour market 87, 89, 92, 96–7, 100–1; work permits 90–1; writing skills 96*t*, 97*t*, 97
unemployment 6, 41–2, 101, 167, 184*t*, 185*t*, 186*t*
unemployment insurance 217, 221
United Farm Workers (UFW) union 217–19
United Kingdom 11, 40, 46, 226; Bulgarian migrants 145; Polish migrants 12, 145, 199 (*see also* strawberry picking in the USA, UK and Norway from employers' point of view; United Kingdom and migrant pickers post-Brexit)
United Kingdom and migrant pickers post-Brexit 6–7, 193–205, 236, 240, 241; Agricultural Bill 2018 194; agricultural and other economic support 194–6; agricultural transition 194; Agriculture and Horticulture Development Board 195; central and eastern European migrants 6, 12, 199; Common Agricultural Policy (CAP) 193–5, 203; community involvement 199; dairy farms 196–7; egg-packers 196; futures: settlement undermined 198–200; horticulture 196–7, 205; Pillar 2 (rural development support) 194; Pillar I (direct income support) 194; rural revanchism 15–16, 198, 200–3, 204; seasonal and migrant labour 196–8; sheep farms 195; 'us' and 'them' 199
United States 9–10, 11, 12, 232; Agricultural Labor Relations Act (ALRA) 217–19; BLS projects 220; Bracero programme 90; Census of Agriculture 219; Census of Population 214; Chinese migrants 216; Filipino migrants 216; Indian migrants 216; Japanese migrants 216; Latin-American migrants 10; Mexican migrants 10, 216–19, 223, 226; undocumented (clandestine) migrants 10 (*see also* farm labour in California; strawberry picking in the USA, UK and Norway from employers' point of view)
unpaid family work 71
unpredictability 81; *see also* precarious status of employment

value-oriented rationality 154
visas 9, 197
vulnerability 229; farm labour in California 223, 227; Italy 60

wages 9, 14, 15, 16, 228–31, 242; agro-pastoralism in Greece, Spain and Italy 75–7, 79–81; average 61; differences between nationalities 57–8; farm labour in California 212, 217, 220, 222, 225; hourly 61; industrial agriculture in Italy 53; internal mobility in rural Norway 184*t*, 185*t*, 186*t*, 188; low and uneven 52; Polish migrants in Germany and Norway 107; postponement until end of working season 59, 230; Romanian migrants in Spain: guest-worker programme pattern of migration 25, 28; Russian migrants in Norway 163, 164; strawberry pickers in USA, UK and Norway 143–6, 148, 150, 155; Thai migrants in Sweden 26, 121–3, 125, 128–31, 129*t*, 130*f*; Ukrainian migrants in Poland 87, 92, 101 (*see also* guaranteed wage; minimum wage)
Weber, M. 154
welfare benefits 6, 10–11, 127
wellbeing improvement; Polish migrants in Germany and Norway 108; Romanian migrants in Greece 38, 40, 42, 45, 46
word of mouth recruitment 28, 56, 76, 234
worker-friendly labour market regulations 144
work ethic 110, 199; *see also* 'good worker' rhetoric
work groups 76
working conditions 7, 14–16, 18, 228–31, 234–7, 242–3; agro-pastoralism in Greece, Spain and Italy 74, 76, 79–81; farm labour in California 214; Polish migrants in Germany and Norway 108–11, 114, 116; Romanian migrants in Greece

38; Romanian migrants in Spain 25, 30; strawberry pickers in USA, UK and Norway 141, 143–6, 150, 153, 155; Thai migrants in Sweden 125, 128; Ukrainian migrants in Poland 92–3, 96, 99

working hours; flexibilisation 58; reduced 3
work permits 88
World Bank 213
World Trade Organisation (WTO) tariff lines for agriculture and fisheries 194